ENDLESS EDUCATION

ENDLESS EDUCATION

Main Currents in
the Education System of
Modern Trinidad and Tobago
1939-1986

Carl C. Campbell

The Press University of the West Indies
Barbados • Jamaica • Trinidad and Tobago

The Press University of the West Indies
1a Aqueduct Flats Mona
Kingston 7 Jamaica W I

© 1997 by Carl C. Campbell
All rights reserved. Published 1997
Printed in Canada
ISBN 976-640-032-6

01 00 99 98 97   5 4 3 2 1

CATALOGUING IN PUBLICATION DATA

Campbell, Carl C.
    Endless education : main currents in the
    education system of modern Trinidad and Tobago
    1939-1986 / Carl C. Campbell.

    p. cm.
    Includes bibliographical references and index.
    ISBN 976-640-032-6
    1. Education – Trinidad and Tobago – History.
    2. Education and state – Trinidad and Tobago.
    I. Title.
    LA505.T8C35 1997   325 . 309

Set in 10.5/13 Grand-Old-Style x27
Cover and book design by Robert Harris

for Sil and Lorraine

Contents

Preface / viii
Acknowledgements / xi
Abbreviations / xiii

[1]   The First Century of the Education System 1834-1939 / *1*

[2]   Post-World War II Adjustments 1939-1955 / *19*

[3]   The Multiplication of Nationals with Degrees 1939-1955 / *46*

[4]   The Return of Dr Eric Williams 1948-1955 / *56*

[5]   The Nationalists in Power 1956-1981 / *69*

[6]   Nationalism and Education 1956-1981 / *81*

[7]   Government Education Policy 1956-1981 / *97*

[8]   The Tobago and Indian Experience 1956-1981 / *130*

[9]   The Primary School and Teacher Training Experience 1956-1981 / *143*

[10] The Technical/Vocational Experience 1956-1981 / *152*

[11] Special Topics in Education 1956-1981 / *167*

[12] An Assessment 1956-1981 / *198*

[13] Epilogue 1981-1986 / *212*

Appendix / 216
Notes / 219
Bibliography / 239
Index / 253

Preface

There is a large body of writings about the history of education in Trinidad and Tobago in the form of theses written for university degrees. Published research in the form of articles in learned journals is very scarce and there are hardly any books on the subject. Recently this author published *Colony and Nation: A Short History of Education in Trinidad and Tobago 1834-1986*; and it was followed by *The Young Colonials: A Social History of Education in Trinidad and Tobago 1834-1939*. The present book (*Endless Education: Main Currents in the Education System of Modern Trinidad and Tobago 1939-1986*) is intended to be a follow-up to *The Young Colonials*. It is hoped that these three volumes will give readers a fairly comprehensive view of the general lines along which education has developed in the twin-island republic.

I have tried to include Tobago as much as possible, but it is likely that the friends of Tobago will remain dissatisfied about the amount of attention given to this island. The written historical records of Tobago are just not as ample as those for Trinidad and it is futile to expect equal attention to Tobago.

I am also aware that almost nothing has been said about the education of certain minority groups like the Chinese or Syrians. A promising section on special education was omitted at the last minute because the research was incomplete. Amazingly also this book has left out of focus (but not out of the study) a class of schools which were once talked about very much, namely intermediate schools. The author comforts himself with the thought that other researchers have been left something to do to complete the history of education in these islands.

This book has been divided into 12 chapters covering the period 1939 to 1981. This is followed by an epilogue on the short period 1981 to 1986. The book ends on the eve of the defeat of the People's National Movement (PNM) in the election of 1986. This brought to an end 30 years of continuous rule (1956-1986) during which the redoubtable Dr Eric Williams was political leader from 1956 to 1981, the year of his death. The remarkably prolonged regime of the PNM, the centre of the nationalist movement in the country, is the subject of chapter five.

Chapter one commences from the ending of *The Young Colonials* and is intended to form an introduction to the subject. It outlines essentially the foundations of the education system and the leading ideas which underpinned it in the century after emancipation. This is not to be thought of as a century without significant change, although the fundamentals of the society remained the same.

Chapter two is intended to show how World War II affected education and how far education policy was reconstructed in new directions – as some thought it should – or continued after the war on the old lines of development. The overwhelming conclusion is that continuity, not drastic change, was most characteristic of the years after the war. This was the inheritance of Dr Eric Williams and the PNM.

Chapter three makes it clear that the small core of university trained personnel in the colony increased in the 1930s and 1940s and that the system of studying for the external degrees of the University of London was crucial to this development. The teaching service was the chief beneficiary of this development, some of the holders of degrees being primary school teachers. It was another stage of educational inflation to which the social system had to adjust.

In chapter four an account is given of the intellectual achievements of Dr Eric Williams and of his emergence in the United States and in Trinidad during and after the war as a spokesman for Caribbean affairs. His early thoughts on West Indian education and on a West Indian university are highlighted, and shown to have a highly nationalist flavour. While the early thoughts of Williams on education are fairly well known because of his book *Education in the British West Indies*, there has been no previous major study of the history of education under Williams and the PNM; this deficiency has been remedied in this book.

Chapters six and seven deal with the actual policies of Dr Williams and the PNM government during their 30 years in power. Other chapters focus on specific aspects like teacher training and technical/vocational education. Chapter ten on the development of technical/vocational education and training takes the reader close to vital questions in the political economy of the nation, especially during the oil boom after 1973. An attempt at an overall assessment is undertaken in chapter twelve

Chapter eight on the East Indians and Tobago is meant to put the spotlight on two major interest groups whose leaders found themselves structurally in opposition to Dr Williams and the PNM. Neither group was afforded the opportunity during the period under study of directing policy at the national level; nevertheless important developments in the Tobago House of Assembly are not overlooked.

There is towards the end of the book a long chapter on special topics which is meant to accommodate discussion of several matters which received inadequate consideration in the general sweep of events. These subjects are rather varied and include something called the unassimilated rethinking in education, namely the main ideas which were mooted but which had not taken any institutional form at the time the study comes to an end.

In the event that the phrase 'endless education' in the title of this book should prove inscrutable, the author wishes to explain that it refers both to a voracious popular craving for secondary education as well as to a sense of overabundant national attention to education policy, though with very mixed results. Education policy was endlessly discussed, and the proof of this national predilection is an amazingly long catalogue of reports of working parties, groups, or committees set up by the government to investigate several different aspects of education policy. A bewildering deluge of recommendations followed, mostly unassimilated in policy. The rethinking on education seemed endlessly detailed. The citizens of the country were not only to be trained, but to be constantly retrained. The phrase 'endless education' also refers to a multiplication of new opportunities in education which moved the society closer to the ideal of the democratisation of education.

It is hoped that a discussion of these matters will enrich the understanding of several important groups in contemporary Trinidad and Tobago. Teachers at all levels need a good grasp of the historical development of the education industry; so too administrators of the system. Government functionaries and clerics who recommend or execute policy can benefit from an analysis of issues and controversies in the past. This study, it is hoped, could serve as a source book in schools, colleges and at the University of the West Indies (UWI). Readers who reside outside the Caribbean and who simply want to know more about the social history of one of the most important English-speaking Caribbean island should find *Endless Education* of more than passing interest.

JANUARY 1996

Acknowledgements

The research for this book was conducted mainly in the following libraries: Library of the UWI St Augustine, Trinidad; Library of the Faculty of Education, UWI St Augustine; the Trinidad Public Library; the West Indian Reference Library, Trinidad; the Archives of Trinidad; the Library of the Ministry of Finance, Trinidad; the Parliamentary Library of Trinidad and Tobago; the Royal Victoria Institute, Trinidad; the National Training Board, Ministry of Education, Trinidad; the Library of the UWI Mona, Jamaica; and the Byrd Library, University of Syracuse, USA.

I am grateful to my colleagues in the History Departments of the University of the West Indies who gave advice. Mr Albert Alleyne and Mr Christopher Modeste of the Ministry of Education, Trinidad and Tobago, kindly gave me interviews, especially on technical/vocational education. Mr Waldron Emmanuel, a retired official of the Ministry of Education, also gave me an interview. I have also benefited from long conversations with Dr Theodore Lewis on matters pertaining to technical/vocational education in the secondary schools. Mr Michael Alleyne, a former official of the Ministry of Education, also read a chapter. Indeed over the course of many years I have spoken to so many persons who were closely associated with some of the events described in this book that it would be futile to attempt to enumerate them completely. I ask for the forgiveness of anyone who helped greatly but whose name I have now omitted. Some of the errors in this book could have been avoided by greater contact with highly placed officials at the Ministry of Education who understood how policies were made and how effectively they were executed. I believe I would have received even more assistance if one political party did not have such a stranglehold on the political life of the nation. I am aware that several government documents relating to the role of international agencies in education remain classified information. I look forward to the future when persons with 'inside' infomation in the churches, the schools, the Ministry of Education or the Cabinet will write their own accounts.

At the Faculty of Education, UWI, St Augustine, Mr Innocent Beddoe was particularly helpful with loans of some of his documents. Various friends and colleagues in Trinidad have offered me accommodation and hospitality on my many research trips to Trinidad in the 1970s and early 1980s and to these people I say thanks.

I am grateful to the UWI for study leave and to the United States Information Service for a Fulbright Fellowship which enabled me to spend six months in the USA in 1984.

This book is intended to be a follow-up volume to another entitled *The Young Colonials: A Social History of Education in Trinidad and Tobago 1834-1939*. Together I hope they will provide a comprehensive history of education in Trinidad and Tobago from emancipation to modern times.

I wish to acknowledge that some materials in this book have already appeared in altered form in my book *Colony and Nation. A Short History of Education in Trinidad and Tobago 1834-1986* (1992) and in *The Young Colonials* (1996).

Abbreviations

ACH	Association of Caribbean Historians
ACP	Associate of the College of Preceptors
BA	Bachelor of Arts
BSc	Bachelor of Science
BIT	Board of Industrial Training
CIC	College of the Immaculate Conception
CD&W	Colonial Development and Welfare
CN	*Catholic News*
CO	Colonial Office
CP	Council Paper
CXC	Caribbean Examinations Council
DAC	Democratic Action Party
DLP	Democratic Labour Party
ECFI	Eastern Caribbean Farm Institute
EDC	Education in Developing Countries
GCE	General Certificate of Education
GDP	gross domestic product
HOR	House of Representatives
ICTA	Imperial College of Tropical Agriculture
IDB	Inter-Americian Development Bank
ISER	Institute of Social and Economic Research
LCP	Licentiate of the College of Preceptors
NIHE	National Institute of Higher Education
NIHERST	National Institute of Higher Education (Research, Science, and Technology)
NJAC	National Joint Action Committee
PDP	People's Democratic Party
PNM	People's National Movement
POSG	*Port of Spain Gazette*
QRC	Queen's Royal College
RVI	Royal Victoria Institute
SERVOL	Service Volunteered for All
TG	*Trinidad Guardian*
TTUTA	Trinidad and Tobago United Teachers' Association
ULF	United Labour Front
UNESCO	United Nations Education Scientific Council Organisation
UNDP	United Nations Development Programme
UNIP	United National Independence Party
UCWI	University College of the West Indies
UWI	University of the West Indies

[1]

The First Century of the Education System 1834-1939

> The position of the Denominations in this Colony is so deeply rooted that it would be quite impracticable to embark on any policy which contemplated ignoring or supplementing their work.
>
> *Governor Bede Clifford to British government*
> *16 June 1946, CO 318/467*

Before and after Slavery

The abolition of slavery marked the real beginning not only of popular education, but of public education. The only public schools which existed before emancipation were two Cabildo (municipal) schools in Port of Spain. Trinidad, unlike Barbados or Jamaica, never had any pre-emancipation endowed or charity schools, founded by rich planters for poor white boys. The island had been an underdeveloped plantation society of new immigrants and conflicting nationalities, without an eighteenth century or pre-emancipation nineteenth century golden age of economic prosperity which could have released the philanthropy of successful planters and merchants. Without endowed or charity schools for poor white boys, there was no history of free coloured youths (people of mixed European/African ancestry) before emancipation struggling to gain access, as at Wolmer's in Jamaica, to all-white public schools. The free coloureds themselves, numerically significant and not without families with large landed property, did not establish any public schools, although there were small private schools for those who had the funds and the interest. One attempt to have a well endowed public school for free coloured children was thwarted by Governor Woodford. Nor were there any significant attempts, in the absence of enterprising evangelical Protestant missionaries, to teach literacy to small groups of urban slaves as sometimes happened in other British Caribbean islands as emancipation neared. In short, emancipation overtook Trinidad before it had achieved enough economic maturity and social confidence in its future as a New World creole society; hence it had not generated endowed public schools for different classes and colours. At emancipation the impulse to provide primary schools for the masses came overwhelmingly from outside, from England; and in explaining the origins of St Joseph's Convent, the first proper secondary school, it might also be maintained that the push came mostly from outside, in fact from Martinique and France.[1]

Trinidad had been a Spanish colony for centuries, but when the English captured it in 1797, more Frenchmen than Spaniards were settled there. The French creoles were the backbone of the planter class and the aristocratic core of the elite whites. The English rulers were determined to stamp an English character upon the polyglot, multiracial society of the island. Education was eventually one of their chosen instruments to anglicise Trinidad.[2] After emancipation, education was developed on the British model; there was no indigenous, traditional education, as in Africa, to pose resistance to the British model. For most of the nineteenth century the Roman Catholic secondary schools of the French creoles (St Joseph's Convent, St George's College, and the College of the Immaculate Conception) borrowed from the practice of French metropolitan schools; but these colleges did not enduringly resist the influences of the British model replicated, as usual, in a watered-down colonial form.

As in England, the Christian churches took the lead in pioneering inexpensive elementary schools (also known as primary schools) meant to effect conversion to Christianity, to improve Christian moral standards, and to cement denominational loyalties as well as to provide literacy. The intention was not to promote upward social mobility since the colony needed a plantation labour force. These primary schools were meant for the black and coloured lower class and from the later nineteenth century for the children of the thousands of Indian indentured immigrants who came to Trinidad between 1845 and 1917 to work on the sugar and cocoa estates. Unprepared to, or incapable of, pioneering their own schools (partly from a sense of powerlessness to shape their own future), the black, coloured and Indian labouring classes had to accept the schools and curriculum provided for them by their betters.[3] These schools ignored the popular culture of the people for whom they were intended, the schools for the blacks and coloureds moreso perhaps than the Canadian Presbyterian Mission schools for Indians. On the other hand, the assumption that any and every aspect of popular African or Afro-Trinidadian culture would be welcomed was unjustified as Captain Cutteridge, deputy director of education, discovered in the 1920s when he published his *West Indian Readers*.[4]

[3]
The First Century of the Education System 1834-1939

Secondary Schools and High Prestige

A separate provision of a few secondary schools developed in the nineteenth century. Although these were meant primarily for the white upper class, in the absence of an impassable colour barrier in schools privileged coloureds of means and a sprinkling of blacks (mostly on scholarships) were able to attend. These secondary schools corresponded to the public schools of England and they all charged fees. The fact that the first such college (St Joseph's Convent) was for girls was a quirk of fortune as secondary education was most explicable as a provision for boys who were then the only sex to have responsible public positions and professional careers. The domestication of upper class and upper middle class women left them with only the careers of wives and mothers during the nineteenth century. But a broadening of career opportunities for educated middle class women came in the 1920s and 1930s. New secondary schools for girls, such as Bishop Anstey High School and Naparima Girls' High School, increased the scope for female secondary education from the 1920s.

In a plantation society based essentially on race, social mobility was always difficult; and secondary education reflected starkly the societal divisions. The main characteristics of this secondary education, whether for girls or boys, were that it was separate from primary school education, meant for a different social group, indeed largely for students of a different race and colour than those in the primary schools. For this reason their curriculum had to be like the public schools of either England or France. Progressively, however, more and more non-whites entered public secondary schools in the 1920s and 1930s, two decades in which the nineteenth century social order was further shaken severely. Bishop's High School, started in Tobago in 1925, was almost entirely for blacks. This astounding variant in Tobago still could not have happened in Trinidad in the 1920s. Nor could a black man become principal of a public secondary school in Trinidad in 1925 as Rawle Jordan, a black Barbadian, was of Bishop's High School in Tobago. Despite this variation, it is still important to keep in mind that secondary education there, as in Trinidad, was controlled by white persons.

Secondary education at its best was also classical education, narrowly modelled on the grammar schools of England and to a certain extent France, but of a high quality on contemporary standards. The establishment of Queen's Collegiate School in 1859 (later to be Queen's Royal College) as a colonial replica of the best English grammar schools strengthened the influence of the English model on secondary education, and all the newer public secondary schools from the 1920s thought of Queen's Royal College (hereafter QRC), and sometimes of the College of the Immaculate Conception (hereafter CIC), as their model.[5] As in the British schools, there was from the 1870s a narrow and insecure bridge from the primary schools to the secondary schools, over which successive handfuls of brilliant boys, most of them black and coloured, passed as free-place scholars into secondary schools. The latter commanded far greater prestige than the teacher training schools which had developed to provide instructors for the primary schools.

Since there was no local university, the three public secondary schools, CIC, QRC and Naparima College enjoyed the highest respect. Even the advent of the first institute of specialised technical training in 1922, namely, the Imperial College of Tropical Agriculture (hereafter ICTA) did not immediately detract from their educational ascendancy. ICTA was essentially a school for the British empire and not for Trinidad and Tobago.[6] As in the English model, it was a long struggle to establish the validity of any but a classical education as genuine secondary education; or to convert the public to the idea that secondary education was a stage of education and not a type of education. This latter view was the unheeded message of white experts and professional directors of education from the days of Marriott and Cutteridge. Director Marriott's attempts to discourage reliance on Cambridge secondary school certificates, and to promote the idea of the untried and untested secondary modern school were met with parental suspicion and indifference.[7]

The steam-driven sugar mills, the new railways and expanding urban life of the post-emancipation years required a fair number of skilled workmen. Many came from the neighbouring British islands. Apprenticeship to trades, outside the family, probably had a stigma attached to it as a result of the legacy of slavery and the reality of Indian indentureship. Until the early twentieth century there was no organised system of training tradesmen, though from the 1850s a small beginning was made through legislation by which boys and girls, often orphans, delinquents or Indians, could be apprenticed to master tradesmen. This was done as much as a measure of social control as to promote skills training. Skills passed often from father to son, or through private apprenticeship arrangements. Technical/vocational education was slow to develop, and had to do so in the shadow of a bookish curriculum both at the secondary and primary school levels.

Despite the introduction first of school gardens, of crafts, then of domestic science and woodwork classes into primary schools from the early twentieth century, the most serious institutional expression of technical/vocational education (the Board of Industrial Training) was characteristically separate and inferior to secondary education. The Board of Industrial Training (hereafter BIT) provided for trades training outside the ordinary schools, and all proposals from the 1930s to the 1950s to annex farms to primary or secondary schools failed to materialise. The Junior Technical School in San Fernando, established in 1943, was the first of its kind and it evolved separately from the ordinary schools for the decade of its existence. It was only under the government of Dr Eric Williams from 1956 that serious attempts were first made, not altogether successfully, to integrate technical/vocational education into the mainstream of secondary education.

It was inevitable that examinations would play a most important role in the selection system since demand for secondary education was consistently greater than the supply. The two leading examinations sat locally were the College Exhibition examination and the university scholarship (Island Scholarship) examination. The College Exhibition caused the greatest anxiety to parents; it selected annually a few brilliant boys for free secondary education. The competitors for the university scholarships were fewer than for the College Exhibitions. The university scholarship examination was a notable event in Port of Spain. Competitive examinations for scarce university education left few pleasant alternatives to the losers who had to fall back, at least temporarily, into the ranks of disappointed youths. Fortunately, from the 1930s the facility to take external degrees of the University of London enabled determined handfuls of these persons to refloat their ambitions.

The fiercely contested examinations for free secondary and free university education brought considerable social and economic returns to those who succeeded, and hence they became powerful channels of upward social mobility for a few black and coloured youths.[8] Up to 1939 Indians and Tobagonians were not substantial beneficiaries. Few had access to the better urban or suburban schools. The College Exhibition and the university scholarship examinations, together with the Cambridge secondary school examinations, aroused much public interest in the performance of schools, and created a climate in which scholastic achievement was lionised by most sections of the society.

The Enterprise of the Clerics

In the English model of education, the private enterprise of churches played a most important part in the provision of primary and secondary schools; and so it was in Trinidad and Tobago. The tradition of minimum government interference, especially in secondary education, passed to Trinidad and Tobago, and to owner-operators (the churches) of denominational secondary schools; this custom remained intact up to the 1950s. Nevertheless this should not blind us to the gradual growth of government interest in, and control over, schools in return for government grants. Primary education fell quicker into the sphere of government; but secondary schools were more resistant. At certain critical stages, the desire of government to control particular aspects of education became so pronounced as to lead to serious conflicts with the churches, especially the Roman Catholic Church. The potential of government schools to work as an integrative force in a racially heterogeneous and religiously divided society was quickly grasped, and there were two outstanding thrusts by government to implement policies based on such a perception. One was made in the nineteenth century by Charles Warner, attorney general between 1839 and 1869, a great Anglophile. The other followed about a century later when Dr Eric Williams, prime minister from 1956 to 1981, looked at the education system from the same vantage point. Warner desired to give government schools an overwhelming role in education in order to integrate the society on the basis of English culture;[9] Williams wished to do the same on the basis of a vague, superordinate Trinidadian national culture still in the making. Williams and Warner both espoused government schools and denounced denominational schools as obstacles to integration. The opposition of the Roman Catholic Church served to restrict and frustrate seriously the efforts of both Warner and Williams.

Before and after emancipation, the Roman Catholic Church, as the church of the majority of Christians in Trinidad, including the French creoles, a powerful white group, had a tremendous amount of social influence. The less powerful Church of England was still a force to be reckoned with because of support from the governors and senior English civil servants. Other Christian churches, such as the Moravians and the Methodists had small but faithful followers. From the later nineteenth century the rise of the Canadian Presbyterian Church, with several thousands of Indian supporters and converts, and, indeed, the increasing salience of other religions, such as Hinduism and Islam, all signalled the deep roots which religious organisations had in the society. The neo-African or Afro-Christian churches, like the Orisha religion or the Shouter Baptists, were submerged or proscribed remnants which had no schools and apparently did not desire to run schools.[10] Their labouring class members sought solace through religion, not power through schools. Since most of the churches had schools or wanted to have schools, the stage was set from the immediate post-emancipation period for repeated battles between churches and government for control and influence over schools and children.

Frenchmen, Englishmen and Indians

From the late 1830s the development of education in Trinidad was characterised by fairly constant tension and sporadic struggles between government and the churches, and between one church and another. The right to have denominational schools became an article of religious faith. In particular the Roman Catholic social doctrine of the preeminence of the family in the provision of education, though more usually stated during the nineteenth century as the primacy of the church, provided a firm philosophical base from which to fight the centralising efforts of Protestant-oriented governments or secular governments. The Roman Catholic Church, as the church of the powerful French creole sector of the local upper class, always stood in the lead of all movements to restrict the expansion of government control of education. Protestant Englishmen's dominance over the machinery of government for much of the nineteenth century made matters worse

The First Century of the Education System 1834-1939

since the clash of government and the Roman Catholic Church thereby assumed the character of a rivalry of nationalities between English colonists and English officials on one hand, and French creole planters, businessmen and professionals on the other. In resisting the expansion of the government's role in education, especially between the 1840s and 1860s, the Roman Catholic Church leaders and their French creole allies were setting limits to the imposition of English culture on a cosmopolitan society. But when compensated from the later nineteenth century with greater social consideration, with the legal entrenchment of the dual system of education and with limited political patronage, the Roman Catholic Church and the French creoles came to agree with the English that English culture should be the superordinate European culture. They all reckoned without the large-scale settlement of Indian indentured workers who retained high levels of Indian culture and thus reconstituted the cultural pluralism of the society on a new and more resistant foundation.

The dual system which allowed both churches and government to establish schools on recognised principles of participation was adopted first in 1870, although adumbrated from the time of Governor Woodford. It provided the fundamental framework within which education up to the secondary level was offered. Paradoxically, the consolidation of the dual system was achieved without the dissolution of doubts about its legitimacy. Apart from the experimental period of government (ward) schools between 1849 and 1869, it was generally assumed by the government – up to the time of Dr Eric Williams – that denominational schools were very essential. However, the churches never commanded financial resources to equal that of the government, although they always claimed greater prudence in spending government funds, often perceived to be nothing but the taxes of church members. Increasing government expenditure on schools became an irreversible trend which gradually strengthened the authority of the government, although on a per capita or even per school basis the grants were not impressive as aids towards maintenance and repairs. The government's power and influence were pushed gently by the directors of education, and grew noticeably from the 1920s. As long as the government did not assert a philosophy of education contrary to the churches', as long as increased government control appeared more bureaucratic than ideological, and as long as vital aspects of the denominational identity of schools (such as real control of teachers, of the curriculum or of the admission of students) were not challenged, the constant tension between government and the churches was contained at tolerable levels of disagreement. Tobago was untroubled by conflicts between government and the churches until 1930, and even then not severely.

The supreme creative function of the conflict between government and the churches, and even moreso among the churches, was to expand the provision of education at both primary and secondary school levels. The churches today find their history of mutual rivalries embarrassing to acknowledge; hence they are more apt to emphasise that they were the first to start schools rather than to proclaim that it was their fierce, unholy competition which provided the chief mechanism for the expansion of the education system. It might even be maintained that, for most of the nineteenth century, the supply of primary school places by the churches and by the government more than the demand from the ex-slave and Indian population explained the growth of the primary school system. In the nineteenth century the rewards for staying in primary school were not so great as to sustain high enrolments.[11] In the early twentieth century, the demand for primary education in urban areas became strong enough to surpass the provision of it by competitive suppliers, and hence urban schools were chronically overcrowded from the 1920s. Outside the urban areas, the unfriendly rivalry of churches was still highly responsible for the expansion of education facilities even in the mid-twentieth century, from which time several motivating factors entered parental calculation and made parental ambition, together with government's political response to it, the wheels which moved the education system forward.

Investment in Schools — Whose Responsibility?

The forces making for increased enrolment in and expansion of the primary school sector had to strain against restrictive ideas of race, colour and class. In a society which was structured essentially on race and colour, a persistent white upper class attitude to the lower class, who were mostly Indians and blacks (and to a much lesser extent coloureds), was that they should not be 'pauperised' by indulgent government provision of free social services, including education. Government officials and the upper class disliked what they thought were the exaggerated expectations of the lower class that government should do a great deal for them; these upper-class people felt it was a mistaken policy for government to subsidise social welfare.[12] These ideas were strongest between the later nineteenth century and World War I, a period of severe economic hardship for the sugar industry.

Strange to say, similar ideas are now resurfacing at the end of the twentieth century, in less vicious forms, in some Commonwealth Caribbean countries as governments seek to reduce expenditure on the social services. But then, as now, there were contradictions and countercurrents and the government itself pursued a mixed policy of laissez-faire and subsidised social welfare. Government expenditure on education and public health did in fact expand. Laissez-faire ideas served not to bar the growth of subsidised social services, but to hamper it. Whatever was done for the welfare of the lower class was done as cheaply as possible. Education for them was not to be overambitious; something was done, but not too much. These attitudes conformed to the essentially conservative function assigned to popular education. The purpose was to spread Christianity, literacy, and as always in education social discipline, preferably without social change. The maintenance of the colonial social structure and the labour requirements of the sugar plantations and sugar companies were compatible with an oversupply of illiterate or under-educated youths. Hence the persistence and even open defence of child labour into the 1930s. The provision of schools fortunately enjoyed a certain autonomy from the plantation system; hence excessively conservative opinions, such as those of Mr E. A. Robinson, director of Woodford Lodge Estates Company, in favour of child labour rather than schooling, did not block the increase of school places.[13] The main mechanism of growth of the education system after emancipation, namely the competitive energies of the churches within a regulatory framework provided by Crown Colony government, was not entirely stifled by planters and merchants.

The improvement in secondary school enrolment in the years between 1834 and 1902 was extremely sluggish. This was basically because the pool of students was limited by the fees charged, and by the society's narrow perception of the groups which qualified for secondary education. The French creole community commanded a larger portion of the potential fee-paying students, and this partly accounted for CIC outdistancing QRC in enrolment. For the most part QRC and CIC had different, but restricted constituencies of students, and the competition between them was more for government grants than for the same students, except for potential university scholarship winners. St Joseph's Convent had no competition at all for nearly a century, from 1836 to 1925. The returns on parental investment from the education of girls at St Joseph's Convent were mostly non-financial; attendance could increase the respectability and marriageability of daughters. Boys acquired higher status from secondary education; finding a useful place in life was not always easy. In the absence of the army as a career (or even the church), a post in the civil service was 'the Promised Land'. Beyond this, brilliant or wealthy boys found their way to British and American universities to become professionals. The possibility of winning university scholarships (Island Scholarships) elicited strong parental support for QRC and CIC.

QRC and CIC

The expansion of secondary school facilities beyond the outstanding original triad of St Joseph's Convent, CIC and QRC owed a great deal to demand from urban middle class families of lesser means than those who habitually patronised these three prestigious colleges. The signs of this demand could be seen in the mid-nineteenth century in the upgrading of the curriculum of the two leading Port of Spain primary schools (called the Girls' 'Model' School and the Boys' 'Model'

School). The demand was also visible by the second decade of the twentieth century in the emergence of a new generation of denominational secondary schools such as Bishop Anstey High School and Bishop's High School in Tobago. Moreover, unaided by government, a development of tremendous importance in secondary education occurred earlier in the twentieth century: this was the mushrooming of mass-oriented private secondary schools. These schools, which soon began to register successes in the Junior Cambridge examination, took the control of the output of graduates of secondary schools partly out of the hands of government and the churches, and were the means whereby several underprivileged youths painstakingly made a name for themselves.

The conflict between church and government in education, between the supporters of denominational schools and the advocates of government schools, expressed itself most dramatically through QRC and CIC. These were the two most famous colleges in the island, and in fairly close physical proximity in the same town. For at least a generation in the later nineteenth century, their leaders yearned to destroy each other's college. In no other West Indian island was there anything like this furious intercollegiate madness. The academic competition between them was not without positive results, and eventually antagonism was transmuted into a more mature, mutual toleration ensuring for the religiously divided cosmopolitan society alternative colleges which its Roman Catholic and Protestant middle and upper classes desired. The esteem accorded these colleges was the highest awarded locally to schools, and for nearly a century the male population could be divided gloriously between those who went to QRC or CIC on the one hand and the rest who did not, on the other. For nearly a century it was impossible to win a university scholarship unless one attended CIC or QRC; and their principals were the most widely respected educators even after the arrival of the professional directors of education. Any assessment today of the relative merits of CIC and QRC is bound to meet with partisan disbelief by old boys of one or the other; but judged by the criteria which they cherished most, namely the university scholarships, the medals, and the House Scholarships, QRC was on top in the period from 1870 to 1939, with CIC having to come from behind in the later nineteenth century, and outperforming QRC in selected years.

Canadian Aid in Education

No fact is as well known in the history of education in Trinidad as the sterling contribution of the Canadian Presbyterian Church to the education of the Indians. They came, they saw and, working partly through the culture of the Indians, they took on, nearly singlehandedly, the education of a race of underprivileged workers neglected on the estates and in the villages. The Canadian Presbyterian Mission put the education of the Indians in Trinidad ahead of that of the Indians in Guyana, the only other British Caribbean country with a comparable number of Indians. To the extent that by 1939 Indians had been brought within the mainstream of the society by education, that superb achievement was almost entirely to the credit of the Canadian Presbyterian Church. In the process of providing a separate education for thousands of Indians, the race consciousness and exclusivism of the Indians, already deep-rooted, were encouraged. The resulting societal divisions, however, were not accompanied by a high level of racial violence between Indians and blacks.

The outcome of the work of the Canadian Presbyterian missionaries, then, was both integrative and disintegrative. But it was their integrative function which was more socially significant because integration might not have happened otherwise. Although their work won them enduring loyalty from scores of Indian families, many Indian leaders from the late 1920s and the 1930s became determined to establish Hindu and Muslim schools as a means of preserving Indian religions and culture against the Christianising and westernising influences of the Christian churches. This put a stop to the growth of the Presbyterian Church, but not before their schools had provided the means for upward social mobility for hundreds of Indians – subject to the restrictive ethics of lingering India-derived notions of caste. Mission education worked best when allied with high caste ascriptive values. Other Indians made it from indentureship to the middle class over the same period by the patient route of business success.[14]

Up the Down Escalator

Between 1834 and 1939 secondary education provided a vital lever of upward social mobility for black, coloured and Indian persons. As the editor of the *Catholic News* insightfully wrote in 1920:

> Every lad who goes through College and enjoys the blessings of Secondary Education rises in the social scale, and drags up with him the circle of his family and relations together with a wider range of friends and acquaintances. A greater sense of responsibility pervades the lot: the children of the next generation are better tended, efforts are made for their better education and altogether valuable assets are added to the State.[15]

It has been well said by Lloyd Best, one of the leading black intellectuals of Trinidad and Tobago, that the business of black people has been in the field of education. This is not to deny the achievements of other racial groups in the classroom. The point is that, short of fortunate marriages, the educational route seemed the only way up for blacks in particular. In fact, scholastic and occupational success enabled men to marry upwards, often to women higher on the colour scale, even to white women.[16] On the whole, black people did not have the capital, the patronage, the experience or the confidence to discover and successfully preserve careers as businessmen.[17] Their neglect of family capitalism, and dislike of agriculture generally inhibited the accumulation of surplus needed to start a business. The blacks were neither satisfied with nor committed to a predominantly economic role in the society as were the Chinese, Portuguese or Levantines.[18] Some exceptions existed, but education as the way up from manual labour, around business into salaried white-collar occupations or remunerative professions was a compelling attraction. This preference for education as the path to social and economic advancement necessitated scholastic achievement by individual members of families, and since this generally was less reliable than intergenerational business success by minority groups, there were many academic failures or dropouts in the family histories of the educated black middle class.

It has been shown that nineteenth century Trinidad had a rather large coloured middle class, many of whom were wealthy.[19] Within one generation after emancipation a new group, of less than a hundred primary school teachers, joined the lower middle class on the basis of achievement in primary and teacher training schools. By the end of the nineteenth century there were not only more teachers including Indians, but black and coloured solicitors, lawyers, medical practitioners, journalists and pharmacists. In the early twentieth century there was recognisably a small but important educated middle class. The blacks and the coloureds who won university scholarships and who were able to establish themselves as respectable professionals were an inspiration to the rest of the non-white people. Their schoolboy scholastic reputations followed them to their graves in a society which never forgot intellectual accomplishment. The Island Scholars, though sometimes in and out of politics, did not provide the political leadership for the non-white community which many had expected, especially in the troubled 1930s.[20] They preferred to advance their own careers and standard of living. However, they did form part of a professional elite which could be used by the British authorities to assist with the administration of social services; their opinions were especially sought after in education. Their social importance must not be underrated simply because they left the work of political leadership of the masses to the less schooled trade union activists.

It is not now possible to establish with a high degree of accuracy the extent of the social mobility experienced by individuals and groups in the century after emancipation. There were no revolutionary changes in the British West Indies in this century. For students and academics of the last thirty years (1960s to the 1990s) inclined to use the socialist revolution, sometimes the Cuban revolution in particular, or generally the abolition of inequality, as the sole or most important test of change, the century after emancipation in Trinidad and Tobago must seem a disaster. The existence of oppressive social, political and economic structures was, after all, the basic cause of the reformist uprisings of the working class in the

1930s. But the continued dominance of a white minority did not preclude perceptible social change and scholars should be wary of writing as though nothing worthwhile happened between 1838 and 1937.[21] How, then, is the balance to be struck between the apparently unchanged predicament of the oppressed Indian and black working class over the century after emancipation, and the thousands of blacks, coloureds and Indians who because of education or success in business had higher occupational status and higher standards of living than their forefathers in the immediate post-emancipation period?

The researcher who has given the greatest attention to the question of social mobility in Trinidad from the nineteenth century into the early twentieth century did so as long ago as 1954. In his insightful sociological study of social stratification in Trinidad, Lloyd Braithwaite concluded that there was social mobility, but not so much as to disturb the structure of Trinidad society as it was at emancipation.[22] If, as is often assumed, Trinidadian society was changing faster immediately after World War II than in the 1920s or 1930s, Braithwaite's conclusion would be even more applicable to the 1920s or 1930s than to the early 1950s. He saw very little mobility from the lower class to the middle class, and when it did occur, he interpreted it more as a function of light skin colour, especially for females, than of educational achievement. Braithwaite apparently saw social mobility among the black and coloured people (excluding Indians) as upward mobility within their existing social class than as movement from one class to another. Race and colour for him seemed to have erected a caste-like society with little mobility across caste/class lines. While acknowledging that educational prowess and success facilitated upward mobility of black and coloured professionals, Braithwaite perceived this as occupational mobility within the middle class rather than social mobility into the upper class which was closed because its members were white. Race, colour and marriage appeared to be more determinant of social mobility (or the lack of it) than education. It does not appear then that Braithwaite was denying the enlargement of the middle class through education; and it might well be that historical analysis over time is more apt to reveal the growth and functioning of such an enlarged educated middle class than static fixed-frame sociological analysis. Braithwaite appeared to have underestimated the cumulative force of education as a lever of change over the century.

The upward mobility of thousands of blacks, coloureds and Indians through education during the century after emancipation meant that Trinidad's society did not remain static. The existence of non-whites who had moved into higher social ranks through education was more obvious in 1939 than in 1909, and more apparent in 1909 than in 1879. The society was increasingly more stratified according to economic classes, though the racial and cultural divide between the Indians and the rest of the non-white community remained in place as well as a measure of caste distinctions among the Indians. Correspondingly, the spread of education moved the society away from what Braithwaite called the paramountcy of particularistic-ascriptive values characteristic of slave societies towards the greater, but imperfect, acceptance of universalistic-achievement values in a less unequal, but still racist society. This was a modernising function of education; it had the effect of modifying the plural society.

Although blacks and coloureds up to 1939 achieved more upward social mobility through education than Indians and therefore came to share more common values with the whites (English and French creoles) sooner than Indians, the fact must not be missed that a minority of Indians, through the schools of the Canadian Presbyterian Church, participated in this incomplete ongoing process of creolisation. These Christian Indians appeared to have placed more value on the Euro-creole Christian aspects of the shared values than on the Afro-creole elements; these Christian Indians of the 1920s and 1930s were probably the parents or grandparents of the Christian Indians whom Yogendra Malik in the mid 1960s (or Selwyn Ryan in the mid-1980s) found to be least opposed among Indians to mixing with blacks and to the principle of interracial marriages.[23]

The Power of the Metropole

Trinidad was a Crown Colony in which there were no elected representatives of the people until 1925. The British government had ultimate power, but in the field of education, if not in others, it left the local governor and Legislative Council to do pretty much as they pleased – provided they could secure the agreement of significant local groups, such as the churches. Before World War I, generally, the secretary of state for the colonies had no established way of formulating policies for education in the colonies. Joseph Chamberlain, a strong secretary of state for the colonies, imposed his own ideas of imperial development on the British Caribbean. Among other things, he wished to promote agricultural education in the colonies. The momentum from his policy rippled throughout the British Caribbean for at least the first two decades of the twentieth century, and in this sense the British government provided the imperial stimulus behind the considerable expansion of interest and practice of agriculture in schools in the British Caribbean from the early twentieth century. Agricultural education was however a special case. One could still maintain that education generally was in the backwater of business between the British government and the colonial government in Trinidad and Tobago; British officials in the colony were left to follow English models which were the only ones they really knew. Throughout the entire century after emancipation, the English model of education exercised a more profound influence on education in Trinidad than the British government itself. The education system of the island was shaped by the colonial government without much direct direction from the British government. In the 1920s there was a higher level of British government interest in education in Africa, and this spilled over by the 1930s into the British government's relationship with the West Indies, creating the context in which the decision gestated in 1931 to dispatch the Marriott/Mayhew Commission to the West Indies. It is a moot point whether or not the Marriott/Mayhew Report of 1931/1932 represented the official policy of the British government. Official British government policy in education was enunciated in respect to Africa rather than the West Indies.

It was not until the labour movement had consolidated itself after World War I that representatives of the workers, some of whom were Marcus Garvey sympathisers, began to challenge the education policies of the colonial government. By this time the movement for self-government was on the boil and Crown Colony government was on the defensive. The teachers, too, began to give unsolicited advice. From that point onwards, education policy had to run the scrutiny of teachers, or self-appointed or elected leaders of the people who brought to their criticism some perspectives different from the obsession of the clerics with the rights of the Christian churches to educate and to have government grants for this purpose. The first call for education to contribute to the dignity of black people came from the labour movement. This was the meaning of the outcry against the Cutteridge reading books for schools.[24]

Curriculum Reform Under Suspicion

Curriculum reform in Trinidad and Tobago was met with suspicion leading to ineffective implementation or postponement of solid ideas into the distant future. In accordance with the English model in which technical/vocational education of school children had never been in popular demand, the curriculum of primary and secondary schools of the nineteenth and early twentieth centuries was bookish and literary, with only slight concession to practical work and that mostly at the primary school level.[25] Efforts to introduce practical and vocational subjects into the curriculum went through three broad overlapping phases in the very late nineteenth century and the early twentieth century, preceded by a less well defined post-emancipation effort. Although there were feeble calls in the immediate post-emancipation period for 'industrial' education, meaning agricultural work more than trades, to be made a part of the primary school curriculum, with the intention of preparing the ex-slaves' children to accept the grinding task of becoming a working class on the sugar estates, these came to nothing. Here the intention was both 'vocational' and pre-vocational: some unskilled work was to be done by the children, but also it was intended to build what was called 'habits of industry', in other words to prepare children psychologically for work, for the benefit of the planters and upper class. The need to implement such socially problematic reforms was apparently reduced by the coming of Indian indentured workers. At any rate, the suspicion of a return to slavery was too strong for such proposals to succeed.

The first phase of serious curriculum reform in the direction of practical and vocational subjects came towards the end of the nineteenth century. It was a time of crisis in the sugar industry and in addition there were many signs of rural unemployment. It was somehow thought that agricultural education might be a means of escape for the depressed sugar industry; hence the renewed call for agricultural education, this time backed more seriously by the British government, did result in the imposition of school gardens on most primary schools. These were adjudged to have been failures by World War I partly because the upper class expected too much from these endeavours, without having improved the income and lifestyles of peasants and small farmers. At the same time that school gardens were introduced, QRC and CIC made marginal and unsuccessful attempts to introduce agricultural chemistry without laboratory space.

Contemporaneous with the introduction of school gardens came the beginnings of trades training by the BIT; and this was the second phase of the drive to introduce practical and vocational subjects. It arose from the greater complexity and variety of technology in the island, from the untrained state of most of the tradesmen and from the demand of the upper class for better workmanship. Trades training was also gaining ground in North America as the best form of education for the urban working class. But it is to be noted that this trades training and its associated apprenticeship programmes was a part-time evening programme, completely separated from the ordinary schools. It was meant to be vocational. Up to 1939 when this trades training programme moved to southern Trinidad, it had substantially excluded Indians. The third phase in the call for curriculum reform in the direction of practical subjects came in the 1920s. It led to the gentle introduction of crafts (or handicrafts, sometimes called handwork) in primary schools. Surprisingly, the intention was declared by the directors of education to be educational, not vocational; the children themselves rather than the employers were seen as the potential beneficiaries, and the practical work to be done was not in agriculture. A wide variety of materials were brought into the classroom allegedly to train the mind by developing the dexterity of the hands. Curiously this method was not used to develop the brains of the upper class children in the island.

Crafts did not drive out the discredited school gardens; rather it was superimposed on them. School gardens and crafts, especially the former, created suspicion in the minds of some parents; but no curriculum reform caused as much controversy as the reading books of Captain Cutteridge who in the 1920s had introduced a certain amount of African or Afro-Trinidadian materials in them, and had moved swiftly from conception to implementation. All these innovations – school gardens, crafts and West Indian *Readers* – met with slow and limited success, despite pedagogical arguments in their favour.

The First Century of the Education System 1834-1939

The Wisdom of Stupidness

Whether in the direction of a localisation of reading materials or the introduction of crafts, the success of the curriculum changes in primary schools depended on the quality of the teachers. It would be erroneous not to recognise that, on the whole, the primary schools of Trinidad and Tobago were better in 1939 than in 1839; it is a mistake to speak of a century of stagnation.[26] In 1966, comparative education expert C. E. Beeby wrote a seminal book in which he developed a model of the stages in which primary schools in developing countries must pass in the life history of a system of popular education.[27] He wrote of a dame school stage in which the teachers were poorly educated and either untrained or barely trained. Teaching would be mechanical and confined to little more than the three Rs. A second stage, called the stage of formalism is characterised by teachers better trained, but still poorly educated. Here the syllabus is rigid, textbooks narrow, examinations strict, and the inspections rigorous. There is a great deal of emphasis on book knowledge, without appeal to the children's imagination. The next stage (the third) is a transition stage on the way to the fourth and last stage (stage of meaning). This latter stage marks modern education in developed countries. In the third stage (stage of transition), teachers are better educated and better trained than in the second stage (stage of formalism) because they have some secondary education and have been to a properly organised teacher training college. In this third stage the teachers begin to have a wider conception of education and they begin to have the skills to take their pupils along with them. There would still be official textbooks, but also supplementary reading materials. Education would be more meaningful without being quite modern.

However severely criticised, especially on the question whether the stages were distinct or overlapping, the Beeby model (revised by Beeby himself in 1980) has the merit of insisting that the trained teacher is the key to change in the quality of education.[28] If we look at the history of teacher preparation in Trinidad, it does seem that there were phases in the primary school system which roughly resembled what Beeby had in mind. For instance, during most of the years between 1834 and 1870, primary schools displayed mechanical learning and the teachers were poorly educated and in several cases untrained. What Beeby calls the stage of formalism bears a resemblance to the system of payment by results between the 1870s and 1921. In this period, the schools did become more formalised, more tightly organised with regular inspections and examinations. The teachers were more trained as certificates were required from all teachers. It was the aim of Director Marriott and Director Cutteridge to take the schools out of this stage into what Beeby calls the stage of transition; but by 1939 most of the primary schools had not reached anything like stage four. Marriott and Cutteridge did raise the standard of teacher education by recruiting some graduates of secondary schools, and they also improved the quality of many teachers by organising a proper

Government Training College, whose graduates were put at the top of the teaching service, as trained certified teachers. Cutteridge thought that his curriculum revolution gave education meaning.

While it might be readily believed that all the schools by the 1890s had been upgraded from stage one to stage two (the stage of formalism), it is debatable how far by 1939 Marriott and Cutteridge had managed to transform the primary school system from something like the stage of formalism into the higher existence they desired. Cutteridge himself believed that he had succeeded, but his critics made unfavourable judgements of the schools of his day. To the extent that Directors Marriott and Cutteridge did improve the quality of the teachers, it is reasonable to believe that the schools had been improved in their time. But by how much? This question of the quality of the primary school of the 1920s and 1930s is still of great relevance today as hundreds of older Trinidadians and Tobagonians are products of the Cutteridge schools. The Mighty Sparrow (Trinidad's leading calypsonian for many years) might in 1963 make fun of Cutteridge's school books (the *Readers*) and of primary school education in his calypso "Dan is the Man in the Van"; he might imagine that bright pupils ran the risk of learning a lot of 'stupidness' from these *Readers*,[29] but the schools then (from the 1920s to the 1940s) were better than the post-emancipation schools.

[2]

Post-World War II Adjustments 1939-1955

> The dual system already exists and has, by and large, worked satisfactorily. We see no reason why it should not continue.
>
> *The Report of the Working Party 1954*
> *(The Missen Report)*

The Agenda of S. A. Hammond

The foundations of the educational system of Trinidad and Tobago as it existed in 1955 were laid in the century after emancipation; and in the decade and a half during and after World War II (1939-1955) there were adjustments, reaffirmations and expansion, but no fundamental change of the system. Following the Butler riots of June 1937 and other disturbances elsewhere in the British West Indies, a commission (the Moyne Commission) that examined conditions in the West Indies put forward two recommendations which might have effected major adjustments in the education system: the government, not the churches, should have control of the appointment and transfer of teachers in denominational schools; and junior secondary schools for the age group 12 to 15 years should be established.[1] These latter schools were nothing else but the secondary modern schools which Marriott and Mayhew had called for in their report in 1931/1932. Neither of these two important recommendations of the Moyne Report was carried out in Trinidad and Tobago in the period under discussion.

Following other recommendations of the Moyne Report, an imperial planning authority called Colonial Development and Welfare was established in the Caribbean to spend the British grant for social and economic development of the West Indies. Colonial Development and Welfare ambitiously set out to rebuild West Indian society. If this aid agency had been allowed its way, the system of education in Trinidad and Tobago would have been recast drastically. Mr S. A. Hammond, education adviser to Colonial Development and Welfare, recommended consistently that little or no funds should be spent on traditional grammar school type of education to satisfy the demand of ambitious parents for the social mobility of their children. During World War II Trinidad and Tobago was involved in a Grow More Food Campaign; more land came under cultivation; and both islands were in a high state of community alertness. Schools were roped into the Grow More Food Campaign. It was a good moment to urge structural changes.

Hammond favoured a radical recasting of the education system which would reform education and rural communities simultaneously and interrelatedly. He aspired to use education to transform social conditions. Hammond appeared to have no doubts about the power of education as a change agent in society. Education, for instance, could insulate the people from the chronic failure of their export oriented economies. T. S. Simey, himself an adviser to Colonial Development and Welfare, wrote in describing the objectives of Hammond:

> The foundation of good education is . . . seen to be, not in an elaborate school system, but in the conservation and right use of the soil by which the people live and the conservation of the people themselves by a stable home and stable family economy, self-supporting by self-subsistence and internal exchange at least to the point that it is not disrupted by changes in export markets.[2]

Declaring the objective to be "the better use of the land and the foundation upon it of better homes and families",[3] Hammond in the teeth of World War II gave adult education (the education of the parents) and community development equal importance with the education of children in primary schools. The war had necessitated a considerable amount of adult education, especially in food production and island security. Without adult education, Hammond claimed, the work of the primary schools was wasted; the curriculum of the primary schools should be strictly related to the activities carried on in the homes and on the farms of the peasant and small farmer class. In fact getting the children to participate in Young Farmers' organisations could do more good than their classroom work; for example, organising the entire community to erect their own school buildings from local materials was Hammond's idea of adult education in action. In this way education could be, Hammond thought, a powerful force in adjusting the life and expectations of the community to the demands of the times. He had taken a more conventional view of education when he was director of education in Jamaica in the early 1930s, but from about 1937 when he became education commissioner for the eastern Caribbean, Hammond had changed views about what should be done. He probably had in mind some African model of the community school, a not unusual sort of comparison for British officials to make in the 1930s and 1940s.

Post-World War II Adjustments 1939-1955

Hammond abandoned all hopes of a fully trained teaching service. In the face of increasing population, he argued that West Indian governments, including that of Trinidad and Tobago, could not afford the recurrent cost of expanding education on the existing system as it stood at the start of World War II. By adopting the English model of education, West Indian governments, according to Hammond, saddled themselves with a system which was not cost-effective. Not even universal primary school education could be afforded. James Marriott and Arthur Mayhew, two English education experts, had run up against a wall of scepticism about the value of their proposed reforms in 1931/1932. If asked, Hammond (like Marriott and Mayhew) would have denied that he was pushing for an inferior type of education; he would have maintained that he wished a more relevant education, one which would improve material conditions and develop the virtues of self-reliance in rural people whom he regarded as the backbone of the West Indies.[4] If war re-energised rural communities temporarily, the reformed primary schools should be the centre for a permanent mobilisation of the people.

Hammond's vision and the agenda of Colonial Development and Welfare did not correspond to that of the education authorities or the politicians. The existing system was English and not African and was already well entrenched and there was no social demand among the people for the type of schools or curriculum that Colonial Development and Welfare cherished. The elected politicians in the Legislative Council had to pay attention to the wishes of their constituents and at any rate it seemed that Hammond and Colonial Development and Welfare had grossly underestimated the financial capability of oil rich Trinidad and Tobago to support a considerable expansion of the education system on the existing model.

It is worth elaborating on what might be regarded as the major success of Hammond and Colonial Development and Welfare in influencing the system of education. The core of Hammond's thinking was that primary schools should help to mobilise the entire community, that education was not just for children, not simply for schools, but for adults and for the community. Hammond meant primarily to improve the material conditions of the people; he was less keen on adult and community education designed to enhance the 'intelligence' or political consciousness of the people. The single most important adjustment that the education system made to Hammond and Colonial Development and Welfare was that the education authorities accepted a responsibility to educate adults and the community, without declaring this education equally important to the schooling of children. As suggested already World War II required a policy of increased adult education. What the education authorities did was to add adult and community education to the education system as appendages, rather than as integral parts of a revamped system; this was not what Hammond had in mind.

A detailed description of the rich and conflictive variety of activities undertaken during and after World War II by the new and ill-fated Social Welfare Department, by Trinidad and Tobago Welfare Ltd, by the Education Extension Service

Department or by other agencies such as the Trinidad Public Library, the British Council and the Extra-Mural Department of the University College of the West Indies is beyond the scope of this chapter.[5] Activities ranged from classes in basic literacy to preparation for external university degrees; from the strictly recreational to the learning of craft skills for profitable self-employment. The degree of interpenetration between adult and community education on the one hand and the normal work of the schools on the other was considerably less than Hammond desired; but he must have been satisfied with the stated objective of effecting social change through self-help. Hammond must have been delighted by the vast proliferation of voluntary rural groups: youth clubs, thrift societies, women's groups, cooperative societies; he must have been pleased with the health campaigns, the cookery classes and the home improvement projects. The schools however had not become rural community centres; autonomous community centres had been erected in some areas.[6]

The Effrontery of Mr Patrick

During the war, while Hammond was advocating drastic overall change in direction, Trinidad and Tobago did get a director of education, Mr Robert Patrick, who tried to make some daring changes in one delicate corner of the education system. Patrick attempted by legislation to enlarge the role of the government in the appointment, dismissal and promotion of teachers in denominational primary schools. He could claim with justification to be acting on one of the important recommendations of the Moyne Commission; but every major education report between emancipation and independence, except the beloved report of Patrick Keenan in 1869, came under the suspicion of the Roman Catholic Church. Since Hammond was at the same time as Patrick, not only recommending a change in direction, but suggesting strongly that government schools rather than church schools should be built with the aid from Colonial Development and Welfare, and in fact that church schools already built partly with government aid should become government property, the Christian churches were extremely alarmed by Hammond and Patrick, and under the forceful leadership of the ultramontane Roman Catholic Archbishop of Port of Spain, Count Finbar Ryan, worked successfully to get Patrick transferred to another part of the empire.[7]

If poor Patrick was chased off, Hammond could be mostly ignored because Colonial Development and Welfare could only give advice; it could not act by itself in any colony, and not a great deal of its funds were allocated to Trinidad. It must not however be thought that the dual system did not undergo changes during and after World War II. The pattern of incremental growth in the authority of government, especially at the level of the primary schools, continued from the

1920s to the 1950s. The persons most responsible for this trend before World War II were the directors of education; but during and especially after World War II certain constitutional changes worked to decrease the power of heads of departments, including the director of education, and to increase the power of the elected members of the Legislative Council. The elimination of the director of education from the Legislative Council was a case in point; but more important, from 1946 the elected members were returned on a system of universal adult suffrage. These elected members could now claim unambiguously to be spokesmen for the masses. This development strengthened the hands of the government in dealing with the churches in the dual system, at the same time that it reversed the order of importance of Legislative Council and director of education in the making of education policy. The Legislative Council now took the lead generally speaking, though the director was still the kingpin of the education bureaucracy. The change was fortified and formalised by the appointment by late 1950 of five ministers of government, one of whom was a Minister of Education and Social Services. The minister was given responsibility for education policy, but control over personnel in the Education Department and in the schools remained with the Colonial Secretary acting in the name of the governor.

Education and the Constitution

In 1946 the colony had universal adult suffrage for the first time and an historic elections the same year, a giant step on the road to decolonisation. A major adjustment in the years from 1946 to 1955 was that the Legislative Council came onto centre stage in education policy with the Minister of Education and Social Services as the prima donna and the director of education as head of the supporting cast. The next step was the evolution of the Cabinet under Dr Eric Williams and the PNM government as the supreme instrument of education policy. Dr Williams and the PNM government took the final steps in shifting responsibility for education policy from the hands of senior civil servants to those of elected politicians. Here what happened in education was only a part of a larger process of the transfer of responsibility for policy from white senior civil servants and the governor to non-white elected representatives of the people. The same thing happened elsewhere in the British West Indies.

It might also be said that constitutional advances towards self-government speeded the recognition of the need to bring nationals into the highest positions in the civil service. Even the oil companies understood this new era. The need to train nationals for senior positions became the ideal after the war. For this and other reasons there came, for the first time at last, open recognition in the Legislative Council of primary school teachers as a reputable and intelligent body of men and women whose welfare deserved the greatest attention. The message of several elected members was the need to eliminate sources of dissatisfaction from among the nearly 3,000 teachers. It was believed in some quarters that teachers had the potential to influence the outcome of elections;[8] and the elected members certainly sought teachers' interest as if they believed it. There followed upward regrading of salaries, the erection of teachers' cottages in increasing numbers; the removal of several anomalies; equal pay for male and female teachers; pension rights on the same scale as civil servants; in fact a general review of the controversial Cutteridge Code of 1935. Captain Cutteridge would have marvelled at the amount of changes favourable to teachers who always, so he thought, wanted something more. On the vexed question of the participation of teachers in politics, a major step forward was taken in 1949, largely at the instigation of the elected members of the Legislative Council. Teachers were allowed to take part in politics as long as it did not interfere with their duties. A teacher could obviously not enter the Legislative Council without resigning; but resignation was not mandatory for teachers who became members of Road Boards or County Councils. As we shall see later in the case of Dr Eric Williams in the 1950s, some teachers felt less restrained than previously to forge political alliances.

The Churches and the Government

An adjustment in the education system arose from the growing weakness in the capability of some Christian churches to find their proportion of the cost of new primary school buildings. The Moravian Church gave up eleven of its schools in Tobago to be administered by the government; the Canadian Presbyterian Church thought about surrendering their schools in Trinidad to the government, since the schools no longer appeared to be contributing to the growth of that Church. Only the Church of England and the Roman Catholic Church among the Christian churches still had the financial power to expand their primary schools. The Christian churches seemed to have lost some of their competitive energies which had expanded the primary school sector since emancipation. At any rate World War II created conditions which suppressed competition among the Christian churches in respect to primary schools. Shortage of building materials, of workmen who sought work on the construction of the United States military bases, as well as the uncertainties of war time, put a damper on new school buildings.

The government made some moves however which manifested a stronger desire to assume responsibility for education: prior to the start of World War II, the government had negotiated a loan to finance education, the first time this was ever done; then in 1945 it legislated in favour of compulsory primary education for the entire colony; after the war also, the government with the encouragement of the British government drafted long term plans for education, health, housing – all indicators of a desire to take a stronger lead in social welfare.[9] Much of these movements were the indirect outcomes of the 1937 disturbances and of new directions in British government's policy. With the coming of the five ministers of government in 1950, including a minister of education, greater power and responsibility, as previously explained, were shifted from Crown Colony officials to the hands of these elected officials. When the government drew up its White Paper on education in 1946 and its plans to use Colonial Development and Welfare funds, it evinced a desire to erect government primary schools rather than to assist with funding new denominational primary schools. However, because of the already very large number of denominational primary schools, government expenditure on these schools continued to be greater than on government schools.[10]

The New Hindu and Muslim Schools

It is well known that the first half of the 1950s saw the sudden birth of as many as 51 Hindu and Muslim primary schools and that by far the greatest number of them (as well as of temples) had been hastily brought into being by the Hindus through the revived and reunited Sanatan Maha Sabha. Bhadase Maraj, a young and astute Hindu who had risen from poverty to wealth over the previous decade, put up his own money to build these Hindu primary schools and by so doing immortalised himself in the Hindu community. Here at last were opportunities for schooling, without the risk of conversion to Christianity. While the Roman Catholic Church, the Presbyterian Church, and the Church of England chose to shift emphasis from primary education to secondary education, the Muslims and Hindus had to start with simple, inexpensive primary schools and so, independently of the government to a large extent, they developed a range of primary schools to protect their religions and hopefully even the Hindi language. Because of the reborn Hindu communal power behind the Sanatan Maha Sabha and the rugged independence of its leader, Bhadase Maraj, at a time when Hinduism was in an assertive mood the Maha Sabha schools sprang up suddenly and tactlessly without reference to the government, thus posing several problems for the government before aid with recurrent expenses was extended. One such problem related to the poor quality of the buildings erected.

The Muslim schools were started one by one (El Socorro, Aranguez, Warrenville, Five Rivers, Lengua) with the advice of the Board of Education and in such an apolitical manner that government aid with recurrent expenditure could be extended to them sedately. The El Socorro Islamic school at San Juan was the pioneer Muslim institution in this series of schools. It was started as early as 1940 by Maulana Nazir Ahmed Simab who obtained permission of Moulvi Ameer Ali to use the Islamic Hall.[11] Not until 1947 or 1949 did it receive government aid, but it was the first non-Christian school to do so. This recognition resulted largely from the quiet but persistent advocacy of Muslim leaders like Moulvi Ameer Ali, Maulana Nazir Ahmed Simab, Abdul Ghany and Noor Ghany. The inclusion of Hindu and Muslim schools into the dual system constituted one of the major adjustments of that system after the war. Ten or fifteen years previously such inclusion would have elicited strong protest from the Christian churches. It was the unpopular Roy Joseph, Minister of Education, who more than any other member of the government, facilitated it for reasons not unrelated to his own political survival.[12] Financial aid to schools was only one of a number of favourable adjustments to the claims of Muslims and Hindus.

Incidentally, it should be noted that the incorporation of these new Muslim and Hindu schools brought back onto the agenda an issue which, if successfully urged, could have resulted in a major change in the education system. This was the long standing, tender question of the role of Hindi. The Samajists, a reformist branch of Hinduism, had always emphasised the teaching of Hindi. The revived Sanatan Maha Sabha provided in the 1950s the strongest organisational base ever for the demand that Hindi be recognised by the government as a second language in schools where Indians predominated or were a significant minority. Simboonath Capildeo, a member of the Maha Sabha Board of Education, himself an expert in Hindi and Sanskrit, was very insistent on the teaching of Hindi.[13] The first half of the 1950s saw the spread of Hindi. In the federal elections of 1958 Bhadase Maraj addressed Indian political meetings in Hindi. Revived Hinduism gave Hindi a high priority, placing considerable importance on it as a means of teaching the tenets of Hinduism. During and after World War II there existed many Hindi classes outside the schools; inside the new Sanatan Maha Sabha primary schools Hindi was taught as well as in Samajist schools and in Canadian Presbyterian schools. But in the end the obstacles proved greater than the special interest of the Sanatan Maha Sabha. As usual, a great hindrance was the lack of commitment of young or westernised Hindus to Hindi; and the stout refusal of government to give it any special place in education. Dr Eric Williams in 1955 condemned the attempt to teach Hindi as racism – a view which he apparently never gave up.[14]

The Indians and Scholarships

During and after World War II Indian primary and secondary schools conducted by the Canadian Presbyterian Church seemed at last to be coming to grips with the challenge of the College Exhibition examination and the university scholarship

(Island Scholarship) examination. Stimulated by an expansion of the number of College Exhibitions, Canadian Presbyterian schools, even rural ones, began to produce College Exhibition winners, or at least pupils who had passed the examination without acquiring scholarships. Vidia Naipaul, the future famous novelist, was one such Indian College Exhibition winner in 1944. Canadian Presbyterian schools at Debe, Union and San Juan in 1949, 1951 and 1953 had College Exhibition winners. In 1952 Canadian Presbyterian schools won nine out of a total of 120 College Exhibitions.[15] The new Hindu primary schools of the Maha Sabha were not ready yet for such academic achievements. By 1945 the acquisition of Cambridge School Certificates by Indian boys was not uncommon. Apart from those attending Naparima College, there were scores of Indian youths at CIC and QRC. Indian girls were by World War II attending Bishop Anstey High School and St Joseph's Convent (Port of Spain) in increasing numbers. Naparima College and Naparima Girls' High School began to turn out in some years, especially in the late 1940s, boys and girls who were coming within reach of the precious university scholarships, once unthinkable prizes beyond the horizon. The warning was first sounded by Sylvia Ramcharan from Naparima Girls' High School who attended Naparima College's sixth form class. In 1943 she came a close second in the race for the university scholarship (Modern Studies Group). The government gave her a compensatory scholarship to study abroad. She was the first female to win a government scholarship for university study overseas. Three years later Kathlyn Smith of Naparima Girls' High School made history by winning the Island Scholarship in the Modern Studies Group, the first girl to do so; the first winner from any school other than CIC and QRC,[16] Miss Smith, became immediately a heroine of the South.

Trades Training in the South

Port of Spain was the political and commercial capital of the colony; the South was its industrial centre. This latter fact became more obvious during and after World War II. An important adjustment in the system of education was the spread of trades training through the BIT to areas outside Port of Spain. Very soon after its foundation in 1907 the BIT became aware, from requests by persons in various rural districts, especially in the South, that there was a need for both registered apprentices and technical evening classes outside Port of Spain. It took some 31 years before the BIT extended to the East (Arima) and to the South. The Butler riots were indirectly responsible because the Foster Commission which investigated the cause of the disturbances recommended industrial education and training for the South, a formula not unusual after any popular uprising. The overextended and underfunded BIT took up the challenge. Between 1940 and 1944 continuation classes and evening trade classes were started in San Fernando, Point Fortin, Siparia, Fyzabad and Arima. By 1948 the number of registered apprentices for the entire colony had grown to 425, more than double what it had been in 1937. Of these apprentices, 189 (44.4%) were in the oil industry, the only large industrial enterprise in the colony, and 30 other apprentices came from firms in and around San Fernando. Hence in respect to registered apprentices the South, the centre of the oil industry, had caught up with the North within eight years.

It was the same story in respect to students in the classes. Indeed by 1955 the balance of apprentices and classes was in favour of the South. The single greatest explanation was the readiness of the oil companies, whose production expanded from about 1935, to take more apprentices and to graft their own efforts at training apprentices, begun independently, upon the programme of the Southern Committee of the BIT. It was not primarily the sugar industry – employing a relatively small number of apprentices – but the oil industry which made possible the rapid expansion of BIT activities in the South. There was a high level of cooperation between the BIT and the oil companies. Trinidad Leasehold Limited, owners of the refinery at Pointe a Pierre, gave assistance with equipment (for the Junior Technical School and more so later for the San Fernando Technical Institute), offered the use of its workshops, and gave permission for high-level personnel to help with the instruction of the evening classes at San Fernando.[17] The oil companies also allowed some of their management personnel to serve on the Southern Committee of the BIT; in return the BIT put on classes in certain centres for apprentices, sent a peripatetic teacher of continuation classes to apprentices working in Palo Seco, Forest Reserve, Point Fortin and at the Usine St Madeleine sugar refinery, and took over from the oil companies the troublesome responsibility of administering relations between apprentices and employers.

It is quite clear then that whereas World War I had a restrictive effect on the BIT operations with a drastic fall in the number of apprentices, the period of World War II was marked by tremendous expansion. To meet the needs of British war machinery the oil companies expanded production, creating new trades and greater need for apprentices and skilled workmen. New opportunities for craftsmen also opened up with the building of the United States military bases which employed at their peak in July 1942 nearly 26,000 persons. Perhaps the displacement of skilled workmen to the bases encouraged some firms to take more apprentices. During the war existing engineering firms and shops had more repair work to do requiring the making of machinery parts formerly imported. The point was that employment opportunities for apprentices, skilled craftsmen and even technicians rose beyond the dreams of anyone in the depressed 1930s. The full employment bubble of the 1941-1943 period did not survive the end of the construction of United States bases.

Post-World War II Adjustments 1939-1955

Trades Training and the Indians

The expansion to the South had two great results – one technical and the other sociological – which must not be missed. First it incorporated Indian apprentices and students into trade classes on an unprecedented scale and the integration of most of the Indians who became tradesmen came via the oil industry, and not via the sugar industry as might have been expected. By 1959 out of 566 apprentices at least 151 or 26.6 percent (judging from their distinctly Indian surnames) were Indians.[18] In 1939 Indian apprentices were probably less than 5 percent. The support which Indian parents gave technical/vocational education especially training in motor mechanics, did not do much to modify the overwhelming public image of the Indians as an agricultural people.

The second major importance of the expansion to the South was that the work of the BIT– its apprentice programme and trade classes – took a further and decisive turn towards the engineering trades at the expense of the building trades. Although oil companies employed a surprising variety of tradesmen, it was naturally the engineering trades which were at a premium. Since wages and career prospects were superior in the oil industry to most other firms, applications to serve engineering apprenticeships were greater than in other trades. In particular, it should be noted that the trades of welding and motor mechanics became well established reflecting the spread of the use of motor vehicles from the 1930s and the newer technologies of metal processing which killed the craft of the blacksmith.[19] Concurrently but independently, the Trinidad and Tobago Electricity Company, based largely in the North, strengthened the trend towards engineering trades by a large firm school of apprentice electricians. The electrification of premises along the Western Main Road was an important development of the 1940s, reflecting the growth of population and housing in these areas. Indian youths in the North were very involved in this apprentice programme of the Electricity Company.

The slower integration of the sugar industry into technical and vocational training not only reflected the relative economic weakness of that industry, but its peculiar structure. A new trade – sugar factory mechanic – was proclaimed, but this job could be seasonal, quite unlike the all-year activity of the oil industry craftsmen. The oil industry also made earlier moves than the sugar industry to foster training at the higher level of technicians. It should be noted that from 1906 the BIT had functioned at the level of craftsmen, but the opening of the Junior Technical School and the growing industrial activity of the oil companies obliged it to begin to function at the higher level of technician – but it proved unequal to this enlarged task and was allowed to wither away – without much gratitude – over an incredibly long period.[20] On the other hand the direct involvement of the Department of Education and the oil industry in technical/vocational education and training via on-the-plant training schools continued to increase. Additionally, in 1949 the United British Oilfields of Trinidad began to train O level graduates (older boys with Cambridge School Certificates) on shortened apprenticeships, and with the probability of promotion to supervisory levels. By the early 1950s the oil industry began to send selected youths to universities abroad to acquire professional training as engineers.[21] A Faculty of Engineering had failed to materialise as an initial component of the University College of the West Indies. This new policy of company sponsored university training lay the foundation for the transformation of the professional and supervisory ranks of the oil industry from white people to local non-white persons.[22]

The Reaffirmation of the Dual System

We come now to discuss some ways in which the system of education was reaffirmed during and after the war. On the whole the Moyne Commission confirmed the validity of the dual system. So too did the Missen Report of 1954. This report expressed its belief in the need for religious instruction as the means towards the building of character in children. Indeed the dual system was thought by the Missen Report to be so well entrenched and to have performed so satisfactorily that changes in it were not worth discussion.[23] Of course the persons who drew up the Missen Report knew that the Christian churches would not accept without a fight any serious alteration of the dual system in favour of the government. Most of the elected members in the Legislative Council, particularly Roy Joseph, Minister of Education, were friends of denominational schools. They did not perceive the churches as agents of colonialism, but as benefactors. If anything they sensed that the white senior civil servants, often heads of government departments, were the enemies, not the white expatriate heads of churches or schools. Also the absence of strong party alliances among the elected members dissipated much of the force of any nationalistic sentiments they may have harboured.

By and large the old pre-war lines of curriculum development in the primary schools were maintained. The drive towards domestic science and woodwork centres was kept up during and after the war. In response to the criticism of the Moyne Commission (and the Moyne Commission was responding to teachers' dissatisfaction), the notion that the curriculum needed to be simplified caught on among the education administrators, after the departure of the man (Captain Cutteridge) who had increased the number of subjects; so too did the idea that teachers should be allowed greater flexibility in using the syllabus; but it is not clear that any subject was officially removed from the syllabus. The subject additions of Marriott and Cutteridge remained, for example crafts, Cutteridge's

Post-World War II Adjustments 1939-1955

Readers, his Geography book, also Daniel's *West Indian Histories*, although they were no longer praised as the panacea for education, and indeed Cutteridge's Geography book, and Daniel's *West Indian Histories* were reported by the Missen Committee to be piled up unused in many primary schools.[24]

One aspect of the problem of secondary education during and after World War II should help to show the extent to which the existing system was entrenched. From the early twentieth century at least a need was seen for a secondary school syllabus to meet the more practical needs of those who were not going on to a university. In the early 1950s that need had multiplied greatly by the growth of industries, and in virtue of the much larger number of students in secondary schools seeking Cambridge Certificates. Directors Hogben and Daniel openly acknowledged the correctness of what their distinguished predecessors, James Marriott and Captain Cutteridge, had been saying previously: too many secondary school students were doing courses not designed for their abilities. The Missen Report of 1954 said the same thing and also recommended the old formula of the secondary modern school, now called the Central school.[25] If the students did not fit the secondary schools, then the secondary schools must fit the students.

It was recognised that a fundamental problem was the social demand for grammar school type of education to which the denominational schools as well as QRC catered out of fear that anything less would cause them to lose social standing and academic prestige. There was no social demand by the people for the secondary modern school (or Central schools) if it meant local examinations and a more practical syllabus. The whole society had got locked into the Cambridge examination syndrome with its emphasis on academic subjects and a foreign cultural orientation. It would require strong leadership from the government to effect changes, but the elected members of the Legislative Council, if they recognised the problem, had no answer. The motto of the elected members at this stage might very well have been to give the people what they wanted in education: it is doubtful if they would have agreed with the Missen Report (to which Director Hayden had contributed) that already (in 1954) there were probably more youths leaving schools annually with the Cambridge School Certificate than the colony needed.[26] The government allowed its second secondary school, St George's College at Barataria (despite its domestic science, woodwork facilities, and expectations to capture children of working class parentage) to be diverted from its original purpose as a secondary modern school into the QRC model, a process helped no little by the redeployment there of ex-QRC senior staff.[27] The government also gave up funds set aside to build a government secondary school at Couva (which might well have been a secondary modern school) to the churches who promised to build two grammar type schools for girls with the same amount of money!

Secondary Education and the Avalanche of Cambridge Certificates

There was considerable expansion of education during and after World War II. Primary schools were hardly affected adversely by the war. Money was not the problem because the government at the start of the war still had much of the loan of $240,000 unspent; the colony's revenues were buoyant for the early years of the 1940s (1941-1945). As is well known, the building of United States military bases brought temporary prosperity to the colony. The number of primary schools in 1937 was 293 and in 1945 it was 292, but enrolment had increased from 72,776 to 91,426 (25.6%). There is no accurate record of the amount of government funds disbursed on primary school building during the war: a conservative estimate would be at least $70,000. Two constraints were the difficulty experienced by the churches in raising their proportion of cost; and the shortage of imported building materials on account of the war. It was sometimes said later that no schools were built during the war. A more accurate statement would be that a few schools were built, or extensions to old schools effected. However this building activity was almost exclusively replacements for old schools demolished. Sometimes a school was rebuilt on a completely new site, for example the Church of England school at St Joseph. The records only show one absolutely new school building (that is one not replacing an old building) during the war: a Roman Catholic school at Morvant. Hence there was an expansion of the number of school places without an increase in the absolute number of primary schools.

The training of teachers did not make much progress during the war. The three training colleges (Government Training College, Naparima Training College and the Roman Catholic Women's College) together enrolled about 140 students, with an annual output of between 50 to 80 trained teachers. Another 20 to 30 students per year could be expected to pass the Teachers' Certificate Examination without entry into the training colleges. During the war it became obvious that the annual output of trained teachers was falling behind the demand. Compulsory education, in the view of some critics, including Deputy Director Daniel, had been prematurely extended by Director Patrick to the entire island in 1945.[28] This pleased the elected members of the Legislative Council, but caught the education system ill-prepared. The number of teachers did increase during the war from 2,055 in 1941 to 2,488 in 1945 to meet an increased enrolment of 11,000 children; but some of the approximately 400 new teachers were pupil teachers, the apprentices who could not be kept out of the system despite declarations of intent to reduce their numbers.

In secondary education there was during the war, and just after it, unprecedented expansion in enrolment. Leaving aside Fatima College, the new school founded in 1945/46, six of the nine recognised secondary schools doubled their student population during the war (CIC, Naparima College, Bishop Anstey High

School, Naparima Girls' High School, St Benedict College and St Joseph College in San Fernando). Bishop's High School in Tobago tripled its population. QRC and St Joseph's Convent (Port of Spain) gained considerably in size. In 1938 the recognised secondary schools had a total of 2,259 students; in 1945 the total was 4,190 and in 1946 it was 4,765. Some of these schools had received government grants to extend accommodation, but what has to be explained is how so many more parents were able to afford secondary education. The proportion of free place students in the recognised secondary schools was 10.5 percent at its highest (1942) during the war; free education then could not have been the explanation. Private secondary schools also increased their student population as well.[29] It is impossible to resist the conclusion that some of the war time prosperity was used by parents to send more children to secondary schools. The fees at QRC remained at $16 per term and at the denominational colleges it varied from this figure downwards. In fact fees had remained stable for a considerable period since the late nineteenth century. Secondary education was heavily subsidised by the government which faced a steep rise in the recurrent cost of the capitation grants to schools.[30] Even so the recognised secondary schools were in great need of more funds in the early 1950s.

The production of holders of Cambridge certificates went along at an increased tempo in the war years. In 1937 a total of 35 students entered for the Higher School Certificate; in 1941 the number was 66 and in 1945 it was 110. The total number of students sitting the School Certificate (both private candidates and those in schools) was 358 in 1937, 607 in 1941, and 1,134 in 1945. These figures represented unprecedented growth rates in the numbers sitting these prestigious external examinations, the only comparable experience being the growth rate in students sitting the School Certificate in the early 1920s. Particularly significant was the rise in the numbers taking Higher School Certificate which had stagnated in the 1920s and 1930s under the maximum of 38 candidates (1935). But it must not be thought that secondary education had become common. Enrolment in recognised secondary schools was only 5 percent of enrolment in primary schools. Arriving in 1945 the new director of education, Sidney Hogben, concluded immediately that secondary education and primary education constituted two different worlds.

The Post-War Expansion Programme

The ten years after World War II may be divided broadly into two periods for our purposes: first, the two years immediately after the war (1946 and 1947) which might be seen from the point of view of education as years of preparation of new plans. These were years when government revenues declined and a White Paper of Education Policy was produced in 1946, but not discussed in the Legislative Council because of insufficient funds; the 'Yankees' went home and wartime prosperity wore thin as the economy wound down to normal. All sorts of government construction works and development plans came to a halt. The government increased taxes. Between 1948 and 1955 (the second of our two periods) the new plans for education were executed, resulting in an unprecedented wave of school building, unusually high levels of government expenditure on education, and the near pacification of the teachers by increased salaries, pensions, paid study leave and scholarships. The golden age of endless education had begun.

Over much of the Western world the post-war years saw massive increases in school enrolments. An expansion of aspirations as well as population growth came together to create a powerful demand for school places.[31] In Trinidad and Tobago there were also specific explanations: elected members of the Legislative Council with voters to satisfy were bringing new pressure on the administrators of education; there were new notions locally and in the Colonial Office in London about turning the schools into aids towards social development and even self-government. The British government reversed its colonial policy between 1938 and 1943 and decided to aid education and social welfare.[32]

Additionally, the buoyancy of the Trinidad and Tobago revenues, after an initial period of difficulty subsequent to the war, plus inputs of British government money through Colonial Development and Welfare, gave the education administrators and the elected members the funds for a major school building programme and higher recurrent expenditure. What could Hammond mean that Trinidad and Tobago could not afford to expand education on the existing model? Maybe he had conflated his analysis of St Lucia or Grenada with that of Trinidad and Tobago. Up in Washington, at Howard University, Dr Eric Williams was thinking that if he had the power he would put on more taxes to pay for more education.

It was not only the elected members who supported the expansion of education which occurred after World War II. The governors and top white civil servants sitting in the Legislative Council were also supportive of increased expenditure on education; in fact even the nominated members representing the sugar and oil industries were generally more alive to the needs of education than previously. The situation had been reached in the late 1940s in which the white ruling class and white government officials had been converted to the inevitability of continually rising expenditure on education. It is important, however, to keep in mind that the increased expenditure was overwhelmingly for primary education and that changes in the elitist assumptions about secondary education, and particularly university education, were not as marked as the amelioration of social attitudes towards the universalisation of primary education. Clearly the state of official opinion generally about education in 1946 or 1949 was different from what it had been in 1930 or 1934. Crown Colony government was in slow retreat. The Butler riots of 1937 had set off at one level a whole series of shocks which increased the respect of white government officials and the white ruling class for the rights of the man in the street; on another level World War II and nationalistic sentiments in India and Africa had changed and liberalised the attitude of the British government to its colonies. For Trinidad and Tobago, as well as for the other large West Indian colonies, self-government was the attainable objective as long as nobody tried to go too fast or to forget that conditions of economic and social progress applied.[33]

Perhaps if a senior white civil servant who had been reluctant to vote money for education in 1932 was asked why he was willing to do it in 1949, he might – apart from the obvious answer that the economic position was more favourable – have mumbled something about a recognition of the importance of education to social development. In the vocabulary of officialdom one can detect most clearly from the 1940s a new use of an old word: development. The colony and its people were to be developed and education was a means to this development. Although the full coming of human capital theory was in the future, understanding of education as a matter of investment as well as an item of consumption was slowly gaining ground as West Indian colonies took long-term sectoral planning more seriously. The conversion of the ruling class and the white officials of Crown Colony government to the idea of development,[34] however limited it might appear today, was one of the most seminal local outcomes of the 1937 disturbances, of World War II, and of the nationalist movements elsewhere in the British empire.

The Priorities in Expansion

The building programme began in 1948. The sum of TT$425,342, a ridiculously small sum of money today, but a worthwhile allocation in the 1940s, was set aside in 1948 for a programme of rebuilding, extensions and repairs of government and denominational primary schools, on a changed formula of two-thirds the actual cost of construction for government and one-third for the churches. Inevitably not all the construction could be done in 1948; so the programme spilled over into 1949, when an even larger infusion of capital was on the horizon. The government funds for the 1948/1949 programme had come from surplus revenues; but in 1949 came an application to Colonial Development and Welfare for TT$1.5 million for schools from the TT$4.8 million promised by that agency for development schemes in the colony. Eventually an education expansion programme of TT$3.7million (including the TT$1.5 million from Colonial Development and Welfare) was rolled into a Five-year Economic Programme (1950-1955) of TT$36 million. The principal source of this large sum was a loan of $28 million. In terms of the amount of money to be expended under various heads, education came second only to the allocation for water.[35]

It was easy enough to establish that primary schools had priority over secondary schools and that secondary schools had a greater claim on funds than a new teacher training college. In respect to primary schools, the first necessity was to improve accommodation in existing schools; second, to erect new schools where none existed previously. Dangerously dilapidated buildings were to be attended to first; then came replacements of dilapidated buildings, repairs and extension to existing schools. Most of the primary schools had been built in the nineteenth century or the early twentieth century, and had suffered from inadequate maintenance. For example in early 1948 the government ordered the closure of 17 denominational primary schools which were considered unsafe.

The programme of expansion of primary schools was first and foremost an upgrading of the provision already made, but in such a way as to extend it. Most of the new schools built were really replacements of old schools. All the absolutely new schools were to be government schools. Increasing the physical space in schools meant of course that schools got larger; gone completely were the accusations of the nineteenth and early twentieth centuries that denominational primary schools were wastefully too small. The Presbyterian Church, the Roman Catholic Church and the Church of England, in that order, obtained most of the funds allocated to churches for primary schools. At the end of the programme in 1956 it does not appear that anyone had a precise idea how many new primary school places had been created. On the eve of the general election of 1956 the financial secretary, who was not a candidate, provided a useful figure: he concluded that "more than 20,000" places had been made available in the five years between 1950 and 1956.[36] This unprecedented achievement in five years brought the government, in the estimate of Governor Rance in October 1955, within 5 percent of full enrolment of the primary school population. It is not clear however if this estimate included the approximately 11,000 pupils enrolled in new Hindu and Muslim primary schools between 1948 and 1955 which had not been incorporated in the government building programme.

The Benches Fill Up

Between 1948 and 1955 enrolment in the primary schools increased by 34,320 pupils (including the Hindu and Muslim schools), or on average by 6,864 pupils per annum. Here was a challenge to teacher training on a scale not before experienced. Not even during World War II had enrolment proceeded at such a tremendous pace. The teaching force expanded from 2,918 in 1948 to 3,951 in 1955, slightly over 1,000 teachers in seven years. There was already a huge backlog of untrained teachers. With an output of about 100 trained teachers per year, the three teachers' colleges fell woefully behind the task of keeping up with the demand. Devising ways of training the teachers was left to the director of education: neither the elected members in the Legislative Council, nor the Minister of Education, concerned themselves with this problem; their attention was on the school building programme which had more voter appeal. The only solution was continued reliance on the pupil teachers with many attempts to raise their standard of training and preparedness. The long standing plan for a new Central Training College and Farm Institute in Trinidad serving the eastern Caribbean had to be scrapped because the expense had become too great.[37]

Secondary schools also recorded increases in their enrolment after the war. Enrolment increased from 4,765 (1946) to 6,109 (1952), including 499 students from three schools (the College of St Philip and St James, St Augustine High School, Holy Faith High School) not in existence in 1946. The Presbyterian Church showed a willingness to invest in new secondary schools; the St Augustine Girls' School (started 1951-1952) was theirs; this school got early recognition by the government, but the Presbyterians also had new 'branch colleges' of Naparima College in Siparia and Tunapuna. Putting aside these new, recognised secondary schools, the increase in enrolment derived not from the big two (QRC and CIC), but from the other recognised secondary schools. The larger secondary schools like QRC and CIC simply could not find any space to put more desks. The parallel growth of private secondary schools indicated that demand was high, but places lacking in recognised secondary schools.

The Dream of Free Secondary Education

In view of the famous association of Dr Eric Williams and the PNM government with the introduction of free secondary education in 1960, it might be well to remember that it was elected members of the Legislative Council of 1949 who first tried to bring it about in the legislature. Curiously, free secondary education was in the mind of Albert Gomes, a white man of Portuguese parentage, who was later castigated by Eric Williams as a politician of little vision. Gomes was leader of the majority in the Legislative Council and a promoter of indigenous art and culture. This "upstart Portuguese" had gone neither to CIC nor QRC, but had in the words of a later commentator an "unorthodox kind" of secondary education in private schools and was more than ordinarily self-taught.[38] In January 1949 Gomes, introduced a motion (seconded by the Indian, C. C. Abidh) which sought to get government to explore the possibility of free secondary education, or to approach this ideal by increasing the number of College Exhibitions. Here Gomes was not really leading the colony, but following a section of the public which hankered after free secondary education. All the speakers in the Legislative Council felt that the second part of the motion (increasing the College Exhibitions) was more practicable than the first part (free secondary education in principle) and indeed the government was already in the mood to contemplate continual and accelerated increases of the College Exhibitions.[39] The most outstanding feature of the debate was the recognition that there was widespread and urgent demand in the country for free secondary education; and when it came to the vote no one, even those who had other priorities in education, wished to be seen as the enemy of such a progressive measure. The motion passed unanimously.

The government never came back with a formal answer about the feasibility of free secondary education; but it was clear when the Five-year Economic Programme was announced that expenditure on secondary education had to take a back seat behind the expansion of primary education. From this point of view the emphasis which Dr Eric Williams and the PNM regime immediately placed on secondary education from 1956 was nothing but a welcomed reversal of the order of priority of their predecessors. The PNM reaped the electoral rewards for free education which were denied Roy Joseph and Albert Gomes. The expansion of primary education in the first half of the 1950s seemed the belated fulfilment of a routine right; the offer of free and expanded secondary education under the PNM government was the unexpected bestowal of a magnificent privilege.

The College Exhibition

Although less money was spent on secondary education than on primary education in the late 1940s the College Exhibition system was progressively widened in the 1940s and 1950s. After settling down at 8 per annum for many years, the number of College Exhibitions inched forward in the late 1930s, stagnated in the early years of World War II at 16 per annum; then went forward again after 1942 by about 6 more per annum to the total of 52 in 1948. Then a far quicker pace of increase, spurred on by the interest of the elected members of the Legislative Council in free education, set in after 1949, leading to a doubling to 100 by 1950 and a further doubling to about 200 by 1955.[40] This was not free secondary education, but the momentum towards it was building. These exhibitions had progressively attained the status almost of a constitutional right and no government could lightly alter them in any way which appeared unfriendly to the aspirations of the people for free secondary education.

It was not only the number of College Exhibitions which increased. Generally more exhibitions were available; denominational secondary schools increased their own exhibitions. Friendly Societies provided some, and the Municipal Councils of Port of Spain and San Fernando returned to the task of assisting with education by supporting exhibitions. There was no adequate compilation of all the avenues to a free secondary education after the war. But clearly an end was coming to the idea that secondary education was only for those who could pay for it. The ideal was shifting to the notion that it existed for those who could benefit from it.

Expansion on the English Model

It has been the main burden of this chapter to emphasise that the education system expanded during and after the war on the same foundations as before the war. Education was still based on the English model. The role of the Christian churches and indeed of non-Christian churches was still of the greatest importance. The dual system was still in place. It is to be recognised however that the government had after the war a greater propensity to think of itself as the driving force in the partnership in the dual system. This had come about because of political and constitutional changes, because of the increasing expense of building schools, and because of greater reliance on planning the social services. Secondary education was still a different kind of education from primary schooling rather than a logical continuation of it. However more children of middle and even lower class parentage were getting some sort of secondary education because of the growth of private secondary schools; and there was a very strong demand by the middle and lower classes for more secondary education, preferably free secondary education. Technical and vocational education still trailed far behind academic education in public esteem, and was slow to develop. However during the war the trades training programme and the apprenticeship programme of the BIT were extended successfully to the South.

The role of examinations in the education system continued to be crucial. Parents still put pressure on teachers to allow their children to take the College Exhibition examinations and parents whose children did not receive scholarships took comfort in the fact that their children's name might have appeared in the published pass list. No way had been found to prevent the College Exhibition from distorting the curriculum of the primary schools, especially the urban and suburban schools which sent up most of the candidates. The Cambridge secondary school examinations (School Certificate and Higher School Certificate examinations) were still the tests which could provide the qualification for many jobs, and indeed employers, with an oversupply of applicants, often insisted on a Grade 1 or at least a Grade 2 certificate. The Higher School Certificate Examination, taken to determine the university scholarships (Island Scholarships), remained the supreme examination in the colony, much more in the public eye than the self-inflicted ordeal of adults studying to pass by correspondence courses an external degree programme of the University of London.

During and after World War II there were sporadic struggles and constant tension between government and the churches about the operation of the dual system. The most obvious example of a flare-up occurred when Director Patrick attempted to carry forward the Moyne Committee's recommendation that government should have control over teachers in church schools, except in relation to their religion.[41] Rivalry between the government and the churches, and indeed among the churches themselves, was still an important means whereby the education system was expanded; but as indicated above, the Christian churches either were in a weaker position than before to conduct this rivalry in respect to primary schools, or they chose to continue it more avidly at the level of secondary schools. The Roman Catholic Church, the Presbyterian Church and the Church of England were till very keen to compete for a share of the secondary school market; and the government seemed willing to allow them to continue as the leading providers of whatever new secondary schools were to be built, whether traditional schools or, if possible, secondary modern schools. On the other hand, the government having stirred up a greater demand for primary schools by compulsory attendance, appeared ready to attempt to satisfy it.

The late nineteenth and early twentieth century notion of the upper class, that each class should directly carry the burden of educating itself without putting a financial strain on other classes, faded into the background during and after the war. The imperial power itself had abandoned the doctrine that colonies should be financially self-sufficient. At the level of primary schools, objections to schooling the masses had disappeared completely from sight; so too objections to the abolition of fees. Fees were retained in certain superior urban, Intermediate schools to ensure a higher quality of education and perhaps to reserve them for a class of people above the labouring man. It is at the level of secondary schools that the measure of social generosity in the country about the democratisation of education should be tested. In other words, if there were restrictive ideas about race, class and colour in education, we should expect to find them at the secondary school level. As long as the normal route to secondary school involved the payment of fees, each family was expected to carry its own education burden. But it was in the post-war years that the momentous question of free secondary education as a principle was first raised and it was noticeably not negated on the grounds that it would pauperise the people, or that it was morally wrong. It was not pushed because the government was judged to be incapable of financing it at a time when the universalisation of primary schooling had not been achieved.

The conflicts and suspicions between the supporters of denominational schools and the advocates of government schools which had been most pointedly expressed through rivalries between QRC and CIC continued during and after the war. This contest was perhaps the most enduring trend in the history of education in the colony from emancipation to independnce. The probability that one of the university scholarships might slip to Naparima College did not diminish the centrality of QRC and CIC to the secondary school system. Nor did the commencement of a university scholarship for girls. There was no reason to doubt that secondary education continued to provide a vital lever of upward social mobility in the colony. It was the foundation for careers in the civil service and for white collar occupations, as well as for the professions or university careers. Before the opening of private enterprise to competitive employment, the civil service provided an incomparable local arena of job satisfaction. It follows from the arguments above about the expansion of the number of successful candidates in the Cambridge examinations, that there must have been continued widening of the educated middle class during and after the war. This strengthened the stratification of the society according to economic classes, but without removing the tough, divisive barriers of race and colour.

Integration and Non-integration of the Indians

It was concluded in a previous chapter covering the century after emancipation that the questionable provision of separate schools for Indians by the Canadian Presbyterian Church had both an integrative and a disintegrative effect, but that the integrative effect was the more significant trend. The Muslim and Hindu schools of the 1950s also had an integrative and disintegrative effect, but it seems that this time the disintegrative potential of separate Indian schools was more socially significant. It was the deliberate social intention of the Hindu and Muslim founders – unlike the Canadian Presbyterian providers – to strengthen Indian religions and cultures and hence the separateness of Indians, if need be, at the expense of national identity and integration. If accused of 'racial' politics Bhadase Maraj would have replied that he did it for the Hindus. These schools also lacked a superior layer of Muslim or Hindu training colleges or secondary schools where Indian sub-professionals and youths ready for university training could be prepared for the competition of life in the world of educated black, coloured and white creoles. The question is not whether these Hindu and Muslim schools helped to spread education, but the direction of their social consequences in so far as this can be calculated. On the assumption that it was at the secondary school level that capability to compete in the non-Indian world was acquired most assuredly, the Hindu and Muslim school effort lacked a powerful integrative tool such as the Canadian Presbyterian Church had in Naparima College. It seems reasonable therefore to believe, in the absence of empirical studies, that the Muslim and Hindu schools of the 1950s had a more disintegrative function than an integrative effect upon the society, however beneficial they were to Indian communities.

Tobago — The Backyard of Trinidad

And what of Tobago? The special position of Tobago in the union with Trinidad seems to invite some discussion about education there during and after World War II. But first some brief remarks about the situation in the 1930s. Bishop's High School, founded in 1925, undoubtedly the showpiece of education in the sister island, remained the smallest of the recognised secondary schools in Trinidad and Tobago. It had to recruit its students entirely from Tobago and free places were few. A successful Tobagonian dentist resident in New York, Dr Sylvan Bowles, funded a few three year exhibitions to it.[42] A new building was completed in 1937 on the hill at San Souci and perhaps this partly explains how enrolment jumped to 82 in 1938. The school still had difficulty in securing adequate staff and the failure rate for Cambridge School Certificate was higher than in the recognised secondary schools in Trinidad; the school did better at the Junior Cambridge examinations.[43] The school was a young struggling college in search of traditions. After only seven years in existence, it already had an annual cricket match between old boys and the students. Notable landmarks in the academic development of the school were the success of Victor Bruce (future governor of the Central Bank) in 1939 in the Cambridge Higher School examination, the first time this examination was sat in Tobago; and the winning of three House Scholarships, one by A. N. R. Robinson, future Prime Minister of Trinidad and Tobago, during World War II.

The number of primary schools in Tobago remained unchanged in the 1930s, understandably since the population was hardly increasing.[44] In terms of enrolment and attendance the system was remarkably static. In fact the number of schools (36) in Tobago in 1938 was the same as in 1920, and there had been no variations between these dates. Every village had a school and new villages were not being formed. Enrolment and average attendance had improved in the 1930s over the 1920s, and in both decades children attended school better in Tobago than in Trinidad. There was overcrowding at Charlotteville Methodist school, and at Des Vignes Road Moravian school in the early 1930s; and in the late 1930s a total of six schools were deemed too small for the attendance. The resident inspectors of schools in Tobago (E. B. Grosvenor, 1933; Rawle Ramkessoon, 1934; H. W. MacAlister 1936/1937) successively called for new and improved, and presumably more commodious buildings. Nothing was done in the 1930s to improve to any significant extent the school buildings of Tobago. Even after World War II, when Trinidad entered a period of large-scale replacement of dilapidated schools and increased school places, Tobago did not witness any significant rebuilding of schools. Partly because its population was not growing as fast as Trinidad's as well as its remoteness from the centre of government, Tobago's need for new school buildings was not given priority.

The work of the resident inspectors in Tobago could be gratifying and frustrating at the same time. There was a sense of community which the inspectors felt; the school system was small enough for most of the teachers and pupil teachers, given enough notice, to get together, whether to be instructed by the Inspectors, or to listen to a talk by an expert from Trinidad. At the same time there were mixed reports on the quality of Tobago schools vis-à-vis schools in Trinidad. Rawle Ramkessoon produced in 1934 a classification for efficiency grants which indulgently made them look quite good; MacAlister took the opposite view in 1937 claiming that Tobago's schools were more like the schools in Trinidad (presumably the rural schools). Apart from Mason Hall government school, established deliberately to be a model school, Tobago's schools did not win prizes in the 1930s in school garden competitions. This led to the suggestion – which was not acted upon – that probably Tobago should have its own school garden competition. During the war however Tobago's schools did make a notable contribution to the Grow More Food Campaign and the island enhanced its position as a supplier of food to Trinidad.[45]

Bishop's High School and Tobago Nationalism

As in Trinidad, secondary education in Tobago grew during World War II when Bishop's High School tripled its enrolment, reaching 228 students in 1946. Enrolment made only small gains over the next seven years. Possibly some of Trinidad's wartime prosperity reached Tobago as remittances from Tobagonians working in Trinidad, and funds from greater peasant sales of food to Trinidad during the war might also have helped. Perhaps the war prevented some children from being sent from Tobago for education. An increased student body put on the agenda the question of a new building on a new site. The college improved its Cambridge examination performance and added the prestigious Higher School Certificate during the war. In 1950 when the school celebrated its twenty-fifth anniversary it was at a peak of its achievement to date. It had under Rev Ivor Jones, its second principal, reverted to its old status as a grammar-school type of secondary school.[46]

Perhaps the most important trend which occurred in Tobago after World War II was the further development of Tobago nationalism. It was an unobtrusive, black creole peasant-based nationalism in an island where only a few people of mixed racial ancestry (coloureds) were present and still fewer whites. Its roots lay deep in the longstanding, particularistic sentiments of the islanders as a distinct society. From the time of union with Trinidad there had existed an integrationist and a separatist view of Tobago's relations with Trinidad. All over the Caribbean new economic, social and political expectations blossomed after World War II;

islands smaller than Tobago were talking about constitutional advance and economic development. Tobago's nationalism sharpened its teeth, not on labour disputes, nor on war against expatriate capitalists, but on accumulated grievances against the unequal development between Tobago and Trinidad.

A. P. T. James, a Tobago partiot, became the spokesman in the Legislative Council in Trinidad for this new stage of Tobago nationalism. He won the sole seat Tobago had in the Legislative Council in 1946, the first election under universal adult suffrage. James, a black man of poor origins, set out to prove that a man with working class and trade union antecedents, without any professional status or university education, could represent Tobago better than anyone previously had done. He carried to new heights of assertiveness the old feelings that Tobago as a separate island had rights beyond those of any other remote rural ward or county of Trinidad and Tobago. The Legislative Council had never seen any more persistent advocate of Tobago. James must have been embarrassed sometimes by the deceptive passivity of the long-suffering public in Tobago itself who seemed resigned to its disadvantages. But Tobago nationalism could spring to life unexpectedly like a released jack-in-the-box. Early in his career as legislator James seemed to be threatening secession, but for most of the period 1946 to 1955 his position was that Tobago was treated unfairly as a part of the colony of Trinidad and Tobago.[47]

James did not press for a superstructure of educational institutions, for example for a teacher training college, such as existed in Trinidad; nor did he request reform of the curriculum to reflect anything distinctive to Tobago. This was to come from his spiritual successors in the next 30 years. He mentioned, but did not insist on, the desirability of a farm school and a second secondary school; in 1952 James asked for a trade school; however on the subject of schools his strongest advocacy was for government to repair on time, as promised, the primary schools it had inherited from the Moravian Church.[48]

Perhaps Tobago nationalism touched education most strongly in the affair of the dismissal in 1954 of Rev Ivor Jones, the black Barbadian principal of Bishop's High School. This episode apparently had much more to it than has ever reached the printed record. Jones was dismissed suddenly by the Church of England Board of Management without adequate public explanation. Petitions from Tobagonians reached various heads of departments in Trinidad, including the Colonial Secretary;[49] and A. P. T. James brought the case to the attention of the Legislative Council. He clearly would have like to see government reverse the decision of the board, but that was virtually impossible. To make matters worse, the succeeding principal, Dennis Beacham, an English expatriate, the first and only white principal, was suspected of racism in his administration of the school. Beacham spent only two years there, and was obliged to leave because of a government inquiry and a certain level of community pressure. It was extremely difficult at this stage for anyone not approved by Tobagonians to hold the principalship, so

Post-World War II Adjustments 1939-1955

sensitive were influential Tobagonians to the behaviour of outsiders resident on the island.

On the matter of technical/vocational education sponsored by the BIT, Tobago was always at a disadvantage. In late 1947 the Tobago Peasants and Industrial Workers Union requested the BIT to commence holding technical classes in Tobago. Perhaps the union had been aroused by the spread of such classes to southern Trinidad. The union felt it could get 50 students at each of the following centres: Scarborough, Roxborough, Moriah and Charlotteville. Gaskyard Granger, its general secretary, asked for classes in engineering, building construction, architectural drawing, commerce, dressmaking, tailoring and animal husbandry.[50] The BIT felt unable to start any technical/vocational classes. A sequel to this was a request from masters of apprentices in Tobago for payment; their case was that without BIT technical classes they were doing all the training. This request was refused. Some good however did come out of these initiatives as by 1953 the BIT had a branch in Tobago, but no classes. Still individuals, especially females doing dressmaking and commerce, sat the City and Guild of London Examinations administered locally by the BIT.

On the eve of the visit to Tobago of Governor Beetham in mid-1955 an anonymous writer from Scarborough produced a list of Tobago's grievances in education. It made no mention of the staff problems at Bishop's High School, but regretted that Tobago had only one secondary school. The absence of trades training was not recorded as a grievance, but rather the absence of one or more farm schools. The core of Tobago's grievances in education, according to this writer, related to the disadvantages suffered by its primary school teachers. Few gained entrance to the Government Training College and usually the exceptions did not return to Tobago after graduation. It was alleged therefore that Tobago had mostly untrained teachers, an outcome perhaps not unrelated to another complaint, namely non-promotion of Tobago's headteachers to the inspectorate. Nor had senior teachers below the rank of headteachers received recognition from the authorities in the form of scholarships to study post-primary methods, although Tobago allegedly had creditable post-primary classes. Finally Tobago winners of College Exhibitions, without additional government support, could not take advantage of secondary schools in Port of Spain. Hence they had no choice but to attend Bishop's High School.[51]

[3]

The Multiplication of Nationals with Degrees 1939-1955

> There are some young men who have matriculated and are taking the Intermediate Arts. There will be more BAs than we can count just now.
>
> *Teachers Herald, November 1933*

Private Study and External Degrees

It was argued in the last chapter that greater participation of the elected members of the Legislative Council in the business of government, especially after World War II, created pressure for the expansion of education and that expansion did take place in primary and secondary education. There were additionally other areas of quickened growth in education; some like adult and community education were partly government sponsored programmes; but the people also made things happen independently of government, at the level of adult and community education and at the level of university education.

An important development was the gradual swell of non-whites holding university degrees. Leaving aside the professionals, for instance the lawyers and medical practitioners, it would be doubtful if there were more than 15 persons holding university degrees in the colony in 1929. Of these probably at least 50 percent would have been whites; yet 20 years later there were 88 persons in 1949 with university degrees in public schools, of whom 20 had external degrees.[1] Most of these 88 persons with degrees were non-whites. The proud holders of honours degrees were a cut above the possessors of general degrees; and holders of external degrees ran a poor second behind those who had resided abroad in universities in advanced countries and sat face to face with learned professors.

The Multiplication of Nationals with Degrees

This multiplication of persons with degrees was satisfying to some persons and threatening to others; down to about 1948 (the commencement of the University College of the West Indies) the government had no responsibility for those seeking degrees except in the case of the Island Scholars. Generally before the late 1940s it gave no encouragement or assistance to private students who wished to study abroad. The government was never the active agent in the emergence of external degrees of the University of London; this was the achievement of enterprising and ambitious individuals, aided by friends and relatives. Indeed had it not been for the elected members of the Legislative Council, the government in 1945 would have shut local men with external degrees out of permanent appointments to the staff of QRC. T. M. Kelshall, a coloured elected member, himself a lawyer, had to declare that a London BA was a fine degree even when obtained extra-murally. To him a London University degree was the same whether the candidate travelled or remained in Trinidad and Tobago. Few people really believed this.

Rawle Jordan, principal of Bishop's High School in Tobago (himself a graduate of residential Codrington College in Barbados), felt that the flaw in the education of those who acquired external degrees was that they were too individualistic; they had missed the "nobler ideal" which was a product of residence in a university college.[2] In outlining the benefits to character of university education in England, the director of colonial students in that country implied all that was supposedly lacking in West Indians who did not have the opportunity of studying overseas. He wrote in 1943:

> ... the average colonial student ... returns home with a feeling of self-confidence and with a store of experience which is invaluable to him and which he can only acquire by residence abroad and by association with home students [United Kingdom students] and with people more advanced than his own. He no doubt returns with a certain feeling of discontent at local conditions and at the prospects before him, but the fault of this lies in the colonies rather than in this country. In normal times [in peace time] the pre-graduate student had the opportunity of mixing with fellow students; he gets to know the mentality of his 'rulers', he loses his sense of inferiority by measuring his own capacities with theirs and if he is himself good material, he returns home much better fitted to make his career alongside European colleagues than would be the case if he had remained in a purely colonial atmosphere. I feel that there is much to be said in favour of pre-graduate studies overseas, particularly in the case of young Colonials who are to enter government employment and take their place in services partly staffed by European personnel. I believe also that the political value of education overseas is also great and that one should not allow 'failures' to outweigh the many successes.[3]

A clear message in the assessment was that those who studied at universities abroad were more employable in the colonies because they understood better the Englishmen with whom they would most likely have to work. Perhaps they had lost their creole narrow-mindedness. On the other hand, it could well be that the director underestimated the capacity of metropolitan residence and university education in England to radicalise colonial students – at least while still overseas. Father Boniface, a Roman Catholic priest, put the deficiencies of the stay-at-home university graduate another way: the holders of external degrees were "text-book perfect – that is about all that they are".[4]

The University of London developed in the twentieth century as the university of the British empire. The uniqueness of this university was that it alone among United Kingdom universities gave external degrees to students who need not fulfil any conditions of residence or attendance at its classes. Perhaps external degrees were in theory available in the West Indies from at least the 1880s, by which time candidates were sitting them in British colonial Africa. Why local persons did not resort to them before the 1930s is not clear; in fact amazingly few persons even in the 1930s seemed to have known about this facility. The opportunity to earn an external degree from the University of London was not mentioned in any official documents from the education authorities before a handful of private persons started passing the examinations. An atmosphere of secrecy also surrounded the availability of certain courses from correspondence colleges in England and the United States of America. No advertisement for these degrees or courses appeared in the local newspapers. Usually it was only when someone succeeded that the identity of persons studying by correspondence courses became known outside the study groups.

Those who aspired after external degrees of the University of London usually tried for degrees in Arts subjects or in Economics; but some worked for Natural Science degrees. Only a handful of persons who went abroad before the early 1950s took courses in Arts, Natural Sciences or Social Sciences, the rationale being that only the attainment of one of the remunerative professions, for example medicine or law, could justify the expense of overseas study. Some students who were studying Natural Science intended to continue in medicine overseas. The most professionally assured group of students were those who were engaged in the study of law. From matriculants to graduates, there was a string of hard working, well-deserving Trinidadians who set out to conquer the odds against success. As J. Wright, an Englishman, himself a graduate teaching at QRC, wrote in 1944:

> Students attempting to take the external examinations of the University of London at present work under many disadvantages. The time they can give to studies is limited since most are engaged in full-time employment. Lacking expert guidance, they are liable to waste much time and effort in ill-directed, and even unnecessary, work. They miss the spur from contact with other students and the confidence coming from an instructor's judgment and experience. Their other great handicap is the lack of satisfactory library facilities. It could even be maintained that the first of their needs is a specialised library.[5]

Whatever the private difficulties or public reservations the possession of an external degree was a major triumph; it was a level of education which was remarkable because so few persons even among the white population had it. It was an era in which holders of first degrees or diplomas proudly placed their letters behind their name in all official correspondence. It was something of a slight to omit these credentials.

Ironically it was the much maligned Cambridge School Certificate examination which articulated Trinidadians into the examination system of the University of London. Excellent performance in certain subjects at School Certificate level could earn exemptions from the matriculation examination of the University of London. Certain levels and combinations of passes in the Oxford and Cambridge Higher School examinations gave exemptions from the intermediate examinations for the external degree of the University of London.[6] Happily World War II brought the added privileges, allowed by the Council for Legal Education in England, of permission for West Indian law students to study and take the bar examinations without having to risk a sea voyage to England. Port of Spain was a centre for this examination.

University Education Overseas

It might be a matter of surprise to learn that the trek abroad for university education continued during the war. In the early twentieth century successful Chinese immigrants sometimes sent their sons to China to be educated, but after the revolution there it was easier to dispatch them to England or North America for first degrees and professional studies. It is reported that eight Chinese boys departed in early 1945 to study in England.[7] This reflected the relative safety of England at that time, but in the early 1940s North American universities were often preferred since they could be reached with less risk. Both Indians and black students resorted to North American universities. In view of the high percentage of Indians who were illiterate, it is interesting to note an increasing incidence of Indians going abroad to study. In 1943 there were about 20 Indian students at McGill University in Canada. In 1948 it was reported that 77 graduates of Naparima College, presumably all Indians, were at universities abroad.[8] Medicine and law were still the favoured fields of study; dentistry was coming into greater favour. In the hunt for degrees by capable holders of Cambridge Certificates, the Indian aspirants to the ministry of the Presbyterian Church could see no reason why they too should not go abroad to university for training. The Presbyterian Church had to change its policy of local theological training for all Indian ministers. Training in Canadian universities became the ideal. The degree of BA or BSc was thought to be well worth having for daughters. Noticeably Indian females began to study for Arts degrees in Canada, in a few cases returning to the island during the war to take jobs at Naparima Girls' High school. A handful of Indian girls left to study nursing. Indian lawyers and doctors who had themselves studied abroad in the first two decades of the twentieth century were in a position to send some of their children overseas; and, as always, the senior Indian headteachers of the Canadian Presbyterian schools made it a religious duty to strive for professional education abroad for at least one of their children, preferably a son.[9] Of course many Trinidadians and Tobagonians who studied overseas never returned to seek jobs in Trinidad and Tobago.

From the late 1940s it became obvious to the government that the approximately 200 Trinidadians and Tobagonians studying abroad in universities represented human resources to be counted and cared for in the expectation that on their return they would contribute to the well-being of the colony. After the war there was a joyous acceleration of the pace of higher education. A list of students studying abroad in 1948 still showed many persons studying law and medicine, but there was a widening of courses to include engineering, accountancy and economics; and there were more nurses than previously.[10] A handful of students, some selected and sponsored by the British Council in Trinidad, were studying educational methods, or the teaching of English, or one of the creative arts, usually for a diploma. Despite increasing incidence of scholarships the great majority of Trinidadian students abroad were financing themselves, usually no easy task. There were poor part-time West Indian law students in London who cut a sorry sight in the student community. Private students in the United States were thought to have some advantages over those in the United Kingdom. Apart from the wider range of colleges and universities with flexible matriculation standards, they had greater hope of gaining scholarships or fellowships, or the chance to work and study. On the other hand it was known that there was no guarantee that qualifications obtained in the United States would be automatically recognised by the government of Trinidad and Tobago. The same dilemma faced the obscure handful of Indians who went to study in universities in India from the late 1940s. Whatever the uncertainties it was always better to have a university qualification in the competition for employment in schools, a training college or the civil service.

Teachers with Degrees

The first sector of the society to benefit from the multiplication of university degrees in the arts and sciences was education. At the top of the education establishment were a handful of administrators who were civil servants. It was very difficult for non-whites to get into this group, but those with degrees pioneered the way. Perhaps the first Trinidadian to get an external degree was the Christian Indian, Rawle Ramkessoon, about 1932. He used it to establish himself in the Education Department and rose from inspector of schools to deputy director of education over a period of some 20 years. J. Hamilton Maurice and C. V. Gocking, both blacks, after acquiring external degrees travelled in the same direction, if not so far, and only after spending several years teaching in secondary schools. The logical job for the man or woman with a degree in the arts or in science, however obtained, was teaching in a secondary school. Such jobs were difficult to get during the war; degrees and character were closely scrutinised and the success of all those degree-less nuns staffing new and old Roman Catholic secondary schools must have raised the question whether character was not often more important than university certification.

After the war it became less difficult to get teaching jobs as it was nearly impossible to recruit white expatriate teachers with degrees. Getting employment was always easiest when racial status or religious loyalties worked in favour of the candidate. For instance, Indian females who had obtained degrees in Canada returned to take up jobs at Naparima Girls' High School. The 1940s on the whole was the first decade in which the higher education of Indian women, with the help of the Canadian Presbyterian Church, began to have an impact on the education of Indian girls in the colony. A sprinkling of degreed Trinidadian males and females began to line up behind the white expatriate principals and white senior mistresses and masters in some of the recognised secondary schools. These graduates, not themselves Island Scholars, set a trend which a few of the Island Scholars of the late 1940s and the 1950s amazingly followed.

An awkward group were those primary school teachers who by local private study acquired unusual diplomas or even external degrees of the University of London. Primary school teachers with ACP (Associate of the College of Preceptors) or LCP (Licentiate of the College of Preceptors) after their name were bad enough and there were 19 of them in 1944. These persons expected some kind of promotion. There were in the same year 12 primary school teachers with university degrees.[11] At a time when the battle to base entry into teacher training colleges on the Cambridge School Certificate was not yet finally won, a primary school teacher with a university degree was a square peg in a round hole. There was little point in such a person looking to QRC for employment as the taint of work in the primary schools could not be erased by a degree, worse if obtained externally. The best chance for such a person was at the Government Training College. Even if successful such a person was not likely to get a permanent appointment right away with only an external degree. The black man, Harry Joseph, only achieved this at the Government Training College after covering over his external degree with the mantle of a Diploma in Education after a one-year sojourn at the University of Southampton.[12]

ICTA Graduates Without Degrees

Had there been a local university in Trinidad and Tobago the multiplication of men and women with degrees would have proceeded at a faster rate. From 1922 the colony had an institution of higher learning, in several ways on par with a university, but strangely not granting degrees. The reference here is of course to ICTA. It is true that the authorities at ICTA jealously guarded its imperial character; still it offered diploma courses for West Indians whose governments made financial contributions to the institution. The success of ICTA in its imperial mission as a centre of research of high international standard and a trainer of Engish postgraduate agriculturists should not be allowed to mask its failures and misgivings as a local contributor to the education system of Trinidad or indeed of the West Indies. A basic failure of ICTA was not to offer a degree course; in other words it failed to be a university. West Indians who sought higher education wanted the prestige of degrees, preferably degrees from metropolitan universities. ICTA was a specialist college for agriculture which was not a profession comparable to law or medicine. It gave neither independence of action nor satisfactory remuneration. ICTA was a bastion of English civilisation in a tropical colony; and it was not well integrated into the community. It was very difficult to reform it or to make it the base for a university of the West Indies, because it was well set in its ways and tightly controlled from England.[13]

During and after the Second World War ICTA had varying fortunes. The war was a threat to the college; staff vacancies could not be filled; new developments had to be postponed; most disturbing was the delayed arrival of English postgraduate students in some years. Only five postgraduate students were there in 1945/1946. The academic year 1943/1944 was a bad one for diploma students from the West Indies. But relief was on the horizon. The Moyne Commission had recommended that after the war all major agricultural research was to be centralised at ICTA and, with the promise of British subsidy through Colonial Development and Welfare, ICTA was set for a new stage of development along old lines. The promised expansion did occur after the war, but it was an expansion more of the infrastructure of buildings and research staff and not primarily of the student population. In the period 1946 to 1951 the physical and academic assets of the college reached the unprecedented high level which the University (College) of the West Indies inherited in 1960 at the time of the take-over of ICTA.[14]

The Question of a University of the West Indies

In February 1944 while World War II was still in progress the question of university education for Trinidad and Tobago was brought into sharp public focus by the arrival of the Irvine Committee. This was a branch of the Asquith Commission on university education in British colonies which was committed to the establishment of colonial universities; hence the Irvine Committee which toured certain West Indian colonies was not inquiring if a West Indian university

The Multiplication of Nationals with Degrees

should be set up, but rather educating itself in order to frame the university which the West Indies deserved. Some Trinidadians clearly believed that Trinidad should be the site of a centralised West Indian university, or at least it should host one of the branches of the constituent colleges of any such university. To some persons it seemed, however, that a university would draw off resources needed to expand primary and secondary education. This was the position of some Hindus (Samajists) organised in the Arya Pratinidhi Sabha. This organisation argued that the elimination of illiteracy and the provision of adequate primary and secondary schools should be the priority because the Indians were too far behind other sections of the community in education.[15] Among the black and coloured people the evidence of support for a local university was abundant although they had not campaigned for it as in Jamaica. Strong support came from civil servants, students and teachers, most of whom had no hope of finding the means to study abroad. Although in the early 1940s no evidence was found in Trinidad of outright opposition by the whites against a West Indian university of the intensity displayed by the editor of the *Gleaner* in Jamaica (or even the same level of official misgiving as in Guyana), it would be an error to believe that there were not detractors.[16] In fact neither Director Moreland Hopkins, nor his Deputy Daniel was keen on a West Indian university; nor was Mr Hammond from Colonial Development and Welfare. However it was not a question of outright opposition, but of conflicting agendas and timing. Generally the resident Englishmen giving advice and leadership on education wished to concentrate on the reform of primary education. Hammond distinctly hinted to one member of the Irvine Committee that the university should be put off for the next five years.[17] As in West Africa doubts about the value of a local university could be disguised as a legitimate concern for proper standards or for the weaknesses of secondary schools; and clearly a university would cost the island governments far more than the University scholarship system, for the benefit of a non-white majority of students.

Among the memoranda presented to the Irvine Committee, that of the Why Not Discussion Group (said to have been made up largely of ex-QRC boys meeting informally) was one of the most intelligent presentations and certainly the most radical. The readiness of Trinidad for a West Indian university was evinced, according to this group, not only by the number of potential matriculants, but by the alleged high demand at the Public Library (in Port of Spain) and the Carnegie Free Library (in San Fernando) for technical books. The country was peppered with literary and debating clubs, and large audiences were guaranteed in Port of Spain for any reputable visiting speaker. A West Indian university, said the memorandum, would raise the level of cultural activities and break the centuries old tradition that trained men must come from abroad. There was a universal desire to go abroad to study, but this often led to permanent residence abroad and hence loss of valuable human resources.[18] Facilities for taking locally external degrees were no substitute for courses in a West Indian university. ICTA was clearly nothing like a West Indian university; the diploma that it offered West Indians led, according to the memorandum, up a "blind alley" of unemployment; hence potential applicants preferred a straight science course at a university abroad.

A West Indian university, however, such as the Why Not Discussion Group envisaged, would be inappropriate without meaningful social, economic and political changes. It could supply teachers for an expanded secondary school system, provided the intention was to replace white expatriate staff with West Indians. A West Indian university would provide personnel for a West Indianising of the civil service, without which, said the memorandum, there could be no political advancement. Research into the history, sociology and economics of the West Indies must be pioneered by a West Indian university. The new gospel of development of the West Indies required a West Indian university. And like Dr Eric Williams, as we shall see later, the Why Not Discussion Group expressed a conviction that to carry out these functions a West Indian university needed to be independent of British university tutelage from its inception. This was the most radical aspect of the memorandum.

The establishment of the University College of the West Indies (hereafter UCWI) in 1948 as a single campus university located in Jamaica created a totally new situation for Trinidadians as well as for other West Indians. An independent university was thought premature by the Irvine Committee. Indeed this was never on the agenda of the planners of the new universities in Africa and the West Indies. UCWI was affiliated to the University of London; hence providing a degree reassuringly approved by the University of London. All external degrees of the University of London already obtained by private efforts automatically gained in status. But the residential nature of the degree programmes of UCWI – which did mean travel overseas for Trinidadians after all – gave UCWI graduates a social edge over holders of external degrees obtained in Port of Spain by unglamorous self-directed studies.

The commencement of UCWI in Jamaica stimulated the government of Trinidad and Tobago to provide more university scholarships to study there. It was now possible to multiply degree holders in medicine, arts and science at a cheaper cost; and as Crown Colony government weakened, the Trinidad and Tobago government from the late 1940s accepted the broad policy that West Indians should be trained for senior positions in the civil service. As popular demand for more secondary schools climbed, the government saw the need for more teachers, which in turn meant more university graduates. Hence the granting of additional scholarships to universities, special overseas training schemes for selected teachers and civil servants. Not all of these persons were sent to UCWI, but sufficient Trinidadians were going to UCWI to make that country second only to Jamaica as a contributor to the student population.[19] In respect to the training of West Indian doctors over which the Irvine Committee had agonised at length, the new UCWI garnered most of the young aspirants from Trinidad and the other

West Indian colonies. In fact the difficulty of gaining access to medical schools in the United Kingdom and Canada provided a strong reason for making the Faculty of Medicine the first Faculty of UCWI.

[4]

The Return of Dr Eric Williams 1944-1955

> Dr Williams has come home and he has brought with him scholarship and learning of which any one, anywhere, however talented, might be proud . . . He has passed from the field of study to the field of action, as Secretary of the Caribbean Research Council.
>
> Acting Governor Renison, 19 April 1944 [Williams 1969: 93]

From Oxford to Howard University

Born in 1911, son of a junior clerk in the Post Office, Eric Williams won a College Exhibition to QRC in 1922. This was the first major prize in a brilliant academic career. In 1931 Williams capped his local academic achievement by winning a coveted university scholarship (Island Scholarship) to study at a university in England. Sent away in 1932 to study History at Oxford University, he distinguished himself as an undergraduate and won awards to do historical research leading to the prestigious DPhil degree of the same university. His thesis on the economic reasons for the abolition of the British slave trade shocked his intellectual superiors at Oxford by rejecting the conventional wisdom which credited British philanthropy as the chief motivating force for this momentous shift in policy.[1] There had been previous Island Scholars in law and medicine, who had won many academic laurels in England; for example H. O. B. Wooding in legal studies at Middle Temple and Dr S. Devenish in medical schools. With Eric Williams it was not simply what was achieved, but how it was achieved. Academic distinction was won through dissent from orthodox views. Unknowingly Williams thus set a model for career development for several young West Indian intellectuals of the future. Still, in August 1939 as he landed in the USA (like C. L. R. James the previous year) from Oxford, just before World War II broke out, there was no reason to believe that his career path would have been different from those other talented Island Scholars who did not return home after the completion of their studies. There was no obligation on Island Scholars of his generation to return to serve the island or to show any interest in the affairs of the colony.[2] Residence in the United States during World War II when a nationalist perspective was common for Third World intellectuals in exile converted Williams into a progressive academic. Additionally, his exceptional talent, hard work and good fortune transformed him from the holder of a precious advanced university degree into an accomplished and recognised spokesman on Caribbean affairs.

If Williams had stayed in England after graduating from Oxford, World War II might have disrupted his attempts to launch an academic career. In the USA he was safe from both induction into the army and the destruction of war. As an opinionated colonial in England in a highly controversial discipline, he might not have been allowed to become a star even if he could have penetrated the outer margins of a British university; but in the USA he was a privileged member of the oppressed black minority which fortunately possessed its own academic institutions and learned journals. As an Assistant Professor of Social and Political Science at Howard University, one of the greatest black universities, he found room for his early articles in the *Journal of Negro History* and the *Journal of Negro Education*. He grasped with both hands the accelerated academic opportunities not uncommonly presented, then as now, by the rich variety of learned institutions in the United States open to talented West Indians who (unlike C. L. R. James) posed no danger to the American way of life.[3] The early book, so crucial in the take-off of an academic career, came in 1942 with *The Negro in the Caribbean*, less an objective analysis than a political statement. This was followed in 1944 by *Capitalism and Slavery*, an elaboration of his Oxford thesis, a brilliant and shocking reversal of the accepted views of the British role in the abolition of slavery. This book clinched his reputation as a scholar.

The Birth of a Caribbean Spokesman

Williams had placed himself in a field of study in which he had no British West Indian competitors in his class. He was the first West Indian from the British territories to undertake research in, and teaching of, West Indian history as a professional career at university level. He dared to be a radical and was able to employ history in the service of politics to get to the roots of the imperial nexus between England and her colonies. He was in a unique position in his generation to exercise an unprecedented sort of leadership. He enhanced this position by his strategy. He avoided the trap of being too insular or too cosmopolitan: his interest went beyond the history of one West Indian island or the British West Indian islands; but at the same time he was not diverted from the Caribbean by the fascination of Africa or Marxism. He did not confine his attention to history, but extended it to literature, contemporary politics and economics.[4] His tours of the French and Hispanic islands, though speedy, gave him first hand knowledge of some of their contemporary problems as well as stimulating contacts with some of the intellectuals of the region. He tended to think from the micro to the macro level; from the island to the Caribbean level. He thus gave a pan-Caribbean perspective to his writings and speeches which was welcomed and rewarded by recognition as a spokesman on Caribbean affairs.

Dr Williams was a representative of much of what passed in the 1940s as progressive thinking.[5] He established a reputation at a time when decolonisation was the burning issue in all the colonies. A war was being fought, it was said by Roosevelt and Churchill, to make the world safe for democracy. The British government was prepared to transfer some of its responsibilities to approved British Caribbean leaders. Williams was in no position to form a trade union; nor did he gather around himself any group of politically conscious West Indians abroad; it was as an individual that he acquired a reputation abroad; he was influenced by progressive black American intellectuals and their activism married to his reputation as a young scholar moved him towards the field of political action. His chance came with the establishment of the Anglo-American Caribbean Commission in 1942. He talked his way into a job there, thus becoming a consultant while continuing his teaching and research at Howard University. By 1948 he ceased working at Howard University, becoming until 1955 a full-time employee of the commission at its new headquarters in Trinidad. The post was fraught with difficulties from the start as Williams tried to combine loyalty to his imperial employers with his anti-colonialist orientation; working with the white imperial backers (the Americans, British, French and Dutch in the expanded Caribbean Commission) of the vested economic interests in the Caribbean, while unmasking (without publishing) those very vested interests with the tools of history and sometimes the research materials paid for by the Caribbean Commission. This was an unholy marriage between a radical nationalist and at best moderately reformist imperialists, which could only have lasted as long because Williams soft-pedalled his views ; also because of the loose articulation of Williams' research portfolio as Deputy Secretary of the Caribbean Research Council (an affiliate of the Caribbean Commission) with the main administrative routine of the Commission. Also the predominating weight of the Americans in the Caribbean Commission, through which was expressed the new supremacy of the US government in the region, protected him from dismissal by the British who were less patient with subversive colonial employees.[6] Williams claimed that he obeyed all the regulations of his employers, but eventually the contradictions exploded in his face.

The opportunity to travel throughout the Caribbean islands created by his research job with the Caribbean Commission enabled Williams to grasp West Indian problems in greater Caribbean perspective; the Caribbean Commission was not obsessed with the West Indian past, but concerned with its present and future; and the specific assignments given to Williams, and those he initiated, led him to research contemporary West Indian problems which his historical knowledge showed him to be deeply embedded in the particular historical experience of the region. History then became a social science in his hands in the fashion of Walter Rodney of later times, but without any socialist or Marxist commitments. Williams was not using social science, as is now fashionable, as a methodology to analyse historical problems, but using the insights of history to illuminate contemporary social and economic problems. That was one sense in which the job with the Caribbean Commission moved him further into the field of practical political action.

Return of a Native Son

When Dr Eric Williams, Associate Professor of Social and Political Science, returned to his native Trinidad in April 1944, for the first time since he departed it in 1932, his advent was unlike that of any previous returning Island Scholar – and he knew it. He delivered a highly successful series of public lectures at the Public Library on the topic "The West Indian Situation in the Perspective of World Affairs". Essentially Williams spoke about the subject matter of his doctoral thesis and of his forthcoming book then in press. He was the embodiment of those who felt from before World War II that West Indian history could be an instrument of self-liberation and a beacon on the road to self-government. Here was an Island Scholar with potential for political leadership. He was the first intellectual produced by the country whose sole focus was Caribbean affairs. He was youthful, energetic, brilliant and confident. Here was a man to be listened to on Caribbean affairs. He had the lustre of success in academic circles in two metropoles, the prestige of an international civil servant from a small country, and he was on the point of becoming the author of a masterful book. Williams had, in the eyes of the Trinidadian, the higher status of a man who had lived abroad for 12 years. He had presumed to question the imperial record of the English in the West Indies; thrown cold water on the traditional colonial middle class belief in the inherent goodness of the Englishman in England; he had invested them with the material motivations of mortal economic men acting in their own interest. He had asserted in his writings and speeches that the oppressed West Indians, descendants of ex-slaves, had contributed by their sweat and suffering to the industrial greatness of the metropole. The message to West Indians was that they were a people of importance. They had played a vital role in the history of the world. The path forward led through the thickets of decolonisation, self-government and a federation of the West Indies. Williams brought West Indian history and West Indian politics together as one thing. A few weeks later in describing to his publisher the tremendous audience reaction to his speech in Port of Spain Williams wrote: "I am not so modest as to deny that some part of the interest was due to the speaker, but at the same time the subject exercised a great attention."[7]

Eric Williams' Agenda for a West Indian University

Dr Williams had definite ideas about education in the West Indies. He felt that the orientation of education in the West Indies was wrong: education was not to serve the interest of the imperial power or the small colonial intelligentsia; it should serve the interest of the masses in the cause of cultural autonomy, political self-determination and Caribbean identity. The first major opportunity to gather his thoughts on this subject into writing came with the appointment of the Irvine Committee to investigate the establishment of a West Indian university. Williams missed the sitting of the Irvine Committee in Trinidad in February 1944 by only two months (April 1944). After taking evidence in the West Indies, the Committee visited Howard University in Washington on its way to McGill University in Canada, and Williams with typical brashness volunteered to give evidence before it (May 1944). Then he incorporated his evidence into a 80-page memorandum, which was later elaborated into a book (*Education in the British West Indies*). Some of his ideas on a West Indian university found an outlet in three articles in the *Harvard Educational Review* in 1945, the *Journal of Negro Education* in 1946, and *School and Society* in 1946. Here it will be possible only to highlight those views which appeared radical, or very opposed to those of the Irvine Commission which had already made up its mind about all the essential features of a West Indian university.

It should be said at once that several of the proposals of Williams on a West Indian university resembled the progressive thinking of the Why Not Discussion Group in Trinidad and it should not be ruled out that he might have had contact with some of its members while on his visit to Trinidad in April 1944. Williams was also obviously impressed with the role of black universities in the education and upliftment of black America.[8] These institutions rather than British universities should be the model for the West Indian university. Williams insisted that the university was not to transmit an abstract 'culture', but to impart an education befitting the needs of society. He outlined some of the current movements in West Indian society which the university should "consciously and belligerently"[9] support: land reform, a diversified economy, full self-government and federation.

A major point was that the university should not be an elitist institution, but should seek to educate the masses. This was his understanding of what black American universities sought to do. "The university should put on overalls, leave the campus, and reach out into every home in the community."[10] Its most important service would be adult education – almost what would be called today a community college. It should not be anchored in the British aristocratic tradition of education, but should be liberated by the American practice of democratic education. Its curriculum should be practical; it should, for example, concentrate on helping farmers. The teaching of agriculture and education would be more important than the graduation of lawyers. The languages of the Caribbean should be studied to facilitate cultural exchange. Pharmacy, social work, music and the fine arts would be taught before the more expensive disciplines of medicine, dentistry and engineering. Every student in freshman year would have to do general courses in "social sciences, humanities and natural sciences, together with a comprehensive course in West Indian life and culture".[11] Williams must surely have been thinking of a four-year degree. A university to serve the particular interest of the West Indies must stand on its own feet from the beginning. It must not be affiliated to any other university; it must be independent. It must reject – like American universities – dependence on the external examinations of London University and set its own examinations. "If the West Indies are to be self-governing what better place to start the process can we find than the university."[12] In all these matters except perhaps the study of Caribbean languages, Williams took exactly the opposite views from the Irvine Committee which recommended strongly in favour of a temporarily dependent, residential university college of 400 to 500 students representing the scholastic elite of the West Indies. Nor were the extra-mural programmes of the UCWI as practical or as politically motivated as Williams would have liked. Williams' university was essentially different from the university of the Irvine Committee or from what was established in Jamaica in 1948.

Williams Crosses Swords with Hammond

While Williams was expanding his memorandum on university education into a larger text, including primary and secondary education, the opportunity occurred to cross swords with S. A. Hammond, the education adviser to Colonial Development and Welfare since 1940. The *Journal of Negro Education* dedicated its issue of summer 1946 to "The Problem of Education in Dependent Territories". Hammond an English educationist with vast experience in Africa and the West Indies wrote an article on "Education in the British West Indies", a Dr J. F. E. Einer wrote on "Education in the Netherlands and French West Indies", and a Dr Lloyd Bauch wrote on "Education in the Territories and Outlying

Possessions of the United States". Eric Williams was given the job of producing a review article on the writing of these men. For the purpose of the present discussion, it will be necessary to deal only with the views of Hammond and Williams. The fundamental differences, as Williams recognised, was that Hammond, an Englishman, employed by an aid agency set up by the British government, was not prescribing for an independent West Indian nation, or even for a self-governing set of islands. Hammond acknowledged without enthusiasm, indeed with cautious scepticism, that self-government was being asked for in the West Indies, but he assumed that the education system was still to transmit British cultural values.[13] After all this was exactly the goal towards which the British Council was working in the colony. Williams wished to use education as a preparation for self-government; the schools should not reflect the colonial culture which was not to continue; they should be change agents in shaping a West Indian culture. Here was already well formed the deep nationalist mind-set on education which was to govern Williams' political life in Trinidad and Tobago.

Hammond angered Williams by the suggestion that West Indians should not aim at European standards in the social services. Within Trinidad at the same time there were creoles, mostly blacks, who were up in arms against Dora Ibbertson, an English woman, who was giving advice on social welfare programmes. In the 1940s there were nationalists in the colony who were distinctly uncomfortable with English expatriates who ventured to chart the course of the future. Hammond's remarks were pointed chiefly at primary education and the training of primary school teachers. His thesis was that the island economies could not bear the cost of expanding primary education on an English model of schooling or teacher training. Such teachers would require European level of remuneration. An important premise of Hammond was that the agricultural economies of the islands, burdened with rapidly rising populations, could not be taxed further to produce additional revenues to finance education. However bad school buildings were, however defective teaching was, recurrent education expenditure by governments was to be reduced, or at least kept in check.

Williams always insisted on the need to raise standards of all types of education. He attacked Hammond's thesis with the argument that income tax rates were too low in the British West Indies; it was absurd to think that maximum levels had been reached. He contrasted the expenditure on education in Puerto Rico with expenditure in the British West Indies which had more people. The British West Indies with a population approximately 50 percent larger than Puerto Rico's spent less than 50 percent what Puerto Rico expended (excluding the University of Puerto Rico). Williams did not stop to inquire whether the funds being spent in Puerto Rico were generated in Puerto Rico. He denied that Puerto Rico was richer than the British West Indies. Trinidad, he claimed, was wealthier in mineral resources than Puerto Rico.[14]

Hammond, as was commonly done at this time by British officials, linked financial self-sufficiency to aspirations for self-government. A too costly system of education, falsely modelled on English standards which were always changing, presumably upwards or for the better, would spoil the islands' chances of qualifying financially for self-government. Williams' reply was that of the nationalist: financial self-sufficiency was a dignified goal for the West Indies, but the British government was morally obliged to give aid in return for centuries of exploitation of the islands' wealth. If the British government did not wish to give aid for recurrent cost like teachers' salaries, it could offer money for research or buildings.

Williams also crossed swords with Hammond on the question of curriculum and examinations, but this was partly because he had not read the many previous memoranda of Hammond (or because he was in a mood to oppose anything Hammond said). Judging solely from Hammond's article in the *Journal of Negro Education*, it appeared that he failed to place emphasis on curriculum reform although approving proposals in the islands for practical studies generally and for a new kind of secondary school (the secondary modern school) linked to agriculture. Williams proclaimed that for him a major reform needed was to put agriculture at the centre of the rural primary school and the rural secondary school, not to turn out agricultural labourers for the plantations, but to spread agricultural skills and to harmonise the social aspirations of students with the agricultural reality of their environment. Hammond, thought Williams, mistakenly, still adhered to a colonial emphasis on the production of an urban intelligentsia through urban based secondary schools.[15] This allegation was in fact the very opposite of Hammond's real position. Williams was very critical of Hammond's contentment with the external examinations of Cambridge University for secondary schools. External examinations were rejected by Williams as the chief source of distortion of the curriculum. He also rejected external examinations at the university level; here, as always, his position was the imperative for an independent university.

Although Hammond himself had been a party to a major dispute with the Roman Catholic Church over ownership of school buildings and control of denominational school teachers in the Windward Islands and Trinidad, he felt that the dual system of education itself was not a major problem. It gave rise, he said, to "administrative inconvenience and untidiness";[16] Hammond wrote in his article in the *Journal of Negro Education* that most people probably felt, like Winston Churchill, Prime Minister of England, that religion could never be taken out of schools. Dual control of one sort or the other was to be found in all Christian countries, Hammond reminded his readers. Eric Williams implied that Hammond had underestimated the power of the minority in the West Indies who wished for state control, hinting that through the democratic process this minority might become a majority. Dual control, retorted Williams, was a matter for the West

Indian people to decide, and not for Mr Churchill. He Williams had a preference for "a fully state controlled system – that is a democratic, self-governing state".[17]

Williams was very critical of Hammond's approval of apprenticeship programmes as the main means of imparting technical/vocational education. Hammond felt that this method was "valid for small communities where the supply of craftsmen must be strictly adjusted to the demand and where neither numbers nor subsequent earning power justify the high overhead costs of technical schools".[18] This line of thought, sneered Williams, was proof of Hammond's failure to rise above the narrow social and economic framework of colonial thinking. Instead of restricting the supply of craftsmen to the demand, Hammond should, had he not been an imperialist at heart, be thinking of how he could create new economic structures which would call for a larger number of craftsmen, and therefore justify technical schools. Here Williams' critique was justifiable, for the value of apprenticeship programmes themselves was not in question. Hammond was accused of being one of those whose thoughts were governed "by the West Indian social milieu in which the plantation system dominated by absentee capital restricts the available land, the colonial connection obstructs the development of secondary industries, and commercial employment is determined by the race of the applicant rather than by his merits".[19]

Williams also took issue with Hammond over adult education. Hammond had indeed said that this was necessary to secure the gains of primary schooling, and in other places Hammond had advocated that parents and communities, no less than children in schools, should be the object of education. But Williams, judging Hammond solely from the article in the *Journal of Negro Education*, felt that his concept of adult education made it "an appendage to the normal educational process, which it is neither obligatory to promote nor culpable to neglect".[20] Hammond's real position on adult education was the very opposite of this, and was a more radical position than would have been acceptable to most of the colonial officials who administered education in the West Indies. Williams gave away the essential difference between himself and Hammond by substituting the term 'mass' education for adult education. At once Williams invested it with a direct, political dimension whereas Hammond thought of it mainly as a mechanism of social and economic development, teaching rural communities how to establish better homes, families and farms. Williams said adult education should not be an aid to the urban intelligentsia trying to acquire external degrees; nor a means of teaching music or other refined accomplishments; it was to teach "good citizenship and responsible living". As a form of political education it would presumably be directed to the goal of self-government.

Education in the British West Indies
The Nationalist Agenda

Williams has given an account of the difficulties he had in finding a publisher in the USA for his book *Education in the British West Indies*. Unlike his previous work, *The Negro in the Caribbean*, it did not have a Pan-Caribbean focus, but was confined to the British Caribbean. This limited its appeal to the United States market. Indeed the book (*Education in the British West Indies*) might be said to be symptomatic of Williams' descent from the wider Afro-American academic stage to the narrower social and political concerns of the British Caribbean. He was on his way home, as he himself puts it, to his "nationalist cradle". Two years after Williams had been posted to the Trinidad Headquarters of the Caribbean Commission, the book was eventually published in a limited edition in Trinidad and Tobago, under the sponsorship of the Teachers' Economic and Cultural Association. It drew heavily upon the reforms of the white colonialist education experts like Hammond whom Williams was anxious to chastise at every turn. No wonder Hammond was vexed with the young upstart, lifting the best ideas of the enemy – Marriott, Cutteridge and Hammond – and reshaping them into assault weapons in the interest of a nationalist creed. On Williams' own account Hammond was "distinctly rude" to him after reading the book.

In *Education in the British West Indies* Williams condemned the literary bias of the primary and secondary schools. The bias should be towards agriculture in the case of primary schools and agriculture, industry and commerce in the case of secondary schools. The curriculum of the secondary schools was criticised for omitting to stress, or even to take seriously, anything West Indian. "West Indian history, geography, economics, community organisation and problems – West Indian culture, in a word – find no place."[21] The 'artificiality' of the British West Indian secondary schools was credited largely to the colonial practice of taking external examinations of Oxford and Cambridge Universities. The English examinations require a "knowledge of Roman history rather than West Indian history, of the British monarchy rather than the Crown Colony system, of empire geography rather than West Indian geography".[22] Technical/vocational education had too small a place in the educational system of the islands. Williams also condemned the practice of using cheap pupil-teachers as a substantial part of the teaching force. Secondary school teachers also came in for a share of criticism. Ability to learn had been equated with ability to teach. And finally the imposition of fees for secondary education and the failure to implement compulsory primary education were named as obstacles to progress.

On the question of dual control of education Williams took the position that denominational rivalry led to the harmful multiplication of inefficient schools where the public interest demanded consolidation. Noting that the churches owned most of the schools in the region, Williams argued that a democratic government must safeguard the superior right of the community as a whole to control the general trend of education, without ignoring the religious sentiments of the people. In other words if a duly elected government wished a state controlled system of education, then as representative of the majority it had a right to enforce such a policy, whatever the churches preferred. This was exactly the situation Williams as prime minister was to find himself in during the 1960s.

It has already been shown elsewhere that there were reformers in Trinidad and Tobago, men of a colonialist mentality, like Burslem, Crehan, Bushe, Hancock, Mackay, Marriott, Cutteridge, Daniel and Hogben who had voiced some of the same criticisms of the education system as Eric Williams.[23] Burslem and Crehan, once the principals of QRC and CIC respectively, had criticised the overly classical curriculum of their own colleges; Bushe and Hancock had been Inspectors of Schools when agriculture was introduced into the primary schools; Mackay had supervised the introduction of science in the secondary schools; Marriott had led the hopeless assault on the veneration of Cambridge external examinations; and Cutteridge had immortalised himself by daring to write local textbooks for arithmetic, reading and geography; Daniel had produced a local West Indian history book, and Hogben had emphasised critically the separateness of secondary schools from primary schools. These men had generated new ideas and introduced a considerable amount of change into the education system over the first fifty years of the twentieth century; but the schools and the education system, which are always difficult institutions to change, resisted innovations. Like so many other social institutions when faced with pressure for change, the schools had absorbed the innovations and the criticisms, and then returned to something nearly like their original state before the changes. There was room therefore for new champions of change to demand widespread reforms, some of which had been called for previously, and partly implemented, by white colonialist civil servants, when Eric Williams was a teenager or undergraduate.[24]

There remained however an inescapable difference between the reform-oriented English education experts in the service of the British empire and the nationalist historian Dr Eric Williams who could claim no expertise in pedagogy. If Williams in *Education in the West Indies* in many areas appeared to be calling for the same kind of reforms as the white English experts – or the Moyne Commission – the awesome difference was that while they worked within the colonial framework, he wished to break through it to a new vantage point of self-government and Caribbean identity for the West Indian islands. There was then a tremendous difference of motivation and consequently in the ethos and measure of change desired. When Cutteridge or Daniel wrote local textbooks emphasising, as they thought, the local environment they justified it on pedagogical grounds; it was pedagogically sound, they would have claimed, to have children learn from the known (the West Indian environment) to the unknown (the wider world). When

Williams called for a more sweeping West Indianisation of the curriculum, his aim was not to improve reading skills, but to increase knowledge of West Indian affairs, impart pride and create the cultural bases for decolonisation and nationalism. For Williams there were apparently no limits to the process of West Indianisation of textbooks; the process was to become central to education policy, not an appendage to it. Marriott and Cutteridge were still committed to transmitting English cultural values; Williams the nationalist, carrying further the concern of the stay-at-home young Trinidad intellectuals of the 1930s who wished to have a genuine West Indian history in the schools,[25] aimed at nothing less than the creation of an independent cultural movement. For Williams colonialism was the enemy.

It is almost incredible that Williams in *Education in the West Indies*, where he championed the West Indianisation of the curriculum, should have omitted mention of the efforts of Captain Cutteridge. The question of the use of Cutteridge's *Readers* was not dead when Williams returned to reside in Trinidad and Tobago in 1948. Williams knew that there were persons in the colony opposed to Cutteridge from a suspicion of all things West Indian in education, at least when proposed by the agents of colonialism.[26] A good opportunity to give some credit to Cutteridge came in Williams' article in 1956 on instructional materials for Caribbean schools, but he missed it also.[27] His obsession with nationalism did not permit him to credit Cutteridge for pioneering changes in the right direction, even if from the 'wrong' motivation. Nor did Williams' personality, especially his intellectual arrogance, lead him easily to acknowledge the debt his own reforms owed to the Englishmen he disliked.

Williams as Political Educator

Williams resided in Trinidad from 1948 to 1955 as an international civil servant. In the development of education in the colony these years were dominated by school building; from 1950 there was a Minister of Education, Roy Joseph. Williams was later to detract from the achievements of Joseph, by alleging that he was too shortsightedly concerned with school buildings, and not with the genuine reform of the education system. If the professional directors of education and the Minister of Education promoted certain types of changes, it was all within the colonial framework – so Williams thought. Ironically a new policy sponsored by these authorities enabled Williams to carry his critique of the education system and of West Indian conditions to a wider audience. The adult education programme (partly the result of Hammond's advocacy) created the ambience for public lectures by Williams, although his lectures were never under the auspices of the Education Department; they were sponsored by voluntary agencies or by the Extra-Mural Department of the new University College of the West Indies which was erected on lines unsatisfactory to him. Williams clearly wished a larger role in political affairs and the question was how far this was compatible with his job as an international civil servant. He politicised everything he touched, whether it was the Trinidad and Tobago Historical Society of which he became president (1950-1954), or the Little Carib Movement of Beryl McBurnie. Williams' increasing involvement in the cultural life of the Trinidad community, culminating in 1955 in a deliberately staged series of public lectures on education designed to boost his image hopefully to thwart dismissal by the Caribbean Commission, had the effect of legitimising his already considerable intellectual claims to political leadership in the country.[28]

Specifically in relation to education Dr Williams in brilliantly crafted speeches took the argument in his public lectures over ground which had scarcely been covered in public forums previously; for example, audaciously back to Aristotle.[29] He excused his own lack of qualification as an expert in education by identifying a catalogue of inconsistent recommendations by past experts. The lesson he distilled from all this was the incontrovertible need for state control of education. The enthusiastic public reception of these lectures, in respectable meeting places like the Public Library and Naparima College (not to mention the later roar of the crowd in the 'University of Woodford Square') furnished the encouragement to move fully into political organisation in 1955. He had become the focus of a considerable nationalist movement in a disunited society. The Hindus were organised under the leadership of Bhadase Maraj. Fortunately for Williams his political skills and his personal popularity were considerable, but it should be recognised that he did not nurture a party from scratch; pre-existing groups, especially of black, disaffected middle class teachers, for example the People's Education Movement led by nationalists DeWilton Rogers and John Donaldson surrendered their organisations, their loyalties and their energies to him; and he built upon these urban black middle class foundations.[30] This new party, the PNM formed in early 1956, won a surprising victory at the polls at the end of that year. Shortly after this success Williams recalled that recently he had been denied the use of a certain school as a venue for a lecture. Now as chief minister he could enter any school receiving public funds.[31] The nationalist historian, formulator of a critique of education, had been pitchforked into a political position from which he could begin to carry through a nationalist policy.

[5]

The Nationalists in Power 1956-1981

> The first prerequisite of party politics in Trinidad and Tobago is the establishment of one good party. Such a party is now being organised; and I am identified with it.
>
> Eric Williams, 13 Sept 1955 (Woodford Square)
> [Sutton 1981: 108]

The Early Nationalist Movement

Although agitation for some form of self-government was almost as old as the English conquest of Trinidad, the history of the modern nationalist movement can hardly be said to have begun before the end of World War 1; and the beginning is incontestably linked with the political career of Capt Cipriani and the labour movement. Under the leadership of this white man, the first group to carry the banner of nationalism was the working class, particularly the black creole urban working class, since it must be said at once that the racial divide between Indians and blacks was the greatest single factor inhibiting unified action of the working class in the process of nation building. From the time the Indians first emerged politically at the end of the 19th century to the eve of independence in 1962, their traditional leaders (who carried the most following) and whoever led the black creoles have disagreed about constitutional reforms, and the transmission of political power and influence from the colonial masters to local hands. Because they were in an underprivileged minority position, had a separate, distinctive culture and religions and looked to India as their true motherland, the Indians, for very good reasons, could not, and did not, take the lead in the evolution of nationalist sentiment for Trinidad and Tobago, and often were fearful of nationalism or opposed to it.[1] The Indians desired change and improvement in their communal conditions, but seemed less dissatisfied with the constitutional status quo than the black urban working class. Cipriani, the white creole, failed to build working class unity between Indians and black creoles, and so too did Rienzi, the Indian, and Uriah Butler, the fiery black preacher politician and nationalist.[2]

With few exceptions the defense of the status quo was led by English government officials, by the English settlers and by the white creoles, especially the French creoles. World War 11, mostly for reasons outside Trinidad and Tobago, created a whole new world more favourable for decolonisation and nationalism than anything existing previously. Politics in England shifted to the left of its pre-war position.[3] But the Crown colony authorities in Trinidad and Tobago were not ready to yield any ground which was not contested by leaders who demonstrated a knowledge of the political system of the metropole and could sometimes talk its political language. Because of the inherent difficulty of uniting the people, because of the toughness of the employer class, the cleverness of the English overlords, and the ineptness of the Indian, black or coloured creole political leaders, the nationalist movement did not advance single-mindedly during or after World War 11.[4] The country did register two important political gains during this period: universal adult suffrage (1946) and the inauguration of the ministerial system of government in 1950. But not a single political commentator has had anything edifying to say about politics between the mid-1940s and the mid-1950s; it is depicted as a quagmire of greed, corruption, individualism, divisions, strife and political immaturity. The passage of politics in the words of a recent researcher was from personal politics to ethnic based parties.[5] Political organisations after the 1950 elections became more openly based on racial considerations. This was the situation which faced the nationalist, Dr Williams, on his entry into politics.

The First PNM Government 1956-1962

The main reason for putting before the reader an account and an interpretation of the long regime of Dr Eric Williams (1956-1981) and the PNM (1956-1986) in the country is to provide the essential context to the remarkable education policies of the government over the same period.[6] Also education policy appears to have been widely accepted within the first five years, and by the end of Williams' life, as the most successful aspect of the PNM regime. It should be instructive therefore to evaluate the political economy over the same period as the education policy; Such an examination will proceed in steps corresponding to the three phases (1956 to 1962; 1963 to 1972; and 1973 to 1981) in which education policy is later to be considered. In successive waves, and then all together the country underwent a political revolution, a social revolution and a massive economic boom. During

The Nationalists in Power 1956-1981

all these years one political party and one prime minister were in office continuously; and therefore neither Dr Williams nor the PNM can escape for a minute from the tremendous burden of total identification of contemporary Trinidad and Tobago with one man and the party over which he exercised a most extraordinary dominance.

Between 1956 and independence in 1962 Dr Williams and the PNM had the greatest impact for good on the society; after independence the shock of PNM conquest was over, and the limitations of the victory had begun to be more readily apparent. For the first time a disciplined party captured power in elections. The PNM was far from being the creation of one man, but its philosophy and its plan of action emanated from Dr Williams; and there was no one of his stature or charisma in the party. It eschewed socialism and nationalisation; under Williams the party was nationalist and pragmatic. The party promised to raise the standard of living by social welfare measures and to create a national community. It declared that it stood for racial equality and for equal opportunity. In the sphere of economic policy, Williams and the PNM decided to join most other West Indian countries in aiming for economic expansion through light manufacturing. The economy was opened up to foreign investment in the so-called strategy of industrialisation by invitation based on the Puerto Rican model. This economic strategy with its large-scale concessions to private enterprise is better known for its differential trickling down effect of benefits than for any equalising effect on incomes or economic opportunity. For all Williams' rhetoric against colonialism he was ready to work with foreign capitalists. The creation of jobs was a prime concern of the PNM; also improvements in housing and health. The main strategy to effect equality was in the field of public employment and in the provision of education: the higher reaches of the civil service were opened to non-whites, substantially for the first time; the whites and near-whites in some cases were retired, or felt obliged to resign rather than serve black ministers of government. That blacks and coloureds got far more of these new civil service jobs than Indians has been the subject of much acrimonious controversy. In the field of education the widening of access to secondary education via the Common Entrance Examination was a democratising thrust capable of exerting equalising pressures on the society. Free secondary education from 1961 was perhaps the single most popular measure ever taken by Williams and the PNM government.[7]

Williams was the most radical nationalist who ever obtained power in the Commonwealth Caribbean and at least for the first five years of his government he revelled in this position as the unquestioned leader of the fight for West Indian nationhood either within the infant federation of the West Indies, or implicitly for an independent Trinidad and Tobago. He and his party identified the chief internal enemies as the same forces which had supported British imperialism and colonialism: the British government officials; the English settlers; the Roman Catholic Church; the white business elite; the white creoles and the backward sections of the black and coloured middle class; also among the ranks of the enemies was the mass media, especially the *Trinidad Guardian*. Although it was part of his plan to carry the Indian working class with him, Williams attacked Bhadase Maraj, leader of the Hindus, and the Sanatan Maha Sabha as reactionary forces, bent on frustrating the nationalist movement. Needless to say who the main external enemies were: the British government, the United States government and, surprisingly, the federal Prime Minister of the West Indies, Grantley Adams. Williams in his challenge to the residual American military presence at Chaguaramas catapulted West Indian nationalism to new and strange heights, with less than anticipated results. Within two years (1958-1960) an accommodation was reached with the Americans, which lowered the temperature and restored the government's focus on its internal enemies. The scholarly commentators, it is said, have still to decide whether the peace made in 1960 was honourable or dishonourable; a victory or a betrayal.[8]

The organisation of an Indian opposition party was inevitable; and it came in 1958. In the elections in 1956 the PNM victory rested on the votes of middle and working class blacks, especially those resident in urban and suburban districts of the North; the whites had voted for opposition candidates or parties; and the majority of the Indians for Indian candidates or the People's Democratic Party (PDP). As far as Indians were concerned, especially Hindus under Bhadase Maraj, the worst had happened: they had fallen under black political domination and expected to be disadvantaged because of it. As in the past most of the Indians were unwilling to exert themselves in a political struggle to create a national government and a national society in which they as a minority expected little or no power or benefits. Their success in the federal elections of 1958 convinced them that the PNM government was really a minority government, and that with greater organisation and a leader to match the 'Doctor' in intellectual stature and 'knowledgeism', the Indians might be saved from black power. Hence the new Democratic Labour Party (DLP) and the impressment of a politically inexperienced Dr Rudranath Capildeo into the role of leader.[9]

Dr Williams made matters worse by his outburst against the Maha Sabha in 1958. In words which rankled for years he stigmatised them as a recalcitrant minority masquerading as the Indian nation and refusing to identify with the nationalist forces of Trinidad and Tobago and the West Indian nation. What Dr Williams and the PNM could have done in the first five years to reconcile Indians and blacks is not clear. It is a moot point whether the desired national community could have been created even by a proportionate sharing out of jobs between blacks and Indians at the expense of party favourites or people of genuine merit. Nowadays the best advice of the experts is that multiculturalism is the only way to lay the basis for the national community; but this was inconceivable in those early days when the compelling presumption of the new government was that colonial culture had to be replaced by one consolidated something which was national and integrated. Either Williams and the PNM were deceived into believing their own propaganda that the colonial masters' policy of divide and rule was the main or sole barrier to Indian-black solidarity, or they remained optimistic that the Indians as a minority would come to their senses and assimilate themselves into a creole oriented cultural core. This did not happen by independence, nor since independence; and it remains one of the biggest challenges to the nation at present. Arguably though, Indian-black relations were better at independence in 1962 than in 1956 or 1958; but it has been suggested that they were better still in 1946 or 1948 under colonial rule than when the nationalists took over in 1956.[10]

Fidel Castro's revolution in Cuba triumphed in 1959. Although Dr Williams came to power two years earlier via the ballot box, his rhetoric against imperialism and colonialism suggested a potential for a measure of ideological extremism not totally unlike that of Castro. 'Papa Doc' Duvalier of Haiti was just beginning to consolidate his regime by corruption and murder, but Trinidadians were either ignorant of events in Haiti, or thought that Williams could not possibly be compared with the Haitian dictator. Williams was branded by his opponents as a communist, a dictator, a godless egotist; he reminded some people of Hitler. Trinidadians were aware that they were living through a bloodless political and social revolution; and the society was seriously divided between those who were for the revolution and those who were against it. Williams did not put property in danger like Castro; and there was no significant emigration of any section of the community as happened in Jamaica under Michael Manley in the late 1970s. Williams declared his opposition to socialism, communism and nationalisation, and invited foreign and local capitalists under the protective umbrella of government concessions to move the economy forward and create jobs. It was the jobs, status and influence of vested interest groups which had been whittled away or which were under threat from the regime.

The best strategy of Williams' opponents was to reorganise, regroup and bring counter-pressure to bear on him and the PNM. The Roman Catholic Church, the white business community, and the Indians, chiefly the Hindu masses under their politico-religious leaders and secular chiefs like Dr Capildeo had considerable leverage in influencing policies, and each of these groups had sympathisers within the PNM. It has been suggested therefore that heated debates occurred within the PNM on attitudes towards opposition groups; and if Dr Williams tended to have his way in the end in terms of policy, it must not be believed that he ruled without restraint. Some of the limits were self-imposed because of his general commitment from his academic training to liberal democracy and a Westminster type of government.[11] His period of residence in the United States between 1939 and 1948 had bred in him a frightening assertiveness and competitiveness and an impatience with delay; and a belief that quick changes were possible. This direct head-on approach to problems and to groups so unlike the hesitant, gradualist

British approach of some of his predecessors, notably Albert Gomes, convinced the Trinidad and Tobago public that a new force had taken over the seat of power. Curiously Dr Williams was at the same time an inscrutable politician, something of an enigma even to those who worked at close quarters with him.

Although he was a determined politician, Dr Williams knew how to compromise; and one analyst has characterised his policies as "accommodative in design and compromising in execution".[12] The question has been raised whether this was deliberate strategy or the result of an ambivalent personality. Whatever its origin, it enabled Williams to play politics with his opponents instead of insisting on some inflexible predetermined policy. This was part of the secret of his retention of political power for a generation. In education policy, for example, the accommodation reached with the churches in the *Concordat* of December 1960 went a long way in attenuating clerical grievances until 1965. Relations with the United States government, after the end of the Chaguaramas drama, went as calmly as if no confrontation had happened; Trinidad and Tobago remained on the side of the West in the Cold War, as indeed its economic policy of industrialisation by invitation dictated. Even a measure of accommodation with the Indians under Dr Capildeo was arrived at in respect to the making of the independence constitution; and then came the struggle between Indians and the PNM for the spoils of office in the highly charged elections of 1961. Dr Williams won a resounding victory.

Williams and the 'February' Revolution

The decade between 1963 and 1973 was the most difficult years of all for Dr Williams and the PNM since they had to face a Black Power movement and army mutiny which nearly toppled them from office in early 1970, and certainly put them on the defensive for at least the next three years. Williams lived long enough to see the black masses listening to other voices in his 'University of Woodford Square'. The genesis of the troubles was not the success of the Indian opposition in or outside Parliament; the Indian opposition politicians in fact were divided and ineffective. The root of Williams' problems was the failure of his economic policies to create jobs fast enough and to secure a serious redistribution of incomes. Concurrently, it was felt by some blacks that the social structures of colonialism, especially the predominance of white creoles in business with the long-standing consequential discrimination against blacks and Indians in employment in private enterprise, had not been destroyed despite the coming to political power of black men, and increased access to education by Indians and blacks. The success of Castro's revolution in Cuba in redistributing incomes and welfare often provided the muted criteria for the assessment of Williams' government. The Cuban model came to rival the Puerto Rican model. Studies subsequently revealed that although

The Nationalists in Power 1956-1981

the Trinidad economy continued to grow after independence at least down to 1969, it was another classic West Indian case of slow growth without economic development; outflows of capital have been shown to have been greater than inflows; the local white business people, though prosperous, had not been converted by cooperation with foreign capitalists into a vigorous entrepreneurial class; unemployment had become more severe in a country noted for the youthfulness of its population. The expectations, especially among black people, of an adequate share in the benefits of the PNM revolution had not been satisfied.[13]

Additionally the radiating influence of the new civil rights movement of blacks in the United States penetrated Trinidad and Tobago and found receptive ground in the black, unemployed youths of the depressed urban areas and in the middle class student population of the newly commenced St Augustine branch of UWI. Stokely Carmichael – born in Trinidad – and the Black Panthers of the United States were heroes among many black youths in Trinidad, and certain high points in the civil rights struggle in North America, for example the trial of the West Indian students in Canada for the destruction of a computer at Sir George Williams University, raised anti-white, anti-establishment feelings to great intensity in the local black community. The Indians took no significant part in the Black Power disturbances.

A group of West Indian academics calling itself the New World Group, centered on the Mona campus of the UWI, but with a branch in Trinidad and Tobago led by rivals, Lloyd Best and Dr James Millette, emerged as a serious focus of scholarly opposition to what was regarded as the neo-colonial policies of West Indian governments, including the nationalist government of Trinidad and Tobago.[14] The unrest among UWI students at St Augustine and the black youths of depressed areas of Port of Spain interpenetrated with the scholarly objections to Dr Williams and the PNM of the New World Group. New black opposition clusters like NJAC (National Joint Action Committee), UNIP (United National Independence Party) and Tapia came to the fore, while the Indian opposition forces watched silently in fear that the new assertiveness of blacks might eventually turn in fury against Indians. The explosion of popular youth protest and marches between February and April 1970 was unlike anything previously seen in the country; it was Trinidad's delayed participation in the waves of youth rebellions in 1968 in North America, England and western Europe. Had the mutinous soldiers of the Defence Force (however non-revolutionary their objectives appeared to have been) succeeded in getting out of their base at Chaguaramas into Port of Spain, the government might have fallen. As it was, Dr Williams by declaring a State of Emergency on the 21 April 1970 managed to stop protest marches, and through a series of repressive measures in the next two years the Black Power movement and its small, armed, residual wing operating in the hills were dispersed or refocussed into feeble movements of Afro-Trinidadian cultural nationalism.[15]

The New Economic Strategy

Even before the Black Power movement peaked in April 1970, Dr Williams and his Cabinet had been obliged to begin the search for a new economic strategy to replace the Puerto Rican model. Williams was obliged to think more in ideological terms.[16] The government turned to the left to find new solutions, and to appropriate some of the positive ideas of the enemy – the New World Group and the Black Power movement. However Williams and the PNM did so without adopting a socialist philosophy, even though some of the measures taken from the mid-1970s (for example, the Peoples' Sector of the economy, meaning small business enterprises and co-operatives under the banner of self-help and self-reliance) were rather like those which Michael Manley talked of in Jamaica under the ideology of democratic socialism. Dr Williams and the PNM also began to speak more about economic independence and a social transformation. In the short run, the quickest hand-out Williams could manage was to increase expenditure on the Special Works Programme which benefited both Indian and black workers; also more Indians were recruited into the civil service and the police. The government in fact was becoming more and more the major employer of labour.

The essence of the new economic strategy was that the government, not the private sector, was to become the prime engine of economic growth. Certain areas of the economy would no longer be open to entry by foreign capital; the government would not allow foreign capital to be employed unless in joint ventures with a meaningful proportion of ownership falling to the government. The purpose was to work for the transfer of major assets and requisite managerial skills from foreign hands to local hands, and thus to encourage the reinvestment of profits in the country. This was part of a general programme of localising important sectors of the economy, including banking and insurance. It was state capitalism, (his so-called "middle road") not socialism that Williams had in mind; but how was it to be financed? Dr Williams could borrow money from international agencies to build schools, but not for economic adventures.

The opposition parties boycotted the election of 1971, and the PNM won all the seats, but only with a voter turn-out of 39%. Hence the legitimacy of the government was challenged at a time when it was already on the defensive on account of the Black Power demonstrations and their aftermath. Dr Williams bought time by appointing a high level Constitutional Commission to make recommendations for a new constitution, and then proceeded to concede two of the key demands of his opponents - the franchise at age 18 and the abandonment of the voting machine – before the Commission reported in early 1974. No elections were called until 1976 by which time the country had adopted a republican form of government, but without any shift to proportional representation, which the opposition parties and the Commission favoured. Lonely, frustrated and embarrassed by financial scandals involving several members of the

PNM, even Ministers of government, Dr Williams announced at his party's convention in September 1973 that he desired to quit the leadership of the party and to retire from politics. That there was no public outcry against this decision, nor any public demand for the return of Williams, might have been due to the fact that Williams never actually resigned and that only sections of his party really cared enough for the 'Doctor'. This situation was a far cry from the widespread popularity of Dr Williams during his first five years in office as the confident philosopher-king and ideologue of the party and the black creole masses.

The Oil Bonanza

The political pundits do not seem to be sure whether Williams really meant to depart from the leadership or whether his was a game to flush out enemies and confirm friends in the party. There was however one good and overwhelming reason for his going back on his word. A sudden and dramatic rise in oil prices, for which Trinidad and Tobago was not responsible, pitchforked the nation from a balance of payment deficit of TT$32 million in 1973 to a surplus of TT$694 million in a matter of months.[17] No prime minister could conceivably give up office voluntarily, while enjoying reasonable health and strength, in the face of such an overflowing treasury, which removed money as an obstacle to the attainment of national objectives. It was now possible to redistribute income and to move nearer to the PNM dream of a welfare state by increasing old age pensions, subsidising food for the poor, public transportation, meals and books for students, and by reducing income tax on certain levels of incomes. At the same time the government began to have the money to implement its new economic policy; to buy majority shares in companies, to set up government companies and lend money to them.

Much to the disgust of the private sector, the government's direct participation in the mixed economy in terms of ownership mushroomed to previously unimaginable proportions within a few years. The government also obliged the banking and insurance industries to localise their operations. More than any other Commonwealth Caribbean state the Trinidad and Tobago government owned the so-called commanding heights of the economy by the end of the 1970s, but it had stopped short of nationalisation as a principle and where it was undertaken, it generally came more as a result of the desire to save jobs. Texaco, the giant oil concern, was left alone, though other oil and petrochemical companies came under joint ownership or full government ownership. After 1975 came the momentous decision, which few Third World prime ministers in a similar situation could have resisted. This was to attempt to shift the economy from reliance on oil revenues to heavy industries in petrochemicals and iron and steel for export using the nation's large reserves of natural gas for energy. It looked like a fairy-tale opportunity to transform the country into a serious industrial nation and the government went ahead with steel, ammonia, and urea plants without regard to cost or soft markets and without adequate local managerial expertise.[18]

The negative and positive effects of the oil boom in the short run were felt by all contemporaries. Unemployment was drastically reduced as the construction industry boomed and the civil service ballooned; everyone, blacks, Indians, white creoles; the private sector – people in Trinidad and people in Tobago – benefited, not equally of course, from increased incomes and new economic opportunities in the growing economy.[19] As we shall see later, a number of programmes to improve technical/vocational training and to enhance the readiness of young people for jobs in industries were undertaken. But as might have been expected agricultural output fell drastically as labour was drawn away from agriculture; the food import bill and luxury spending on imported consumer goods reached unprecedented heights; so too did prices of all goods and services. From 1974 to about 1981 Trinidad and Tobago enjoyed a high level of prosperity, but without solving its fundamental problems. As in all such boom periods corruption and financial scandals, some in very high quarters, came to light, though not sufficiently into the light of day to lead to prosecutions or convictions. Everybody had a better life, or so it seemed.

The prosperity of the country raises the question whether it was an appropriate moment for the politics of the opposition to turn sharply to the left. Presumably hard times provide more fruitful ground for socialist ideologies. The elections of 1976 which occurred almost in the middle of the years of prosperity were marked by the late reorganisation of the opposition forces, including the incorporation of one part of the traditional Indian opposition, the DLP into the United Labour Front (ULF) which declared itself a socialist working class party. While the PNM campaigned on its past achievements and Dr Williams partly by distancing himself from some members of his own Cabinet whom he stigmatised as "millstones" around his neck, the ULF, the chief opposition party, campaigned by rejecting the state capitalism of the government as a spurious form of ownership and calling on the electorate to support genuine nationalisation of the means of production and genuine transformation of the social structure. The country failed to be persuaded and the PNM was voted back into office.[20] Any analysis of voting patterns, however, would reveal the old principle of race first running ahead of attempts at Indian-black working class solidarity. As usual the Indians would have done better by being more united.

The End of Dr Williams

By the end of the 1970s Dr Williams was himself increasingly a lonely, sick, frustrated man; some of his isolation was self-imposed and self-gratifying. He still had great influence within the PNM in terms of policy direction, but he could not prevent party members from straying from party ideals by being greedy, inefficient, without principles; PNM was the party in power, but no longer was it occupying higher moral ground over other political groups. The spoils of office were there for the taking in the oil boom, but Williams personally, as always, remained above financial corruption. A major source of disappointment to him was to see before his very eyes his old colonial enemies still strongly entrenched despite the rise of black men and Indians: the Roman Catholic Church was still a powerful institution; the private sector was still dominated by local whites, despite the success of some Indian businessmen; Indians, especially the Hindus still defined themselves outside the national community he was trying to build. Foreign capitalists in the form of the multinational corporations were formidable forces to negotiate with, and if Williams kept his eyes on the trade statistics he would have seen that despite his windows to Cuba, China and the Soviet Union, Trinidad and Tobago did more business with the former occupants of Chaguaramas, the United States of America than with any other country.[21] He could not escape the colossus to the north. The nationalists had in fact brought about a national society, but by the standards of decolonisation which Williams had set himself and the party, his movement had been a failure. Williams might very well have been the only Third World Prime Minister to have died in office, so desperately saddened, at a time when his country was enjoying such prosperity.

To the consternation of many, the PNM was retained in power in the elections of 1981; they had won without Dr Williams; and indeed it has been suggested that sympathy for Williams who died in March 1981 might have worked to the advantage of the PNM. George Chambers who became political leader and Prime Minister was very much unlike Williams in most important respects; he was very ordinary, without any claims to being an intellectual, without any charisma; it seemed unlikely that he could, under the best of circumstances, keep the opposition out of power for much longer. When the PNM was voted out of office in 1986 in a landslide loss, it was the result of the long desired, but elusive alliance between the Indian opposition party and organised parties of black creoles opposed to the PNM The Indians had to share power with blacks in order to take power. Exactly how much political clout the Indians had in 1986 within the National Alliance for Reconstruction (NAR) was the subject of immediate specuation and doubts; but as a group they never come so near before to the commanding heights of the political system. This position coupled with the outgrowing of their inferiority as a demographic minority in the country, put the Indians in a unprecedentedly favourable position to pursue their vested interest.

After years in the political wilderness A. N. R. Robinson as Prime Minister in the new government found himself obliged in 1986 to pick up the pieces of a collapsed economy, still functioning at a level substantially above that of other Caribbean island nations and most Third World countries, but only a shadow of its former self during the oil boom of 1974 to 1981. The last years of the PNM in office coincided with the final collapse of the regime of high oil prices, first to tolerable lower levels and then to still lower levels which could not support the standard of living of the people, or the financial obligations of the government.[22] The PNM under Chambers choose to keep government support for its welfare programme to the needy sections of the population for as long as possible, and although some subsidies were knocked off, the government resisted a general programme of retrenchment of expenditure. Using hindsight many ordinary Trinidadians and Tobagonians and of course the economists came to realise in the harsher economic climate of the mid-1980s that Williams' audacious, nationalist, economic thrust into a programme of heavy industries ten years previously had backfired into a financial millstone around the neck of the economy. The high prices on international markets envisaged for the products of the petrochemical, iron and steel plants simply had not materialised, and the government had to subsidise them with millions of dollars annually. Oil at reduced prices is still at the heart of the economy, not heavy manufacturing. With dwindling revenues and high indebtedness the government of Robinson had to undertake painful scaling down of the welfare state, plus a partial withdrawal of direct government participation in the economy. How far the country would go back to relying on the private sector, once again, to be the main engine of growth was still unclear in 1986.

[6]

Nationalism and Education 1956-1981

> I see in the denominational school the breeding ground of disunity. I see in the state school the opportunity for cultivating a spirit of nationalism among West Indian people and eradicating the racial suspicions and antagonisms growing in our midst. I place the community above the sect or the race.
>
> Dr Eric Williams, Trinidad Guardian, 18 May 1955

The Government Restricts Church Schools

It was argued previously that government gained increasing control over denominational primary schools from the 1920s to the mid-1950s, but that it did not seek to exercise a similar level of control over the denominational secondary schools or the denominational training colleges. It was also contended that the dual system consolidated itself and added a new dimension in the 1950s with the admission of Hindu and Muslim primary schools. Under PNM government, and especially after independence in 1962, government control over the dual system was taken to new heights, until it looked as if that system itself was threatened.

In an ethnically and politically divided society such as Trinidad and Tobago, it was unthinkable that a nationalist government under Dr Eric Williams could overlook the transforming potential of education. The battleground of the nationalist struggle was said by Dr Williams to be the schools. The secondary schools were to be "the cradle of the new nationalism..."[1] Williams and the PNM hoped to use the education system to bring about social integration and economic progress, the former chiefly by bringing youths of different races and classes into the same schools,[2] and the latter by downplaying the colonial grammar school type of secondary curriculum to the benefit of technical/vocational education befitting a country bent on industrialisation. The centralisation and consolidation of government power over education was an important aspect of a multifaceted process of nation building common to Third World countries in the post-war era. The opponents of Williams, especially during his early years in office, attributed to him and the PNM a desire to gain unfair political advantage by manipulating the content of the curriculum. Not being socialist or communist, Dr Williams and the PNM failed to explain boldly the full extent to which they expected a national system of education to socialize the youths of the new nation into new loyalties, for example fidelity to the political philosophy of the regime, or to its economic structures and social objectives. But obviously the nationalist government desired to re-educate youths in some fashion into new allegiances to the nation presumed to be superior to their parents' commitments to sub-national groups and associations.

It might add clarity to suggest at the outset that the PNM government's relationship with the churches in matters of education went through two broad phases: first there was a phase of challenge to the churches; this was marked by high feelings of nationalism, by open controversy and mutually hostile accusations climaxing in the Education Act of 1966. Within this period there was an accommodation and relative peace after the Concordat of December 1960. Then there was a second phase, which might be dated from the early 1970s in which the government and the churches became less hostile, but not friendly partners in the dual system. The accession to leadership of nationals in the Roman Catholic Church and the Church of England in the early 1970s certainly facilitated this phase; while the PNM government, from the renegotiation of the Chaguaramas base agreement, lost some of its nationalistic fire as it settled down to the enormously difficult task of government. But there were nevertheless serious disagreements between the government and the churches in the 1970s, but not so much over the control of education as over money and respect for the rights of the churches as subordinate partners in education.[3]

In the first phase of PNM government's relationship with the churches (1956 to about 1972) the essential question settled was that of final control of the education system; this was put in the hands of the government through the Minister of Education and Culture. The post of director of education was converted into the less important and less imposing title of chief education officer. In this phase it cannot be said that a new structure of education actually existed; that came in the second phase (1973 to about 1981) with the introduction of the two cycle secondary education on the so-called national model. The churches were invited to convert some of their secondary schools to conform to this model, but they hesitated or resisted down to the mid-1970s. This resulted in mild embarrassment of the government rather than heated conflict between state and church. The government could ignore the resistance of the churches. It knew it had the finances, especially after the start of the oil boom from 1973, to fund an expansion of government secondary schools along the desired lines. At the same time it became clear that the government did not intend to use its control, acquired in the first phase, to alter seriously the denominational character of the church schools. The quarrel on the level of high principles receded, but what never changed in the PNM government, while Williams was alive, was the political will to strive for control of the entire system.

A quick macro glance at the outcome of the PNM regime (1956-1981) in terms of the reorganisation of the dual system might be in order before a micro investigation of the struggle between the government and its partners in the dual system. The government reversed decidedly the long established tradition in primary and secondary education for the churches to build more schools and provide more new places than the government. Within ten years (1957-1967) it had increased government primary schools to a total outnumbering that of the Roman Catholics, the most vigorous of the denominational school providers; within this period it created more additional school places at the primary level than all the churches. In fact from 1957 to 1967 the churches hardly built new primary schools. However they still provided more school places in primary education than the government, so large a lead had they at the time Dr Williams came to power. It was strictly in the provision of additional places that the government excelled. The churches still had more primary schools than the government; for instance in 1977 they had 352 schools and the government had 113. This meant that the government had 24.3 percent of the schools in 1977 whereas in 1956 it had only 16.8 percent. After 1967 the government went on to consolidate its premier position in the provision of new primary and secondary school places.

At the level of secondary education the efforts of the PNM government produced more staggering results in a shorter time in terms of overtaking of the churches. Starting from the paltry number of 3 government secondary schools in 1957 (QRC, St George's College and the San Fernando Technical Institute), the PNM raised the number to 21 in 1967, only two fewer than the denominational colleges. After 1967 the PNM government consolidated its new ascendancy in secondary education with a range of new junior secondary schools and senior secondary schools, each costing more money than the churches could afford. It was not only a case that the government directly and indirectly discouraged the building of denominational colleges, but the cost of building secondary schools had become so exorbitant that not even the Roman Catholic Church could easily find its share of the estimates.

By 1963 the reversal of the position of the government vis-à-vis the churches in relation to the building of new institutions was even more pronounced in teacher training. Starting with one college in 1957 (the Government Teachers' College), the government by 1963 had three training colleges, producing many more graduates than the church controlled colleges. The PNM government also threatened the future participation of the churches in teacher training by asserting the right to discontinue their teacher training facilities. It eventually induced denominational training colleges to close their doors. The churches at least could not complain that they were ever encouraged by the PNM government to expand their training schools. The revolution in the position of government vis-à-vis the churches as providers of secondary education and teacher education within the dual system was bound to affect their relative power in practice. However the greater control of the entire education system originated from the political will of the PNM and particularly from Dr Williams. The will to control was prior to the actual reversal of the trend towards denominational schools. The political determination to control and consolidate the entire education system (even before the supervisory personnel actually existed in the Ministry of Education) led to the Education Act of 1966 which brought denominational secondary schools under the inspection of the government.

The control of denominational school teachers was a key point in the dual system. At the time the PNM came to office the government had no control over the appointment of teachers in denominational secondary schools beyond checking the suitability of their academic qualifications. Teachers in denominational secondary schools were put by the Education Act on the same footing as teachers in denominational primary schools; that is, the government was the final authority in their appointment, transfer, promotion and dismissal. The government agencies in charge were the Teaching Service Commission and the Ministry of Education. The role of the Teaching Service Commission, inter alia, was to standardize the criteria by which teachers were employed, promoted or dismissed, and this regulatory function represented a major victory for government control. This was part of measures to unify the civil service. In the actual running of denominational secondary schools after 1966 the churches managed to keep effective control of their staff. Normally the denominational school boards had their nominations for staff appointments accepted by the Teaching Service Commission. No Roman Catholic was appointed principal of a Church of England school against the will of the Church of England board; nor was any Hindu appointed principal of a Roman Catholic school against the will of the Roman Catholic board. The government did not use its authority to disrupt the denominational character of the school staff.[4]

Who Should Control the Secondary Schools?

The government also successfully asserted a right to control the admission policy of the denominational secondary schools; separate entrance examinations for each college were abolished and the government and churches negotiated an enduring system whereby 80 percent of the first form intake of denominational secondary schools had to consist of successful candidates in the Common Entrance Examination. This was done in the famous Concordat of December 1960.[5] But there was misunderstanding about the use of the remaining 20 percent. The words of the Concordat indicated that the principals were free to choose the remaining 20 percent normally from those who had passed the Common Entrance Examination. Most principals, desiring to retain some control over admission to their schools, at first interpreted this more liberally than the government intended and hence the prime minister was able in Parliament to decry their selection of students who had not passed the Common Entrance Examination as evidence of class and racial prejudice in the school system, inherited from the colonial regime. This he angrily denounced as a national scandal. It is not clear however if all denominational school principals ceased immediately to admit students who had not passed the Common Entrance Examination.[6]

The curriculum and even textbooks of denominational secondary schools also fell under the final control of government; and importantly, students who were not of the faith of the denomination owning the school were protected from the proselytising zeal of the clerics. Hitherto only pupils in the primary schools enjoyed such legal protection. It would be a mistake, however, to believe that the government, through its school officials, tried to dictate the internal organisation or textbooks of denominational secondary schools. There was an immense gap between the assumption of final authority in law and its use in practice.

Since the authority of the government before 1956 was already ample in relation to denominational primary schools, the PNM's upgrading of government authority here was not as sensational as in the area of secondary schools. The Minister of Education was clearly given power to regulate all aspects of primary education, and this was a new power. Also all denominational schools, primary as well as secondary, had to furnish accounts of the expenditure of government grants and provide whatever information the Minister of Education required. Considering the heated protest of the Roman Catholic Church in 1930 against any requirement to account for government grants, this provision elicited remarkably few complaints in the mid-1960s, but the explanation was probably that the churches had more vital areas of their rights to defend.

The acquisition of these new powers by the government was not accomplished without public agitation more intense in 1965 than any previous controversy over education policy. This episode was not simply a struggle of QRC supporters against CIC supporters; nor of denominational primary schools against government primary schools. Nor was it a bureaucratic expansion of government power without any ideological declarations as in the 1920s and the 1930s. It was a struggle between the churches and the government at the highest level: at the level of the heads of the churches and the Cabinet of the country. It was a struggle in which each side declared conflicting ideologies fundamentally incompatible. In previous quarrels between the churches and the government over their respective authority in the dual system nothing like this type of confrontation had materialised. The result was that some of the claims seemed remarkably new although as ideologies they were old. For instance, the Roman Catholic Church's claim that the family and not the government had primary responsibility to provide education appeared quite novel, but was based on long-established Roman Catholic social principles.[7] Catholic families (and presumably families belonging to other Christian denominations) were free, according to this doctrine, to establish denominational schools which had legitimate claims upon revenues (citizens' taxes) paid to the government. The supporters of this position were able to get a clause inserted into the independence constitution of 1962 allowing as one of the fundamental freedoms the right of parents to provide schools of their own choice. On the other hand the right of a constitutionally elected government to control education in the national interest as defined by itself seemed like a revolutionary declaration in Trinidad and Tobago in the mid-1950s, but was hardly more than what any nineteenth century European government had asserted in its bid to create a nation state.

In the mid-1960s, as on all previous occasions, the Roman Catholic Church took the lead in defence of denominational schools. As an international organisation of great age it had the longest tradition among the Christian churches of ecclesiastical resistance to governments and the most coherent social philosophy in the name of which to organise group action. In Trinidad it had the most denominational schools and the support of the largest number of Christian citizens; the clash between the government and the churches in the mid-1960s was essentially a clash between the government and the Roman Catholic Church. It was a clash between two organised and disciplined institutions, one very old and the other very young, the latter fortified by the consciousness of being the lawfully elected government and the leading edge of the nationalist thrust, especially after the sweeping election victory of 1961. The government was also sustained by the driving energy of Dr Williams, the prime minister, who was personally opposed to churches and especially to the churches' divisive role in education. A serious difficulty was to disentangle Williams' personal views from those of his party. The charter of the PNM took a more tolerant view of the churches' role in education than Williams himself. After his lectures throughout the colony in 1954 and 1955 he was often branded by Roman Catholic priests as a godless enemy of denominational schools.

Colonialism and the Churches

The origin of Williams' anti-clerical, anti-denominational school views must be traced to his study of West Indian history which convinced him that the Christian churches had traditionally supported the white colonial ruling class.[8] Since he was determined to end colonial rule he had to confront the churches, especially the Roman Catholic Church. All the churches however, Christian and non-Christian, had tenacious social roots in the country, with vibrant religious and lay organisations. The requirement of winning political power through the vote induced Dr Williams and the PNM to adopt a policy which from the outset demanded the retention of denominational schools though in a decidedly more subordinate position. Dr Williams could not terrorise Roman Catholic priests like his contemporary 'Papa Doc' in Haiti. At no time was it the declared policy to destroy the dual system by nationalising church schools as was done in Guyana in 1976, or by excluding them from government assistance. The difficulty for the churches was that they could not predict how far Dr Williams and the PNM would go, once the government was allowed to assume new powers; and it looked unwise to separate the party's programme from the predisposition of the man who dominated it, or from a handful of temporarily powerful, secularised civil servants in important ministries. Down to the late 1960s the government was poised for confrontation, regarding the white expatriate heads of the churches, especially the Roman Catholic Archbishop of Port of Spain, Count Finbar Ryan, as meddlesome foreigners, who had no right to determine the shape of the education system. The problems of the dual system did not end when two nationals, Rev Clive Abdullah and Fr Anthony Pantin, became the local heads respectively of the Church of England and the Roman Catholic Church. These men would not have found it to their liking to oppose the government on the question of ultimate control of education; but they were willing to appeal for public support, as they did in 1974, against government's neglect of their claims for more funds and greater consideration as partners in the dual system. Bishop Abdullah threatened to call a Church of England school strike in 1974; and for the first time the Church of England temporarily took the lead in rallying the churches, Christian and non-Christian, against government's neglect of their claims. For the first time in the history of the churches they had in July 1974 a joint meeting on education. A full page advertisement in the *Guardian* in October 1974 was rather a cry for sanity in government's policies than a call-up of supporters to do battle against the government.[9] The situation in 1974 was totally dissimilar from that in 1965. In 1974 the Christian churches were more like a wounded giant in retreat than a confident gladiator accustomed to victory.

In the course of the controversy between the government and the churches, especially in the late 1950s and the 1960s, Dr Eric Williams made some biting accusations against them. Denominational education was said to be divisive because religious divisions very often coincided with racial and even social divisions. The most obvious case was that Muslim or Hindu schools catered entirely for Indian children; and Presbyterian schools almost entirely for Indians. Some of the Church of England and Roman Catholic secondary schools educated the children of the white upper class, but not exclusively. The children of educated black, coloured, and less often Indian, middle class, plus scholarship winners of all races and classes, also attended these schools. Within these sectored alignments of classes and races with certain schools, there was room, it was alleged, for personal contacts, colour prejudice, family influence and non-academic considerations to pollute admission policies.[10] In fact gratitude to certain families for financial contributions and religious loyalty was openly acknowledged as a legitimate sentiment by principals of denominational secondary schools.[11] No clear definition of the cultural foundation of national integration ever emerged, but the latter was insistently said to be a prime objective of the government: the creation of, to use other phrases thought equivalent, a national community, a national unity. What was abundantly clear, however, was that in education national integration involved the mixing in the same schools of children of different denominations, races, colours and classes.

Another accusation against denominational schools was that clerical managers had grossly abused the rights of teachers, especially primary school teachers. Ironically, however, the government in 1956 had more authority over the relationship between clerical managers and primary school teachers than over the relationship between secondary school teachers and managers (or principals and/or Denominational Boards of Management). Since primary school teachers sprang from the masses and were black, Indian or even coloured, discrimination against them by white clerical managers had not only a class dimension, but sometimes a racial quality as well. There was a long queue of mature teachers in the mid-1950s who would swear that they had been unfairly transferred or deprived of promotion because they had not taught Sunday school or evinced excessive religious loyalty.[12] The answer of the government was to give the Public Service Commission (after 1968, the Teaching Service Commission), on behalf of the government, final jurisdiction in the appointment, transfer, promotion and dismissal of all teachers.[13] To the suspicion that the government would itself discriminate against teachers the stock reply was the alleged unimpeachable integrity of the Public Service Commission or the Teaching Service Commission. The Minister of Education and either of these Commissions were, in the name of the government, to be the guardians of the rights of students and teachers to equality of opportunity and treatment. Since the government could always exercise close supervision over government schools which had no religious interest to foster, the social and political objectives of the government could, it was felt, be more easily attained in government schools; hence these were to be favoured in any expansion programme.

Schools and Social Integration

The claim that government schools united, or at least had the potential to unite, the population, while denominational schools divided it, goes back to the immediate post-emancipation era when the Englishman, Charles Warner, tried to frame an education policy. Warner was very opposed to denominational schools, and it should be recognised that since the era of Charles Warner, Prime Minister Eric Williams was the greatest opponent of denominational education who had any considerable political power or influence. Williams would be the last person to claim any affinity with an Anglophile like Warner, the epitome of the colonial rule which he so stridently opposed; nevertheless Warner was seeking a system of education which would integrate the divided society on the basis of English culture. Williams wished to integrate on the basis of a national culture still to be created. This was a far more difficult task, especially as Williams had to think of integrating the Indians who in relation to education were treated as if they did not exist by Warner, the man who did so much to ensure their coming as labourers. To Warner, integration meant unity without cultural diversity; Williams and the PNM were less sure in the late 1950s and 1960s about the nature of the national integration they sought. Both Warner and Williams were in their time the greatest exponent of nationalism in Trinidad: English nationalism and Trinidad and Tobago nationalism respectively. Both men found the Roman Catholic Church and the French creoles formidable obstacles to their policies.[14] In addition, Williams had to face the ineluctable opposition of the Indians in the wider society.

The Roman Catholic Church had defeated Charles Warner in the 1860s by appealing to the British government and to friendly governors. Nearly a century later, the campaign of the Roman Catholic Church failed to result in the defeat of Williams in the election of 1956. Having won power the PNM allayed fears by proceeding gradually. In bringing pressure on its denominational partners in the dual system, the PNM government appeared to practise the fine art of taking one step backwards and two steps forwards. Or were these manoeuvres simply the erratic outcomes of the ambivalent personality of Dr Williams? Whatever the origins, the effect was to take steps in opposite directions at different times. For instance, two steps forwards were taken after the brash Maurice Committee Report of 1959 provided the basis for government proposals in Parliament in July 1960.[15] It looked then as if the denominational character of the church schools was about to be utterly eroded; then perhaps with the election of 1961 in mind the government took one step backwards to the Concordat of December 1960. The churches were confirmed in their ownership of their schools; negotiations were to precede changes. The churches led by the Roman Catholic Church appeared to have saved the denominational character of their schools.

Then after independence and before the election of 1966 another two steps forwards were taken in the furious year of 1965. A Draft Education Act and accompanying Code of Regulations were put before the public sparking off a level of controversy over education never before witnessed in the country. When the dust settled after the passing of the Education Act of 1966 there was still a dual system, but the relative power of government and churches had shifted further in favour of the government. The denominational character of the church schools remained. It was even possible for some people to think that the legislation had consolidated the dual system instead of uprooted it. Others expressed a contrary view: the Education Act was a time bomb which would one day explode and demolish the denominational partners in the dual system. Even in the 1970s, a quieter decade for church-state relations than the 1960s, some remnants of the technique or unplanned outcome of one step backwards and two steps forwards might still be discerned. The commencement of the implementation of the Draft Fifteen-year Education Plan in 1970 without any serious amendments to meet the criticisms of 1968 was two steps forwards; then came a greater willingness in the mid-1970s to modify the plan, partly on the insistence of the churches. The political will of Dr Williams and the PNM to control and dominate education policies was wisely tempered by political caution. An alternative interpretation to this stop-and-go process is to credit it, not to any conscious wisdom, or even to ambivalence in the Political Leader, but to the failure of the government to overcome the institutional strength of the churches, in other words to the genuine social limitations of the power of the PNM government.[16]

It seems clear that one longstanding argument for the existence of church schools, namely that they saved the government money by their participation, was gradually weakened by the rising proportion of both building and recurrent cost met by government. A critical stage was reached after the oil price revolution gave the government far more financial resources than the churches could ever dream of commanding at a time of escalating building costs. This happened in a period when the government had lost much of its bitterness against the churches; nevertheless the logic of preponderating government financial contribution, actual and potential, led to the preparation of a new formula of ownership and management for certain denominational schools.

The Strange Career of Joint Management

About 1977 discussions were commenced which led the dual system into a new and (down to 1981) indeterminate direction. After World War II the government had increased its share of the cost of denominational school buildings from a half to two-thirds, without any change in the management of such schools. By 1977 the government possessed vast revenues, the churches little or no money, and many denominational primary schools badly needed repairs. It was the first time since the dual system started in 1870 that the government could face squarely the financial responsibility of taking over all the schools the churches possessed and repairing them to a satisfactory standard.[17] The question now was how much more than the two-thirds share should government bear and what changes in management should become necessary? The government was thinking of providing as much as 90 percent of the cost, or even undertaking the full cost (100%) of repairs or of rebuilding. The churches desperately wished an upward revision of government's share, but without any change in management. Failure to come to any agreement after anxious discussions led the Roman Catholic Church in late 1977 to offer to hand over seven of its primary schools to the government, without any mention of change in management. By March 1978 the Roman Catholic Church refined its position on these seven schools; they should be under Joint Management (government/Roman Catholic and certain community groups) under the 'umbrella' of the Roman Catholic Board of Control, with the right of access of Roman Catholic priests to give religious instruction to their co-religionists. The government set up a committee chaired by Dr C. V. Gocking to investigate and report.[18]

In this committee serious differences developed between some members of the government team and the church representatives. The latter decided that compensation to the government for schoolhouses which had appreciated in value subsequent to government-aided repairs was out of the question. This point arose when the question of the property rights of government and the churches in school buildings erected by both was discussed. The major problem however concerned the nature of the Joint Management arrangements and how schools under it should be named. Some government representatives, wishing to emphasise the government's preponderant financial contribution to the new school buildings (government was to contribute 100 percent of the cost), felt that government should have a majority on the Management Board and that the name of the schools should exclude the name of the Roman Catholic Church. These matters were left to Cabinet to decide, but it was agreed to have a two-tier management system with a Central Joint Management Board and a Local Advisory Board for each school.[19]

The subsequent history of the submerged question of Joint Management is shrouded in confusion and up to 1985 it was not clear from the written evidence how such schools as were said to be under Joint Management were actually managed.[20] A central problem was the absence of any legislation to authorise Joint Management. The Education Act of 1966 was not amended and Joint Management rested on agreements signed by administrators and heads of churches. Before the government could complete its policy on Joint Management, the Roman Catholic Church offered to give over another twelve primary schools whose repairs were also beyond its means and the government undertook to pay the full cost of repairs before the finalisation of the Joint Management arrangements. Since some of these schools had to be rebuilt from scratch on new sites, completely at government expense, it might very well have been asked why such schools were not simply designated government schools and all talk of Joint Management forgotten. This was the sort of question which could have divided top civil servants and Cabinet ministers. One can guess that Dr Williams himself would have favoured making them government schools; but it is not clear how close he was to these discussions with the churches. Indeed the government – or maybe more accurately its representatives in the talks – did a strange thing: an offer was made to put all government primary schools under Joint Management, thus giving the churches a role in the management of government schools; a totally unexpected suggestion in light of PNM education policy since 1956. It might well be that at last the management of schools as well as the promotion of students' moral welfare were being recognised by the government (or its representatives) as areas in which the churches traditionally had skills far superior to those of lay managers (notwithstanding the irony that concurrently the churches were experiencing a real decline in their own school management capability). However, this unprecedented proposal appeared contradictory to recent withholding of government funds for school repairs which – in the eyes of the Roman Catholic Church – forced that Church into a financial corner from which it had to escape by offering Joint Management arrangements.[21]

A question which the historian of the dual system has to face is how did Joint Management impact on the ongoing contest between the churches and government: was it to save church control of denominational schools or to enhance government control of denominational school? All along some churches believed it was a government ploy: this was the view of the perennially suspicious Hindus and the Seventh-Day Adventists, who refused to consider the Joint Management formula for their schools in need of repairs.[22] The government certainly showed a desire to have Joint Management; suspiciously, it wished to negotiate separate agreements with each church using the Roman Catholic agreement as a model. By 1981 it was said that a total of 40 schools had been fully repaired by government and put under Joint Management: Roman Catholic, 14; Trinidad Muslim League, 1; Ayra Pratinidi Sabha (Vedic), 1; Presbyterians, 4; Methodists, 4; Fundamental Baptists, 1; Church of England, 3; and the remainder unclear.

The death of Dr Williams in early 1981 might have helped to put to rest any covert desire to use Joint Management as some thin edge of a new wedge of further government control of the education system. A committee set up before Williams' death under the chairmanship of Victor Bruce, but which reported after Williams' death, appeared to have bowed to all the wishes of the churches, although it had no church representatives on it. It said that increased government funding of denominational schoolhouses, presumably including those funded 100 percent by government, should not necessarily lead to government ownership of the buildings; it hinted that government should perhaps be regarded as the mortgagee of the property rather than its owner. The committee accepted the churches' view that ownership of school buildings was essential to maintaining the denominational character of the school. The committee also agreed that no useful purpose would be served by changing the name of a school brought under Joint Management. In other words a Roman Catholic school, even after being completely rebuilt on a new site with government funds exclusively and put under Joint Management, was still to be called a Roman Catholic school.[23]

On the micro level of the Joint Management question, there was one problem clearly foreseen: it concerned the appointment, transfer and dismissal of teachers. The churches were faced with the real possibility that a Joint Management Committee might outvote the church representatives on it and propose to the Teaching Service Commission the appointment of a teacher who was on religious grounds unacceptable to the church whose school had been converted to Joint Management. It was while solutions to this difficulty were being examined that the searchlight was thrown on a long established rule of the Teaching Service Commission requiring it to take religion into account in approving or disapproving the recommendations of Denominational Boards of Management when appointing teachers. This was now said to be unconstitutional since it infringed the rights of citizens (applicants) to equal treatment. The position of Dr Watkis of the Law Reform Commission was that the constitution had to be amended. The view of the churches was that this was a small point which could be ignored, meaning that things could remain as they were. They were more interested in devising ways of bringing to the attention of the Teaching Service Commission the views of church representatives in cases where they had been outvoted in the Joint Management Boards. All these difficulties in the Joint Management system were unresolved up to 1986. One final word on Joint Management: it came under discussion about the same time as the economic thrust of the government via joint venture. Joint Management was joint venture in education. Hopefully the economists cogitating on joint ventures in the economy will find the subject less obfuscated than Joint Management in education. The only thing which was absolutely clear in 1986 was that schools under Joint Management received 100 percent government funding.

If the churches lost ground as financial contributors to the dual system and hence found their position weakened in this respect, there still remained an old ground on which the nationalist state could not defeat them. One argument for denominational schools had long been the widely accepted belief that the churches through religious instruction made an irreplaceable contribution to the moral welfare of the country. Naturally in the 1960s little or no stress was placed by the PNM upon this contribution while challenges were being made to the churches' ascendancy in education. But from the 1970s, the government was more willing to acknowledge that it could not provide the moral welfare which the churches could. This truth had always been recognised by parents who consistently supported church schools as superior moulders of character in desirable directions. While therefore the traditional arguments that churches could build schools cheaper than government suffered some erosion in a time of great inflation, the case for church schools as superior character builders remained unshaken.

Differential Prestige of Secondary Schools

It might be useful here to discuss as well the relative academic prestige attached to government schools and denominational schools. The material for reaching a judgment hardly seems to exist in the case of primary schools. In the nineteenth century there were so few recognised secondary schools that differential prestige among them was not a major problem. Such a situation arose from the 1920s when more secondary schools were added and thought to be of lower prestige than QRC, CIC or St Joseph's Convent. With each wave of new secondary schools the problem of differential prestige assumed more importance. As boys' schools QRC and CIC traditionally remained in a class by themselves maybe for a longer period than their academic performance merited; what became absolutely clear was that the newer government secondary schools established between 1958 and 1971 – not to mention the junior secondary and senior comprehensive schools of the 1970s – did not have the academic esteem of the pre-1958 denominational secondary schools. This was understandable and had less to do with the denominational or government character of the schools and more with the age, traditions and experience of the schools and their staffs. Before 1954 QRC had carried alone, quite successfully, the burden of comparison with the larger number of denominational secondary (boys') schools. From the late 1950s the lower achievement of the increased number of new government secondary schools made the performance of denominational secondary schools look better than ever.

The system of recruiting students into secondary schools also worked in favour of those schools already better patronised by children of middle and upper class parents. The parents of the top 15 percent (or some other variable percentage) in the Common Entrance Examination (which replaced the College Exhibition Examination) were guaranteed entry for their children to the secondary schools of their first choice. Since the children of the professional and semi-professional middle class parents tended to do well in these examinations, it was these children who had the schools of their first choice and they naturally selected the colleges with the best academic record and prestige, which were QRC and the older denominational colleges founded in the nineteenth century, plus Bishop Anstey High School. These students in turn, either from their academic performance or social behavior, helped to maintain the attraction of these schools for other parents. And so the cycle of recruitment, good performance and recruitment continued. A lower tier of preferred schools (essentially the government and denominational five-year schools) was the prize of the next 10 percent (or some other variable percentage) of Common Entrance winners. And last of all came the rest (or most of the rest) who were sent to junior secondary schools. These latter schools had the potential to develop a similar cycle, but with children of the working class predominating in them. The vast expansion of secondary education was bound to bring a lowering of the calibre of students who attended secondary schools.

Before the era of exceptionally high examination failure rates in the senior comprehensive schools, Fr Lai Fook, Principal of St Mary's College, had warned that in reality

> only a relatively small proportion of the school population has the ability to follow with profit courses leading to the GCE O level whether in purely academic subjects of the Grammar school type or in the more practical subjects which are taught in Technical Colleges.[24]

The newer government secondary schools and especially the junior secondary schools of the 1970s had to carry the burden of the academically weak and most indisciplined students from the primary school system. The exceptions to this generalisation only proved the rule. No way has yet been found to establish parity of esteem between the older schools and the new secondary schools. Because the schools were unequal in performance and prestige the expansion of opportunities in secondary education was not quite the same thing as the equal opportunity in secondary education which was desired by the government.[25]

Did a National System Exist?

In considering the relations between education and nationalism from 1956 to 1981 it might not be superfluous to ask if the dual system still existed in 1981. Who was assisting who in 1981? The term 'dual system' was never popular with the PNM government which insisted that a national system of education had been put in place in the new nation, but obviously without the elimination of competitive denominational authorities as in Guyana.[26] There were important government documents, for example the Draft Fifteen-year Education Plan (1968-1983) which refused to mention denominational schools as a separate category of schools. The visitor to the Ministry of Education who asked for a list of schools in 1981 was likely to get one in which government schools and church schools were undifferentiated. This was unthinkable even as late as the 1950s. The word 'partnership', and sometimes the phrase 'joint partners', were usually employed instead of the phrase 'dual system'. Sometimes official descriptions of the education system adopted the technique of assigning denominational secondary schools to the so-called 'old' or 'traditional' sector of the system, and government secondary schools to something called the 'new' or 'national' sector, more recently with 'national' left out.[27] The denominational secondary schools (as well as the denominational training colleges before they closed) constituted a parallel provision to the national system, linked to the national system, but not completely integrated into it. Apparently the same might be said even of denominational schools under Joint Management. In conclusion one could maintain that an incomplete national system and a constricted overlapping dual system existed side by side in 1981. The unique arrangements introduced by the Concordat turned out to be very durable. Some of the social factors which have favoured the semi-autonomous role of the churches in education still existed in 1981, and this suggests that denominational schools should persist unless a radical 'Left-wing' government (totalitarian or nontotalitarian) comes to power. The drive to have government schools should also persist as long as government espouses the ideal of an integrated national community. It will be a matter for the future whether the government drive for uniformity of system will overcome the churches' preservation of their interest through institutional diversity. Some educationists believe that "the idea of a single common school is dead or dying in the densely populated parts of the Western, English-speaking democracies".[28]

[7]

Government Education Policy 1956-1981

> The original Education Plan formulated some ten years ago . . . was designed on the basis of a small, relatively poor, developing country to provide a reasonably good education for many of its citizens, but within very limited resources. This situation has changed completely. Trinidad and Tobago is now on the threshold of achieving its critical mass in one field of high level technology and large-scale industrial development. Any educational plan must recognise this with urgency.
>
> *Prime Minister's proposal to Cabinet on education, 18 September 1975*

Expansion over Reorientation 1956-1962

Some of the main directions of government policies in education in the first term of office (1956-1961) were already adumbrated by the writings of Dr Eric Williams before he entered politics. In 1956 as the PNM approached the task of winning political power at the polls, it made political promises of two types in respect to education: there was a promise of reorganisation and a promise of expansion. The goal was to raise academic standards while achieving a system of education more suited to the political, social and economic needs of the country which included the need for an "integration of the diverse elements"[1] of the population. The PNM also promised to produce highly trained workers, to widen representation on the Board of Education, and to raise the status of teachers. A greater number of years in school was promised to the nation's children.[2] The government would not abdicate its responsibility for education to the churches.

Reorganisation was impracticable without expansion. The declaration by the PNM that everyone had a right to education was a commitment to expansion. The promise to enforce compulsory education at the primary school level was meaningless without an increase in the number of primary schools. There was to be an expansion of science and of technical and commercial education; an expansion of teacher training facilities; a large increase in the number of scholarships abroad to train professionals, and free secondary education for all those who could benefit from it. But this expansion was not to erode the civil right of parents to choose the kind of education that should be given to their children and to send them to schools of their own choice.[3] This caveat was inserted in the PNM charter to disarm criticism from the churches and their supporters who feared a godless, totalitarian education policy from a secular and nationalist government. The implied promise was that denominational schools were safe.

As might be expected reorganisation and expansion could not be equally pursued at the same time; reorganisation would require investigation, and a large local commission of inquiry, comprised of nationals, was immediately established under the chairmanship of J. Hamilton Maurice, a black nationalist ex-school teacher. Expansion however could not await the result of this inquiry. No inquiry was needed to conclude that more schools were required. In Trinidad and Tobago, as well as in some other Third World countries, the expansion of education in the 1950s and early 1960s was less the result of educational planning than spontaneous political and social demand.[4] There were no specific enrolment targets for secondary or university education. What has been called the "revolution of rising expectations" was underway; the people of Trinidad and Tobago wanted more opportunities for education and a newly elected government enhanced its popularity by catering to their demand. In fact, in the period under discussion (1956-1963), it might be said that expansion outdistanced reorganisation in all but one respect. Since a leading characteristic of the expansion was the provision of government schools, both primary and secondary, at a faster rate than denominational schools, a reorientation of the balance of power between the partners in the dual system did occur. Through the distribution of funds (and before any legislation took place) the government expanded its input into the system and hence its control over it. By 1963 the churches were completely on the defensive.[5]

In the early years of the period 1956 to 1960, however, the Christian churches were able to increase their number of secondary schools within the dual system faster than the government because they already had private schools outside it, which could be quickly brought within it. Hence in 1956 and 1957, five additional denominational secondary schools (Holy Name Convent, St Benedict College [San Fernando]; St Joseph's Convent [St Joseph]; Iere High School and Naparima College [Tunapuna]) were brought within the dual system. By 1963 the churches had 20 recognised secondary schools, whereas in 1956 they had 12. The rate of expansion of secondary schools however was more furious in respect to government schools which rose from 3 in 1956 to 15 in 1963. These new government secondary schools (originally three-year schools), which were sometimes described confusingly as Central schools, sometimes as secondary modern schools (or modern secondary schools) continued the trend, started by St George's College, of taking secondary education outside central Port of Spain to the suburbs and to rural areas. Located in Diego Martin, St James, Woodbrook, Rio Claro and Scarborough (Tobago), these 'free' schools can be said at once to have been the pride of the government's expansion of education down to 1963. They facilitated progress in respect to two other election promises, namely to extend the school life of children and to work towards the magical goal of free secondary education for all those who could benefit from it.

The traditional ladder by which poor boys and girls won themselves free secondary education was the College Exhibition (after 1961 the Common Entrance Examination). The number of these was expanded from 255 in 1956 to 1,000 in 1960, and to 3,547 in 1963. The expansion of opportunities in secondary education made it necessary for the government to negotiate with the churches an agreement covering control of admission into denominational secondary schools. This was done in December 1960 in the famous Concordat which provided that 80 percent of the annual intake into these schools would be drawn from successful candidates in the Common Entrance Examination; and the remaining 20 percent would be at the discretion of the principals who would normally select students who had passed the Common Entrance Examination.[6] This latter examination, largely itself a standardised objective test, was substituted for the College Exhibition examination from 1961. The College Exhibition examination had been designed to select a few very bright children; the Common Entrance Examination selected students who could benefit from secondary education. The expansion of free places determined by the Common Entrance Examination plus the agreement about admission ratios with the denominational schools signalled a decisive start to widespread free secondary education from January 1961. Because places were limited, competition was stiff and anxiety of parents and children was hardly less severe and damaging than in the case of the College Exhibition. Despite endless government declarations of the undesirability of an examination at 11+ to select for secondary schooling, it proved impossible up to 1986 to run the education system without the Common Entrance Examination.

Expansion of primary schools was characterised between 1956 and 1963 by a thrust to have government schools such as had not been seen since the 1870s. In 1956 government had 68 primary schools; in 1963 it had 97; this was a much faster rate of growth than the increase of denominational primary schools from 336 in 1956 to 358 in 1963. Enrolment in all primary schools moved from approximately 155,000 in 1956 to approximately 208,000 in 1963, without the promised redeclaration of compulsory education. The draw-off into the new secondary schools was not enough to prevent an undesirable pile-up of children above age 12 in the primary schools. A short term alleviation of the plight of these children was the reform of the curriculum of the 12 to 15 age group to include the teaching of mathematics and Spanish, a sort of pre-secondary school introduction which it was hoped these children would find interesting.

In respect to both secondary and primary education, members of the Parliamentary opposition accused the government of stifling the growth of denominational schools. This was a half-truth: at the level of both primary and secondary schools, the churches were improving their provision, thanks to grants from the government for buildings, repairs and laboratories. The Christian churches could not reasonably complain that in the First Five-year Development Plan (1958-1962) their schools were neglected financially. But undisputedly the government, unlike in the period 1950-1955, when the Minister of Education, Roy Joseph, had been friendly to the expansion of denominational primary schools, had decided that the main provision of schools at all levels should be government schools;[7] and additionally the PNM government adopted more stringent procedures before agreeing to denominational requests for government aid, the intention being that government, not churches, should decide on the location of schools and the adequacy of school buildings. Ignoring in some cases pre-PNM government procedures, the Hindu Maha Saba had in the early 1950s erected certain school buildings which were deemed substandard by the PNM government which refused to provide money to pay their teachers, or to admit them into the family of the dual system.[8] The government found itself in the embarrassing position of refusing to aid these Hindu schools, some of which were unoccupied, while having to admit that there was a need for more school places.[9] The black dominated government of Dr Williams was indirectly accused of racial prejudice against Indians, who constituted the actual or potential beneficiaries of these Hindu schools.[10] The government rejected such insinuations, pointing to the fact that already the Maha Sabha had some 50 schools recognised and aided by government, not to mention Presbyterian schools which had many Indian children. The position of the government was that churches should conform to the education policy of the government, not government to that of the churches.

The PNM government had promised to increase science, technical and commercial education as integral parts of secondary education. The only technical school in existence in 1956 was the San Fernando Technical College. The Chaguaramas Trade School, a gift from the United States government, was accepted and run by government by mutual agreement from 1961 to 1964 when it was superseded by the John Donaldson Technical School in Port of Spain. A Polytechnic Institute was also constructed in Port of Spain. Like the San Fernando Technical College, the John Donaldson Technical School could train craftsmen, less so technicians and no engineers. The Polytechnic Institute (a sixth form school), which had both day and evening classes, was designed to teach mathematics and science and to prepare students for entry into natural science courses of the UCWI and other universities.[11] It was not itself a technical school, but was useful in preparing students for entry to technician or engineering courses. The entire field of technical/vocational education was left to the government, without any challenge from the churches. The BIT, which in the past had prime responsibility for technical/vocational education, continued to function in the background, but it came under the direction of the Minister of Education.

In the same spirit of the recognition of the importance of technical/vocational education, the government accepted the offer to take over the Shell Oil Company's Apprentice Trade School in Point Fortin (renamed the Point Fortin Vocational Centre).[12] A great limitation on technical/vocational education was, as usual, the shortage of properly qualified teachers. It is to be noted that although Dr Williams in his book *Education in the British West Indies* (1951) had insisted on the importance of agricultural education, the government at this stage placed little or no emphasis on it, despite the provision of 50 farm scholarships to the Eastern Caribbean Farm Institute. The emphasis of government economic policy was on industrialisation, not agriculture. Contrary to Dr Williams' views in his book, responsibility for agricultural education was allocated to the Ministry of Agriculture instead of to the Ministry of Education, and little or nothing was done for agriculture in primary schools.

The PNM had accused the colonial authorities in the past of selecting for professional training only a handful of persons. Expansion of opportunities for professional or advanced training abroad in certain desirable fields, capable of assisting with the economic development of the country, became a guiding principle of government: 56 additional Island Scholarships (university scholarships) were granted for study overseas between 1956 and 1961, and 91 Development Scholarships, chiefly to civil servants and teachers, were awarded over the same period, also to study abroad.[13] Never before had so many students been given overseas awards in such a short time. These awardees were bonded to return to serve the country. A nationalistic government wished to further economic development using the human resources provided by nationals. So many new scholarships for overseas study were granted that political opponents became suspicious that PNM supporters or their children might be unduly favoured in the selections.

The expansion of schools in the late 1950s had outdistanced more than ever before the availability of trained primary or secondary school teachers. No systematic provision existed locally for the training of technical/vocational teachers. In 1957, a total of 2,723 of the 4,441 teachers (61.3%) in the primary schools were untrained; 1,232 of the untrained teachers (45.2%) had not gone to secondary schools; 264 (21.4%) were pupil teachers. Only 1,897 (42.7%) of all teachers had completed courses of secondary education. The annual output of the three teacher training schools, one of which was government-owned, was about 100 teachers. Dr Patrick Solomon, Minister of Education, said in Parliament in April 1957 that about 2,000 teachers had the qualifications to enter training colleges, but had no chance in the near future of getting a place.[14] When faced with a similar problem in the late 1940s the government had increased the intake into the one-year course at the Government Training College. The answer of the government was to commence a one-year Emergency Teacher Training College in Port of Spain and to set on foot plans to build a new government teachers' college near Arima. Mausica Teachers' College was opened in 1963. Naturally the government was unfavourably disposed to the increase of denominational teacher training facilities. Control of teachers was a crucial area of rivalry between government and the churches and it was not to the advantage of the government to strengthen the churches' teacher training capacity.

The ratio of trained secondary school teachers was very low since traditionally it was felt that a university graduate was already equipped to teach secondary school without any professional training as a teacher. The government was lucky enough if it could get university graduates; and it did not get enough. So that the expansion of secondary education in the late 1950s and early 1960s was characterised by a low ratio of university graduate to non-graduate teachers, especially in the new government schools which sought to follow the older, better established denominational secondary schools into the path of academic subjects and Cambridge external examinations. The upgrading of secondary school teachers' salaries in 1956 helped and graduates of the UCWI from other territories sometimes migrated to Trinidad and Tobago to receive a higher salary. Then as now the shortage of science and mathematics teachers was most marked.

There were interesting developments in university education in Trinidad. As part of the renegotiation of the Chaguaramas base agreement, the United States government had committed itself to aid the construction of a College of Liberal Arts. This opened on the grounds of ICTA at St Augustine in temporary buildings in 1963, while the previous year a Faculty of Engineering had been commenced on the same site. The merging of ICTA, the College of Liberal Arts, and the Faculty of Engineering into a territorial branch of the UCWI significantly boosted the opportunities of Trinidadians to have higher education without leaving their own island, while at the same time it increased the financial burden of the Trinidad and Tobago government for higher education.[15]

Dr Williams had indicated in his book *Education in the British West Indies* that the British Caribbean colonial tax structure placed too great a strain of indirect taxes on the masses, and too light a load of direct income taxes on those who could pay. Naturally increased taxes formed no part of the PNM election promises, but the country was faced with increased income tax to help finance the Five-year Development Plan (1958-1962). The government had not been successful in attracting loans since its political ideology was suspect. Recurrent expenditure on education rose from TT$10 million in 1955 to approximately TT$20 million in 1961. The capital budget for education was about a half million dollars in 1958, nearly TT$2 million in 1959, a little under TT$4.5 million in 1960, and just over TT$6 million in 1961.[16] Expenditure of this order on education was unprecedented, and bore witness to the fundamental commitment of the government to education. Yet the total actual expenditure on education during the period of the First Five-year Plan (1958-1962) was only 6.1 percent of total expenditure on all programmes.[17] The government took as its prime role the provision of basic infrastructure for the expansion of industry and agriculture (roads, electricity, water); and of the smaller amounts spent on the social services, health and housing each attracted twice as much expenditure as education.

As already indicated reorientation of the education system was promised, but not achieved in this initial period of the PNM regime. The government at first waited upon the findings of the Maurice Commission which was laid in Parliament in August 1959. This report was the basis for certain proposals for education which the government put before Parliament in July 1960. One recommendation of the Maurice Report, accepted by the government, but never really implemented called for the decentralisation of the administration of education by the establishment of Local Education Districts, each with its own Department of Education and its own Local Advisory Board.[18] The Local Education Districts and Local Advisory Boards were allowed by the Education Act of 1966, but the core of the recommendation had been the decentralisation of the machinery of administration and the transfer of substantial authority to the local Advisory Committee and the local Education Department. This recommendation ran counter to the centralising drive of the nationalist government and it was a matter of surprise that it was accepted at all by the government in 1960.

Although the government always insisted on its right, or more precisely the Cabinet's right, to decide education policy, it was prone to appointing committees and working parties composed of nationals. Although a less ingenuous interpretation of later committees and working parties is possible, the idea at this time was to widen the input of people into the remaking of the education system. Before 1956 the Board of Education was normally unrepresentative of any vested interest but the churches, and indeed it was only after prolonged criticism that teachers got a single representative from 1934. The PNM government wished to see parents, employers, trade unionists and delegates from local government institutions on education committees, whether at the local or central level. Perhaps there was a conviction that the more persons invited to give opinions, the less dominant would be the voice of the churches.

Implicit in the Maurice Report – which was a nationalist document in a period of strident PNM nationalist rhetoric – and in the government's acceptance of it, was an unwillingness to acknowledge that in education matters the status of people as members of churches was superior to their status as citizens. The nation was more important than churches; national integration more vital than the corporate integrity of religious bodies. This philosophical assumption abolished the force of religious majorities in the making of education policy. For instance, from the inauguration of the dual system in 1870 the religious group possessing a majority in a district was held to have an irrefutable right among the churches to priority in the establishment of a denominational school in that district. The Maurice Report and the government were minded to see such a religious group as primarily a collection of nationals without any prior right to a government aided school outside the requirements of the nation as determined by the government. It was the Local Committee made up of many persons of different faiths (or of no religious affiliation at all) which was to approve the applications of religious groups (or other groups) to establish schools aided by government. The imposition of a Local Committee in each Education District would have placed a transforming distance between the government and the Denominational Boards of Management. The Local Committee was to mediate between government and the churches. Previously, government and the churches stood face to face in the dual system as the two authorities in education; as the two providers; as the two partners. The Maurice Report and the PNM government implicitly downgraded the Denominational Boards of Management (the arms of the churches in education) and upgraded other groups and individuals who had no direct management of schools, as legitimate participants in the making of policy.

The logic of the downgrading of the Denominational Boards of Management was the assertion of a right and a power by government to demand the use of denominational school buildings, and to oblige Denominational Boards of Management, where necessary, to convert their schools into types of schools conformable to the models developed by the government. Almost no other recommendation of the Maurice Report elicited as much anger from church supporters as this line of thinking which threatened the very ownership of school buildings by the churches without any mention of compensation.[19] Legalised theft was how one angry opposition parliamentarian described it.[20] The right to commandeer denominational school buildings formed one of the proposals in Parliament in July 1960, but a few months later the government backed off this issue in the Concordat of December 1960 which secured to the churches the ownership of their school premises. Down to 1985 the PNM government was unable or unwilling to force any denominational secondary school to become either junior secondary school or senior comprehensive school. Almost as reprehensible to the churches was the recommendation of the Maurice Report that denominational secondary schools be administered by government, which the government itself refused to do.

Both the Maurice Report and the government served notice that the existing denominational secondary schools with their emphasis on arts subjects were unsatisfactory and due for change. What was called the secondary modern school was clearly more desirable, although it is now clear how little practical work actually took place in these schools. The Maurice Report and the government generally favoured a mixture of academic and practical subjects in the same school, whether it be the secondary modern school or the comprehensive school. In the late 1950s and early 1960s the expansion of opportunities via the secondary modern schools was really to redistribute secondary education and to break its colonial structure rather than to train manpower for industry or the economy.[21] There was however confusion surrounding the development of a new type of secondary school, not least because group manpower demands as a motivation for technical/vocational education gradually superseded in the mid 1960s the provision of it as a social service for individual consumption. There was, according to the government, to be new emphasis on technical/vocational education to fill the demands of the economy for trained manpower; but this type of technical/vocational education was seen by the government from the mid 1960s to the mid 1970s largely as a separate provision in technical schools or vocational schools than as an integral part of either secondary modern schools or comprehensive schools.

Dr Williams' proposal that West Indian history be compulsory in all secondary schools and that it be taught in the teacher training colleges constituted an interesting attempt to reorient the curriculum to boost the political consciousness of the youths of the country. West Indian history was the only arts subject which the government seemed anxious to push in post-primary schools. Elsewhere the emphasis was to reorient the curriculum to practical and vocational subjects. Dr Williams' political use of West Indian history as a critique of colonialism and as the discipline which most informed his political speeches in Woodford Square raised the suspicion that the teaching of it might somehow serve the political interest of the PNM.

It is worthwhile to observe the response of the parliamentary opposition, largely composed of Indians, to the PNM proposals for expansion and reorientation of the education system. There was no disagreement about the need to reorient the curriculum away from academic ('bookish') subjects. Technical schools, agricultural schools, vocational schools were the talk of the day while parents hurried to send children to learn academic subjects and take Cambridge examinations in academic subjects. The main criticism of the government related to the rate of increase of the schools and to its discouragement of denominational schools. The parliamentary opposition cared more for rapid expansion than for niceties such as adequate building standards or planned location of schools. The 'intellectual government' was taunted for its delays in fulfilling targets; it was said, often with some truth, that the rate of provision of new primary school places from 1950 to 1955 was greater than from 1956 to 1961; that Roy Joseph, the much despised Minister of Education in PNM election rhetoric, had facilitated the building of more schools than the scholar politician Eric Williams.[22] Excessive planning and investigation by the PNM government and slow bureaucratic procedures by the Ministry of Education and the Ministry of Works were deplored. The promise of some members of the Parliamentary opposition was to liberate the creative energies of the clerical school providers which had done wonders in the past. The country owed, it was said, a tremendous debt of gratitude to the churches and white expatriate teachers for their contribution to education.[23]

Reorientation Over Expansion 1963-1972

Of the three broad periods in which government policies are being considered, namely 1956 to 1962, 1963 to 1972, and 1973 to 1981, the most difficult for the government was 1963 to 1972. This was basically because the balance of emphasis between actual expansion on the one hand and plans to reorient the education system on the other hand shifted in favour of reorientation. This meant delays and promises of a new future while existing problems piled up, for example, shortage of school places at all levels as population increases continued unabated, swelling unemployment and unemployability of youthful school-leavers, and growing political dissatisfaction, especially among young people, leading to the ripening of the Black Power movement in 1969/1970. The PNM government after independence seemed to have slowly lost its way among the many intractable social and economic problems. As suggested previously, the failure of the government's economic strategy to create jobs and redistribute income was at the root of the disturbances.

The continued expansion of primary school places was characterised in this period by a near total cessation of new denominational primary schools. Government primary schools led the way slowly from 99 schools in 1964 to 113 in 1970. There was a slowing down of the rate of provision of new schools and additional school places. The emphasis in respect to denominational primary schools seemed to have been on rebuilding rather than on the erection of additional schools. The government came to have a greater share of the total number of primary schools, though the churches still made by far the greater provision. The pile-up of students in primary schools as well as criticism of the provision of schools by the parliamentary opposition led to a situation in which the government readily confessed to a 16 percent rate of overcrowding in primary schools. Two answers were offered: the first was to use a double shift system in the more congested districts and the second was to point to a near future when the construction of junior secondary schools would draw off thousands from the primary schools. Although the government did not think the overall position discreditable, there were always spokesmen from the parliamentary opposition, most often Indians, who could point out overcrowding of schools and shortage of school places in their constituencies. As in the late 1950s and early 1960s their solution was to liberate the energies of the churches by generous grants to them and a free hand to build schools on a crash programme. The government refused to do this. The number of denominational primary schools in the dual system showed almost no change between 1964 and 1972.

In respect to the expansion of secondary education between 1964 and 1972, it could also be said that there was a slowing down of the rate of growth, especially after 1966. The government increased the number of its secondary schools from 16 to 21, and the churches improved theirs from 20 to 24. Between 1966 and

1972 there was little change in the number of secondary schools or of school places. The increase in the number of secondary school places between 1964 (20,327) and 1971 (27,987) was smaller than the increase between 1957 (9,081) and 1964. This necessarily meant a slowing down in the rate of growth of students entering secondary schools via the Common Entrance Examination. The explanation was that decisions taken to reorient the secondary school system into a two-cycle system had put a brake on the expansion of government secondary modern schools and on the traditional type of denominational secondary schools.

Although there was a tremendous gap between the demand for, and the supply of, trained manpower and a great deal of excitement over the imperative of new vocational schools, there were no new technical schools in this period (1964-1972) – though the opportunities for technical/vocational training at lower levels were vastly expanded by special provision in four trade training centres. The Black Power demonstrations and the February 1970 revolution convinced the government that a special effort had to be made to increase the employability of youths. A new tax, the 5 percent unemployment levy, from 1970 enabled the government to mount courses at the assistant craftsman level in trade training centres. But it was soon found that there was a high drop-out rate from these courses.[24] The Ministry of Agriculture also organised four youth camps for boys in which agricultural skills were imparted with vocational intentions to disinterested participants. However expansion in technical/vocational education also awaited reorganisation.

There were no such restraints however in the areas of admission to teacher training programmes at the St Augustine campus of UWI and in overseas scholarships. At St Augustine the enrolment of nationals in Arts courses increased sizeably between 1964 and 1971; those studying agriculture doubled though from an alarmingly low base; engineering students doubled; there was a five-fold increase in natural science students; social science studies, commenced in 1965, tripled; while a small start was made in 1968 with studies for the Diploma in International Relations. The award of overseas and local scholarships continued significantly high, there being for instance provision for 535 scholarships and study leave awards by government in 1970, with emphasis on accounting, engineering, agriculture, hotel management, quantity surveying and health services. The increase in the number of primary school teachers trained was less impressive. A vast problem in teacher training confronted the government as it contemplated the reorientation of the education system.

The outstanding achievements of the period 1963 to 1972 were in the areas of progress in the reorientation of the education system. The areas most subject to rethinking (as indeed since the 1930s) were secondary education and technical/vocational education, in other words the middle of the education system. Two outstanding developments took place, one so quiet and internal that it missed the glare of publicity. At the John Donaldson Technical Institute in the afterglow of national independence, and under the inspiring leadership of Dr Norbet Masson and Albert Alleyne, a reorientation of the courses and examination of the two technical institutes took place, after a disastrous start in 1962/1963. This reorientation led to the abolition of the external examination set by the much criticised City and Guild of London Institute and to the historic establishment of a very problematic National Examination Council for Technical and Vocational Education. All this happened before the advent of the Caribbean Examinations Council (CXC) to challenge the role of external examination like GCE of London in the academic subjects.[25]

It was through the John Donaldson Technical Institute and the energetic principalship and extended advisory services of Masson that leadership in technical/vocational education was taken back from the South and passed on to the overburdened Ministry of Education. However at both technical institutes progressive thinking ran far ahead of physical infrastructure or teaching power of the general staff, resulting in the equally little publicised fact that these institutions actually did far more training at the craft level than at the technician level. In the second half of the 1960s and in the 1970s the two technical institutes were strangely exempt from the public debate over technical/vocational education, overshadowed by the troubles of the junior secondary and senior comprehensive schools; and the cross-fertilisation of ideas, if any, between the UNESCO Mission, the Planning Unit of the Ministry of Education and the expanding technical/vocational bureaucracy at the said Ministry remains inscrutable.

The key new development in this period (1963-1972) was the introduction, after independence, of serious planning of a short-term and long-term nature. The National Planning Commission under the chairmanship of Prime Minister Williams was formed in 1963 and the planning capability of various government ministries was improved. This was partly a reflection of the optimistic internationalisation of planning in the 1960s, including educational planning in the Third World, encouraged by the United Nations and its agencies.[26] Educational planning supposes that education is an investment in human capital, a vital instrument in modernisation and economic growth. The planning expertise was first provided by a UNESCO team which was invited to the island in 1964. UNESCO was actively interested in the training of education planners, encouraging international aid agencies to favour those countries which had integrated, overall plans. UNESCO advised the establishment of a small Planning Unit in the Ministry of Education. This was immediately acted upon, and with the help of a follow-up one-man mission in 1965 from UNESCO, the unit began an exercise which culminated in the Draft Fifteen-year Education Plan 1968-1983 (hereafter referred to as the Draft Education Plan). No education plan as detailed or as ambitious had ever been seen in the country before or subsequently. It envisaged capital expenditure of TT$171 million, and recurrent expenditure of TT$1.1 billion in fifteen years.[27] As might be expected, it proved too far-ranging and too long term to be anything but a broad guide for future action. It was not long before public pressure and political consideration overturned some of the assumptions and priorities of the plan.

One of the outstanding contribution of the UNESCO Planning Mission of 1964 was to assist the government in sorting out the model of secondary education which it finally adopted. The history of recommendations about such a model can be usefully taken back to the Marriott/Mayhew Report of 1931/1932, which suggested a new type of secondary school, namely the secondary modern school, with two distinct stages, a free junior course for the age group 11 to 15 years and a paid senior course for older children. Then the Moyne Commission of 1939 introduced the phrase junior secondary school only to have it literally shelved for the next 25 years. The Missen Report of 1954 meant virtually the same thing as the Marriott/Mayhew Report and the Moyne Report, but preferred the confusing nomenclature of Central schools.[28] In effect secondary modern schools, junior secondary schools, and Central schools meant the same thing: schools which gave a broad, diversified, non-specialist, practical and academic education to a wide cross-section of the less academically gifted children between 11 and 15 years of age. This new type of school was to coexist with denominational secondary schools and QRC, sometimes called secondary grammar schools (or later senior secondary schools). All these reports envisaged the existence of separate technical schools even when they might not have called specifically for them.

The Maurice formula for secondary education was complex and confusing. The Maurice Committee of 1959, not without serious differences of opinion among its many members, tried to be different by recommending that something called the comprehensive school should be the main type of secondary school; but there were also to be Central schools, secondary modern schools, and technical schools; and the existing secondary grammar schools, whether denominational or government, were to be converted to Central schools or secondary modern schools. The comprehensive school was to combine academic and technical/vocational subjects under one roof and it recommended itself socially as the common melting pot of the races and the classes. The Maurice Committee obviously saw the comprehensive school as subordinate in status to the existing secondary grammar schools and even to the Central schools.[29] The government, it appears, did not like Maurice's conception of a comprehensive school, but the idea of Central schools was completely accepted, indeed it was the main model the government itself was working on, not altogether successfully, in its establishment of government secondary schools in the late 1950s and early 1960s. All the reports before the 1964 UNESCO Mission clearly called for a new type of secondary school; the question was whether the existing grammar schools were to continue unreformed or to be reformed.

The UNESCO Mission recommended that junior secondary schools and comprehensive schools should be adopted, along with the existing secondary grammar schools and technical/vocational schools. A difference however was that the comprehensive school was seen as not merely parallel to the junior secondary schools, but a continuation of it in the sense that children could move from the junior secondary schools to the higher forms of the comprehensive school. And so the first breakthrough in the evolution of the two-cycle secondary education system, with comprehensive schools following the junior secondary schools, was made.

The follow-up one man UNESCO Mission of 1965 firmly adopted, along with the local planners in the new Planning Unit, a two-cycle secondary system; but the nomenclature of the school in the second cycle was stated to be senior secondary schools rather than comprehensive schools or senior comprehensive schools. (In fact the UNESCO Mission seemed to have regarded the label 'comprehensive' as a methodology more than a school.) It can then be said that by 1964/65 the government was being advised to have a two-cycle secondary education system, comprising the junior secondary school for children 12 to 15 years of age, and the senior secondary school for those between 15 and 18 years of age; but the concept of the junior secondary school was more clearly defined than that of the new senior secondary school since the junior secondary school was a reformulation of the secondary modern school, and additionally there were to be vocational schools following on from the junior secondary schools. The problem was always what to do with the existing grammar schools, denominational or government. The idea was to convert them into one or other of the parts of the two-cycle system. But there was an additional flaw: if technical/vocational education was really to be projected as an integral part of secondary education with parity of esteem, why were separate vocational schools necessary?

A more decisive definition of the two-cycle secondary system was provided by the local planners of the Draft Education Plan 1968-1983; the principle was enunciated that all children were to be educated up to age 14, that is up to the junior secondary schools. the junior secondary school was to be followed by the senior comprehensive school which would provide a broad range of academic and practical/agricultural/technical/commercial courses with the option to specialise in one aspect of the curriculum. In truth both the junior secondary school and the senior comprehensive school had a comprehensive type of curriculum, the difference being that the comprehensive range was intended to discourage specialisation in the junior secondary school, but to facilitate it in the senior comprehensive school. In 1967 and 1968 the government had at last a definite model of the secondary school sector which it accepted in Parliament. The first requirement was a range of junior secondary schools and this became priority number one, financed by two World Bank loans, from 1968 to 1972/1974. The range of junior secondary schools could theoretically be obtained in two ways: either new schools had to be built, or existing government and denominational schools (including Intermediate or even primary schools) had to be converted. Even on the assumption that the Denominational Boards of Management would be amenable – and they were not – most denominational schools could not be usefully or conveniently converted. A new range of junior secondary schools would be costly and slow to come into place, but there was no other way. The only advantage of this slowness would be time to persuade the churches to fall in line with the 'national model' at the higher level of the senior comprehensive school. Here again the government was to be disappointed. The era of the junior secondary schools began in 1972, though two government secondary schools had been converted by 1971. While being on the defensive politically after the election boycott of 1971, the government was able to launch a new education offensive. The grand political advantage of the two-cycle system, with the junior secondary as the first cycle, was that it raised the real possibility of universal secondary education up to age 14. The junior secondary school was good politics. But the appetite of the public for a full course of secondary education leading to external certificates (GCE O level, for example) was quite strong. It took some time before the terminal nature of junior secondary education for most students was unmasked as a national problem.

If the country could afford enough junior secondary schools it would be able, it was said, to abolish the Common Entrance Examination. It was envisaged that all the junior secondary schools would be double shift schools, notwithstanding the many clearly understood social inconvenience and educational disadvantages of such a shift system. The plan was for all the students of the Junior secondary schools to follow a common curriculum without streaming them. This created a lot of consternation among the teachers, school managers and parents as it was feared that bright students would be held back with the mediocre ones. Only 35 to 40 percent of these students at age 14, through a locally designed examination, would be allowed to pass on to the senior comprehensive schools for specialised training in either academic, technical or commercial subjects. It was when the students got to the senior comprehensive school that they would take GCE O levels in two years, and a few would go on even to the A levels. But these external examinations would only apply – temporarily – to the academic subjects; the technical/practical or commercial/agricultural courses were to be tested by a local examination and eventually all examinations would be devised and marked locally under the aegis of the UWI.

The technical equipment of the senior comprehensive schools rendered them very expensive and the thinking of the government planners was that to reduce per capita cost these schools had to combine many types of courses with a large student population. The educational value was expected to be opportunities for cross-fertilisation of certain academic and technical courses; the technical/agricultural/commercial courses would benefit from association with the prestigious academic courses, thus making them more acceptable as secondary education. The social benefits of combining different types of courses were expected to be like those at the junior secondary level, namely that of bringing together children of different races and social classes under the same roof.[30] The government hoped to achieve, through the two-cycle secondary system, the integration of the diverse racial and social elements of the population. At this stage of the PNM regime, integration was coming to be better understood as simply mutual understanding and tolerance (something more like multiculturalism) rather than a single consolidated national culture.[31]

The Draft Education Plan suggested that advanced technical and vocational training should be developed in the existing technical schools in Port of Spain and San Fernando (the John Donaldson Technical Institute and the San Fernando Technical Institute) as well as at the Eastern Caribbean Farm Institute (agriculture). It did not call for a separate provision of technical schools. The government obviously found something wrong with this aspect of the Draft Education Plan, because in 1968 it set up a Tripartite Committee to work out a vocational training programme at craft level, taking into consideration manpower requirements and apprenticeship schemes. By 1969 the government had to hand a manpower survey of 1968 – which was not available to the planners of the Draft Education Plan – in other words, a crude inventory of the national deficiency in trained manpower at the craft and technician levels. Using these estimations, the Tripartite Committee recommended the establishment of a National Training Board and six vocational schools;[32] government decided to construct 15 vocational schools. A relevant but unanswered question was then the following: did not these vocational schools become part of the Education Plan? If not, why not? In December 1970 it was said that this programme of construction would stretch over four years. Unfortunately the National Training Board to advise the Minister of Education and develop craftsman training was only established in February 1972. Clearly the proposal had become a victim of the political emergency consequent on the revolution of February 1970.

The government had always spoken of vocational schools as desirable; and in the rapid spread of community centres in the mid 1960s, it was often said by government officials that these would serve as craft centres as well. The problem with technical/vocational education which made it the most difficult to organise was that the society had little experience with it; and there was a considerable amount of confusion about the various levels from operatives, craftsmen, up to technicians or sub-engineers. It seemed impossible to integrate all the various types of technical/vocational education into the mainstream of secondary education, and the government from the late 1960s to the mid 1970s had at the same time the apparently contradictory policy of integrating technical/vocational education with academic education in the senior comprehensive schools, while planning to establish a separate range of vocational schools. In the end the former plan prevailed, as from about 1974 the government abandoned the scheme of building vocational schools without having completed the construction of any.

The Education Plan (1968-1983) dealt only briefly with the tremendous task of providing trained teachers for the practical/vocational/technical/agricultural subjects in secondary schools. The ordinary teacher training colleges were apparently seen, if expanded, as capable of producing, via a compulsory study of one practical/vocational or technical/agricultural subject by each student, the teachers needed for the junior secondary schools. The plan to staff the junior secondary schools with non-university graduates was a sure sign that at best they were only half-way between primary school level and a traditional secondary school level. For the senior comprehensive schools the planners looked to the St Augustine campus of UWI for graduates with the Diploma of Education. An important step forward was the idea of using the two technical institutes as the bases for training technical/vocational teachers. It was recognised, however, that the training of teachers of technical subjects, a long neglected and problematic matter, would require a separate and extra provision backed, as in the past, by foreign expertise or overseas scholarships.[33] This training was unfortunately left for the future.

So far only a reorientation of the structure of secondary education has been discussed. There were also attempts to reorganise curricula, and a significant influence upon these efforts was the onrush of the Black Power movement in 1969 and 1970. One issue agitated by students and youths was the inadequacies of curricula in schools. The NJAC, the leading Black Power organisation, fervently took the position that the existing curriculum destroyed the souls of black people. The rejuvenation of education required, it was said, the re-education of youths. The message of NJAC and the National Organisation of Revolutionary Students did reach secondary school students in Port of Spain and its environs. The most serious student disturbances occurred at Woodbrook Secondary School where the students demanded the teaching of more Caribbean literature and history and more Afro-Indian studies. Black Power slogans appeared on walls of some schools; also underground school newspapers circulated in schools. Some students in Port of Spain joined street marches instead of staying in school.[34] Student unrest made it urgent to reassess what the secondary schools were doing and such unrest was part of the reason for the government-sponsored Conference on the Secondary Schools in 1971 at which student delegates were admitted and allowed to give their views of the education system. This latter feature made it a historic four-day conference chaired by Dr Eric Williams himself.

Arising from this conference a Working Party chaired by Fr Pedro Valdez, principal of CIC, and comprising parents and students, was appointed to look into certain aspects of secondary school curriculum. It is possible to use government's acceptance of certain recommendations of the Valdez Working Party as indicators of the direction in which it wished to reorient the education system. Government endorsed the teaching of agriculture in primary schools as the base for agricultural studies in secondary schools. The plan was to include agriculture in the Social Studies programme of primary schools with the addition of practical work, including gardening where possible in the higher forms. It was at the junior secondary school level that school gardening competitions were envisaged; again (as in the primary schools) the technique would be to tack on agriculture to the Social Studies programme, but with greater emphasis on agriculture as a science. In this respect a marriage was called for between agricultural studies and the General Science courses. It was argued in the Working Party that without greater attention to agriculture than was envisaged in the Draft Education Plan, the specialisation in agriculture which was one of the options at the senior secondary level could not be properly achieved. All senior secondary schools (including urban schools) were to engage in agricultural studies, care being taken to link it with the biological sciences. To maximise the use of expensive equipment the idea of a Central senior secondary school specifically for agriculture was mooted. The aim was to produce career agriculturalists below the university level. Farm schools to produce small farmers would do the junior secondary school curriculum in agriculture with added emphasis on practical animal husbandry and repair of farm machinery.[35] There can be little doubt that the unrest among youthful sympathisers of the Black Power movement had increased the Working Party's sense of urgency that youths be given practical life skills to enhance their chances of employment.

The recommendation for agriculture in secondary schools by the Valdez Working Party (1972), accepted by the government, seemed to carry forward to greater detail the outlines of the curriculum for agriculture to be found in the Education Plan. In respect, however, to the Working Party's recommendations on industrial, technical, vocational or commercial education there seemed to have been some contradictions with the ideas of the planners of the Draft Education Plan. The Valdez Working Party wished to have both industrial arts (woodwork, metalwork and draughting, for example) and vocational subjects, but especially the latter, taught in a more job-oriented fashion in the junior secondary schools. It thought of these activities as vocational, not prevocational. It concluded that for the majority of the junior secondary school students there would be no further formal education. The Valdez Working Party also spelt out in detail the type of vocational studies which could be carried out in separate vocational schools, or presumably in senior comprehensive schools when they materialised. In short it was all for more practical work in all secondary schools. A major problem with curriculum reform was that everybody could always think of something to add to the curriculum, but very little, if anything, to take from it.

The government also agreed to promote the study of the history, literature and culture of the West Indian peoples, including the French and Hispanic Caribbean. This involved the study of French and Spanish as languages facilitating communication. It must not be thought that some, or indeed most, of these subjects were not already being taught in secondary schools. The accepted recommendations were a summation of what was desirable, not a programme of absolutely new studies. The government had also long ago decided that West Indian history was of the greatest importance and was to be compulsory in all secondary schools. It was also thought desirable to have students exposed to the history, literature and culture of Africa and Asia, not through a separate programme, but via the Social Studies courses as well as the geography courses. This might be viewed as a concession to the Black Power movement, while reassuring the Indians that India would not be forgotten.[36]

All these plans and reports made the PNM government aware of the tremendous deficiency in textbooks to meet the needs of the new orientation of the curriculum. There was the problem of new textbooks for the older academic subjects, especially those with West Indian content. At the start of the PNM regime Captain Daniel's *Histories of the West Indies* and Captain Cutteridge's *Readers* and geography books were still used in the primary schools, though not exclusively. Who was to write the new textbooks? Worse yet, there were new technical/agricultural or commercial subjects in the secondary schools. Progress in this field was extremely slow at first. It was easier to set up a bookmobile service, plus a Publications Branch of the Ministry of Education than to produce the academic materials for new textbooks. The writing of such textbooks is still in progress, and if anything, there now appears to be a confusing oversupply of titles in some disciplines.

It had long been recognised that a new approach to examinations was necessary. The government was advised to look to UWI and the long talked about CXC as the institutions to prepare new examinations to replace the external examinations of secondary schools long carried on by the Cambridge syndicate, and more recently by the University of London through its GCE programme. Examinations set by the CXC were not ready even in a few subjects until 1979; still it was a matter of policy in the period under discussion (1963-1972) to avoid extending external examinations to the many new technical/vocational subjects to be placed in the secondary schools. These subjects, anyway, it was recognised, could be better examined by tests administered by the secondary schools themselves, incorporating the practical and theoretical achievements of the students, with comments on their course work. Students would be given a certificate relating to the different technical/vocational subjects they had passed. Hence the problem of testing technical/vocational courses pushed thinking away from the concept of a single certificate covering a number of subjects passed at the same time and in the direction, first charted by the GCE, of certification for individual subjects, not necessarily passed at the same time. A problem which received little or no attention, was how to achieve standardisation of the tests to be administered in the various secondary schools.

In the 1920s the country first adopted what came to be known as the bursar system of training primary school teachers. It involved government scholarships to secondary schools for young intending teachers who subsequently entered a training college or received special instruction in teaching from selected headteachers. This scheme was the first feeble step to the slow emergence of the lowly teacher training schools as post-secondary institutions. This did not mean that the training schools took every subject to a higher academic level than the best secondary schools, but that new subjects related to the art of teaching, for example pedagogy, were taken up in a post-secondary mode by more mature students and staff. The consummation of this ambivalent process was reached under the PNM government when training colleges began to produce teachers for secondary schools: junior secondary schools and senior comprehensive schools. The projected expansion of secondary education and of the teaching of technical/vocational subjects within secondary schools was on such a large scale that it was impossible to continue to look only, or mostly, to university graduates to provide the permanent teaching force. Indeed the status of the teacher as a trained practitioner seemed to have become more important than the status of the teacher as a university graduate. The government accepted the ideal of training via in-service courses for all university graduates in the teaching service, and all other teachers as well should be trained. The ideal was a fully trained teaching service. The government also accepted the idea that the training schools' main business was to teach teachers how to teach and to evaluate the work of students, and not to be a substitute for secondary schooling.

In this chapter we have maintained that proposals to reorient the education system outdistanced the actual expansion of the system. Although the parliamentary opposition consisting mostly of Indian members did not perform particularly well on the whole, in relation to education its spokesmen were abe to make some telling points. It was not impressed by proposals to reorient the education system; it usually demanded a faster rate of expansion. Certain parliamentarians were able to demonstrate a shortage of primary school places in their constituencies.[37] There was the publicised case of a Mrs Marjorie Bishop, who for two years tried unsuccessfully to get her two daughters into a primary school in the San Juan area.[38] The expansion of secondary school places was laughed at by the parliamentary opposition as grossly inadequate; the Common Entrance Examination, the perennial butt of the critics, was said to have been discarded in England from whence the government borrowed it; the government's proud boast of free secondary education meant little in practice, it was said. The promised technical/vocational schools had not materialised. The PNM government, it was alleged, was actually educating in 1968 fewer students per thousand available than was the case in 1956.[39] The double shift system in some primary schools was strongly condemned as inconvenient and as an obstacle to accomplishment. The curriculum had not been revised after 12 to 14 years of PNM government; so an anti-colonial government was still using a colonial curriculum.

The parliamentary opposition was able in this period (1963-1972) to hit the government's education efforts harder and more effectively than ever before because there was far more planning than implementation in evidence.[40] The answer from the government benches was to trot out impressive statistics of increased school places and grants and to point to the Draft Education Plan. The government members admonished the parliamentary opposition to wait until the government's plans were implemented. Government members, if anything, thought they were going too fast, not too slow, in education. As before, government refused to adopt any emergency measures suggested by the parliamentary opposition,[41] or to give any countenance to the grand solution favoured by it, namely to give the churches all the resources they needed to expand education.

It remains to say a word about private secondary schools. Numerically they were important and by 1957 they produced about 700 students per year with Cambridge School Certificates. The government appointed a committee in 1957 to investigate them and to recommend a plan to give aid. If the report was ever submitted, no action was taken in Parliament. Like other schools they were by the Education Act of 1966 subject to the jurisdiction of the Minister of Education. The view of Dr Williams and the government seemed to have been that they could not give government aid to profit making institutions; it was partly to prevent profit making that all schools had to submit accounts of expenditure of government grants. In the meantime the expansion of private secondary schools continued to keep pace with the expansion of government and denominational secondary schools from the point of view of numbers of students. For instance in 1964/65 the total number of students in government and denominational secondary schools was 20,299 and in the registered private secondary schools it was 16,450. Between 1956 and 1967 private secondary schools had increased from 21 to 77, a faster rate of increase than government and government aided denominational schools. There were more private secondary schools in Tobago than government and denominational secondary schools. In giving an account of its stewardship in 1968 to a government committee investigating private secondary schools, the Association of Principals of Private Secondary Schools produced figures to show that, between 1956 and 1966 in relation to London GCE O level and the Cambridge School Certificate, their performance was about half as good as that of the government aided secondary schools and nearly on par with the Intermediate schools.[42] Members of the parliamentary opposition by the late 1960s had formed the opinion that the correct government policy was to offer financial aid to the private schools as allegedly was done in Barbados. Private secondary schools, however, did not conform to the national model the government was aiming at. The government however changed its mind slightly after the oil bonanza: soft loans became available to private schools, a policy then said conveniently to be consonant with the constitutional right of parents to provide schools of their own choice.

Expansion and Reorientation 1973-1981

Between 1973 and 1981 the balance of government education policy between expansion and reorientation shifted back in favour of expansion; and this time the expansion was more spectacular than between 1956 and 1963. The years of preparation in the mid 1960s and early 1970s paid off in an impressive range of new secondary schools which threatened to make a reality of the principle of universal first cycle secondary education. In order to build the first set of junior secondary schools the government had to turn in 1968, before the oil boom, to the World Bank for a loan. Ten junior secondary schools each with a double shift system were expected to be completed in time for the beginning of the school year in September 1971. But they were delayed and it was in 1972 that these new giant schools opened their doors. Never before were so many new secondary schools opened at the same time as in 1972; and their new style curriculum represented a curriculum revolution in secondary education of unprecedented proportions. And unprecedented controversy over the structure and quality of secondary schooling also began. No secondary schools had ever suffered as much criticism on secular grounds as the junior secondary schools under the double shift system. A new era in secondary education had begun.

In 1972 the government also took a loan from the Inter-American Development Bank (IDB) to construct vocational and farm schools. Suddenly something happened to put the policy of external borrowing to fund school building in a new perspective: towards the end of 1973 there began a revolution in world oil prices which in a few months brought unimaginably huge revenues into the coffers of the government. The estimated revenues from oil for 1975 alone was TT$1,184.2 million, almost 50 percent higher than the total oil revenues (TT$786 million) for the eleven years between 1963 and 1973. Put simply, in the words of Dr Eric Williams, money that was unavailable before 1973 for normal development needs became available after 1973. In 1974 the government set out to spend TT$121.6 million on education, although the Minister of Education was still talking as if funds were short. This sum was larger than the total budget of the country in 1957. The government abandoned overall economic planning and set up large Funds to finance specific projects in various sectors of the economy. An Education Fund of TT$300 million was soon established and there was more money still available.

By the end of that year (1974) there were 11 new junior secondary schools, and this number climbed to 16 by 1975 and to 22 by 1979, moving the number of children in them from 6,962 in 1972 to 35,676 in 1979. The government moved nearer the target in the Draft Education Plan 1968/1983 of a 90 percent intake into first cycle secondary education from primary schools. Perhaps most parents had not read the Education Plan carefully though it was extensively discussed in the press. Towards the early months of 1974 as the first batch of junior secondary school students were approaching their final year in school, the concern was raised about further secondary education for the nation's children (although the public was not yet fully aware of the oil fortune) in anticipation of only the planned 30 percent intake into the senior secondary schools. The issue of how the secondary

Government Education Policy 1956-1981

school sector was to be organised and of how students would pass from the junior secondary schools to the senior secondary schools constituted something of a crisis in 1974 and 1975. The appetitite of working class parents for secondary education had been wetted and they wanted more of it for their children. If the government had simply stuck to its plan of selecting a part of the junior secondary school graduates of 1975 via a 14+ examination, there might have been a large-scale loss of popular support for the government which it could ill afford with an election scheduled for 1976. Popular demand for secondary education ran ahead of the government's plans; the government now could hardly plead lack of money; and this was the only obstacle which ordinary citizens understand in education. The churches looked to the government to find a solution, confident that the problem was of the government's own making. They had warned from 1968 against a two-tier secondary education system[43] and continued to hammer home the message of the superiority of the all-age secondary school over the junior secondary school. The government tried to get the churches to convert some or all of their secondary schools into senior secondary schools. The churches showed no willingness to do this: the one effective negotiation weapon the government had, short of public opinion, was the severe financial straights of some of the churches. Since at least 1971 they had been begging desperately for increased subsidies and in 1974 they displayed their disgust publicly.

The subjects which the government advanced for discussion at a hastily convened National Consultation on the Education Plan held at Chaguaramas in October 1974 reflected the direction of government's thoughts on education; and its priority was not more funds for the churches. This was the second time in three years (the first being 1971) that the government had adopted the device of a conference to diffuse criticism, placate opposition and hopefully gather public support for its views.[44] Following the lines of a famous Eric Williams' speech on education at the Seventh-Day Adventist College in Maracas Valley in August 1974, the government was thinking that it needed to invest more heavily in technical/vocational education to make the best use of its oil revenues in new heavy industrial plants. It emphasised that there was an oversupply of GCE O level graduates in non-technical and non-vocational subjects. It meant to throw part of the blame for this outcome on the churches and their traditional grammar schools. The argument was that the senior secondary schools, both denominational and government, were being used to produce misfits.[45] Ministry of Education officials were working on a list of government secondary schools which were to be converted into junior secondary schools or senior secondary schools. The churches were expected to cooperate.

The churches could not afford to be seen as entrenched obstacles to reform. They declared sympathy for both technical and vocational education and for the idea of comprehensive schools, but preferred all-age secondary schools (also called five-year schools) to the two-tier system.[46] In 1975 the government had extensive consultations with interest groups about the organisation of secondary education. In these consultations (undertaken before Williams announced his policies of September 1975) the choice seemed to be between the two-tier comprehensive secondary school system (favoured by government, the Secondary School Teachers' Association and the Public Service Association) and the all-age comprehensive school (favoured by the churches, the Trinidad and Tobago Teachers' Union, the National Parent Teachers' Association, and the Chamber of Commerce). But all these groups still retained the idea of also having separate vocational schools. For the churches, the Trinidad and Tobago Teachers' Union and the Chamber of Commerce, the all-age comprehensive school obviated the problem of what percentage of the 14+ age group would continue with secondary education; among the supporters of the two-tier system, the Public Service Association wanted 60 percent of the 14+ group to go to senior secondary schools (about double the percentage in the Draft Education Plan); and the Secondary School Teachers' Association of Trinidad and Tobago seemed just to want the Education Plan implemented, meaning the 30 to 40 percent transition.[47] What was Dr Williams to do? The junior secondary schools were a reality. Denominational all-age schools were also a reality. More 'science and technology' was the number one priority of Dr Williams. The easiest way out was to build on the government junior secondary schools with government senior secondary schools: and the most effective way of doing this was to relinquish the idea of separate vocational schools and to guide everything and everybody from the junior secondary schools into the senior secondary schools. It followed that the separate vocational schools would have no clientele, hence their abandonment.

The existing junior secondary schools with their shift system, in their infancy, were easy targets of attack: badly staffed, lacking university graduate teachers, completely without any traditions as secondary schools, without external examinations on which to cut their teeth, they appeared, despite their well planned new buildings, more like schools for older primary school children than as secondary schools. These schools also became objects of controversy. They were schools for the people; the people welcomed them, but preferred other schools. junior secondary schools, the churches' spokesmen said, were unstable and would continue to be unstable institutions, with too rapid a turn-over of students.[48] They would be the breeding ground of mediocre students. No church wished any of its secondary schools to be downgraded to a junior secondary school. But becoming a senior secondary school was not upgrading either, for this could only be done by losing the lower forms (forms I-III) of such schools, and opening up such a school to annual invasions of inadequately socialised, mediocre students from the junior secondary schools. The churches urged the government to appoint a Working Party to revise the Education Plan.

It was the government which made most of the concessions in 1975, but not on what was then the most vital points, namely the two-tier secondary school system. Nor on the indispensable need to retain the unpopular double shift in many schools. Parents were promised five years of free secondary education, the government characteristically making the commitment before it had seen its way clearly to all the new places.[49] This was the best known, most important, single change in the Education Plan. It was a major revision; a most important upgrading of government's commitment to the concept of secondary education for all. It pacified parents; for October 1975 the churches agreed to take an extra fourth form of junior secondary school graduates into each of their secondary schools. The churches in return did get increased subsidies, as well as the re-examination of the Education Plan they had requested.[50] The entire body of junior secondary school graduates for 1975, after taking a non-selective 14+ examination, at the last minute was squeezed into government technical/vocational schools (300 students), into government senior secondary schools (4,620 students on double shift), and into other government and denominational secondary schools (680 students). By far the greatest number were placed in government schools of one type or another.[51] What was to happen to the next batch of junior secondary school graduates in 1976? About 10,000 such students were on the horizon.

The Working Party to review the Education Plan was under the chairmanship of Dr St Clair King of UWI, Before it could report, Dr Williams himself intervened and turned the education policy of the government in a direction which made it even more difficult for churches to change any of their schools to senior secondary schools, even if they wanted. The government had negotiated an IDB loan to build seven vocational schools, and three farm schools. Three others of the latter type were to be funded from local revenues. The government felt that in the light of the oil bonanza and the decision to go into heavy industry, science and technology would have to be given a higher priority.[52] With little done to build the separate vocational schools beyond site identification, Dr Williams introduced another major revision of government's plan (if not quite the Education Plan) in mid 1975: this was to drop the idea of separate vocational schools for specialised craftsmen as socially undesirable, educationally backward and economically costly, in favour of the incorporation of this type of training, including the specialised crafts, into the senior secondary schools now to be renamed senior comprehensive schools.[53]

Even senior Ministry of Education personnel did not seem to know, or did not care to tell, how this decision of the most critical importance for education was reached. It might have been taken independently by Williams, or more likely on the advice of the funding agency, the World Bank. It was not reached as a result of the mid 1975 consultation with the Teachers' Unions and the churches; for these latter discussions did not centre on the development of plans for technical/vocational education, but on the question of the two-tier secondary school system.

Once this decision was taken the next step was to mount a crash programme of "unprecedented magnitude" to construct nine senior secondary (comprehensive) schools in one year. Special committees were set up; red tape was cut; only one of these schools (Malick) was ready for October 1976, but the others were nearing completion. Something unusual had happened; never before had so many public buildings been erected in so short a time. The government was in a self-congratulatory, euphoric mood by November 1976, and in the elections of that year it campaigned on its record in office over the previous 20 years. Progress in education was thought to be the most substantial achievement of the government between 1956 and 1976.

The plan adopted was to send in children as the new senior secondary buildings were near completion and to make up lost time by extra classes in the summer vacation of 1977. The country was experiencing a building boom fuelled by the oil prosperity. By 1977 there were 14 of these new, giant schools, each characterised by elaborate buildings and equipment. The capital expenditure on one senior secondary school was about TT$8 million, excluding the cost of equipment and furniture (approximately another TT$1.5 million). Inflation added greatly to the cost. Nevertheless it must be recognised that as educational plants nothing like them in size, modernity and complexity had ever been erected in the country. That was what the government meant by saying that these buildings and equipment presented the opportunity to bring some "dignity" to vocational training and increased salience to technical education.[54]

The large-scale draw-off of students from the upper forms of primary schools, plus a lowering of the birth rate had a significant impact on the school population of the primary schools.[55] This stabilised itself in the very early 1970s and then started to decline slowly, with the result that whereas 227,254 children were enrolled in 1970, the corresponding figure for 1978 was 181,863. Consequently, overcrowding went down to just 2 percent in 1975/1976. The number of primary schools stopped increasing after the early 1970s. The task then was not to increase school places at this level, but to tackle the large backlog of government and denominational school buildings in need of repairs or replacement. A bigger than ever disparity between the quality of primary school and secondary school buildings had been brought about by the new government secondary modern schools of the early 1960s and even more so by the junior secondary and senior secondary schools of the 1970s. Many of the primary schools were still unpartitioned one roon structures. Repairs were facilitated by the availability of TT$300 million in the Primary School Building Fund and far less so by an aborted third World Bank loan in 1979. In fact the government declared its willingness to provide 100 percent financing for the repairs or rebuilding of denominational primary school toilets and drinking water facilities. In respect to the old formula of two-thirds government contribution to the building and repairs of denominational schools, the government was ready to increase its portion as long as the aided school conformed to 'national norms'. The massive oil revenues in the hands of government and inflation in the cost of building and maintaining schools had put the government in a position where it could put pressure on the denominational schools. But the churches were not willing to cooperate on the issue of the two-tier system.

There were two other types of schools undergoing expansion between 1972 and 1981. The explanation given for the rise of what was called 'composite' schools, a sort of hybrid combining junior secondary schools and senior comprehensive schools, was that they suited remote and sparsely populated rural areas such as Cedros, Toco and Tabaquite where the school population was too small to support the two-cycle secondary education system. The technique apparently allowed the teaching of, or at least the possibility of teaching, subjects peculiar to the district. For instance, at Toco there was a request to include fishing on the curriculum.[56] Only a handful of composite schools existed.

Some belated progress was made with nursery schools, but since there was little political capital to be gained, these schools were totally in the backwater of government's propaganda about its education policy. Indeed the government for about the first 14 years (1956 to 1970) left this level of education to village councils, private enterprise and voluntary organisations using the community centres. About 1970 the government announced plans for a National Pre-school Education Project, with 100 centres for about 5,000 children between ages 4 and 5 years. But progress was slow and the budget for it small. The Van Leer Foundation of Holland offered assistance. By 1976 there were ten centres, with plans to establish more.

In the area of teacher training the major development was the building of a large teacher training college at Corinth in southern Trinidad. The government had decided that the proper thing was to have only two large government training colleges, one in the South and the other in the North. The one in the North would be located at Valsayn for 640 students. Construction at Valsayn was completed in 1978. By 1975/1976 it was estimated that 64.3 percent of primary school teachers were trained and the government was hoping to have a fully trained teaching service by about 1981. With the reduction of the primary school population, the training schools were increasingly being looked to as sources of trained teachers (non-university graduates) for the secondary schools. If these secondary schools, especially their technical departments, were taken into account in the estimation of needs – and they were by the St Clair King Working Party of 1976, – then the nation was far from being able to supply the teachers needed. In particular, the demand for trained technical/vocational teachers had skyrocketed; belatedly – and for the very first time in any systematic manner – the local training of technical teachers was begun at the John Donaldson Technical Institute in Port of Spain. A new wing of this institute enabled the government to start part-time training of technical and vocational teachers (with the exception of agriculture). Surely now these teachers would be trained in the realities of how things were done in Trinidad and Tobago rather than in metropolitan countries!

The programme of overseas awards in selected areas in which the nation was short of expertise continued with 1974 being declared 'Petroleum Year'. Twenty scholarships leading to qualifications in petroleum technology and related studies were awarded, and a number of scholarships were given to study special languages. In 1976 the number of Island Scholarships (university scholarships) based on A level results was temporarily increased from 10 to 19 to mark the country's accession to the status of a republic. In 1978 one of the many funds set up with the oil revenues was a Scholarship and National Training Fund of TT$15 million. Higher education, like secondary education, was being guided by manpower considerations. The government however could not find enough suitably qualified candidates to award scholarships in certain critical fields like mathematics, the physical sciences, and specialised crafts, and most of the money from an IDB loan (1972) for an overseas revolving fund had to be returned unused. At UWI St Augustine there was expansion in the Faculty of Engineering and by 1978 a fund was established with TT$15 million to initiate building of a University medical complex at Mount Hope, near to St Augustine, to include a teaching hospital, schools of medicine, dentistry, veterinary science, pharmacy and nursing.[57] Up to 1985 most of these facilities had not been completed.

At this point we will consider a number of miscellaneous examples of expanded services or of initial decisions to expand services. Up to 1985 the PNM government had not constructed the new National Library promised since at least 1979, but school libraries were improved, including sixth form libraries. Increased funds were spent on sports in schools, with a number of coaches appointed to serve schools and communities. Hitherto the government had only given money for sports; in the late 1970s it began to take part in the organisation of sports. Annual sport clinics were held at Chaguaramas gymnasium; and a Division of Physical Education was set up within the Ministry of Education. The government decided to establish a National Foundation in Arts and Culture and a National Theatre. These did not materialise.

It might be well to consider here increased attention to the health and physical welfare of students at primary and secondary schools. In the rebuilding of primary schools attention was given to space for medical and dental treatment. The provision of school meals predated the advent of the PNM, but with increasing revenues the government was able to extend this programme until the budget of 1978 carried the large sum of TT$113 million for school feeding, far more than the entire annual budget for education in the 1960s. The aim was one well balanced meal per day for each student. Money was no problem. The long debates in Parliament brought to light the tremendous difficulty of organising one meal a day for some 300,000 students. Up to 1981 the full programme had not come into existence; the money was available, but not the machinery or the experience. The free meal represented an attempt to redistribute income and spread the benefits of the oil bonanza. So too were the increased book grants which cost the government TT$22.1 million between 1973 and 1978. Still in terms of benefits to each student the grants seemed small. Schoolbook and school uniform grants were increased to TT$40 (1978) and TT$70 (1977) per annum for each primary school and secondary school student respectively. The first school bus service existed from the 1930s, but this was only transportation from school to practical training centres. A school bus service from home to school and back, introduced in 1966 with 18 buses in 11 areas, was extended steadily to 243 buses (1978) serving 78 areas. In 1978, 89 new buses were assembled locally to join this fleet.

It is time now to consider the question of ways in which the education system was in fact reoriented, or was to be reoriented in the future. A new primary school curriculum was devised by the Ministry of Education and academics from UWI in 1975; it included language arts, mathematics, social studies, general science, nutrition education, physical and creative arts. The general science curriculum included agriculture, and the mathematics was new maths. It appears that the guiding principle was to provide a smooth integration with the curriculum of the junior secondary schools. This new curriculum raised the question of the reorganisation of the curriculum of the teacher training colleges.

In the area of secondary education a significant decision was to give up plans for a range of vocational schools separate from the junior secondary schools. This meant that the specialised craft training which the government now thought more indispensable than ever, in view of the decision to go into heavy industries, had to be moved into the senior secondary schools (which then became senior comprehensive schools with specialised crafts). In the Education Plan the senior secondary schools were going to combine academic courses with "basic disciplines and scientific education on the basis of which the employer would build his specific job training rather than the specific training at school . . ."[58] The more specialised crafts would be offered only in the technical colleges and in the comprehensive schools in evening classes. At the time when the Education Plan was drafted the planners could only have been thinking of light industries; by the mid 1970s the country's industrialisation plans had become suddenly more ambitious and the aim of educational planning at the level of secondary and post-secondary education was more than ever to produce the trained manpower which heavy industrialisation would require. The answer was thought to be the senior comprehensive schools, especially those with specialised crafts.

These expensive schools with their machinery and workshops required new concepts in the maintenance of schools. The maintenance and repair of the machinery, and in fact the training of technical instructors to use the machinery, proved more demanding than the resources immediately available. The government met the problem by contracting with a United States firm to maintain and repair the machinery, provide security and train local personnel for three years. The problems of management of schools with as many as nine laboratories, 80 teaching stations and 13 buildings and as many as 1,500 students were altogether more enormous than the difficulties usually encountered in smaller secondary schools of four or five buildings and 250 to 450 students: the government had to arrange seminars for principals, vice principals and senior staff. Towards the end of 1981, some of these schools were divided experimentally into departments with departmental heads to facilitate better management.

As might be expected, the early batches of students passing through the junior secondary schools and the senior comprehensive schools were 'guinea pigs' of the new system. They had to start classes before all the machinery was in place and before the teachers of technical subjects were properly trained. Their accomplishment after leaving the schools was recognised to be so limited that they were offered continuation classes starting in 1978, with the hope that more of them could sit O levels and the national craft examinations in 1979. The government also supported extension classes in 19 centres designed to help students and adults pass GCE O levels. The government thus gave school leavers additional chances to acquire the qualifications they had failed to get at school, and the early graduates of the senior comprehensive schools needed this as their results in the GCE examinations were generally unflattering. As is well known government at this stage had turned its back on overall planning in favour of a project-by-project approach to development. An interesting development was a scheme to rope in the students who had specialised in a craft into apprenticeship schemes in industries to provide on-the-job training in these various projects. Government construction projects were to take on construction apprentices from among the graduates of the senior comprehensive schools; so too were the foreign firms erecting the many new structures made possible by the oil bonanza. As each batch of graduates emerged from the two-cycle secondary school system, the question arose whether they were more employable than the graduates from the parallel government and denominational secondary schools which were still concentrating on academic subjects.

It has already been suggested that the availability of large capital funds and abundant petrochemical resources led to a decision to enter heavy industries which in turn increased the urgency to produce skilled industrial workers. Since the government intended to invest heavily in iron, steel, petrochemical and fertiliser plants which would require ideally an infrastructure of science teaching and research of a high order, the question arose what other institutional support for such a programme was available outside UWI which was a regional institution. The government complained that the balance of studies was too much in favour of Arts-based rather than science-based subjects[59] and at any rate the business of the university was not sufficiently under its control. The answer of Dr Williams and the PNM government was to conceive a new institute called the National Institute of Higher Education (NIHE), later to become the National Institute of Higher Education (Research, Science and Technology) (NIHERST).

The relationship between Dr Williams and UWI had never been without tension even in the years when he was its pro chancellor. The UWI was never sufficiently the kind of university which he had sketched in his book *Education in the British West Indies*. It had not been independent from the start; it was not on his criteria sufficiently oriented to the service of the community through practical programmes. Possibly Dr Williams had abandoned some of his earlier ideas about the role and nature of a University of the West Indies, but he was not the person to reverse his opinions completely. The PNM government from the early 1960s would have gone ahead with its own liberal arts college if UWI had not decided to develop a campus in Trinidad. Equally threatening all the time was the government's insistence on the need for all types and stages of education (except nursery schools and private schools in practice) to be under the control of the government. The nationalist government was pathologically wedded to the idea of integration: it disliked deviations from its 'national norms'. A university campus at St Augustine largely financed by the Trinidad government, but only partly under its control, was always a misfit; a sort of obstructive, secular, 'denominational' school at a higher level. The bid to restructure UWI with a view to having greater Trinidad governmental control over an autonomous St Augustine campus was the belated consummation in higher education of the long pursued, integrationist government drive in education. The possession of enormous government revenues by the mid 1970s and the decision to go into heavy industry furnished the plausible excuse that Trinidad had special needs sufficiently different from those of the other contributing territories to warrant an autonomous campus. Certain leading politicians in Jamaica, for example Hugh Shearer, Edward Seaga and Michael Manley, for other reasons had already come to a similar conclusions about the UWI campus in Jamaica. Dr Williams was on bad terms with these Jamaican political leaders.

Without the Trinidad government's control over an autonomous St Augustine campus, the level and ease of coordination thought desirable between UWI and the new National Institute would be impossible. The committee set up to draft proposal for the National Institute argued that between independence in 1962 and 1976 about TT$13.4 million in capital grants and TT$179.6 million in recurrent expenditure had been made available to UWI (all campuses) by the Trinidad government; over the same period a substantial amount was expended by the Trinidad government and the private sector on scientific and technological research in an uncoordinated manner which dissipated efforts and reduced the impact of research on the development of the country.[60] The idea was to invent a new institutional framework which would bring under one controlling authority, scientific and technological research then done by different government ministries, statutory boards and government teaching institutions. Hence research would be the primary activity of NIHERST, but government spokesmen also said that it would train 'para-professionals', persons between the university level and the worker.⁶¹ Once NIHERST was formed, the next indispensable step would be a restructured UWI to give the Trinidad government the control needed to turn the St Augustine campus, in association with NIHERST, into an instrument for development suited to a rapidly industrialising nation. Sometimes it sounded as if the St Augustine campus of UWI was almost to be a part of NIHERST and not vice versa. The publication of the White Paper in 1977 outlining the NIHERST project was a development which the university could not ignore. Senior officials of UWI doubtlessly saw NIHERST as a danger to the university. While the prime ministers of contributing countries, UWI officials and special committees debated the new structure of the University, the NIHERST project was stalled on paper, materialising in law in a much watered down form only in 1985, after the university had been restructured, that is decentralised. Dr Williams had died in March 1981, and the oil boom was over; the future of heavy industry was unclear. A new political party came to power in 1986 with the new idea that what was needed at the tertiary level was a community college – to be called the Community College of the University of the West Indies. NIHERST, if not dead, was buried alive.⁶²

The tone of two Ministers of Education (Carlton Gomes, and Dr Cuthbert Joseph) by the mid 1970s was overly self-congratulatory. The government by the mid 1970s habitually congratulated itself on its achievements in the field of education, particularly in secondary education. Trinidad and Tobago, it was frequently declared, compared favourably with other Latin American and Caribbean countries; it was a model nation in this respect. There was no parliamentary opposition between 1971 and 1976. Once the two-tier secondary school model was in place the criticism that the government had not made adequate provision for the graduates of the junior secondary schools to continue their schooling crumbled. While the United Labour Front (ULF) poured scorn on the new joint venture economic policy of the government, a consensus was developing that the government had effected tremendous improvements in the provision of education.

There was however a new and promising direction for parliamentary criticism. Senator Louise Horne raised a query which the Minister of Education seemed reluctant to answer: how was it that students were leaving the primary schools illiterate?⁶³ And of course everybody could legitimately wonder if anything but frustration awaited the thousands of graduates of secondary schools who would not be able to find a job, not even a technical job, in the capital-intensive, energy based industries which were the new kingpins of the government's development strategy. Senator George Sammy, himself an engineer on the teaching staff of UWI, expressed scepticism about the success of the proposed NIHE. He reminded the Senate that the National Scientific Council and the National Council for Development had both failed and these were the predecessors of NIHERST. He said he saw no reason why NIHERST would succeed simply because it was larger.⁶⁴ On the whole, however, it seems that criticism of the education system in Parliament had receded from 1976 to 1981. The quantitative achievements in education had largely silenced the critics who had all along tended to agree with the government's direction of curriculum reform. To some extent criticism both inside and outside Parliament was turning towards the quality of education, and the Minister of Education had what he thought were adequate replies. The government was taking steps to raise the quality of education.

We turn now to a discussion of some of the measures that the government began to take in the hope of raising standards in the schools towards the end of the period 1973-1981. In 1978 a local committee of experienced educators headed by Dr C. V. Gocking was appointed to inquire into the entire system of teacher training.[65] It was the first time that an inquiry had been conducted solely and specifically into teacher training and the results were expected to form the basis for reforms. At the end of 1981 the fruits of this were not yet evident. The government hoped to bring down the pupil/teacher ratio in primary schools to a position comparing favourably with developed countries. Also a review team was set up to look into the possibility of converting junior secondary schools into all-age single shift secondary schools (in other words into five-year schools). In 1979 a UNESCO team returned to the island to give advice on the management of the education system and on a variety of other problems. It was hoped to submit all these reports to the National Council on Education which would make a comprehensive review of the system. No such review was undertaken; or if undertaken, no report was published.

One problem which could not await such a review was the shortage of teachers, and this was to be met partly by the re-employment of retired teachers on short contract and by the recruitment of teachers, foreigners and nationals, from abroad. To meet the problem of inadequate parental and moral support for the thousands of working class children from deprived homes then in secondary schools, greater emphasis was put on family life education, and a guidance counselling programme became a recognised branch of secondary school activities, with many new school posts created for this service. The government believed that having put a 'national' system of education in place, the problem was to increase the capability of students to benefit from it.

[8]

The Tobago and Indian Experience 1956-1981

> I have talked to many people both in Trinidad and in other parts of the West Indies, and also in Europe about Tobago. Whenever I am asked where I come from my answer was simply Tobago.
>
> A. P. T. James (Legislative Council, 15 December 1953)
>
> In Trinidad, the school system [of the Presbyterian Church] has made a very considerable contribution [to Indians], but it has not been successful in building up a strong indigenous self-supporting church after a hundred years.
>
> Garth Legge, Report of a preliminary survey of the Presbyterian Church of Trinidad and Grenada, October-November 1965, p. 85

Indians' and Tobagonians' Perceptions of Self-Identity

At first sight there appears no obvious link between the predominantly black population of Tobago and the Indians which would justify a consideration of their experiences under the PNM in the same chapter. Only a handful of Indians resided in Tobago, and Tobago is not even geographically near those parts of Trinidad dominated demographically by Indians. It has been argued elsewhere that from its incorporation into the state of Trinidad and Tobago in 1889, the island of Tobago was subjected to integrationist and separatist perceptions of its identity, which shaped people's verdicts about the condition of education in Tobago.[1] Those who saw Tobago as essentially a part of Trinidad, like Toco or Manzanilla, usually failed to see any disadvantage which the island suffered in point of education on account of its physical separation from Trinidad. The perception of Tobago as a separate entity from Trinidad led usually to the notion that it needed special facilities in education. The highest expression of the separatist outlook appeared among Tobagonians themselves, giving rise to the conviction that

Tobago had insufficient schools, or needed varied types of schools to meet its needs. Hindu and Muslim leaders of Trinidad campaigned from the late 1920s for their own denominational schools teaching Hindi and Urdu to protect their religions and culture. The Hindus and Muslims were belatedly allowed their own schools within the dual system, but the teaching of Hindi and Urdu was not officially endorsed; and no assistance was offered for Hindu and Muslim secondary schools.

The Tobagonians were also partly pacified by the establishment of Bishop's High School in Tobago in 1925 and by a resident school inspectorate. The separatist drive of Tobago and of the Indians which went beyond education presented challenges in different forms to the nationalist government of Dr Eric Williams. It should not be overlooked that Tobagonians and most Indians lived rural lives to a large extent, and perhaps similar instinctive perceptions arising from their material environment helped to shape their persistent alienation from an urban based government in Port of Spain.

Tobago and the PNM

The separatist outlook among Tobagonians increased under the PNM regime until Tobago had to be given a form of local government with an elected Assembly. This happened in 1980. Before long it became quite clear that the powers of the Tobago House of Assembly fell far short of what the leading Tobagonian politicians thought Tobago should have in order to direct its own essential affairs within the union with Trinidad. The question of the ultimate constitutional relationship between Tobago and Trinidad is obviously not yet settled. A key to the concern of the PNM government for Tobago has been the fate of the PNM in general elections in Tobago itself. Three broad phases can be detected: an opening phase (1956-1961) marked by the defeat of the PNM in Tobago in the elections of 1956; then a middle phase (1961-1976) in which the PNM won two parliamentary seats in Tobago in the elections of 1961, and the third phase (1976-1981) when it lost the two seats. It cannot be said however that the shape of government policy in education in Tobago conformed to these phases; but the PNM government's broader attitude of sympathy for, or indifference towards, Tobago oscillated according to electoral loss or success in Tobago. Enthusiasm for all sorts of Tobago projects, including education, rose and declined according to political calculations. The abolition of the Ministry of Tobago Affairs in 1976 was widely interpreted as a sign of Dr Williams' aloofness to Tobago after losing the two parliamentary seats there.

Just as Trinidad found in Dr Williams a hero and intellectual leader from 1956, so Tobago soon discovered in A. N. R. Robinson, a native son, a defender and protector of its interest. Between 1946 and 1961 the chief spokesman for Tobago was the less educated A. P. T. James; after his election victory of 1961 in Tobago, Robinson, a university trained economist, succeeded fully to the mantle of James; but Robinson was an ally of Dr Williams as well as a high ranking member of the PNM who eventually became its deputy political leader. In time Robinson had to choose between loyalty to Dr Williams and loyalty to Tobago, and he chose the latter. Hence from the early 1970s another factor in the fluctuating relationship between the government in Port of Spain and Tobago was the break between Dr Williams and Tobago's leading politician. Robinson after an abortive attempt to challenge the PNM in Trinidad through his own party, the Democratic Action Party (DAC), built up his political base in Tobago itself, eventually withdrawing from the Parliament of Trinidad and Tobago to become the leader of the Tobago House of Assembly.

The dissatisfaction of Tobagonians with the PNM government expressed itself at various levels: the great majority simply wanted a better deal from the government, specifically more development funds, a minority espoused one or another type of self-government, and a handful took a stand for an independent Tobago.[2] Tobago has not escaped some of the wider political and economic movements in the Caribbean over the last 35 years. The growth of nationalism in the Commonwealth Caribbean has been stronger at the insular level than at the federal level: the West Indian federation broke down because of insular nationalism. Where smaller islands found themselves yoked politically and constitutionally to larger islands, their relationships with these larger islands came under strain, notably in Anguilla's bid to secede from St Kitts. It was easier for insular politicians based in smaller islands to challenge the newly independent or semi-independent governments under which their islands fell than it had been to challenge the British government in colonial times. The rising expectations of a better standard of living, of social and economic development to transform economies, provided insular opposition movements with the criteria and the motivation to resist the ruling regimes on larger islands. The items of dissatisfaction in Tobago were numerous: since everything was controlled from Trinidad, everything which went wrong in Tobago or was deficient in any manner, be it roads, the electricity supply, the bus service or the steamship link, was the fault of the government in Trinidad.[3] In Tobago also a tinge of nostalgia for the old elected Assembly, once possessed but lost in the transition to Crown Colony government, provided an emotional rallying point and a lost privilege to be reclaimed through a strong Tobago House of Assembly. Tobago had, after all, in this Assembly, a form of self-government which Trinidad never had even at the moment of its imperial absorption of Tobago.

The integrationist and separatist views of Tobago's relations with Trinidad continued during the Eric Williams era. Williams started on the right foot by being the first head of government in Trinidad to admit that Tobago had a regional problem different from Mayaro or Toco and the right to expect compensation for past neglect. Dr Williams made himself Minister of Tobago Affairs during the late

1950s and early 1960s and a special Development Plan for Tobago appeared.[4] In June 1957 came in Parliament Williams' famous sympathetic analysis of the Tobago predicament in historical perspective. His argument was that the colonial governments of the past had betrayed Tobago. This was music to the ears of A. P. T. James, the sitting opposition member of Parliament for Tobago, but it also spelt danger for him. Dr Williams intended to undercut James' popularity by accepting the thesis of unequal development between Tobago and Trinidad. The outcome in terms of improvements was what mattered to Tobagonians: they believed that there was an implicit contract between Tobago and Trinidad in which the obligation of Tobago to continue as a part of the unitary state was dependent on tangible benefits. No other part of Trinidad and Tobago could take such a contractual view of its civic responsibilities. After the oil boom began, its benefits did appear in Tobago, but not on a scale to satisfy Tobago's leaders.

The chief spokesman for Tobago during the first term of the PNM (1956-1961) was A. P. T. James, the Tobagonian who had defeated the PNM candidate in 1956. James was himself the sponsor or benefactor of a private school which he wished to have aided by government. He was unsuccessful. James continued from 1956 through to 1961 to do what he had done between 1946 and 1956. If anything, he was more addicted to the separatist view of Tobago. James continued to ask for the development of Tobago, including more secondary schools, especially with a technical/vocational curriculum. Training in agriculture (a farm school) and in the trades was still felt to be basic needs of Tobago, unfulfilled by Bishop's High School or by the practical training centres. Since transportation was difficult within Tobago, James wanted a secondary school on the windward side of the island, preferably at Roxborough.[5] He also repeated pleas for the speedy repairs of the ex-Moravian schools which the government had acquired on lease. The request was granted, but the further development of secondary education had to await the unfolding of the government's First Five-year Development Programme (1958-1963).

Education Policy in Tobago

The government, which took naturally the integrationist view of Tobago's affairs, did not regard Tobago as having any special education problems. It thought that certain industries in Tobago needed special attention, for example tourism. But there was no special needs identified in education by the government, although much later Mr Victor Wheeler, principal of the Roxborough government school ineffectually attempted at the National Conference on Education at Chaguaramas in 1974 to impress on the audience the unique applicability to Tobago of rural education with a technical/vocational bias.[6] Other principals of secondary schools in Tobago held similar views. Apart from a farm school at Kendal, the government's education policy in Tobago was to reproduce the system of primary and secondary schools in Trinidad. There was never apparently any question of replicating the tertiary institutions found in Trinidad itself. The first major step forward after 1956 was the establishment of a government secondary modern school at Scarborough, with the same range of practical subjects, for example, woodwork and domestic science, as were to be found in contemporary sister foundations in Trinidad.

The pride of Tobago's education structure was Bishop's High School, a Church of England secondary school founded in 1925. For a generation before the advent of Dr Williams to power, this school had been the main local mechanism for the emergence of a local black middle class. A major turning point in the history of this school between 1956 and 1981 was its removal to new buildings on the present site. It gave the school vastly improved accommodation facilitating the teaching of more science subjects. Down to the early 1960s the school was still dependent on staff from Barbados and England, qualified natives of Trinidad being notoriously unwilling to work in Tobago. Tobagonian nationalism and common sense manifested themselves in efforts to build up a staff of Tobagonian natives, necessarily the ex-students of Bishop's High School itself. This process was assisted by university scholarships to promising non-graduate staff members paid for from funds set aside for this purpose by Dr Sylvan Bowles, the outstanding benefactor of the school.[7] He had been persuaded by Mr Blackett, the Barbadian principal (1957 to 1974), to shift funding from scholarships to the school to scholarships from the school to UWI. At the start of the 1980s the school was in the unprecedented position of having past students comprising 75 percent of its staff, of whom 38 percent had benefited from Bowles university scholarships. Concurrently lay participation in the management of the school became more Tobagonian. Bishop's High School was obviously so thoroughly Tobagonian that it could not be altered by the authorities in Port of Spain without careful consideration.

The PNM government eventually established in the 1960s two secondary modern schools, Scarborough government and Roxborough government schools; and then in the early 1970s Tobago got its first and only senior comprehensive school, at Signal Hill. In the shift over to the two-tier secondary school system in the 1970s there were fears, needless as it turned out, that government would downgrade Bishop's High School to a junior secondary school.[8] The government at one time (1975) was planning to convert Scarborough and Roxborough government secondary schools into composite schools to complement the senior comprehensive school at Signal Hill. Eventually Scarborough secondary school was converted into a junior secondary school to complement Signal Hill senior comprehensive school (which did not have specialised crafts), and Roxborough secondary school became a composite school. Tobago thus had one of each type of secondary schools: one denominational secondary 'grammar' school (Bishop's High School); one composite school (Roxborough); one junior secondary school (Scarborough); and one senior comprehensive school (Signal Hill). It did not have though a specialised technical/vocational institute. Tobago also had a farm school, a few youth camps and trade centres. It could not escape the problem of inadequate staffing of secondary schools, lack of trained teachers of technical/vocational subjects; nor could the schools halt the drift from the land, nor the migration of young people to Trinidad. Quantitatively Tobago appeared in the 1960s and early 1970s to have received its share of the PNM expansion of education; and there was nothing except cost to prevent Tobagonians from attending schools in Trinidad. All Tobagonians who wished training as teachers or as technicians had to cross over to Trinidad. Tobago never got the supra-structure of specialist post-secondary institutions which Trinidad possessed.[9]

One area of government expansion which benefited Tobago so clearly that it did not form the subject of complaint was the increase of opportunities for secondary education via the Common Entrance Examination. It appears that the cut-off point for 'successful' Common Entrance candidates in Tobago was set at a lower level than in Trinidad. It was later alleged by John Donaldson, Minister of National Security, that some parents from Trinidad sent their children to Tobago to prepare and sit this examination in order to improve their chances of success.[10] It is possible that this 'indulgence' of Tobago was the result of special pleas. At least one well known teacher in Tobago, Lionel Mitchell, had expressed the view in December 1956 that Tobago should be treated separately in respect to College Exhibitions (forerunner of the Common Entrance Scholarships). It is possible however to see this favourable situation in Tobago as the result of the greater availability of places in secondary schools for the 11+ age group than in Trinidad; but this early advantage did not endure into the later 1970s or 1980s.[11] Failure to provide the projected school places under the Education Plan led to a shortage of secondary school places, resulting in Tobago being able to admit only about 40 percent (not 80 percent as in Trinidad and Tobago) of the 11+ age group into its secondary schools.[12]

As in the days of A. P. T. James (1946-1961) unequal economic development, not unequal educational provision per se, was in the forefront of Tobago's grievances against Trinidad. The epiphenomenal character of complaints about education did not mean that they should be underestimated. Some Tobagonians wanted to have Tobagonians in control of educational institutions in Tobago and there was always the objectionable brain drain from Tobago to Trinidad. A. N. R. Robinson, when moving a motion for internal self-government in Tobago, complained in Parliament in January 1977 as follows:

> Every gifted young person in Tobago has to leave the island. The whole system brings them out, so they cannot give of their talents to the villages . . . If you are a teacher you cannot study for a degree in Tobago; you cannot have any form of higher training;

you have to come to Trinidad. If as a young person you want some form of technical training you have got to leave Tobago and come to Trinidad. That is the definition of colonialism.[13]

Associated with the desire to control schools in Tobago was a conviction that more knowledge about Tobago's history and folklore would be channelled through the schools, if they were administered by a local authority. Tobago did constitute an Education District of the unitary state of Trinidad and Tobago with officers of the Education Department residing locally; but these civil servants took orders from Port of Spain. In the division of power consequent upon the establishment of the Tobago House of Assembly, a measure of authority over schools, short of overall policy direction, was transferred to that Assembly. For example, the schools' nutrition programme and repairs and maintenance were under the control of the Tobago House of Assembly. But the legislation setting up the Assembly seemed ambigious on certain other points; and the extent of Tobago's authority over schools – as over other matters – remained in doubt.[14] Up to 1985 the Tobago House of Assembly had done nothing to put Tobago's culture into the schools; the Tobago House of Assembly yearned for total control of education in Tobago.

Dr Williams and the Indians

It is notorious that Dr Williams and the PNM were seen by the majority of Indians as an aggressive Afro-Trinidadian party and government and that despite early sporadic attempts to reach out to the Indian majority, Williams and the PNM, even after they had taken into alliance some of the Muslim Indian leaders, confirmed the Indian stereotype of them as a black dominated party and government.[15] In the six elections between 1956 and 1981, all of which were won by the PNM, it might even be true that there was a tendency towards increased use of Indian candidates by the PNM and of black candidates by the Indian opposition party or parties; but these interesting developments could not conceal the basic division of political allegiance along racial lines which have solidified in the country – at least before the election of 1986. The prolonged PNM dominance of government must be taken against a little publicised, but most important fact which cannot fail to produce further political changes in the country. The birth rate of Indians has been known to be higher than that of other races in the country for most of the twentieth century. Indians were a substantial minority, moving slowly from nearly 33 percent of the population at the start of the century to about 39 percent in the middle of it. By 1980 the Indian population was almost as large as the black population.[16] The age of the Indian minority predicament had come to an end.

Dissatisfaction and frustration for the majority of Indians arose from failure to capture the government through elections, or even to get a share of the civil service jobs to which their numbers and importance seemed to entitle them. Perhaps now nothing less than an Indian prime minister can satisfy this longing for political centrality. The blame for electoral failure was at different times placed by Indians specifically on the voting machines, or generally on fraudulent elections, on inappropriate distribution of seats, unfair constituency boundaries, bribery and political corruption, or on the division of the Indian vote among opposition parties.[17] Failure to capture political power meant an inability to shift their culture from a tolerated, even encouraged subcultural position, onto centre stage as the core of the national culture of Trinidad and Tobago, or as its most essential ingredient. The PNM government undoubtedly went further than the British colonial ruler it replaced in recognising some aspects of Indian culture. The independence constitution guaranteed freedom of religion; one Hindu festival and one Muslim festival were recognised as public holidays; still the relentless drive towards the acceptance of western culture has not been halted. As in colonial times, the Indians were expected by Afro-Trinidadians to move to Western ways of doing things; sociologists and anthropologists no doubt can find examples of Afro-Trinidadians who have adopted some aspects of Indian life styles, but there would be many more obvious examples of westernised and creolised Indians, of Christian Indians, for example, who apart from looking like Indians, were substantially undifferentiated in a cultural sense from Afro-Trinidadians. The cultural dilemma of the Indians in general under the PNM was how to maintain a fair share of Indian cultural input into the national assimilative cultural melange,[18] and assertive Indian youth groups had the additional problem of how to remain Hindu at all cost.

Education and the Presbyterian Church

At the onset of the PNM regime the country still had a small Presbyterian Church with a large number of Christian (Presbyterian) Indian schools, and a large Hindu and Muslim population with a small number of Hindu and Muslim schools. Most of the Indian school population attended Christian or government schools. The school building programme of Bhadase Maraj and the Maha Sabha Board of Management, or of the different Muslim school organisations, was never able to reverse this basic situation during the period 1956 to 1981; in fact the expansion of government schools at the primary and secondary levels led to a higher proportion of Indian children being taught outside Hindu and Muslim schools. On this level the government was successful in stemming the tide of Hindu and Muslim separate schools after World War II, and hence indirectly stanching the new revival of Indian cultural consciousness consequent on the independence of India. But the Hindus and Muslims did increase the number of their schools, notably their primary schools. These gains appear to have been at the expense of the Presbyterian Church which expanded its provision of secondary schools, but not substantially its primary schools.

The leaders of the Presbyterian Church who were by the late 1950s predominantly Indian ministers, partly educated in Canada, experienced some difficulties, as in Guyana, in deciding on an education policy in the face of the nationalist thrust of Dr Williams and the PNM towards a greater role for the state in education. In the mid 1940s when Director Patrick had imprudently challenged the role of the churches in education, the Presbyterian Church had responded with an internal debate in which one group advised the surrender of all Presbyterian schools to release the church from the weight of a school system, grown too large, it was said, for the church to carry it on simultaneously with its real mission of evangelisation through the word of God. It was decided however to continue with the schools. A decade later, after universal adult suffrage had reduced the influence of Christian Indian leaders, the Presbyterian Church undertook a similar exercise with similar results. This time a leading voice in favour of trimming the church's commitment in education was the Indian Presbyterian cleric, Rev Roy Neehall: he wished to see what he regarded as a 'school-church' turned into a 'church-school'.[19] These reassessments in the mid 1940s and 1950s also sprang partly from doubts as to the value of the schools in building up genuine Christian converts to Presbyterianism in the face of the Hindu and Muslim revival. The Presbyterian Church membership remained small; the church was able to express its presence more powerfully through its schools and numerous educational associations.[20] It was easier for Indian Presbyterian ministers, far more westernised than Hindu and Muslim leaders, to think of surrendering a slice of the denominational achievement in education to the Afro-Trinidadian government. Some of these Indian Presbyterian ministers responded positively to the appeal of the PNM for a new loyalty to the nation under the leadership of Dr Williams. They were sympathetic to the notion that relaxing the churches' hold on schools was a requirement of decolonisation. Another sentiment which encouraged the reassessment by the Presbyterian ministers was ecumenism, which allowed the Presbyterian Church to proclaim itself more an advocate for Christianity than a promoter of the Presbyterian branch of Christianity. It appeared from this perspective that as long as the schools were not lost for Christianity, the education work of the Presbyterian Church would not have been in vain. In the end, however, Presbyterian schools were not handed over to the government.

Maha Sabha Schools and the Nation

The Hindu and Muslim religious leaders had no qualms about the expansion of their schools in the face of the black creole nationalism of the PNM. By the time the PNM came to power in 1956 the first burst of new Hindu and Muslim schools was over; and it was a question of gathering financial resources for another big drive forward. Only a few new Hindu and Muslim schools were opened in the early years of the PNM regime. The attitude of Williams and his government toward Hindu and Muslim schools was most instructive. The nationalist regime preferred at all times government schools to denominational schools whether Christian or non-Christian. Williams in his election campaign in 1956 had referred to the Maha Sabha schools as political cells of the PDP, his Indian political opponents, chief of whom was Bhadase Maraj.[21] Earlier in his public lectures from 1952 to 1954, he had pronounced most emphatically his total opposition to the teaching of Hindi or Urdu in the schools. This amounted in his mind to Indian racism which would inhibit the building of a national identity. The English language was to be the common language of the new nation. About six years later, Dr Williams put his views less offensively in a speech marking the centenary of the Indian poet Tagore. He said:

> From time to time the question has been mooted of the teaching of Hindi in Trinidad's schools. My own view is that this is infinitely less significant than the inclusion of Indian history and literature in our curriculum. All of Nehru's great works are available in English. Gandhi's teachings and his educational philosophy are available in English. Tagore's poems and plays are in part available in English ...[22]

In other words he was still opposed to Hindi. In addition to the cultural and political reservations which Williams and the PNM had against Hindu and Muslim schools, there occurred some unfortunate remarks about the building standards of these schools which were to embitter the Indian leadership for years to come. During the election campaign of 1956 some PNM persons – who was the first is not clear – made an invidious comparison between the Maha Sabha school buildings or some of them, and cowsheds. The PNM government showed a stubborn unwillingness to take some of these Maha Sabha schools within the dual system because they had been built without regard to the government's standard of school building and would, it was felt, require repairs in less than the usual time.[23] The government was chided for having what was called a 'dog-in-the manger' attitude.

The Indian Parliamentary Opposition

It has already been shown that Indian opposition members in Parliament in the first two terms of the PNM government (1956/1966) argued in favour of a liberation of the creative force of the churches, Christian and non-Christian, as the traditional providers of education. By a strange twist of fortune Hindus, whose participation in the dual system had been anathema to the Christian churches up to the 1930s, were now the foremost parliamentarian defenders of Christians' and non-Christians' role in education. This strategy was of course a defence of their own Hindu interest. Particular Indian members of Parliament made suggestions in Parliament as follows: Simboonath Capildeo in December 1956 said that the time was ripe for a complete overall of the education system; A. S. Sinnanan felt in April 1957 that the government should consider the introduction of free secondary education; L. F. Seukaran advised in April 1957 that the whole education system needed changing, noting that there was a need to develop technical education, and he declared himself, unlike other Indian members, in favour of government control of the education system; Dr Rudranath Capildeo, the Indian 'brains' recalled from university teaching abroad to oppose the 'knowledgeism' of Dr Williams, bitterly criticised the Common Entrance Examination in December 1963, and called for all children to go to secondary schools; Balgobin Ramdeen, very much the opposition parliamentary spokesman on education from 1961 to 1966, denounced the government's distaste for expatriate teachers and advised it in November 1964 to build cheap schools fast. On 28 May 1965 Ramdeen, obviously in rejection of the Maurice Report, moved – unsuccessfully – for a commission to investigate education and decide how to increase the churches' contribution to it. Denominational education, he felt, was an antidote to communism. Simboonath Capildeo called for a Hindu and Muslim teacher training college in May 1965. In the debates in 1965 and 1966 over the controversial Education Act the majority of Hindus, in and outside Parliament, were opposed to the government's plans, but Muslim leaders tended to agree with the government.

The above suggestions by Indian parliamentarians were in the nature of positive recommendations. They have been presented here as opinions of individuals because the Indian opposition was not noted for coherent statements of party policy in education. Because the Indian opposition never formed the government, it never had to implement policies and the country never had the opportunity of knowing if it really had alternative policies to those of the PNM. The two clearest policies which seemed to command the respect of almost all the Indian parliamentarians were support for a strong church input into education, and the reform of the curriculum in the direction of more technical/vocational education. Dr Rudranath Capildeo's speeches on education were more remarkable for the number of examples drawn from recent education debates in England – which he obviously knew better than anyone else in Parliament – than for any alternative programme to that of Dr Williams and the PNM. Simultaneously with the positive suggestions were, as one might expect from an opposition, bitter criticism of the slowness with which the government provided new schools and school places; and veiled accusations of favouritism in the distribution of scholarships and of discrimination in the priority given to various locations for schools. As was characteristic of much of public life in the country, open accusation of racial discrimination in education was taboo; but clearly a feeling that PNM education policy was anti-Indian in some respects resided only two inches below the surface of the speeches of some Indian parliamentarians. The disguised charge of racial discrimination, for example, could take the form of accusing the government of building schools in the urban areas while neglecting rural villages.[24] Everybody knew that rural villages meant rural areas heavily populated by Indians.

There came a time however, not easy to define, possibly in the later part of the third term of the PNM government (c. 1966-1971), which signalled a decline of Indian unwillingness to speak of racial prejudice in government policies. It could possibly have been a reaction of the Indians to all the talk about Black Power. The Education Plan had also been publicised. In 1968 and 1969 Bhadase Maraj and Rampersad Boolai, close associates on the Hindu Maha Sabha School Board, requested a technical school for central Trinidad, Chaguanas being the favoured location. They also wanted another technical school for Sangre Grande; and they did so in language which locals would understand to be clear calls for schools for Indians since Chaguanas and Sangre Grande were heavily populated by Indians.[25] Boolai could name with justification several locations in his constituency of Nariva where many scores of Indian children were without any neighbourhood primary schools. But the biggest surprise in terms of Indian demand for something which would benefit Indians alone came from Hans Hanoomansingh in December 1970 when he called for a full debate on the teaching of Hindi and Urdu in Indian schools.[26] Nothing had been heard about this in Parliament since the PNM first came to power. Hanoomansingh never got his debate; and there is no indication that the majority of Indian parliamentarians would have supported him. At any rate the Indian opposition was absent from Parliament by the following year. The re-emergence of the idea, however might, have been symptomatic of residual sentiment for these languages in schools as necessary preservatives of Indian culture in the countryside.

When the Indian opposition returned to Parliament in 1976, the new government junior secondary schools and senior secondary schools were already a reality; and so the opposition parties had missed the chance to speak in Parliament about the education crisis of 1974/1975. It seemed that the existence of a vastly expanded secondary education system blunted opposition to inadequacies in the government's provision of schools. Indians of course did criticise weak points in the Education Plan, but the criticisms tended to be undifferentiated from those of non-Indians. This observation should not deceive us into thinking that Indian grievances in education were at an end. Dissatisfaction with the formal curriculum existed and with the lack of progress in fostering multiculturalism in schools. In the words of one Indian female critic, the Hindu presence needed specific recognition in the schools.[27] There were within the informal culture of some schools many nagging, submerged problems arising from the unresolved questions of which culture – Afro-Trinidadian culture or Indo-Trinidadian culture – should prevail in schools with Indians and black children. Such problems were treated more like domestic problems within schools than like public problems in the nation. While new active organisations of Hindu youths in the 1970s and 1980s worked to preserve Hindu culture, in the process criticising the pro-Afro-Trinidadian tendencies of some schools,[28] their grievances in education did not reach any sustained level of national propaganda. Hence on the public level it appears that by 1981 the PNM government had more difficulty with Tobago over education than with the Indians. This was partly because the problem of Tobago was a ripe, public problem of greater political urgency than the chronic, social, submerged problems of balancing the cultural interest of Indians and Afro-Trinidadians within the education system in Trinidad itself.

Schools and Social Integration

A number of questions remain to be asked about the experience of the Indians in respect to education during the prolonged regime of the PNM. There is no easy answer to them. Did Hindu, Muslim or Presbyterian schools become less racially exclusive than previously? Were government schools of the 1960s and 1970s able to bring Indians and non-Indian children together under the same roof on a larger scale than before 1956? Did the schools play any significant role in creating interracial understanding and tolerance after 1956? These are questions worthy of research. Since the Indian population has moved from a minority position to a position of near parity with the black population, it is now more legitimate than ever for the Indians to ask if the schools run by other racial groups have become less racially exclusive. Did these latter schools have a greater proportion of Indians than previously? Some impressionistic answers seem possible, but ultimately empirical work will be necessary to give decisive answers. Christians did not normally send their children to Hindu or Muslim schools; this made Hindu or Muslim schools almost entirely populated by Indians. Additionally these schools were deliberately meant to be non-integrative. It was possible for an Hindu or Muslim child to attend certain primary and even secondary schools without rubbing shoulders with a non-Indian classmate; but this would be impossible at the level of the technical schools, the teacher training colleges, or the St Augustine branch of the UWI. One gets the impression that Presbyterian schools, particularly secondary schools, were fairly well populated by non-Indian children. The new giant government secondary schools remained sufficiently large for a genuine mixture of the races in the country. One gets the impression that these schools have definitely contributed to the breaking down of exclusive education for either Indians or blacks. On the whole there seems to be less racially exclusive education going on in 1986 than in 1956.

[9]

The Primary School and Teacher Training Experience 1956-1981

> New standards are also being introduced into primary schools construction and siting. Nineteen seventy-five saw a new syllabus for primary schools. The back-log of untrained teachers in this sector has been almost cleared. In one very important area, however, that is in Teacher Education and Training, things have stood still.
>
> *Report on Teacher Education and Training for Primary Level (January 1980, p. iv)*

The Subordination of Primary Education

The most obvious thing about primary education between 1956 and 1981 was its utter subordination to secondary education. It got less capital funds, less government attention, less public notice than secondary education. The battle for the universalisation of primary education was already substantially won, though overcrowding posed a problem in several schools, with a need for additional schools in a few localities. A great many primary school buildings were badly in need of repairs,[1] but expenditure on primary education was subordinated to the need to expand secondary education. Throughout the nineteenth century and for most of the first half of the twentieth century, the link between the manpower needs of the economy and the education system was made at the level of the primary schools because these were the first and last schools attended by the working class, hence the last schools before entry into the work force. If schools had to teach the habit of regular work, or habituation to agricultural routine, or skills of peasant agriculture or crafts, it had to be the primary schools (which then were truly elementary in the sense that they did not lead to a second level of schools). If plantation agriculture was to be assisted by the schools, it had to be the primary (elementary) schools – if one of course left out ICTA.

The goal of universal secondary education involving the removal of teenagers from the primary schools to secondary schools released the primary schools from the intolerable burden of preparing children for the work place.[2] This situation had advantages and disadvantages for primary schools; the advantage was that these schools were now available for genuine reforms dictated by pedagogical considerations; the disadvantage was that primary schools could be neglected in the drive to match educational output at the secondary level with the manpower needs of the economy. Primary schools, beyond the provision of basic literacy, became irrelevant to national economic development; and to the extent that religious instruction was de-emphasised they also lost some of their purpose as institutions which moulded character by moral education. Indeed primary schools progressively got another main purpose beyond literacy: this was to train and select the winners and the losers in the Common Entrance race for places in secondary schools. The Missen Report of 1954 provided a comprehensive critique of primary schools; they were failing to produce a "lively, reasonable and thinking child at 12 years of age".[3]

Reforms were slow in coming. The first direction of attempted reform in the late 1960s was towards the reorganisation of timetables and classroom teaching, with a view to having specialist teachers giving instruction to different grades as in secondary schools. The initiative for the first attempted reform grew out of a proposal by Dr James Maraj of UWI St Augustine, in what came to be known as the Caribbean Plan. The most important new feature was the use of specialist teachers in art, craft, music, drama, physical education and remedial reading in special afternoon sessions. Inevitably however the use of specialist teachers would have involved revision of the syllabus of these subjects. The focus of the plan on paper was administrative; when however the plan got international funding from the Carnegie Foundation, and a team of local and foreign experts, including Maraj, set about testing the plan in certain selected schools from 1968 to 1971, it appeared to be at least as much about new teaching methods and syllabus as about reorganisation of timetables and regrouping of children or staff.[4] About 80 primary schools all over the country apart from the ten project schools were drawn in varying degrees into the Carnegie Project in School Organisation. An elaborate report on the experiment was produced; but apart from the use of a few specialist teachers by some headteachers, no practical long term results followed from the project.

The explanation for this very meagre result is not clear; perhaps the proposed reorganisation was too radical. One possible problem was that the project, though approved, was undertaken outside the Ministry of Education; and if any result were to follow, it would have to be appropriated by the Ministry of Education. It was quite a new thing to have a local experiment of this scale outside the jurisdiction of the education authorities. Its findings were treated with the official silence from the education authorities which often characterised government reaction to the many reports by local Working Parties.

The second direction of reform was in the revision of the syllabus leading to the preparation of a New Primary School Syllabus in 1975. This reform was undertaken under the auspices of the Ministry of Education by experts in various subjects. In July 1975 the New Primary School Syllabus was made public and at least one section of it, the Language Arts syllabus, stirred controversy because of its revolutionary attitude towards the teaching of language.[5] One of the defects of this Language Arts syllabus, according to one of its originators, was failure to accompany it with any literature which teachers could use to implement it. This observation was true about the entire syllabus, with perhaps the exception of the Social Studies section. The New Primary School Syllabus of 1975 was therefore only a guideline for the future. Teaching materials were not ready; equipment and facilities to teach new syllabi were lacking; most of the teachers were not psychologically prepared for it; the teacher training colleges had not reorganised their own courses to prepare trainees to teach in the manner envisaged by the new syllabus. For instance trainees in most cases lacked the knowledge to teach general science and new maths. It followed therefore that implementation of the new syllabus in the primary schools in the late 1970s was very slow and was not complete by 1981.

The Dominance of the Common Entrance Examination

A serious problem of primary schools between 1956 and 1981, namely the presence of a high proportion of untrained teachers, was gradually ameliorated in the 1970s. Overcrowding of classrooms, however, remained a serious hindrance to productive and enjoyable work. Inadequate buildings, often of the open hall type with makeshift partitions if any, continued to be a major obstacle to education of quality. Inability to repair several of these schools was, as we have seen, one of the main factors behind the appearance of 'joint management' proposals in the late 1970s. Primary schools were grossly undersupervised by inspectors and government primary schools had substantially only their headteachers as on-the-spot managers. The quality of a primary school in the eyes of the public was judged by its ability to 'pass' pupils in the Common Entrance Examination.

The greatest single criticism made of primary schools as a whole in the period under discussion was that their work was distorted by preparation for the Common Entrance Examination.[6] In the very early twentieth century when the number of children taking the College Exhibition Examination (the forerunner of the Common Entrance Examination) was relatively small, it was more a particular teacher than primary schools as such which prepared children for these examinations; the glittering credit went to particular teacher or teachers first and then to the school in which they taught. As numbers taking the Common Entrance

Examination at each school grew much larger, often above 100 pupils, the preparation of pupils became much more the function of the school than of any one outstanding teacher though, teachers of extraordinary reputation still existed. Since everyone now had a right to sit the examination, everyone was a potential winner; but since only a few had the ability to win without special preparation, all had to be specially prepared and the earlier the preparation started, the better appeared to be the candidates' chances. The Common Entrance Examination down to 1981 consisted essentially of objective tests of intelligence supposedly beyond preparation;[7] but teachers and parents have acted on a contrary assumption, although Common Entrance question papers were not public documents.

The particular drawback to this preparation was that it was limited to the same subjects (Arithmetic, English, and 'Intelligence'), and to the same methods of answering (multiple choice questions and blank-filling work) as the Common Entrance tests themselves. Two unsavoury consequences followed: many schools did not follow the normal curriculum prescribed for primary schools, but rather the Common Entrance subjects. Another deleterious effect was that testing became very frequent, sometimes becoming a substitute for teaching. For example, English composition which was not tested in the Common Entrance Examination (down to 1981) was not done regularly except in the lower grades. Examinations have always, and presumably will always, exercise an influence on what is taught in schools; sometimes however the degree of influence amounts to a suffocating stranglehold, and this was the case with the grip of the Common Entrance Examination on primary schools in the 1960s and 1970s. As in the case of the impact of the Cambridge external examination on QRC and CIC in the late nineteenth century and early twentieth century, the dominance had the convenience of serving as a yardstick to judge the 'efficiency' of the school. The quickest way of forming an opinion of a primary school in the 1960s and 1970s was to ascertain its performance in the Common Entrance Examination. The public primary schools that had the highest percentage of passes attracted children from far and wide; and since there was no zoning of primary schools, it followed that schools with good Common Entrance pass rates were often overcrowded.

Clearing off the Backlog of Untrained Teachers

The most talked about, the most spectacular development in teacher training between 1956 and 1981 was the clearing off of the backlog of untrained teachers in the primary schools; second in importance to this as a trend was the means whereby this miracle was accomplished, namely the centralisation and concentration of teacher training facilities into two large government colleges. Additionally there was in some respects a raising of the academic standards of large numbers of trained teachers, partly through the higher entry qualification which became general during this period. Instead of entering with the minimum of a Teachers' Provisional Certificate mostly acquired by way of the pupil teachers' examinations, all pre-service candidates had to achieve five O level passes at least, including English, before admission. Entry into teacher training by way of the pupil teacher system came to an end in 1959 (though it took some years for candidates already in the system to pass through). This period therefore (1956-1981) saw the large scale realisation of the dream of former directors of education, Marriott and Cutteridge, for trained teachers with secondary education. In this sense the entire system became as it were a 'bursar system'. The teacher training colleges had at last emerged fully as strategically higher institutions than the secondary schools, though some of the latter went on to do sixth form work. Associated with this higher entry qualification was a change from the dominant pre 1963 pattern of in-service training to a new model of predominantly pre-service training, plus some in-service training (1963-1975). But then there was a return to complete in-service training (1975-1981).

Training for Secondary School Teachers

In respect to the secondary school level of teacher training, the dominant patterns over the period were the inauguration of an in-service Diploma in Education for university graduate teachers, based at UWI; and the development of technical/vocational teacher education at John Donaldson Technical Institute in 1979. The development of a UWI campus in Trinidad enabled the university to become involved in teacher training both at the level of the teachers' colleges for primary school teachers, and the training of university graduates as teachers for the secondary schools. This was an outstanding contribution of the UWI to education over the last 30 years; the Faculty of Education provided supervisory service over the teachers' colleges' examinations and teaching practice; and with special funds from the government of Trinidad and Tobago started a Teachers' Centre, and an in-service Diploma of Education programme, including instruction in school management for principals and vice principals. The idea that all university graduates intending to teach should have professional training gained firm root, especially after student protests and complaints against teachers and curriculum during the height of the Black Power movement. But unlike the training of primary school teachers the Diploma in Education programme at UWI was incapable of training graduate teachers fast enough to keep up with the expansion of secondary education.[8]

The Consolidation of Teacher Training

At the start of the period in question (1956) there was one government training college and three denominational training colleges with a total output of about 300 trained teachers annually.[9] To speed up the training of teachers a non-residential branch of the Government Teachers' College was established in Port of Spain to give a special one-year Emergency course, sometimes to candidates with GCE A level qualifications; this Port of Spain Teachers' College was for in-service training; the first big break forward into a rapid multiplication of trained teachers came in the years between 1963 and 1973, a decade which belonged to Mausica Teachers' College, then the key to the government's strategy of pre-service teacher training. This was a residential college for young male and female teachers between 18 and 25 years preferably. It became the largest training college, with an output of about 110 students per year, increased further in the late 1960s to meet the junior secondary school challenge. Mausica then usurped the leading role of the Government Teachers' College, a role which the latter had monopolised for about a century.

By the time of the Education Plan it was declared that the way forward was to concentrate and economise on teacher training facilities by having two other colleges – government colleges – in addition to Mausica: a new government college in the North and another in the South. All denominational colleges getting government aid as well as the Government Teachers' College and the Port of Spain Emergency College were to go out of existence. The official rationale was reduction of expenditure; but the nationalism of the PNM government was unfriendly to church participation in the area of teacher training. Eventually the projected three medium size colleges (about 400 students each) were converted into a strategy for two new government colleges each larger than Mausica which was to be closed. Again the explanation was economic efficiency; but perhaps certain problems at Mausica were not unrelated to the decision to close this college. The ideal of pre-service training at Mausica had apparently not worked as well as it was anticipated: as with the bursar system of the early 1920s the award of seniority and higher remuneration to young inexperienced Mausica graduates sparked resentment and complaints from older untrained teachers with long service. Doubts had also developed about the commitment to teaching and the overall quality of these younger teachers, some of whom had gone to Mausica directly from secondary schools.

Student unrest at Mausica in 1974 might have cooled enthusiasm of the authorities for a residential campus of young full-time trainee teachers. Clearly there was in the two new government colleges of the 1970s (Corinth and Valsayn) a return to the old formula of in-service training as the dominant pattern. Again the justification (avoiding pre-service training at the new colleges) was to accelerate the clearing off of the backlog of untrained teachers. Incidentally this elimination of the backlog was not as simple as it might sound: it was an exercise which needed careful planning as young, newly recruited teachers, put in temporary posts to substitute for untrained teachers sent to teachers' college, constituted a new group of untrained teachers. After a few years the two new large size government colleges solved the problem rather suddenly about 1982/1983, when only a handful of untrained teachers could be scooped up to form the first year intake. Untrained teachers had been called up systematically to enter the training colleges rather in the manner of compulsory military service. An unforeseen factor was the slowing down in the 1970s of the birth rate which checked the need for increased number of teachers in primary schools. The clearing off of the backlog of untrained teachers was a point of pride for the government, but its accomplishment was something of an embarrassment since it appeared to have caught the government itself by surprise. It was however a development of historic importance in education; since slave emancipation there had always been a large backlog of untrained primary school teachers.

The Christian churches did not mount a public campaign to save Naparima Training College or the Roman Catholic Women's College. Carrying them on was by admission of the Presbyterian Church and the Roman Catholic Church an onerous financial burden. There was some representation to the government to keep open Naparima Training College and later the Roman Catholic Women's College, or alternatively to allow the establishment of an ecumenical teachers training college.[10] But this was contrary to the government's plans. Only the Caribbean Union College (run by the Seventh-Day Adventists) which was not assisted normally by the government retained a small teacher training unit (and in fact opened the way for trained teachers to a local degree programme given externally by an American university). The Roman Catholic Church and the Presbyterian Church were unable to fight this issue since the government had presented its position as purely a matter of financial efficiency. The elimination of the churches from the field of teacher training was a landmark in the secularisation of education; the idea that the churches had a peculiar role to play in the moral education of teachers, though still alive, was now without institutional means of expression. Particular churches could still bring their beliefs to bear on teachers through special seminars and of course through church attendance; but these means were less regular and systematic than through a residential training college.

The ideal of a residential period of teacher training as essential to the formation of Christian morality and a cooperative personality in a teacher was also blunted after the closure of Mausica Teachers' College. The idea that the teachers in training were a select group of persons – almost like trainee ministers of religion – drawn from a larger body of unworthy aspirants was also lost in the large scale, nearly automatic admission of teachers to training colleges on a system which did not even require their personal application for training. The rapid call-up to training colleges was a significant new stage in the gradual erosion of the conception of the teacher's job as a sacred calling instead of a paid profession. Any teacher who had the academic qualification to enter a teacher training college could embark on the training programme. Teaching over a long period had progressively separated itself from the religious role of preaching and from clerical requirements of personal religious commitment, or fervour. Many teachers still exemplified admirable religious virtues and lifestyles; but it does appear that the process of secularisation of teaching took big steps under the PNM regime in consequence of the democratisation of teacher training opportunities. There still existed an undeclared Code of Ethics for teachers; the government, the teachers themselves and the community have certain ideas about the public behaviour expected of teachers; the point is that this discipline is no longer associated necessarily with religious morality and religious commitment.

The Durability of the Model of Teacher Training

Almost everybody would agree that amazingly the model of teacher training remained largely unchanged throughout the education revolution of the years between 1956 and 1981.[11] A new syllabus was adopted about 1970, but this came before the peak of the education changes of the 1970s. The coming of junior secondary schools and senior comprehensive schools with large infusions of technical/vocational subjects, and the new primary school syllabus of 1975, were changes of the 1970s. At first sight it appeared incongruous to have juxtaposed a stable model of teacher training in teachers' colleges and a rapidly changing education system. The first extenuating observation is that these rapid changes were mostly in the area of secondary education, and therefore needed not affect the preparation of teachers for primary schools. It was not that work at these colleges was entirely unaffected by changes in the schools. After all an extra year's work was added in industrial arts, home economics and agricultural science for a few teachers going on to the junior secondary schools. But the internal adjustments were minimal compared to the vast increase of teacher trainees; and an adjustment like the addition of elective subjects in 1960 might not strictly have been relevant to the preparation of primary school teachers, but to their self-preparation for university entrance via GCE A levels.[12]

The primary schools did not change too much until the 1975 syllabus. But when this syllabus was agreed on, the teachers' colleges seemed slow to react; and certainly a new orientation in the teachers' colleges' syllabus did not precede the new syllabus of primary schools. The basic design of the colleges' curriculum did not change between 1970 and 1981; but the output of teachers was vastly increased. At best it might be said that the teachers' colleges, unlike the secondary schools, avoided the confusion of simultaneously reorienting syllabus drastically while undergoing vast expansion. By the time the Gocking Commitee of 1978/1980 came to making recommendations for changes in teacher training, the nature of the problem to be dealt with had altered vastly; there were by then (1980/1981) only a few (about 138) untrained teachers; and they had insufficient qualifications to enter training college. The primary problem had then become not how to train new teachers, but how to continue the education of trained teachers; how to institutionalise the concept of life long education.[13]

After conceding the durability of the model of teachers' colleges between 1956 and 1981, critics usually divide themselves into two camps: a minority (as in the critique of technical/vocational education) complained that the very design of the training was faulty; but most critics confined themselves to showing up deficiencies in the implementation of the design. The most consistent criticisms of those who felt that the design was faulty involved the old dilemma of the proper balance between genuine professional training on the one hand and improvement of the knowledge of the students on the other.[14] They complained that in the case of the training colleges too much emphasis was placed on increasing knowledge and too little on professional training. Teachers should be taught essentially how to teach. Often the work of a teacher training college looked too much like the advanced forms of secondary schools. The critique of lack of professional training led to suggestions to improve teaching practice by replacing evaluation of teaching practice by college tutors with active and collaborative assistance to the students during teaching practice; also there have been vague suggestions that examinations should be redesigned to test the competence of students as teachers rather than their knowledge.[15] Another suggestion was the discontinuation of the unfortunate practice of selecting university graduates without teacher training as teacher educators in the teacher training colleges. (Failure to conceive of teacher educators as giving a higher service than secondary school teaching led to insufficient differentiation between their remuneration and that of secondary school teachers.) Critics including the Heads of the teacher training colleges who tended to point out deficiencies in implementation, complained about the academic weakness of the students at entry, especially in mathematics and English, and also about general difficulties of translating theory learnt in the colleges into practical classroom teaching. Explicitly or implicitly all critics wished to raise the standard of achievement of the students in the colleges.[16]

[10]

The Technical/Vocational Experience 1956-1981

> We recommend in principle the incorporation of vocational schools into some secondary schools to form a comprehensive or a multi-lateral school . . .
>
> UNESCO *Education Planning Mission, 1964*

The Location of Technical/Vocational Education

The overwhelming new development in technical/vocational education between 1956 and 1981 was its progressive march into the public secondary schools, slowly between 1956 and 1972 and with chaotic rapidity after 1972. No other aspect of curriculum reform over these 30 years, not even the new primary school syllabus, was as sensational or as controversial as the firm insertion of a wide range of technical/vocational subjects, including the specialised crafts, into many secondary schools, principally government secondary schools. This was done in the name of economic development, and in the cause of decolonisation; it was a sort of final overthrow of the colonial grammar school as the ideal type of secondary education. The move was intended to link education to the world of work, to match educational output with manpower needs of the nation for skilled craftsmen and technicians. But it might also be viewed as the inescapable handmaiden of the other revolution in secondary education, namely the progressive trend towards the universalisation of secondary school experience. An academic (or 'bookish') syllabus would be inappropriate for the great majority of children in an expanding secondary school sector.

At the time when the process of insertion of technical/vocational subjects into the secondary schools was accelerated, an international literature warning against the easy assumption that formal vocational training in schools was a credible or predictable instrument of economic development in the Third World was already a reality;[1] but either this literature was little known in Trinidad and Tobago or slightly regarded, because no public doubts were expressed by the education authorities or the ministers of government about the compelling relationship between the development needs of the economy and the vocationalisation of a substantial sector of secondary school curriculum.[2] Perhaps the oil boom of the post 1973 years which dramatically provided the capital for a substantial measure of industrialisation masked the weakness of the assumption that the insertion of technical/vocational education into formal secondary school educational programmes was a reliable instrument of economic development, while at the same time it created the need for an enlarged stock of skilled craftsmen and technicians. The problems of technical/vocational education in secondary schools, as understood by the local educators, arose in relation to the type of training which should be provided – especially the degree to which it should be specialised or generalised training; and not from doubts about the validity of technical/vocational education and training in formal secondary schools as a contributor to economic progress.

It is possible to interpret a good deal of the history of technical/vocational education and training between 1956 and 1981 in terms of attempts to decide where it should be located in the formal education system; whether separately from the secondary schools in its own institutions, or conjointly with the traditional secondary schools' curriculum inside secondary schools. There was never any question of shifting the entire education system over to a technical/vocational base. One facet of the issue of location was the degree of technical or vocational education and training which should be given, particularly inside the public secondary schools; that is, the extent to which such training should be pre-vocational and general, or strictly vocational and specialised. But this latter aspect, submerged in the 1960s, only surfaced as a major issue from the late 1970s; and up to the mid 1980s remained secondary to the more socially absorbing question of where technical/vocational education and training should be located in the formal education system. The traditional colonial way of dealing with technical and vocational education – when it was provided – was to keep it outside the secondary schools in apprenticeship schemes, or in separate institutions of an inferior reputation to the secondary schools. This was because technical/vocational education was not considered true education, and was intended for working class boys. After Dr Eric Williams came to power, the removal of most children above the age of 11+ from many primary schools to junior secondary schools swept the traditional primary school type of technical/vocational education out of the domain of the primary schools and into the arena of the junior secondary schools.

Secondary Modern Schools and Junior Secondary Schools

There was never any question whether technical/vocational education and training should be introduced into the junior secondary schools. The appearance of this type of secondary school in 1972 represented up to that point the most substantial insertion of a technical/vocational component into the sphere of the secondary school. There was no confusion about the level of technical/vocational work most appropriate to the junior secondary school: it was always clear that it was to be pre-vocational and general rather than specialised and vocational. The insistence that all students of the junior secondary schools should do all the subjects of the diversified programme (the common programme) meant that the technical/vocational component was compulsory, the only non-technical schools in which this was the case.[3] Since the largest group of 11+ children passed through the junior secondary schools, the development of technical/vocational education as an inescapable component of studies there drastically altered the education experience of youths between the ages of 11 and 14 years. Woodwork, metal work, and domestic science in the upper grades of primary schools from the 1930s to the 1960s had not been as unavoidable.

The earliest insertion of technical/vocational education into the secondary schools however came not with the junior secondary schools, but with the five government secondary modern schools started in the late 1950s and early 1960s. It took the traditional patterns borrowed from the primary schools of industrial arts, namely woodwork, metal work, technical drawing, and domestic science (home economics) for girls. Some agriculture was attempted at Diego Martin secondary modern school. This injection of technical/vocational education was minimal in size and not designed to meet any calculated manpower needs. Very few students in these schools experienced technical/vocational education, and there was resistance to it by parents and students:[4] there were very few entrants in these subjects for Cambridge examinations or GCE O level examinations. Indeed there was a shortage of teachers who could take students up to O level standard. The great body of technical/vocational teaching still remained outside secondary schools, in the San Fernando Technical Institute, the evening classes of the BIT, and the various apprenticeship schemes and firm schools.

Indeed it might have appeared that the government intended to strengthen technical/vocational education outside secondary schools, for the next major step forward was the construction of the long projected technical institute (the John Donaldson Technical Institute) in Port of Spain. The coming under the control of the government of the Chaguaramas Trade Centre and the Point Fortin Trade School represented changes in ownership and management from a foreign government and private enterprise respectively to the Trinidad and Tobago government.[5] The addition in the 1960s of youths camps confirmed the ascendancy of the pattern of providing technical/vocational education in separate institutions outside secondary schools despite the technical/vocational input into the new government secondary modern schools. By the start of 1972 the balance of location of training had not changed: most of the technical/vocational education was being done outside the secondary schools, though the government was committed to changing secondary school curriculum in the direction of practical and vocational programmes at the expense of traditional academic studies. The trade training centres of the early 1970s, partly a response to the Black Power movement, also went in the direction of a separate provision for technical/vocational education outside the secondary schools.

Plans for Separate Vocational Schools

As previously mentioned, a major leap forward in the process of moving technical/vocational education into the secondary schools came with the inauguration of the first junior secondary schools in 1972. But this step was preceded by a period of rethinking and planning between 1964 and 1969 which provided much of the ideological underpinning for developments in the area of secondary education after 1972. This period was characterised by the work of a UNESCO team of education planners in 1964, followed by another UNESCO expert in planning in 1965, and importantly by the establishment of a Planning Unit in the Ministry of Education and Culture in 1964.[6] A seminal outcome was the new idea of education planning with an eye on the need to match trained personnnel to manpower needs. The UNESCO experts were in favour of putting most of the increased technical/vocational education and training into the secondary schools at both junior secondary level and senior secondary level, while continuing to supplement the growth of technical/vocational education in separate Technical Institutes.[7] The UNESCO Mission apparently did not reflect exactly the thinking of the government on the point of location of the main thrust in technical/vocational education. While planning pre-vocational studies in junior secondary schools, the government's main thrust in its Second Five-year Development Plan (1964-1968) was mostly in the direction of a separate provision for increased technical/vocational education in vocational schools. This was also the view of the government appointed Tripartite Committee investigating technical/vocational education.[8] The Education Plan (1968-1983) prepared by the Planning Unit under the inspiration of the UNESCO experts purported to finalise the thinking of the UNESCO experts. However no mention was made of the proposed new vocational schools. But technical/vocational training was considered the most important reforms of the secondary school curriculum, with the technical/vocational studies (but not specialised crafts) being placed firmly within the new senior comprehensive schools to be built for about 30 to 40 percent of the junior secondary school graduates. There was something curiously strange about the silence of the Education Plan in respect to the proposed new vocational schools as the government had already approached the World Bank for a loan partly to build these schools[9] and Dr Williams had talked a lot about new vocational schools on his Meet the People Tour of the mid 1960s. Who was in charge of education policy in the mid 1960s? The 'Doctor' (Eric Williams), the Cabinet of the country, or some civil servants in the Ministry of Education?

The Volte-face on Separate Vocational Schools

The plans for the new vocational schools were alive as late as August 1974. They were mentioned in Williams' famous speech in that month at Caribbean Union College in Maracas Valley. Between the speech in August 1974 and September 1975 when the government completely cancelled the plans for new vocational schools there occurred a volte-face in government's thinking about the location of its major technical/vocational thrust. Already one vocational school at Chaguanas was under construction, but there was still time to turn back from the full range of separate vocational schools.[10] What made the government turn back from the separate vocational schools is more problematic. In the speech at Maracas Valley in August 1974 Dr Williams declared that a crisis point had been reached in denominational and government secondary schools (excluding the junior secondary schools) which sent up students for the O and A level GCE examinations in the traditional academic subjects. Too many students were failing to get five passes or even one pass. At any rate the nation was said to need not more GCE successes in traditional academic subjects, but progress in technical/vocational studies and of course the traditional science subjects. Hence the government was probably reconsidering its intention to build a new range of senior secondary schools with traditional subjects to continue the education of selected junior secondary school graduates.

Up to August 1974 the scheme which the government (not necessarily the education planners in the Planning Unit) had in mind was obviously as follows: continue the education of some junior secondary school graduates in new government senior secondary schools (and presumably in existing government or denominational secondary schools); build separate vocational schools to continue the education of a portion of the junior secondary school graduates. The decision not to strengthen the ascendancy of traditional subjects in senior secondary schools by building new government senior secondary schools was not in itself a vote to eliminate the proposed vocational schools. It was possible to cancel the new government senior secondary schools and retain the plan for new vocational schools. Some of the Christian church leaders would doubtlessly have preferred this development which would leave their five-year secondary schools in a strong position in the education system. But according to Carlton Gomes, Minister of Education, speaking at the National Consultation on Education in 1974, the World Bank thought that Trinidad and Tobago should have only two technical institutes – which already existed. This view from a powerful funding agency could hardly have been ignored lightly. The government eventually decided to cancel the vocational schools and to put the normal technical/vocational curriculum of the cancelled vocational schools into the new government senior secondary schools, now renamed senior comprehensive schools. But as indicated earlier, it is not clear how the government reached this decision, or if Dr Williams acted on his own.

Although unprecedented high revenues from oil were on hand, the government in view of double digit inflation and shortage of contractors and skilled workmen in what was a general building boom could not construct in the mid 1970s a new range of senior secondary (comprehensive) schools as well as new vocational schools for basically the same age group. The calculation that too few students would attend each vocational school to justify the high cost of such a school migh thave been crucial in killing the vocational school plan; but all the social and even pedagogical arguments for putting technical/vocational education under the same roof as the traditional academic subjects were already at hand in the Education Plan.[11] It was democratic; it worked in the direction of equality of treatment in education; it looked like it might increase the prestige of technical/vocational educaton by associating it within the same school with the prestigious academic subjects. The government's thrust into heavy industries as a result of the oil bonanza suggested the need for many more skilled craftsmen and technicians than the country possessed.[12] Already (by 1969) it had been estimated, before the oil boom, that if the economic targets of 1973 were to be met, there would be a need for about 37,000 craftsmen and 5,000 technicians in the economy.[13] With the increased industrial activity, especially in construction, after the oil boom started, many more of these categories of workers were thought to be needed. In as far as the annual output rate of a large senior comprehensive school of some 1,200 students would normally be greater than that of a technical school of 400 to 500 students, it seemed that the former was a more appropriate instrument for the stage of economic development in which the country was embarking. Hence in 1975 the question was sealed: forward with technical/vocational education in the senior comprehensive schools, and this meant in practice, not only pre-vocational level, but the specialised crafts as well.

Enter the Senior Comprehensive School

Nothing like this had ever happened to secondary education; it was a curriculum revolution in the secondary schools. But it was to take place in fact only or mainly in the new government sector of the secondary school system; how far it would occur in the denominational secondary schools was a matter for subsequent negotiation. Clearly owners of these schools had not responded cooperatively to the government's idea that they should follow its model of secondary education by converting their schools into either junior secondary schools or senior secondary schools. Now they were to be asked to add a heavy dose of technical/vocational education to any of these schools which were converted into senior secondary schools. The insertion of technical/vocational education into the senior comprehensive schools for about 55 to 65 percent of the students (45 percent pre-technical and 10 to 25 percent specialised crafts), on top of the technical/vocational input into the junior secondary schools, turned the balance of technical/vocational studies in the nation decisively in favour of location inside the secondary schools rather than outside in separate institutions.

The technical/vocational programme in a senior comprehensive school was as follows:

Pre-technical level:

General electricity, woodwork, metal work, general draughtmanship, agricultural science, surveying, commercial studies (shorthand, typing, accounts), clothing, textiles, fashion and fabrics.

Specialised craft courses (for those senior comprehensive schools that had them):

Auto mechanics, machine shop welding, electrical installation, masonry, construction/carpentry, plumbing, air conditioning, refrigeration, domestic electronics and dressmaking.

The problem of the depth of technical/vocational studies to be engaged in by the various schools, institutes, or centres which imparted it, was second in importance only to the question of the location of technical/vocational studies inside or outside the secondary schools.[14] The education system and teachers had long been accustomed to the teaching of subjects like physics, history or literature in formal educational institutions; and over many years local and foreign examinations of academic subjects had distilled and refined understanding of the level of knowledge appropriate to these subjects at various stages of the students' life.

The same could not be said about technical/vocational subjects, for example welding, dressmaking, carpentry or refrigeration. In the Third World wherever technical/vocational education was tried, it was not unusual to find a considerable amount of disorder and confusion in the curriculum. This arose from the very novelty and unfamiliarity of teaching these subjects in the classroom, but also it must be admitted that since specialised technical/vocational education was geared to the work place there was a greater need to define aims more clearly than in the case of academic subjects. From the 1950s to the 1980s the vocabulary of technical/vocational education had received considerable clarification, particularly in respect to the distinction between craftsmen and technicians, but there was for many years a great deal of confusion about the meaning of terms such as industrial arts, vocational education, pre-vocational or pre-technician education; and whereas no one felt the need in any of the many reports on education to define English literature, or chemistry, it was not unusual to find glossaries in reports on technical/vocational education. In fact technical/vocational education still means different things to different people; and its varied providers – government technical institutes, private enterprise trade centres, youth camps, trade centres, junior secondary schools, and senior comprehensive schools – established at different times, administered separately in practice despite the growing supervisory function of the National Training Board since 1972, had served to multiply the varieties of perceptions of technical/vocational education.

The 'Generalists' and the 'Specialists'

Another factor of great importance was the varied sources from which technical/vocational education teachers were drawn, whether recruited locally or abroad. Up to 1986, and despite the development of technical/vocational teacher training at the John Donaldson Technical Institute from 1979, there was no practice comparable to the teacher training college tradition of entry into the teaching of technical/vocational subjects through a single well-known training process, or from common academic antecedents.[15] Nor was a system of local examination of technical/vocational coursesestablished long enough to solidify the teaching of various subjects into a set pattern. The rapid rate of technology change also exercised an unsettling influence on technical/vocational education. For example, machinery within the schools might be outdated compared to those actively used by the leading firms in some industries. A fairly recent challenge to technical/vocational education is computer education which had to be grafted on unsettled levels of training in older branches of applied science, technology and craft work.

How much technical/vocational training and education to be given, at what stage, to whom and with what purpose constituted serious problems. The systematisation of technical/vocational education and training had a special challenge to it of a kind not directly posed now in general education in either the arts or the sciences. Since it was considered more vocational than general education, there was need for closer integration between it and industry, between it and manpower needs, between it and economic development strategies. There were more problems in defining the level of training appropriate to craftsmen than that appropriate to technicians. The training of the technicians was left almost exclusively to the technical institutes. Despite the fact that some persons turned out as technicians in Trinidad and Tobago did not possess enough practical experience to fit the British origin of the term, their training was not haunted by doubts about the degree of on-the-job experience which might be concurrently or subsequently necessary to complete their qualification. The training of craftsmen was dispersed in different kinds of institutions; was susceptible to more internal gradations of achievement, and was bedevilled by its relationship with on-the-job experience concurrently or subsequently to formal institutional education.

The best and most recent example of difficulties over the level of training of craftsmen occurred in the senior comprehensive schools. When asked what it meant by "limited specialised craft training" in the senior comprehensive schools, the government said it wished for in-depth training in a certain (limited) number of crafts.[16] This meant that the senior comprehensive schools were to train some youths of 14 to 16 years to be masons, welders, plumbers and so on, and not merely to give them an introduction to the general skills related to a number of crafts. Between 1975 and 1985 this was what the senior comprehensive schools with specialised craft training attempted to do. But by at least 1979 considerable doubts had developed about the wisdom of specialisation at as early as 14 years of age.[17] By the early 1980s ideas about the superiority of general craft training over specialised craft training for the age group 14 to 16 years were gaining ground, particularly the concept of the distillation of general training from a cluster of related crafts. Rethinking in Trinidad and Tobago on this subject was catching up with the drift of the international literature. Between 1979 and 1984 the conviction grew among a few educators in Trinidad that craft training in the senior comprehensive schools was too specialised altogether, or that specialisation should start later, at perhaps age 16 years rather than age 14. Even the junior secondary school technical/vocational programme was, according to this view, to stress more basics than it did: the Richards Committee of 1984 recommended that a new technical/vocational syllabus be devised in the long run to integrate separate industrial arts programme of woodwork, metal work, and technical drawing into one subject.

The Implementation of Specialised Craft Training

The problems of organising technical/vocational education in the junior secondary schools and the senior comprehensive schools, particularly in the latter, were varied and largely unresolved up to 1985. Everybody with any acquaintance with technical/vocational education in these schools between 1972 and 1981 would agree that its delivery was extremely problematical. There were at least two ways of interpreting what happened: one line of criticism already noticed stressed that the design of technical/vocational education for the schools was faulty; that too much emphasis was on specialisation too early at the expense of general technical education. This was the view of the generalists, some of whom were regarded by certain National Training Board personnel as university academics not grounded in the reality of the situation. The other view, which was that of certain persons at the National Training Board, was that the trouble was not with the design of technical/vocational education, but with its implementation. According to this view, if there was anything wrong with the design, it was largely because the Ministry of Education, which was in charge of technical/vocational education in these schools until 1980, did not understand what the National Training Board intended.

At the heart of the argument about faulty implementation was the lack of any pilot scheme, or of any deliberately phased introduction of technical/vocational education. Particularly in the senior comprehensive schools a wide assortment of technical/vocational subjects was thrown into the schools all at once, or as many as possible at once, without any time to find out what should be attempted first, or how much of it at first. The resultant confusion was immense. Added to the newness of technical/vocational education was the fact that many of the students coming up into the senior comprehensive schools from the junior secondary schools were poor achievers in general education, inadequately numerate or literate. The majority of technical/vocational instructors were not trained as teachers; there was a lack of supervisors from the Ministry of Education. The installation and maintenace of equipment was problematic. Some students who wished to become welders had to do auto-mechanics; some who saw themselves as future refrigeration specialists had to settle to become plumbers and vice versa. Worse yet, some students better suited for specialised craft courses could find no place in any such course.[18]

There was a surprising amount of indifference and snobbishness on the part of many overburdened principals of senior comprehensive schools towards the new technical/vocational wings and their seemingly strange teachers. for the most part the principals were university-trained persons, with academic degrees, who could not or cared not to cope with technical/vocational teachers some of whom appeared to be social misfits in the teaching fraternity. In some cases a senior comprehensive school was really not one school, but a number of schools, with the technical/vocational wing not being the prestigious part of the school. The curious thing as one researcher has shown was that each of the major streams of the senior comprehensive school with specialised crafts might easily have thought that it was the disadvantaged stream and that other streams were favoured above it.[19]

A major problem with technical/vocational education in these schools, not always perceived by the public, concerned the integration of the technical/vocational staff (some with stronger antecedents as craftsmen than as grammar school graduates) with the more traditional academic staff; all the social prejudices in favour of academic subjects or against technical/vocational subjects were encapsulated in these schools, sometimes, it would appear, in the staff rooms. The public heard more about the inappropriate, unused equipment – so often found in projects funded externally; of the shortage of technical/vocational teachers, of the unpreparedness of semiliterate students to deal with technology, and of the high failure rate in the examination of the National Examination Council. A mere decade (in the case of the junior secondary schools) or half a decade (in the case of senior comprehensive schools) was clearly not enough to get right the enormous experiment of introducing several technical/vocational subjects into new schools. If the glare of publicity on the failures and confusion of technical/vocational education fell more on the senior comprehensive schools than on the junior secondary schools, it was not because the latter got it right, but because the senior comprehensive schools were the last stage before immersion into the world of work. Some of the graduates of the technical/vocational streams of the senior comprehensive schools, immediately after leaving school, felt the need, or were advised, to go back as evening students to do the same sort of work they had just 'completed' in school.

Schools and On-the-job Training

Another aspect of the implementation of technical/vocational programmes in the schools concerned the question of the balance between formal institutional training and on-the-job training. Those technical/vocational educators familiar with the international literature on technical/vocational education might have been acquainted with the considerable misgivings of leading metropolitan authorities about the value of formal pre-employment institutional training as a preparation for the work place. Skills as practised at the work place might be too complex to be adapted to classroom teaching in schools. Formal institutional education versus on-the-job training, however, was not a major issue in Trinidad and Tobago, but the issue underlaid some of the confusion in the tremendously difficult task of implementing technical/vocational education. Everybody was willing to subscribe to the great importance of on-the-job training; but few would have gone as far as to see firms and industries as the leading sectors in the twin sector (firms/schools) training system.

There must be considerable doubts whether firms/industries generally saw themselves in this exalted role as the leading sector of the training system. Most persons, while stressing the importance of on-the-job training, would have agreed that the schools should be the leading sector of the training system. The task of the National Training Board and the government was to construct a major on-the-job training scheme to encompass the large number of students in technical/vocational streams in secondary schools and of course youths who had already left schools who might have been unemployed. The organisation of such a scheme by the National Training Board – a questionable substitute for traditional apprenticeships – had at best mixed fortunes. At the peak of the on-the-job training scheme in 1978 and 1979, a sizeable number of youths, perhaps as many as 3,000, did get useful training in the construction industry, each for about six months.[20] The quantitative needs of the construction industry for this type of workers might have been met. These workers were insufficiently trained. It is doubtful if more than a handful of these trainees ever succeeded in the examinations of the National Examinations Council. Qualitatively the O level graduate section of the on-the-job scheme enjoyed a more satisfying mix of special classes and on- the- job training in the new energy based industries.[21] Despite the broadening out of the on-the-job training programme to include a few other industries, it remained true that the new energy based industries and the old construction industry at a new level of activity were the two industries which most supported the programme. It is to be noted, however, that the construction boom did not last long enough for enduring careers for many youths to be based firmly on it; and in the case of the energy based industries, after the construction period, they were not labour intensive enough to employ many of the technical/vocational graduates.

The secondary schools had the capability of turning out faster many more persons than could be integrated into any nation-wide on-the-job training scheme. Some of the technical/vocational graduates of the senior comprehensive schools were integrated into on-the-job training opportunities after leaving school. It was the productive worth of the trainees as workers more than the government cash incentive which attracted participating employers. As always, industry remained convinced that it could do a superior job of training skilled persons than the schools; some firms were willing to do it for their own immediate benefit and most would not have admitted any national responsibility for training on a wide-scale beyond their own needs. The argument that industry has a financial responsibility of the highest order to pay for technical/vocational education generallygained no widespread acceptance anywhere.[22] The successful organisation of a large-scale on-the-job training scheme for thousands of technical/vocational graduates was really incompatible with voluntary participation of industry and of youths.

Technical Institutes, Youth Camps and Trade Centres

It remains to look briefly at the variety of opportunities for technical/vocational education apart from the secondary schools and to comment on some of their problems and achievements. Leaving aside the Faculty of Engineering at UWI St Augustine, the two technical institutes (the San Fernando Technical Institute and the John Donaldson Technical Institute) were at the top of the technical/vocational network. The John Donaldson Institute was opened in 1962, but like its older sister institute it suffered from severe shortage of qualified instructors in the 1960s. The earlier youth camps (leaving aside the El Dorado camp for girls in 1975) were founded about the same time as the John Donaldson Technical Institute: (Persto-Praesto in 1964; Mt St George in 1965; Chatham in 1966; Chaguaramas in 1968). They represented another attempt to spread technical/vocational skills by low cost out-of-school systems to underprivileged, unemployed youths. The trouble with youth camps which were originally intended to be essentially agricultural was that landless youths could find no jobs on the land except on family farms. Also, the standard of work was too low, and the image of these institutions was tarnished insofar as they were confused with reformatories.[23] Hence their graduates did not stand a good chance in the competition for jobs. The Certificate of Assistant Craftsman was not respected, and this was usually the highest level of training in youth camps which were institutions remote from the public.[24] As institutions of the 1960s started before the Black Power movement peaked, they showed the concern of the government to prepare youths who had dropped out of school for the job market. On the other hand the urban trade centres, whether government run or operated by private parties, were largely creatures of the government's or churches' reaction to the Black Power movement. These trade centres, concentrating mostly on the building trades, were the non-residential counterparts of the rural youth camps and suffered from the same twin disadvantages of poor academic standards and low social prestige.[25] Private technical/vocational schools, run by the churches, made their appearance in the 1970s, but were too small and underfinanced in most cases to catch the public's attention, though they contributed to the increase of opportunities to learn a skill in the building trades.[26] SERVOL (Service Volunteered for All) eventually became the most successful of these projects.

It would not be irrelevant to ask the difficult question how far technical/vocational education gained in social status over the years between 1956 and 1981. It possibly did; but it was still a socially less acceptable form of education than the traditional training in the arts and natural sciences. In Trinidad and Tobago, as elsewhere in Third World countries which turned to technical/vocational education to solve unemployment and aid economic development, the planners ran up against a high wall of social support for the traditional subjects.[27] The demand for technical/vocational training was not primarily coming from the population at large, but from government, education experts and some special interest groups; and most of these advocates did not sent their children to such schools. A factor compounding the obstacles to the growth of recognition for technical/vocational subjects was its association with the education of the poor, the underprivileged or the academically less gifted. Technical/vocational education was not the education of the select few, but of the masses, and it was the masses who carried the scars of experimentation in technical/vocational education in the various institutions.[28] The government ruse of denominating the San Fernando Technical Institute as a secondary-technical school between the 1950s and the 1960s never convinced parents. The selection system for secondary schools reinforced annually the historic legacy of technical/vocational training as the lot of the less favoured majority, indeed as the alternative to true education. The population to be educated on the technical/vocational model was gathered in largely from 'failures' in the selection process or programmes for academic schooling. Persons attempting to use technical/vocational education and training as an alternative route to higher education soon discovered how poorly articulated it was with entry into universities.

The Case of Agricultural Education

With the formation of the National Training Board in 1972 agricultural education became administratively linked through this Board to technical/vocational education. Prior to 1972 the BIT had nothing to do with agricultural education. This grouping of agricultural education and technical/vocational education was not a marriage of equals: agricultural education was the poor relation of technical/vocational education and training; indeed it was only loosely articulated with technical/vocational education. Anyone reading the writings of Dr Eric Williams before 1956 might easily have concluded that agricultural education would have been at the centre of the reorientation of the curriculum of the schools away from the academic to the practical.[29] But nothing was done beyond a few scholarships to strengthen or expand agricultural education down to 1968. Not in the primary schools; not in the new government secondary schools of the early 1960s (with the exception of Diego Martin secondary) where industrial arts, technical drawing and domestic science (home economics) comprised the types of technical/vocational education which predominated. Agricultural education in the youth camps, even at Chatham which was specifically designated an agricultural youth camp, was in disfavour by youths;[30] tutors were badly lacking and the camps were not self-sufficient in food.

Whereas private industry/manufacturing enterprises offered some assistance to craft or technician training, private enterprise farms gave no such support to agricultural education. An exception was the West Indian Tobacco Company's support of a project at Persto-Praesto Youth Camp. The proportion of persons employed in farming was falling in the 1950s and 1960s. Only the government offered employment to graduates in agriculture (usually from the Eastern Farm Institute, a regional school) at the craft or technician levels as junior employees in the Ministry of Agriculture or as extension officers. School-leavers usually thought about finding a job rather than about acquiring skills leading to self-employment. Wages in agriculture, except as employees of government, were low; as always, poor remuneration in agriculture made it unattractive to students. The social demand for agricultural training was traditionally low, and before the Education Plan the government's strategy was chiefly dominated by the desire to give the people the type of education they wanted. A problem of choice which was not new was that the instructional needs of practising adult farmers (who had no time for formal education) seemed greater and more immediately rewarding as investment than those of youths who might never work the land.

Despite the lower profile of agriculture than technology in the technical/vocational package, it would be true to say that like all other practical subjects the dominant trend in agricultural education over the period 1956 to 1981, and particularly since 1972, was to bring it into the secondary schools. By being part of the common junior secondary school curriculum, agricultural science at the pre-vocational level was made compulsory for the section of the age group 11+ to 14+ who were in junior secondary schools; in the senior comprehensive schools where it was optional, agricultural science was inserted at the pre-technician level and also as one of the specialised crafts. At technician level it also existed at the Eastern Caribbean Farm Institute. The difference between agricultural education and trades training – apart from agricultural training being examinable mostly through the CXC – seemed to have been the lack of controversy about agricultural education: this suggests public indifference as well as a perception of it as less important for national development. Very few, if any, examples of problems in technical/vocational education in the various reports of Working Parties were drawn from agriculture. Persons with academic background in agricultural education did not become senior in the government education hierarchy and have never been chairmen of Working Parties. Obviously the National Training Board did not have the tradition or sufficient experience in agricultural education to interfere decisively in agricultural education in the secondary schools. The policy of the National Training Board in agricultural education apparently was to keep a lower profile than in trades training

In the late 1960s and early 1970s every statement of government policy for technical/vocational education included mention of the construction of three farm schools. Only one was ever constructed, namely the Kendal Farm School in Tobago. This government farm school and the privately owned Trinidad Tesoro Farm School provided respectively a two-year residential course and a one-year non-residential course at the assistant craftsman level in farming and animal husbandry. The teachers usually came from the Eastern Caribbean Farm Institute. This latter was always seen as the key institution at the technician level. This institute was a post-secondary, post-GCE residential school with a two-year course in either agriculture or forestry qualifying persons for middle level jobs in the Ministry of Agriculture and the teaching service. In 1964 the future of this institution apparently was in doubt; the students were few (46 of whom 12 were from Trinidad); the fees were high (TT$2,800 per annum) since the entire recurrent cost had to be met from it; and the financial and managerial arrangements were about to collapse with the demise of the West Indies Federation.[31] New arrangements were made to restructure its financial and managerial base and this included assistance from UNDP in the 1970s. It survived to become the chief source of agricultural teachers for the new agricultural science courses of the junior secondary and senior comprehensive schools.

[11]

Special Topics in Education

> Certainly we cannot expect Government to look after art before education, sanitation, public utilities and the rest. Art is still the stepchild at the foot of the table. But we had hoped that having laboriously laid the foundation for a national culture long before the Government, which is now a national Government, had come into being, we would have been given a far more sympathetic ear.
>
> Beryl McBurnie (*Sunday Guardian*, 1 August 1966)

Religious Instruction

Considering the long involvement of the Christian churches in the ownership and management of schools, it was natural that religious instruction played a considerable role inside the classrooms and in the debates of education policy-makers. The view of all the churches, especially the Christian churches, was the nearly impossible ideal that religious instruction must be integrated into the teaching of all subjects; that schools must have a religious atmosphere; that religious instruction must be delivered primarily by classroom teachers themselves whose own lives should exemplify the influence of religion. The Roman Catholic Church went further than other Christian churches in insisting that all its members must send their children to Roman Catholic schools where available.[1] During and after World War II certain social problems, which had not been very obvious previously, mounted to nearly crisis proportions. For example, there was venereal disease among adults and crime among youths. The former was undoubtedly connected with the presence of United States military personnel in the island and the consequential growth of prostitution;[2] the explanation of the crime was more complex. Scholars have spoken of a breakdown in the social order due to displacement of large sections of the population, either to make way for the bases, or to work on the bases. Thousands of deprived and poor young people came to maturity at a time of prosperity and greater circulation of money in the early 1940s. There was increased violence in the ghetto districts of Port of Spain, some of it connected with rival steel bands, a musical invention of lower class males of the town. Suffice it to say in the words of Governor Hubert Rance there seemed to have been a "failure of character in the difficult years which have followed the War".[3]

As governor he was particularly disappointed in the civil service where corruption had reached a new height for a country which had a long history of financial scandals in government departments. The remedies suggested for this social crisis included bringing back judicial whipping for certain categories of criminal offences and more religious instruction in the schools. The director of education, Mr Sidney Hogben, distinguished himself after the war by his consistent support for heightened programmes of religious instruction in the schools. In 1949 the government passed a law to include religious instruction, subject to a conscience clause, on the official curriculum of primary schools.[4]

This legislation marked a major reversal of a century old government policy of excluding religious instruction either completely from government schools (1849-1890), or from the official curriculum of government and government aided denominational schools (1890-1949). The ability to execute this new policy in 1949 without any public protest must be related to something not easily admitted by the clerics. Generally the society took organised religion seriously in the nineteenth and early twentieth centuries. Obviously this was substantially less true by the mid 1980s. The secularisation of public opinion and the decline of religious rivalries among the Christian churches were slow growths; and are subjects worthy of separate research. Clearly by the 1940s the middle and upper classes were less committed than in the 1920s to the thesis that Christianity, preferably their own particular branch of it, should prevail at all cost.[5] This secularisation of thought in the colony was part of a wider movement in western Europe and North America. It is possible that the Hindu and Muslim religions were less affected than Christianity. There were of course contradictions and countercurrents. It is important not to equate the waning of Christian religious passion and animosity with an eclipse of the willingness of lay persons to defend their denominational interest when called upon by the clergy. The clerics could still mobilise a considerable amount of public opinion, but only against the government in defense of religiously defined social issues, not against rival churches on creedal grounds. The point is that government in releasing teachers from the long standing prohibition against direct religious instruction in government schools was not stirring up a hornet's nest as it would have done had it attempted the same thing in 1847, or 1902 or 1925.

Dr Eric Williams and the PNM were accused in the mid and late 1950s of being godless aspirants to power and a godless government. Williams' own view was that religion and education were two separate things. The action of his government reflected this position, but with the usual compromising concessions to the churches. The government tended at first to ignore religious instruction and then it showed a preference for excluding it, but generally the best characterisation of PNM attitude was that it showed little or no interest in it. The syllabus for primary schools in 1957 included religious education and character training; however the new Primary Schools Syllabus of 1975 had no place for religious instruction on the timetable, though morality and character training were not neglected.[6] Nor did religious instruction find a place on the timetable of government teachers' colleges, a grievance that the churches never forgot. The government conceivably could have attempted to legislate religion completely out of all government schools, but it did not do it. The attitude of the government was not to give the question of religion in schools the salience of a policy. Hence contradictions were allowed to prevail.

In all church schools the PNM government introduced a conscience clause, but this was not done in anger, but as a part of the making of the Concordat and secondary school regulations. The conscience clause suggests that the government expected, or was not totally opposed to, churches or principals organising religious instruction for co-religionists. The churches continued religious instruction in their schools, but a great variety of practices prevailed in respect to students of faiths other than that of the religious group owning the school. Dr Williams himself was sceptical of the churches' claim that their schools had a special denominational character, citing the large number of students who belonged to other faiths. The denominational character of some church schools was indeed endangered by too few denominational supporters among the staff and students.[7] Where culture was closely intertwined with religious faith, as in the case of the Hindus, devising a satisfactory way of giving religious instruction in a multi-religion school to all the students who desired it was a formidable task for which even the clerics had no eager appetite.

In the development of government secondary schools from the early 1960s there was no regular place for religious instruction, nor any provision for worship before or after the regular curriculum. At some government secondary schools however religious worship was squeezed in at odd times. A great deal of what happened in such schools depended on the particular principal, or the availability of teachers wishing to volunteer their services. This absence of firm regulations positively in favour of religious instruction struck the clerics very forcibly in relation to junior secondary schools and senior secondary schools which taught thousands of children many of whom were under no proper parental control.[8] Juvenile delinquency on a large scale in secondary schools, particularly government secondary schools, was something which came into being in the 1960s and escalated in the 1970s. As the recipients of most of the first generation working class secondary school children, the new government secondary schools had to face problems of social control of the school population which were less obvious at denominational secondary schools of smaller size. The PNM government did not resort to religious instruction as an aid to social control, though it encouraged family life education which had a religious ethos.[9]

The PNM government's record in respect to religious instruction can be interpreted differently by different persons. Its indifference to religious instruction might be seen as an attack on religion by those who feel that religious instruction in schools needed the positive support of government; alternatively, the apathy might be viewed as a new form of government neutrality different from the one practised in the nineteenth or early twentieth century in that it was predicated on the decline of religion as an emotive force in the society. The difficulties that the churches faced by 1981 in restoring the vitality of religious instruction in the schools were not simply of the government's making: they were part of the general crisis of organised religion in a materialistic society in which the majority of persons, including teachers and some clerics, had developed doubts or a plurality of views about important questions of dogma and morality. Children in school were no longer satisfied with religious instruction which called for unquestioning recital of catechisms or obedience to precepts not always observed by their elders.[10] Some branches of the Christian churches have tried to devise new courses of religious instruction or to retrain teachers, but there was a crisis of a shortage of teachers of religion no less serious for the churches than the shortage of technical/vocational teachers for the government. The difference was that in so far as the shortage of teachers of religion was a problem for the churches and not for the government, it was not brought to the attention of the general public, and if it had been, there would have been no public outcry. Yet the public valued denominational schools for their attention to moral education and discipline.

Women and Education

It is fairly well known that World War II provided female primary school teachers with new opportunities to tighten their hold on the profession. The need for more teachers arose mostly from rapid population increase, arising partly from immigration from the smaller islands. Many of the new teachers were women. Even some married females who had been forced to retire because of the rules against them were recalled temporarily to fill difficult rural slots. Female teachers were then nearly 50 percent of the total teaching force of the primary schools.[11] This proportion of female teachers was maintained until in the 1970s the number of females exceeded males for the first time and stayed ahead. The oil boom of the 1970s provided men with more remunerative employment outside the schoolroom.

Special Topics in Education

World War II also stimulated new thinking about the role of women in society. While there was greater concern for equal civil rights in education for women teachers, the society was still a long way off from thinking that women had a right to the same kind of education as men. Women were perceived to have distinctly different education needs and career goals from men. Hence, if anything, there was a need to introduce gender differentiation in curriculum at primary and secondary school levels.[12] On the other hand two 'gender' grievances in particular needed to be addressed: equal pay for women and the right of married women to stay in the teaching service without loss of status or pay. Lower pay for women dated from at least the immediate post-emancipation era; the beginnings of the practice of expelling married women from the teaching service is more obscure, though it was borrowed from England. A new stage in the government's determination to enforce this practice was reached in the infamous Code of 1935 drafted by Captain Cutteridge, the director of education. The male dominated Trinidad and Tobago Teachers' Union and Teachers' Journal never fought this injustice. The same can be said about the issue of unequal pay. A grave outrage was the loss of pension rights and gratuities by female teachers forced out of the service on marriage. Post-war elected politicians were more sympathetic to the plight of female teachers than Crown Colony officials. The acquisition by women of the right to vote in 1946 spurred on politicians like Roy Joseph and Albert Gomes to make the defence of teachers, male and female, a part of their political platform, and some female teachers associated with the Teachers' Economic and Cultural Association and the People's Education Movement agitated enthusiastically but quietly on their own behalf, especially for equal pay. The question of loss of pension rights was the first to be remedied; then unequal pay was ended and last of all discrimination by expulsion of married female teachers.[13]

The era of regular despatch of females abroad for university education began, it appears, in the later 1930s and it was not brought to a halt by World War II. The Canadian Presbyterian Mission's connection with Canada, which had worked so well for Indian males from the early twentieth century, began to work for Indian females in the 1930s and 1940s. Best placed were Indian women from well-off families or higher caste families, including those with fathers or brothers who were already professionals. A handful of Indian females, the second or third generation descendants of Indian immigrants, acquired Canadian university degrees and returned to assume teaching posts at Naparima Girls' High School. Indian women going abroad to study also showed strong inclination to study medicine, sometimes in England.[14] On the other hand nursing, which provided in the 1940s and perhaps until the 1970s the biggest block of female students abroad, was not a favourite area of study for Indian females. It became very popular with black girls. In 1948 about 32 percent of Trinidadian students studying in the United Kingdom were females and they were doing mostly nursing and medicine. Among female students in Canada the Arts subjects seemed most popular. These studies, plus those done in Trinidad, indicated the major areas of employment for educated females: health-care related professions; child-related professions like teaching, and also secretarial services.

The coming to power in 1956 of Dr Williams and the PNM was greatly aided by women;[15] but the PNM (within which women had stereotypic, inferior roles) did not, in its campaign declarations, regard women (either as students or as teachers) as occupying any specially disadvantaged position in the education system. The public issue was additional secondary schools for children, not equal access to secondary schools for girls. Dr Williams' expansion of education at all levels was to the benefit of girls. New government secondary schools since the early 1960s have invariably been coeducational. The deficit in the provision of secondary education for girls which existed since the post-emancipation years was sufficiently eliminated for gender questions about the relative access of boys and girls to secondary schools to be a non-issue. In fact the nice balance between intakes of girls and boys into secondary schools as a result of the Common Entrance Examination was contrived – without protest or comment. Vastly increased access to secondary schools by girls was a considerable achievement, but one almost entirely lost within public acclaim of the general societal gains in secondary education.[16] The deficits in female secondary education were in 1986 qualitative rather than quantitative. Of course the inadequacies of the past were still reflected in the statistics for the educational achievement of adult women. There were more women than men in 1965 and 1971 without any formal education. Also slightly more than one and half times as many males as females obtained secondary school certificates in 1965 and 1971.[17] It is also well known – to speak of two other levels of education – that there was a big gap between the number of university trained males and females: five times as many males as females in 1965 and four times as many in 1971 had university training.

Technical/vocational education in Trinidad first grew up on the margins of the education system mainly through on-the-job apprenticeship schemes and evening classes in technical subjects. Females found very little place in it down to the 1970s except in secretarial (or commercial) subjects. Still, because the teaching of technical/vocational subjects was mostly outside the normal schools, it did not create a significant gender divide at the level of secondary education between girls and boys. The coeducational secondary modern schools from the late 1950s began to create a new situation; and it got worse with the technical/vocational thrust from the 1970s. Within the senior comprehensive schools the concentration of girls on domestic science (home economics), dressmaking, or secretarial studies was very pronounced. Athough curiously women were allowed into the urban trade centres from the late 1970s – and these centres concentrated on the building trades – within the senior comprehensive schools a handful of girls only came forward for traditional 'male' specialised craft training in, for example, the building or engineering trades. This was not the fault simply of the schools, but of the entire socialisation of women and men.[18]

Indication that the incidence of female participation in the building and engineering trades could increase by active encouragement was provided by an interesting case. Sometime about 1980 the attention of the National Commission on the Status of Women was called to a government advertisement inviting for young persons to apply for training in carpentry and masonry. Through the intervention of the Ministry of Labour, the commission secured the stipulation that the applicants could be either male or female. The advertisement attracted 26 females and 222 male applicants for carpentry and 10 females and 164 males for masonry. Twenty-three of the female applicants for carpentry and all 10 females for masonry participated in the training. This case was regarded as a triumph for the commission and proof of the need to re-educate society not to exclude women from certain jobs.[19]

Education, The Creative Arts and Libraries

There was no mention of drawing, singing, music, drama or dancing in the shortened reports of the directors of education during World War II. Where these activities already existed there is no reason to believe that the war disrupted them; and their further development after the war strongly indicates their survival through it. In the decade between 1946 and 1956 drama in secondary schools made little or no progress. There was a long tradition of Shakespearean performances, regular or sporadic, by secondary school drama groups, and such plays continued but without any significant new developments, although the secondary schools Drama Festival gave informal support from the late 1960s.

Dancing took an interesting turn in the schools. After pioneering the introduction of Afro-Caribbean and Afro-Trinidadian dance forms in the controversial Little Carib Theatre in Woodbrook, Beryl McBurnie, a teacher, was allowed after her return from a British Council scholarship to make a tentative start in teaching these forms.[20] There was no enthusiasm for Afro-Caribbean or Afro-Trinidadian dance forms in the white expatriate directors of education and it was probably with relief that one of them reported in 1952 that due to McBurnie's absence from the island her classes had stopped, but that other conventional dance courses formed a regular feature of the work of the Government Training College. As Michael Anthony remarks, with some degree of exaggeration, "the whole of the middle and upper classes, in fact anyone who had any pretensions to refinement, looked upon all forms of local art, customs and culture as 'uncivilised' ".[21]

There was no mention of any Indian dances even in the Canadian Presbyterian schools. Cultural traditions might have posed some obstacles to dancing by Indian girls. Afro-Trinidadian and Afro-Caribbean dance threatened from the start to be a powerful art form expressive of a desire for an independent cultural movement and for political self-determination; and the more conservative section of the middle class distrusted its cultural value. What remains enigmatic, however, was the extent to which any form of dance had really invaded the schools. It might be that dance was the creative activity least practised in primary schools. The only reports of dancing were in Roman Catholic girls' secondary schools: folk dancing at St Joseph's Convent (1948) and dancing at Holy Faith Convent in Couva (1953).

Music and art made substantial progress between 1946 and 1956. In the case of art there was a fascinating leap, not made by all students or teachers, from drawing to art. The most reasonable explanation was imitation of England where art education came into vogue after World War II. A key to the turn in art education in Trinidad and Tobago was the appointment of a specialist lecturer at the Government Training College. Mr Alladin, the art officer (later director of culture), was extremely active; he is credited to have been the single greatest influence on art education for about 20 years.[22] This unprecedented continuity in the teaching of art modernised many teachers' approach to it. Alladin did derive assistance from the British Council which at that time appointed its own art officer; also from the trained art teachers individually and from the Art Teachers' Association. Although art exhibitions appealing to a more select audience did not have the mass impact of Music Festivals, they became a regular part of the cultural fare of the country. Examples of children's art were taken around the island on exhibition and also abroad.

The mass impact which art exhibitions lacked was attained by the Music Festivals of the post-war period. Before World War II the emphasis in the schools had been on improving singing and increasing students' ability to read music; and in the absence of resources and the will to purchase instruments for schools – although the number of schools with pianos increased – this line of development had to be persisted with after the war. What changed was the level of organisation of the teaching of singing and music, marked by the appointment in 1946 of a music officer, and in 1952 of an assistant music officer, and the inauguration of islandwide biennial Music Festivals, starting in 1948. The music officer like the art officer, did in-service training with the teachers at the Government Teachers' College and Naparima College; and the teachers in turn produced the school choirs and soloists who formed the core of the Music Festivals. In the early twentieth century the schools had staged agricultural shows and craft displays; these advertised certain activities within the schools. But the Music Festivals were from the 1950s the most successful form of presenting a creative art activity in schools to the public; hundreds of students were involved; the festivals were

Special Topics in Education

important as theatre; items could be recorded and rebroadcast; prizes had the imprimatur of a foreign adjudicator. Choirs which were consistently successful, like the choirs of St Joseph's Convent and Bishop Anstey High School, made a local name for themselves.[23]

A missing dimension in all these Music Festivals was an Indian element. If the stereotype in some parts of the Education Department of the Indian as an untalented singer continued from the 1920s into the 1950s, it was not expressed in the director's reports. However Presbyterian schools which could be assumed to have many Indian students were not frequent winners in the festivals (not even Naparima Girls' High School); and the extent of their participation is not clear.[24] Apparently Indian musical modes were excluded from the festivals despite the popularity of Indian music in Indian films. It might be that self-exclusion by Indians, as well as exclusion arising from the dominating influence of other racial and cultural groups, was at work. Needless to say that musical instruments and modes as distinctly lower class as steel bands and calypsoes were ignored. These were then quite unthinkable as forms of cultural and musical expressions fit for schools.

Art and craft were casualties of the education system after the 1960s. The pressure of preparation for Common Entrance Examination drove art out of primary school classes for older children; and the transfer of the majority of children above the age of 11+ years from the primary schools took craft out of the ambit of these schools. All junior secondary schools did art and craft, but the senior secondary schools and the still more traditional five-year secondary schools did art more than craft, because the former was more prestigious than the latter. The nature of programmes everywhere depended less on syllabus and more on the strength or interest of the particular teacher.[25] Unlike singing, art and craft need considerable permanent floor space for storage and display; and they could not be engaged in without the purchase of materials. It was widely acknowledged that the supervisory power of the Ministry of Education over the development of art and craft in the schools was seriously diminished when the Division of Culture was removed from the Ministry of Education and placed in the Ministry of Sport and Culture, without replacing the art (or drama) officers or supervisors taken from the Ministry of Education.[26] The art and drama officers of the Ministry of Sport and Culture paid attention to the wider community, not necessarily to the schools. In fact one needs to understand distinctly that inadequacies in the teaching of cultural subjects within schools coexisted with important gains in these matters in the wider community. This was very true of drama where little progress was made with the secondary schools Drama Festival, while important advances towards a West Indian theatre were in train.

There were two major criticisms of the teaching of cultural subjects from the 1960s to the 1980s. The PNM government brought technical/vocational education within the schools, especially the new government secondary schools. The creative arts were not similarly integrated within the general educational framework; and this means that they were taught in a haphazard, irregular and spasmodic manner, blossoming and wilting according to commitments to public performances or festivals.[27] The other important criticism was the disappointing failure of the government to establish a Cultural Training Centre or Arts Centre, along the lines, for example, of the Jamaica Cultural Training Centre. In the 1950s, when Trinidad and Tobago looked like the capital of the Commonwealth Caribbean in a variety of indigenous cultural expressions, particularly in the creating of a West Indian theatre, there was no other call so clearly articulated, so insistently made by local supporters of the creative arts, for example the young Errol Hill (and later Dereck Walcott), than for a centre, a home for the arts, a properly constructed centre of teaching and learning, not a temporary shed or an abandoned market. It was understood to be a necessary part of the outpouring of nationalist sentiment in the 1950s and early 1960s, in the the search for roots and identity which the Little Carib Theatre in Woodbrook exemplified. The centre never materialised even with an intellectual as the prime minister. Apart from Carnival – and Best Village shows often tainted organisationally at the grassroots by PNM political patronage – the PNM government did not offer strong leadership in the evolution of a cultural policy for the nation. Possibly the government was afraid to confront the issues of multiculturalism in government sponsorship of the arts.

School libraries at the level of primary schools are essentially very recent creations, in fact since the oil boom of the second half of the 1970s. Governor Lord Harris in proposing his education scheme in 1851 mentioned the desirability of a library in each primary school, but this objective was forgotten for more than a century. None of the three basic requirements for a school library – space, books and a librarian – could be afforded; and this remained the fundamental reality in most primary schools down to 1986. At the same time small, poorly housed libraries sprang into existence in the recognised secondary schools from at least the early twentieth century, and apparently did so as aids to preparation for Cambridge external examinations. No government grants were given for these; laboratories were assisted by government before school libraries. Hence the three basic patterns which characterised school libraries by the mid 1980s became evident quite early: the inadequate provision in the assisted secondary schools was vastly superior to anything in the primary schools; the provision of library facilities in secondary schools was geared towards students preparing for examinations, especially the older students; and very little, if any, government grants went towards school libraries of any sort.

In searching for an explanation of the tremendous gap between the demand of school children for library service and the supply, especially during the PNM regime, the researcher is tempted to place a considerable amount of blame on the famous or infamous lack of integration of the three library services of the country, and on the amazing and shocking failure of an 'intellectual' government to establish a national library;[28] but if a higher priority had been given to school libraries and mobile library service much more could have been achieved by each library service even in the face of administrative disunity; but school libraries, like the cultural subjects discussed earlier, were left behind in the drive to expand education opportunities, especially at the secondary school level. From about 1977 a more positive implementation of school libraries, under the supervision of the Central Library, in new government secondary schools of the 1970s, coupled with a lively rate of training of nationals as professional librarians at the Library School at UWI in Jamaica, introduced a new situation of promise. So too did recent plans for a unified library service.

Private Secondary Schools and Education

Since the early twentieth century private secondary schools have played a significant role in education. The nineteenth century private secondary school operated by individuals for profit took a very limited number of students taught usually by one teacher, more often white than coloured. It also characteristically aspired after social exclusiveness, and could often achieve it because of its small size. However there was at the beginning of the twentieth century a strong demand for secondary education in Port of Spain by parents who either could not afford the fees at CIC and QRC, or could not get their sons admitted into these colleges. At the same time a few black and coloured youths who graduated from CIC or QRC decided to invest in private secondary schools as a form of business.[29] They aimed for a mass market from the descendants of the ex-slaves and ex-indentured workers. Hence the birth of a new type of private secondary school whose social importance was to spread opportunities for secondary level or quasi secondary level education at a cheaper rate to hundreds who could not otherwise have afforded it.

The first return of private schools in 1936 showed a total of 89 such schools, some of which appeared to be at a primary school level. There was a nearly total lack of official information about private schools during World War II and immediately after it; but when official attention was turned on them in the late 1940s they occupied nothing less than a most remarkable position within the secondary school sector. From what has already been said about the circulation of money in the country during World War II, and particularly when the military bases were under construction, it might be guessed that private secondary schools found an expanding market. By 1949 there were 21 registered private secondary schools with 2,886 students enrolled.[30] This latter number was about half as many as the total enrolled in the ten public secondary schools. Osmond High School with 994 enrolled students was second in size only to CIC; Progressive Education

Institute (461 on roll) was about as large as Bishop Anstey High School or Naparima Girls' High School. Of 17 private secondary schools in what was called Category B (schools where students had to pass a preliminary test before being allowed to sit Cambridge School Certificate) only Ideal High School and Haig Girls' School had names which went back to the 1920s. These were the second generation of mass oriented privately owned secondary schools of the twentieth century. They now had a few teachers with degrees from the University of London, plus quite a few of their own superior graduates.

Not only had the private secondary schools grown to a significant proportion of the total number of secondary schools, but their contribution to the annual crop of Cambridge Certificates was remarkably high because this was literally their sole business. It was mainly private secondary schools which threatened to create the first 'oversupply' of Cambridge Certificate holders. By the early 1950s they could be expected to gross about 500 Cambridge Certificates per year, rarely of the highest quality, but of a standard from which the recipients could attempt to construct a brighter future. It is not accidental that most of the primary school teachers of the 1940s and 1950s who had secondary school education had come through Naparima College, Naparima Girls' High School, or the private secondary schools.[31] The explanation was that these schools still drew from a lower social strata on the whole than CIC, QRC, St Joseph's Convent, or Bishop Anstey High School. Indians and blacks were the two groups who found it most difficult to find places in the civil service or commercial enterprises of urban merchant houses. These groups were available for teacher training.

According to Director Hogben certain changes in the Cambridge examination regulations from 1949 originated with the Cambridge Syndicate and not with himself. He felt constrained to explain because the regulations looked socially hostile to the flow of Cambridge Certificate holders from the private schools. The new regulations required a preliminary examination to be taken one year before the Cambridge examination by those students who did not come from schools assigned to Category A.[32] Henceforth a Cambridge certificate was to be marked by an A or B according to the type of school from which it was won. The preliminary examination also served to weed out the weaker candidates who had caused Cambridge examiners to make adverse remarks about the poor standard of English. Only two private secondary schools, namely Mt St Benedict and Holy Name Convent made Category A for the first few years; by 1953 they were joined by the Regent School at Pointe-à-Pierre. It so happened that these schools represented the older tradition of more expensive, more exclusive private schools, with a better class of children, often whites, than Progressive Educational Institute or Osmond High School. The emergence of official categories was a reassertion of the idea that a proper secondary education was more important than the acquisition of Cambridge Certificates. (Rather like the contemporary restriction of City and Guilds of London Certificates to 'Theory Only' because of the inadequacies of workshops and laboratories in which apprentices of the BIT did their practical training.) The Cambridge Syndicate, it was said, wished to insist that its normal certificates were not won by secondary schools which did not teach the traditional virtues of the English grammar school type of secondary schools. In the post-war years, secondary education was still assumed to supply predictably its recipients with desirable social attitudes, with a firm grasp of written and spoken English, and a measure of cultural refinement normally associated with the upper class. Some schools could wondrously perform this miracle even when the students failed their examinations; others could not.

In 1958 after the PNM government took over, there were more private primary schools (often called preparatory schools) than government primary schools (115 private primary schools and 68 government primary schools), but total enrolment in the private schools was about one-third of the enrolment in the government schools. The average preparatory school had 55 pupils; the average government primary school had 460 pupils. The more remarkable role of private schools was in secondary education where they formed the greatest number (23 schools) with 7,089 students. Remarkably, private secondary schools educated about 41 percent of all students receiving secondary education. By 1964/1965 their share of students had increased to 45 percent, and the number of private secondary schools had grown faster than any other type of secondary schools. The growth reflected the large gap between the need for secondary school places and the provision made by the churches and government.

But the situation changed in the 1970s. The expansion of government secondary school places in the 1970s and 1980s to nearly 80 percent of the 11+ age group of primary school children, put the majority of private secondary schools, including some of the commercial schools, out of business. However students failing to win places in any public secondary schools, and moreso the large number of candidates who failed GCE and other examinations in the public secondary schools, preserved a role for a reduced number of profit-making private secondary schools run by adaptable owners. Through these schools, unsuccessful students got several chances to pass examinations. A few private schools survived for reasons of social exclusiveness. Some of these in the late 1970s were Roman Catholic schools, not surprisingly since that church had the strongest tradition of social elitism in private schools. Despite much heart searching immediately after the Black Power 'revolution', the Roman Catholic hierarchy remained indecisive about the future of private schooling for well-off supporters. Apparently failing finances had at least as much to do with the demise of one or two of these elite private Roman Catholic schools in the 1980s as changes in ideology. A new social force in the 1980s was a handful of highly religious black Muslim private schools.

It is a matter of surprise that the PNM government which was nationalistic and desirous of more control over the education system left such a substantial portion of the system without new regulations. Two investigating committees in

1957/1958 and in 1968 were set up by the government to probe private schools, but neither report was made public. It is alleged that the report of 1968 was suppressed because it revealed scandalous levels of abuse and profiteering by some owners of private secondary schools. Nor did the PNM government accede to requests in Parliament for subsidies to private schools; after the oil bonanza it was proposed to offer soft loans to specific private schools, but the government maintained the long standing policy of denying assistance to profit-making schools. Another reason for not giving aid was the concern of the government for equal educational opportunity and for a more practical technical/vocational curriculum. Private schools admitted children who had not passed the Common Entrance Examination, or who already had five years of secondary education in public secondary schools, or had parents who consciously chose private schools for social reasons. The government in 1982 accepted the thinking of a ministerial team that it would be inequitable to aid such students while other persons had received no secondary education.[33]

The Management of Education

Clerics emerged quite early as the typical managers of schools and the Roman Catholic religious orders had a reputation as the best school managers. The management of government primary schools was problematic for the entire nineteenth century and could not be said to have improved until headteachers were recognised as the real managers. This recognition took a considerable time because non-whites under Crown Colony government and in a racist society were thought (with a handful of honourable exceptions like Dr Arthur McShine) incapable of managing any public institutions. The beginning of the appointment of non-whites to the lower ranks of the inspectorate from the 1920s was a landmark in their upward climb in the education bureaucracy. By World War II Christian Indians (Presbyterians) were higher up the managerial ladder of the Education Department than blacks or coloureds.[34]

The modern successors of the inspectors and assistant inspectors of the nineteenth and early twentieth centuries were the school supervisors. Between the 1950s and the mid 1960s the nomenclature shifted from inspectors to education officers to supervisors. Undoubtedly the emphasis of government since the later 1950s was to bring the secondary schools under closer control by extending the system of supervisors to them. This was a major reversal of the nineteenth and early twentieth century emphasis and led to a situation in which the secondary school supervisory service, though numerically very weak and overcentralised, become more salient than primary school supervision. Previously, principals of secondary schools were always recognised as the paramount managers of their schools, indeed almost beyond supervision by government officers.

Denominational Boards of Management which became established features of school management in the 1930s sometimes come into the limelight because of parents' and even students' protest at the site of schools, usually over poor school furniture, school buildings or toilets, or over suspicious transfers of teachers. Such protests were usually directed against boards, though government might be partly responsible for the grievance. Boards were however sufficiently invisible institutions not to feel directly public pressure; usually it was the government which did something to break the impasse between boards and disgruntled parents. The emergence of parents, whether organised or not in Parent Teachers' Associations, as factors in the management of schools was a reality from the 1940s, not always welcomed by headteachers or chairmen of boards, though too democratic and potentially useful to be opposed.[35] Far more troublesome was the interposition of a radical teachers' union, the Trinidad and Tobago Unified Teachers' Association (hereafter TTUTA), into the sphere of school management. This union, as the representative of the majority of classroom teachers in primary and secondary schools, claimed more assertively than any previous teachers' union the right to be consulted on all aspects of education policy before implementation – a claim which the government rejected. In short the management of education, even in respect to routine affairs, became, because of the larger size of schools, the self-direction of teachers, the militancy of TTUTA, and the interventions of students and parents, more problematic than ever.

It remains to mention the question of the management of the Education Plan of 1968-1983. This was an extremely difficult task for which there was no precedent in the country. The planners from the start warned of the critical shortage of personnel of all types at the Ministry of Education to implement the plan: the expansion of the school system at all levels further outran the management capacity of the overcentralised Ministry of Education and the Ministry of Finance. Cost over-runs of school buildings in a time of inflation was endemic. This was a major problem in the aborted Third World Bank loan. The Ministry of Education could not manage efficiently the greatly expanded education industry. The problem of managing technical/vocational components of the education system seemed to require a ministry of its own as was evidenced by the indecisions, delays and poor implementation of the National Examination Council for Vocational and Technical Education. The Ministry of Education was often blamed as if it was something different and apart from the government. Indeed it looked as if the Ministry of Education, having produced a plan and spawned several committees, had to be rescued in its execution by the personal interventions of Dr Williams, or by the report of one Working Party after another, composed of persons outside the core of official planners and bureaucrats. The St Clair King Working Party Report of 1976, looking back on the implementation of the Education Plan between 1968 and 1976, felt that there had been too many delays, failure to supervise programmes and projects, also too little consultation, presumably with the churches, and too much silence about the intention of government at crucial times. These were only some of the shortcomings of government. The planners had to work within the political culture of the PNM and Dr Eric Williams himself. No planner in the Ministry of Education could wisely consult with the heads of churches in periods when Dr Williams had chosen to ignore the particular planner or the churches. On crucial issues in education only Dr Williams could break silence. His method of consulting with the people, of having 'democracy' in education was seldom useful to planners. National consultations were of little or no use as means of defining policy; they were politically motivated, useful to a point in diffusing public anger or outflanking clerical opinion.[36] Perhaps their most enduring legacy was the creation of a culture of national educational consultations not found elsewhere in the Commonwealth Caribbean. Sudden action in setting up Working Parties obliged to proceed at breakneck speed was usually followed by a wall of silence about which recommendations, if any, had been accepted or rejected by the government. Dr Williams might then intervene personally and put new items on the agenda for action which superseded in urgency the unexecuted part of the plan. But the general quantitative goals of the Education Plan were largely achieved.

The Unassimilated Rethinking 1976-1981

Here we will deal with a variety of important matters. They relate mostly to attempts at qualitative improvements in the education system, but were not assimilated into the education system as policy down to 1981. There was rethinking about the Common Entrance Examination. Almost immediately after its commencement in 1961 there were complaints that many teachers in primary schools were neglecting those subjects which did not form any direct part of the examination; and the practice of special classes and special coaching sessions for candidates distorted the normal work of the schools. For example, geography, history and essay writing formed important parts of the primary school curriculum, but were not tested in the Common Entrance Examination. Pupils were arriving in secondary schools with very inadequate writing skills. Since it was logical that teachers and parents would make every effort to have children succeed in such a vital examination, the solution advanced in 1966 by Dr L. T. Green, a consultant, was to include an essay type question in the Common Entrance Examination.[37] This would, he thought, oblige teachers to take essay writing seriously, although it would pose some inconvenience in scoring and standardisation of marks in an examination which otherwise consisted of objective tests. Green did not advance any drastic solution for the neglect of subjects like history and geography, and the essay type questions were not included.

Special Topics in Education

To make matters worse the primary school curriculum was reformed in 1975 to make it wider on the academic side. General science and social studies were added – a development partly negated by the confinement of the Common Entrance Examination to only two subjects: arithmetic and English. Other abuses not so noticeable at the time Green reported were noted by the 1970s. For instance, in order to advance children to grades IV and V to prepare avidly for the examination, certain children were allowed to skip grades, thus reducing their exposure to some aspects of the curriculum in order to concentrate almost exclusively in grades IV and V on English and arithmetic. The St Clair King Report of 1976 recommended that the Common Entrance Examination be based on all the subjects, including practical subjects done in the primary schools. The solution proposed by a special team of investigators (the Examinations Review Committee) led by Dr C. V. Gocking and appointed by the government in 1978 was to incorporate an examination in general science and social studies into the examination.[38] These recommendations had not been implemented by 1981.

The double shift system in the junior secondary schools was one of the most unpopular aspects of the education expansion under the PNM regime. In 1975 a government-appointed committee to investigate measures to alleviate the problems of the double shift system reported. The measures it advocated were very complicated and none was adopted by 1981. A very controversial rethinking emanated from a small committee of Dr C. V. Gocking and Mr Edgehill in 1981. The notion that GCE O level performance was less than satisfactory was born in the 1960s and became the fixed opinion of most educators in the 1970s. Dr Williams, before becoming prime minister, had been extremely critical of external examinations, such as the GCE, but he never took drastic steps to bring these examinations to an end except in as far as his government gave slow support to the CXC. The government wanted to raise the academic standards of the schools. It was therefore a matter of some shock when this Gocking/Edgehill Committee declared in effect that the real problem was that GCE standard was too high and ought to be replaced by an examination, presumably local, which could be passed by students of lower ability than the 20 percent of upper secondary school forms for whom the GCE examination was originally designed. The nation was informed that the need to devise new examinations had been recognised even in England, the home of the GCE, and that a Secondary School Certificate had been put in place to test 40 percent of students below the 20 percent catered for by the GCE examinations. This was what CXC should be doing, said the Gocking/Edgehill Committee.

The CXC which had commenced in 1979 with a few subjects had set standards which could be met theoretically by only the top 20 percent of students who sat the General Proficiency papers, and for the next 20 percent below these there was the Basic Proficiency papers. The expansion of secondary education had brought into the pool to be tested students of a far greater range of ability than previously, and ironically expectations of their performance at the GCE had been misguidedly raised, said Gocking and Edgehill, by the arbitrary tradition that passes in as many as five subjects taken simultaneously constituted the minimum satisfactory school performance. This constituted, it was said, a standard higher than the Cambridge School Certificate of the pre 1964 period. The call to revise standards downwards was not heeded by the end of 1981; teachers and parents thought mainly of how to get more children to pass GCE as it stood; Gocking and Edgehill maintained that the way forward was to set an examination which more students could pass.

Nursery education, meaning the education of children between 3 and 5 years of age was in a state of neglect, disorder and government indifference. The Child Welfare League, a voluntary agency, had interested itself in nursery education from the 1930s, and up to the start of the 1970s the field was entirely in the hands of such voluntary agencies, not always directly connected to a church. In the expansion of education no systematic provision had been made for government nursery schools, or for government assistance to non-government nursery schools. However in the 1970s with the flush of increased oil revenues the government began to promote this type of school in community centres. Hence by 1978 there were 30 government-supported nursery schools established in community centres, and staffed by nursery aides. Additionally there was a large but undetermined number of privately owned and operated day care centres, and nursery schools ranging in quality from dame schools conducted by well intentioned but inadequately trained females to the model nursery school at San Fernando, run by the Nursery School Association of Trinidad and Tobago.[39]

A committee on teacher education (the Teacher Education Committee) chaired by Dr C. V. Gocking, and set up by the government provided in early 1980 a framework of ideas within which nursery education could be made to advance. This committee saw nursery education as having a great potential to overcome the socioeconomic disadvantages of lower class homes; organised nursery education was not only needed on psychological and pedagogical grounds, but as a measure of social reform. The idea was that government should incorporate nursery education as a normal part of the system of education stretching from age 3 to age 18 and spanning nursery education (3–5 years), infant education/school (5–7 years), junior school (7–11+ years), and secondary education (11+–18 years). Since the committee envisaged both privately owned (whether by individuals, voluntary agencies, or industries) and government nursery schools, it was essentially asking for the mechanisms which governed the dual system to be extended to incorporate nursery schools. In the belief that there were underutilised primary school plants, it was recommended that after a survey of the need for nursery school places, such primary school buildings should be modified to suit the needs of nursery schools. Industries, presumably those which employed female workers on industrial estates, were invited to establish modern day care and nursery school complexes. An immediate beginning in part-time training of nursery school teachers could be made with the existing staff of such schools, including some of the operators of "private non-assisted dame school type of schools"; but a higher grade of staff, for examples, principals and teachers in charge, could be obtained by full-time training over six months of teachers already in training colleges. Eventually however, and this was the major recommendation of the committee, the training college curriculum had to be revamped to provide specialization from year two for teachers of nursery schools. It was envisaged that a further specialization would be feasible after a third year at college, and the UWI St Augustine, might be asked to run degree courses in education with a high component in nursery education. No action was taken on the recommendation of this committee by 1981.

New ideas about the training of primary school teachers also materialised in early 1980 from the same government appointed committee which made recommendations on nursery education. The most essential idea was the need to institutionalise the concept of life long education of teachers. Practical arrangements should be made for some teachers to continue studying at the training colleges beyond the Teachers' Diploma up to a specialist Certificate in Education, and even to a degree in education given jointly by the colleges and UWI. At the same time all teachers who had already been trained should get the opportunity, through leave or scholarships, to return to the training colleges for short courses, from a few days to many weeks, to upgrade their skills and knowledge of teaching. Prime groups for this periodic upgrading would be persons, for instance married women, due to re-enter the profession after a period of absence. The basic idea however was that all teachers, at least once every ten years and hopefully soon once every seven years, should be encouraged back to the classroom at the teachers' colleges. There was no hint of compulsion in the recommendation, but clearly what was being recommended was novel in its scope and in the evident desire to integrate and institutionalise post-Teachers' Diploma studies in the training colleges.

This plan to raise the standard of teacher education and training by additional provision for further training came about partly because of the amazing clearing off of the backlog of untrained teachers in the primary schools. In 1980 only about 138 untrained teachers, all of whom did not have the qualifications to enter training colleges, remained as teachers in the system. It was in the context of excess physical plant and underutilised training college staff that the government-appointed committee chaired by Gocking saw the opportunity of putting these facilities back to work essentially to retrain, upgrade and improve teachers already in possession of the basic Teachers' Diploma. It was an attempt to shift teacher training into a 'postgraduate' mode. There would still be a small number of young teachers entering the training colleges to get the basic Teachers' Diploma, but on the assumption that the primary schools only needed to replace trained teachers lost by attrition, the committee envisaged this type of training as the minor activity of the government teachers' colleges.

It must be clearly understood that the clearing off of the backlog of untrained teachers in the primary schools was an achievement specific to teachers in this type of schools only. The government-appointed committee mentioned above, under the chairmanship of Dr C. V. Gocking, also made recommendations on the training of teachers in secondary schools, technical colleges and further educational institutions. These latter included trade centres, vocational centres, youth camps, and UWI extra-mural classes. Here the task was to train, not to retrain, and so the committee advocated a vast expansion of training opportunities for persons who did not already have the basic teacher training which they should have had. The increase of the number of trained secondary school teachers (all university graduates) required expanding postgraduate teacher training at UWI St Augustine. The main thrust of the teacher training programme of the Faculty of Education, St Augustine, was in the teaching of part-time post-graduate in-service Diploma of Education students: here the Gocking Committee recommended an increase from 100 per year to 150 students per year; there should also be a full-time pre-service Department of Education programme for 100 graduates. It also recommended 50 students per year in a new Certificate of Education programme; also 10 students per annum in a Diploma of Education programme. These latter two programmes would be one year in duration, and designed to produce specialists in certain areas of teaching. For persons already holding degrees in education, the recommended postgraduate continuation was the degree of MA or MEd designed to encourage research, and the acquisition of research tools to be applied later in educational research. About 10 students were to complete this programme each year.[40]

The last major area of university involvement in the preparation of teachers for secondary schools was to be the introduction of new types of undergraduate degrees involving other Faculties apart from the Faculty of Education. For instance, the four-year conjoint degrees of BA Diploma of Education and BSc Diploma of Education would require taking courses in the Faculty of Arts or the Faculty of Natural Science. The advantage of such degrees over the traditional route of a degree plus a subsequent Diploma in Education was thought to be the chance of an earlier application of teaching skills to the corpus of knowledge learnt at the university level.

It was not explicitly said, but it would appear as if the two Government Training Colleges were to handle the remaining aspects of the expanded teacher training programme. For instance, short induction programmes for untrained teachers, graduate or non-graduate, who were just about to start teaching in secondary schools. Teachers at farm centres, or social welfare offices, or teachers of an adult education class of the Extra-Mural Department of UWI – in short anyone who taught in further educational institutions who did not have university entrance requirement, or who were possessed of it but wished to upgrade their teaching skills short of a university degree or diploma. All such persons should be trained to teach by the teachers' colleges. Very few, if any, of these recommendations from the Gocking Committee had been implemented by 1981.

The St Augustine Campus of UWI

UWI started as a single campus regional university located in Jamaica, with Faculties of Medicine, Natural Science and Arts beginning teaching in 1948, 1950 and 1952 respectively. If the Irvine Committee had visited Trinidad in 1960 instead of 1944, it would obviously have taken a more favourable view of the readiness of the country to be the site of a university. There was a demand for a university then at a more irresistible level than in 1944. Dr Williams had given from about the mid 1950s a special dimension of intellectualism to the politics of creole nationalism and had opened his own 'University of Woodford Square', with himself as the unchallenged 'professor'. He was the only Commonwealth Caribbean prime minister who had a past as a university professor and who could have been called an intellectual. His government prized university degrees as qualification for the teaching and civil service; and Williams' political opponents in Parliament sought to outdo him by proposing two full universities for Trinidad, one in the north and one in the south, with travelling academic staff.[41] Under these circumstances it was inconceivable that university-level teaching would not have erupted in Trinidad, which already had ICTA on an appropriate site at St Augustine.

The start of the 1960s saw the birth of several new independent nations in Africa and strong movements everywhere in the colonial world for faster progress towards independence. It was the start of a decade of euphoric dreams of rapid economic development for new nations through industrialisation. Within the Commonwealth Caribbean, island nationalism triumphed in the early 1960s at the expense of regionalism. The Federation of the West Indies broke up in 1962; Dr Eric Williams and the PNM returned to power in Trinidad in a resounding electoral victory in 1961; the creole nationalism of Trinidad under the inspiration of Dr Williams peaked in that year in the struggle against the United States military bases; Jamaica and Trinidad became independent in 1962; the government of Guyana indicated that it would withdraw from the UWI. In this context the common services of the defunct West Indies Federation, including the single campus residential UCWI (independent from 1962) had to be restructured.[42] It did not appear capable of sufficiently rapid expansion to meet the needs of several independent island states.

The gregariousness of institutions of higher learning came into play as soon as ICTA became the Faculty of Agriculture of UCWI. A one-Faculty campus was untenable. On the international scene, movements of importance which impinged on the development of a university campus at St Augustine included the availability of substantial financial assistance and technical aid directly to the new nation of Trinidad and Tobago, from sources apart from the United Kingdom agencies. Aid was forthcoming for engineering, science and technology and the humanities. Hence Trinidad and Tobago's claim to other faculties became stronger. These considerations, plus the greater level of industrialisation of Trinidad over Barbados, which had no oil industry, and prolonged inconclusive discussions with Jamaica over its plans for engineering, made it reasonable to site the Faculty of Engineering in Trinidad. The upshot was the emergence of a multi-Faculty university campus in Trinidad between 1960 and 1963 with three major sectors: a Faculty of Agriculture (1960); a Faculty of Engineering (1961); and a College of Arts and Science (1963).

The inflow of students into Engineering and Agriculture, was not solely from Trinidad; but in the case of the College of Arts and Science the students were drawn almost completely from Trinidad and Tobago. It was therefore when the College of Arts and Science started in 1963 that the new university presence at St Augustine began to impact on a wide cross-section of occupations and age groups. The establishment of this college changed the whole scope of local post-secondary educational opportunities.

Hamlyn Dukhan, a local educationalist, wrote in October 1984 on the twenty-first anniversary of the College of Arts and Science, about the impact of the college in 1963. He remembered that:

> To many a citizen the news of the educational innovation was regarded as almost 'unbelievable', 'inconceivable', 'impossible' . . . People of all ages, young and old, male and female; people in the teaching service, the public service and private sector who had left secondary school or had 'stopped studying' more than two or three decades ago, but who still had the fire of academic ambition blazing within them, and of course, had the necessary university entrance and faculty requirements, jumped at the opportunity.[43]

In some respects the branch of the university that developed at St Augustine was more like the university that Dr Williams had in mind in 1944 than the single-campus university in Jamaica between 1948 and 1960. The branch at St Augustine from 1962 was part of an independent university. The College of Arts and Science had a small evening programme; it also prized general degrees over special degrees (then called Honours Degrees); the grouping of subjects into divisions instead of individual subject departments (as in Jamaica) was partly the result of the relatively small size of the St Augustine staff and partly a reflection of efforts, especially on the Arts side, to encourage a mix of the academic fare offered to students. Survey courses were introduced on all campuses for Arts and Science students, in the hope of broadening their views of the world and the Caribbean.

Of great importance to Dr Williams personally – in fact on his urging – a survey course in West Indian history became mandatory for all students in the College of Arts and Science. The West Indianisation of many courses was accelerated; the

Special Topics in Education

same thing can be said about the university staff. All this must have pleased Dr Williams, though there were other sources of tension between UWI and himself. Less pleasing to Dr Williams was the fact that the politics of opposition to his party found bases on the St Augustine campus; so too did the Black Power movement of the youths, culminating in the highly charged events of the academic year of 1969/1970 filled with students' boycotts, lockouts, meetings and marches. The Black Power movement was not centred on the St Augustine campus, but the fact that several of its leaders, including its generalissimo, Geddes Granger, were students on campus encouraged a wide level of student participation; the black power students gave the campus community, not always rightly, the reputation of a hotbed of political opposition to Dr Williams, the PNM and neocolonialism. Still, within six to nine years of its commencement the St Augustine campus had helped to stir up a political storm against its chief architect, Dr Eric Williams.[44]

The figures for the enrolment of Trinidad and Tobago nationals on the St Augustine campus between 1960 and 1969 indicate that the College of Arts and Science had the largest number of nationals, with students in the Arts subjects leading the way. By having an evening programme for the BA. Qualifying and BSc Part One examinations, enrolment in Arts and Science immediately outdistanced registration in the Faculty of Engineering and lapped several times the number in the Faculty of Agriculture. Enrolment of Trinidad and Tobago nationals in the Faculty of Engineering was greater than enrolment in the Faculty of Agriculture; and when teaching of the Social Sciences began in 1965/1966, enrolment of nationals for BSc Economics and the Diploma in Management Studies immediately was slightly larger than enrolment in the Faculty of Agriculture.

This scale of enrolment of nationals, descending from the highest in Arts, through Natural Sciences, Engineering, Social Sciences and lastly to Agriculture, remained the basic pattern until towards the mid 1970s (1973-1975) when Social Sciences overhauled enrolment in Engineering. The first nationals to graduate with local degrees obtained without crossing the seas were in Agriculture (1963), Engineering (1964), Arts (1966) and Natural Sciences (1967). The numerical impact on the society of the early waves of graduates was first felt on a large scale when 80 nationals graduated in Arts in 1966. In a single graduation Trinidad and Tobago had acquired as many Arts graduates as about 80 percent of all the nationals who had graduated in Arts at the Mona campus in Jamaica between 1952 and 1964.[45]

As might be expected the sector of the education system that benefited most directly from the development of a university campus at St Augustine was secondary school teaching. The route from secondary school to one of the teachers' colleges and then to teaching in a primary school was now extended, sometimes after a few years' pause, by hundreds of teachers, to the St Augustine campus and then to posts in secondary schools. Hence the availability of locally obtained degrees was a lever of upward social mobility; and since the Trinidad government paid all the fees of nationals at the St Augustine campus, the university there was the culmination of the framework of 'free' education from primary school to university for those (the increasing minority) who could take advantage of higher education via basic qualifications or meritorious performance.

Nationals graduating in Natural Science and in Engineering were able to move into well-paid jobs in private industry, especially the oil industry. In the first few years (1964-1969) the production of civil engineers kept up with the other branches, but then was outdistanced by them until the construction boom of the late 1970s. At a time when the government was committed to planning the economy, the early graduates in economics were thought particularly well-suited for certain posts in the civil service. The considerable expansion of secondary schools in the later 1960s and 1970s would have been impossible without the flow of graduates from the College of Arts and Science at St Augustine. In the Education Plan (1968-1983) the planners were able to look with confidence to the St Augustine campus to provide an adequate supply of secondary school teachers throughout the period of the plan.

The expansion of enrolment of Trinidad and Tobago nationals at the St Augustine campus in the 1970s outdistanced greatly the figures achieved in the 1960s. Two broad periods can be discerned in the rate of enrolment of nationals in the Faculties of Engineering and Social Sciences: incremental advance before the oil bonanza and large-scale advances after it, particularly after 1976/1977. The oil boom started in late 1973, but naturally it took a few years before enhanced revenues at the disposal of the government began to show on the campus in new buildings and enlarged enrolments of nationals.

The Faculty of Agriculture followed a different trend. The incremental advance of enrolment of nationals in the Faculty of Agriculture continued from 66 students in 1970/1971 to 82 students in 1973/1974, to 116 students in 1975/1976, with a falling off in 1976/1977 to 77 students due to changes in the degree structure. The remarkable expansion of total (nationals plus others) student enrolment in this Faculty was in the early 1970s due to its relative underutilisation at a time when financial stringency led to restriction of admissions to other and more attractive faculties. These restrictions were not applied to the Faculty of Agriculture. It is not therefore that agriculture as a profession for men was more popular among West Indians in the 1970s than in the 1960s. The number of female students however grew sharply, perhaps because of lower social expectations of remunerative employment in agriculture. After 1977/1978 came enrolments of nationals above 200 students per annum. This large increase after 1977/1978 was the direct result of the technique of a pre-agriculture year adopted from 1975/1976, and also to a lesser extent the greater availability of scholarships from the government. The proportion of nationals enrolled in this faculty changed from 46.8 percent (66 nationals out of 141 students) in 1970/1971 to 66.6 percent (226 nationals out of 339) in 1979/1980.

The enrolment of nationals in the Social Sciences moved slowly in the 1970s until 1977/1978 when it shot up to 286 students, a level maintained until 1980/1981 when it went up by a massive leap to 429 nationals. These figures do not tell the full story as a high percentage of students from other faculties took courses in the Social Sciences. Social Science courses enjoyed in the 1970s a remarkable popularity, as the unending fever for marketable skills in private enterprise spread on all three campuses. A significant new programme at St Augustine was the MSc in accountancy from 1975/1976, but this was not responsible for the high enrolments. More to the point was the commencement of an evening programme for the Part One of the BSc degree in 1978/1979. Almost all these students in the expanded Social Science programmes were nationals.[46]

The 1970s brought good fortune to the Faculty of Engineering. This Faculty had been the antithesis of the Faculty of Agriculture: it was oversubscribed. Built to hold 250 students, it had a total (nationals plus others) of 386 in 1975/1976 in more or less the same floor space. It was relatively poorly articulated with the two technical institutes compared to the connection of Arts and Natural Sciences with the 'grammar' type secondary schools. Graduates of the technical institutes might find that they were not qualified to enter the Faculty of Engineering, or to succeed in the competition for entry. Nevertheless the predilection of the government for technical/vocational education in the 1970s and the vast expansion in the construction industry enhanced the claims of the Faculty of Engineering to be an indispensable agent of economic development. (Its graduates did not usually go into teaching.) When the massive oil revenues removed money as a restraint on new buildings, more staff or higher student enrolment, the academic leadership of the Faculty grasped the golden opportunity with both hands: in the light of the decision to enter heavy energy-based industries, the study of engineering and technology appeared as the key to the entire transformation from an underdeveloped to a developed country. Large-scale deficits in every branch of engineering were identified – perhaps excessively.

Plans in 1976 for a massive increase in enrolment to 840 students, of which 615 places would be reserved for nationals, would have made the Faculty the giant of the campus by 1978. But the time allowed was too short for all the new inputs, including essential buildings, to be made by 1978; but a positive beginning to increased enrolment of nationals was made from 1976/1977, and it rapidly led to nationals moving from 41.9 percent of total enrolment in engineering in 1975/1976 (162 nationals of 386 students) to 60.4 percent in 1978/1979 (339 nationals of 561 students). This expansion was still in progress in 1985 though the financial strength of the government had been sapped by falling oil revenues. It is to be noted that all the capital and additional recurrent cost of the expansion of this Faculty came from the Government of Trinidad and Tobago, and not from the other territories contributing to the university. It should also be remembered that along with the new buildings and increased student intake came new undergraduate programmes in agricultural, industrial, and petroleum engineering and unprecedented, high activity in postgraduate teaching and extension services to the engineering community outside the university. The year 1980 was the year when the potential effects of the expansion of nationals in engineering was seen for the first time. A total of 85 nationals graduated in engineering (mostly civil engineering), a number far in excess of anything any other Commonwealth Caribbean territory could boast.[47]

The expansion of the enrolment of nationals in Arts and Natural Science was incremental for the entire 1970s, and did not benefit significantly from the oil bonanza. In fact from at least the mid 1970s government officials felt that there was an oversupply of Arts graduates. This appeared partly to match the alleged oversupply of secondary school holders of GCE certificates in Arts subjects. It seems that the expansion in engineering diverted some potential recruits for the Natural Sciences into Engineering, causing enrolment in the Natural Sciences to level off in the second half of the 1970s. So that while many Arts students could prepare for job opportunities by reading for as many Social Science courses as regulations permitted, some potential Natural Science students had to enter another Faculty.

The oil bonanza also brought the beginning of a new medical school near to the St Augustine campus. The principle of decentralisation of the last two years of clinical training of medical students had already been yielded, so that a number of medical students, mostly nationals, were attached to the Port of Spain General Hospital. What was aimed at from about the late 1970s was a hospital and a medical school, the latter on a scale larger than the medical training facilities in Jamaica. For this Mount Hope Medical Complex, including training in medicine, dentistry, veterinary science, pharmacy and advanced nursing, the government was able to put aside TT$15 million, TT$30 million and TT$200 million in 1979, 1980 and 1981 respectively.[48] Still this was far from enough to finance the many buildings (about 70) which had been completed by 1985. Because of the massive investment of the Trinidad government and its desire to control the Mount Hope Complex (now called the Eric Williams Medical Science Complex), the academic relations between the complex and the Faculty of Medicine in Jamaica were only slowly worked out, and for years the university authorities in Jamaica were not sure what was to happen. Up to 1980 no students were admitted, though a maternity hospital started functioning. Trinidad and Tobago had by 1986 the physical infrastructure to train a large number of health service personnel, but there remained considerable doubt whether the scheme could still be executed in full in view of reduced government revenues. The vastly increased spending on the Faculty of Engineering and the Mount Hope Medical Complex helped to explain why the restructuring of the university to allow for greater campus autonomy and separate campus financing seemed most urgent to the Trinidad and Tobago government.

It remains to mention one other significant programme which started before government oil revenues expanded. This was the in-service training of graduate teachers for the Diploma of Education. A handful of university staff was attached to a local branch of the Institute of Education from 1963; and as elsewhere they saw their main function as the improvement of teacher education. This took the form of research and advisory services, and not training for a university degree. As the increasing enrolments in the College of Arts and Science produced more and more teachers for secondary schools, the backlog of secondary school teachers untrained in the art of teaching became formidable. As teachers could not be spared from the schools, the programme had to be in-service; but the scale of the programme was completely inadequate to the task of making any considerable impact on the sum of untrained university graduate teachers. At no time since the commencement of the programme was there substantially more than 100 students, which meant that the annual output of new graduates in Arts and Science was greater than the annual intake of graduates into the in-service programme, not to mention the backlog.

The vast expansion of all the faculties at St Augustine and the appointment of more senior academic staff naturally put on the agenda, or perhaps more accurately kept on the agenda, the whole question of decentralisation versus centralisation in a regional university. While the St Augustine campus was born in the cradle of Trinidad government nationalism, the true origins of the movement for the decentralisation of the university lay with the academic staff from the 1960s. They were bewildered by the uncertainties or rigidities of the new, largely unplanned relationship with the Mona (Jamaica) headquarters into which they had been thrust innocently. There were endless staff debates about what could be done at St Augustine without Mona's approval and what could not be done. But staff concerns about decentralisation did not centre on separate campus funding; it was not really about money or financial accountability or even appropriate curricula for national development. It sprang from what appeared to be unworkable regulations or bureaucratic red tape. The politicians applied pressure for decentralisation afterwards, but their focus was on some thing different.

Dr Williams grew less enchanted with the university in the 1970s. It had spawned some new political opponents; it was a political centre of 'subversion'. Ideological differences and variations in economic policies and financial strength among Trinidad, Barbados and Jamaica induced strains in the management of the regional university. The government of Trinidad accused the university of a lack of financial accountability, a charge which the university did not leave unanswered. Williams expressed disgust with the 'prattle' that arose in Jamaica about democratisation of the university. Jamaican governments under Hugh Shearer and Michael Manley seemed to have wanted greater control of the Jamaica campus to rid it of 'subversives' (in the case of Shearer), or to 'democratise' it (in the case of Manley); and Dr Williams, especially after 1974, desired greater power over the St Augustine campus to pursue the special interest of Trinidad and Tobago as a rapidly industrialising nation with the capacity to pay for a higher standard of living. In effect Williams too wanted decentralisation – meaning greater campus autonomy and separate instead of pooled financing of each campus. The Government of Barbados was also openly critical of the university, but was not the prime mover for decentralisation euphemistically called restructuring. Since it was a political question, the governments had to take the lead and the university authorities had to follow; the question was how fast could they follow. Restructuring – with much fears for the regional character of the university – at first came gradually, and subsequently with a rush to a new decentralised structure in 1983/1984 after the Trinidad and Jamaica governments became impatient with the university authorities.[49] However decentralisation had been so gradual – and the talk of restructuring so long and dreary – that many academic staff members (perhaps unlike senior university administrators) did not perceive the academic year 1983/1984 as a turning point in the history of the university. Many did not know their institution had been restructured.

In retrospect, one can argue that up to the later 1970s the development of the St Augustine campus was an undisputed success story. The unfortunate collapse of government revenues in the 1980s cast a shadow over that campus, but the university was accustomed to living with such shadows. What gave the saga of the St Augustine campus a unique dimension of audacity was the awesome implantation of the unused Mount Hope Complex, perhaps too massive even with a healthy oil economy. The Mount Hope Complex was and remains a salutary example of excess.

Comparative Perspectives

There are two obvious regions of the world from which a study of education in Trinidad and Tobago could benefit by way of comparison. Leaving aside the metropole which provided the education models, it seems worthwhile to compare Trinidad and Tobago with other English-speaking Caribbean territories and with West African and East African states. It was clear from the Marriott/Mayhew Report of 1931/32 that with the exception of Barbados no island in the eastern Caribbean had any schools or education systems which were thought superior to what existed in Trinidad and Tobago. Barbados and Trinidad and Tobago in some respects were in a class by themselves above the other eastern Caribbean islands. Barbados was thought by Marriott and Mayhew to have performed better than Trinidad and Tobago in respect to expenditure on education, resulting in its having the best school buildings and equipment.[50] Barbados in 1937 spent a higher percentage of its budget on education than Trinidad and Tobago, though the latter spent more money on a per pupil basis. As the young Eric Williams wrote in 1942 "the education of Barbados is severely classical at the secondary level, and Barbadian classical scholars, white and colored, have attained well deserved fame in England".[51] Barbados however was behind Trinidad and Tobago in teacher training facilities and in the quality of its management team in education. Marriott and Cutteridge as directors of education in Trinidad and Tobago were unsurpassed in the contemporary eastern Caribbean. Barbados in fact only got its first director of education in 1943. A weak spot in the Trinidad education framework was the Indian population which was described by the Marriott/Mayhew Report as "educationally backward" relevant to other sections of the population. Despite the inadequacies of the provision for the Indian population, Trinidad and Tobago and Barbados preserved their position of leadership in education in the eastern Caribbean from the 1930s down to their emergence as independent nations.

In the post World War II period and especially after independence, the vast expansion of education at all levels, the greater complexity of the different parts of the education system, the abolition of annual reports of the Ministry of Education by the PNM government, combined to throw the comparative picture into greater uncertainty. Contemporaries might be justified in stressing the tremendous common problems in the Eastern Caribbean of meeting the demands of a more clamorous population for adequate education, especially at the secondary school level, than the advantages of one territory or the other. It seems fairly certain however that buoyant public revenues of Trinidad and Tobago and the oil windfall of the 1970s, plus the consistent interest of Dr Williams in universalizing primary and secondary education placed Trinidad and Tobago in a clear position of ascendancy in the entire English-speaking Caribbean. On the barometer which has since the 1960s become the single greatest indicator of West Indian education systems – the percentage of the 11+ age school population passing into 'free' secondary education – Trinidad and Tobago outpaced the other islands, with a figure of virtually 80 percent admission into all types of government and denominational public secondary schools. Also Trinidad and Tobago in the post-independence era provided the highest percentage of primary school enrolment in the English-speaking Caribbean.[52] The quality of education was another matter; here the massive examination failure rate of enlarged secondary school populations in traditional external examinations formerly taken by the few becomes the talking point rather than any perceived differences of academic performance of the children of different islands. Finally it must not be forgotten that despite vastly improved electronic and printed means of communication between the islands and a three-campus university, the Caribbean sea and the Caribbean past divided rather than united the islands; in matters of education, no less than in other areas, each West Indian territory still had highly educated citizens largely ignorant of developments in other islands.

For purpose of comparison with Trinidad and Tobago only ex-British colonies of West and East Africa will be briefly considered: Ghana, Nigeria, Sierra Leone, Kenya, Tanzania, Uganda, Zambia and Malawi. These countries, with the exception of Ghana, gained their independence in the early 1960s, at much the same time as Trinidad and Tobago. The period of colonisation by the British had been shorter in these African countries than in Trinidad and Tobago; the immense size and populations of these African countries discouraged British government efforts for education; colonial governments entered the field of education, dominated by the missionaries, at a later period than in Trinidad and Tobago; and the racist theories of African mental inferiority went unchecked for a longer period of time into the twentieth century than in the West Indies. Hence the record of education provision, at every level, was much better in Trinidad and Tobago from the 1930s to independence than in any African country between the Sahara and South Africa.[53] In the early 1960s illiteracy rates for persons 15 years and over were between 70 and 75 percent in Uganda; between 75 and 80 percent in Ghana, Zambia and Kenya; between 85 and 90 percent in Nigeria; between 90 and 95 percent in Malawi, Sierra Leone and Tanzania. In Trinidad and Tobago it was negligible. The populations of these African countries were so massively larger than Trinidad and Tobago's that the percentage of their primary and secondary age cohort actually in school could not be as high as in Trinidad and Tobago. The advantage of Trinidad and Tobago in secondary education was particularly pronounced.

All over the Third World there was from the 1960s to the 1980s a mighty expansion of educational facilities such as was never witnessed previously. A part of the gains was unfortunately negated by rapid population growth. From the early 1960s, which the United Nations declared to be the first Development Decade, education planning under UNESCO sponsorship came into vogue, the intention being to use education as an instrument of national development. It is clear that in terms of quantity Trinidad and Tobago was able to preserve the lead in education which it had over the above mentioned African countries on the eve of independence. The simplest way to understand the difference was to examine the incidence of primary education. The most outstanding feature of African education policies was the struggle in the 1970s to attain free universal primary school enrolment, at a time when Trinidad and Tobago having satisfied itself on the level of primary school enrolment was concentrating on secondary education.[54] A striking contrast was the achievement of a cadre of fully trained primary school teachers in Trinidad and Tobago, at a time when African countries had a vast number of vacancies for primary school teachers and a low percentage of trained teachers. Like Trinidad and Tobago some of the African countries started out after independence by putting great stress on secondary and higher education in order to meet high and middle level manpower needs; but a big difference was that Trinidad and Tobago, unlike the African countries, already had a very high level of primary school enrolment.

Special Topics in Education

Citizens of Trinidad and Tobago might find it hard to understand that down to 1980 secondary education was not free in West or East African countries (except Tanzania from 1975) and that in some countries, or in parts of some countries, primary education itself was not free or not free for all grades. Tanzania's commitment to socialist policies led to a deliberate restriction of secondary and university education in favour of primary education and adult literacy. S. A. Hammond and Colonial Welfare and Development would have liked such a programme for Trinidad after World War II, but not for a similar political reason. Civil war in Nigeria in the late 1960s and in Uganda in the 1970s damaged education facilities and dispersed teachers; the financial burden of large military establishments, like the destructive effects of civil wars, was something unknown in Trinidad and Tobago. A survey of university student protest and government repression of academic staff and students in these African countries (with the possible exception of Tanzania) makes the troubles on the St Augustine campus in 1969 and 1970 read like perfect peace.

It would however be short-sighted not to mention the ways in which the education policies of Trinidad and Tobago were similar in the 25 years after independence to those of African countries. A pervasive common point was the government's concern to inject a higher level of technical/vocational training and education into the whole education system and to use tertiary institutions to produce the trained manpower needed. Continuing parental emphasis on academic subjects threw up everywhere hurdles in the way of official policy. Everywhere government control over education grew at the expense of church and private school proprietors, even in Kenya with its strong traditions of independent schools. The cost of education was a heavy burden on the treasuries of all these countries, though oil rich Nigeria, like Trinidad and Tobago, was able to turn its revenue windfall directly into the expansion of secondary schools and higher education. Vastly expanded enrolments put pressure on facilities and created the need to devise new examinations, and complaints of lower standards of examination performance were endemic in Trinidad and African countries alike. It is to be noted that some African countries anticipated Trinidad and Tobago in the creation of their own Examination Council: the West African Examination Council for example. A very common problem was that posed by the failure to match output of graduates from the primary and secondary schools with opportunities for employment in the formal economy. A difference though was that in African countries, because of gross underdevelopment of secondary schools to absorb the expanding primary school population, it was at the level of primary school graduates that the crisis of unemployment was most severe. Tanzania reduced the size of this problem by a close integration of primary schools with agricultural labour, and by compulsory residence of the overwhelming majority of graduates in villages. To varying extent some of these countries had to establish national youth service to discipline youths and encourage patriotism.

[12]

An Assessment 1956-1986

> In respect of education the critics have had a field day – nothing has been done, education is a mess, schools are in poor shape, teachers are demoralised and unhappy, the curriculum is bad, the students are failing their exams, nothing works.
>
> Dr Eric Williams, *Address to Special Convention of the PNM, 25 January 1981*

The Failure and Success of the PNM

There have been several crude quantitative assessments of government education policy between 1956 and 1986 in terms of funds expended, school buildings, school places or trained teachers; and of course the findings of various Working Parties set up by the government constituted a sort of self-assessment.[1] What there have been precious little of are systematic, sociological or educational evaluations of specific aspects of government policies. The few studies of this kind were conducted mostly by university students and staff undertaking research for higher degrees, or for scholarly publications; and such findings have not made any impact on education, on administrators, or on the general public.[2] In this chapter the procedure will be to make a crude assessment of government policies, followed by a review of the scholarly evaluative studies of the impact of education policies. However, the first step will be to examine some recent assessments of the entire PNM regime with a view to putting the achievements in education into some sort of perspective.

The death of Dr Williams in March 1981 triggered attempts to evaluate him as a man, a leader and an ideologue. The end of the long PNM regime of 30 years in 1986 called forth another round of scholarly assessments, this time of the entire PNM era, conveniently presented to the public as studies to mark the twenty-fifth anniversary (1962-1987) of the independence of the nation.[3] In 1988 Selwyn Ryan, the leading scholar of the modern politics of Trinidad and Tobago, concluded

An Assessment 1956-1986

that the most appropriate way to evaluate the PNM regime was to look at it first in relation to what it set out to do, then in relation to what it could reasonably have achieved, and lastly, if only implicitly, in comparison with other Third World countries. Ryan came to the conclusion that judged by their own overambitious objectives the PNM failed badly; judged by what was attained in the circumstances they had some reasonable success, and judged by what happened in most Third World countries the PNM achieved much.[4]

It seems possible to use Ryan's findings to suggest degrees of failure of various PNM policies in relation to their overambitious objectives. The most abject failure was in the objective of promoting and maintaining morality in public affairs. The 30 years in office were littered with corruption and financial scandals. A palpable failure also, second only, it appears, to the absence of morality in public life, was the inability of the government to create what it sometimes called 'national integration'. The extremely ambitious goal of consolidating the cultures of the Indians and the blacks into a national whole eluded the government. About midpoint in the spectrum of failures came the shortfalls in the attempts to industrialise the country and create jobs. In short the strategy of industrialisation by invitation disappointed, and so too did the extravagant and expensive thrust into heavy industries after the oil boom. So where did the PNM government have the least degree of failure? Undoubtedly Ryan points to the political objective of creating a "coherent system of party politics", and in promoting and maintaining democracy.[5] Party loyalty after 1956 meant more than before 1956.

Of special interest to a study of education are Ryan's conclusions about the failure involved in respect to the stated aim of creating "careers open to talent". In Trinidad this question is often assumed to be the same as "Did the Indians get as many jobs in the civil service as the blacks?" or (on a more refined level) "Did the Indians get a proportionate share of jobs in the civil service?" Ryan's own impressions are that blacks got jobs easier in the civil service and that racism was so strongly entrenched that, had the Indians been the chief recruiters for the civil service, they presumably would have recruited more Indians than blacks.

The apparent failure to ensure careers open to talent was curiously juxtaposed beside outstanding success in opening up secondary, post-secondary and university education to the lower class in shares to Indians and blacks which have not seriously been contested on the grounds of racial discrimination. One purpose of giving vastly increased number of Indians, blacks and others increased chances for post-primary education was to ensure equality of opportunity, the logical antecedent to careers open to talent. In discussing the work of the PNM regime in relation to what could be reasonably attained in the circumstances, Ryan gives full credit to their record in education, to the size of the quantitative achievement in terms of new schools and additional school places, noting that from necessity the quantitative achievement would militate against qualitative achievement, hopefully the next step forward.[6]

It followed that on the criteria of what could reasonably be achieved in the circumstances, the PNM's record in promoting party politics and democracy was of a high order if marred by some oppressive legislation and states of emergency. However on any criteria, their record in keeping corruption out of political life stood condemned. In relation to the promotion of the cultural life of the nation (in contradistinction to formal education) the PNM never promised much and delivered precious little. For years parts of the historical archives of the nation (presided over by the disgruntled archivist) were in rotting disarray on the ground floor underneath the Office of Dr Williams at Whitehall, without his doing anything to save the archives, and in the end a proper archives was not built. Even though Dr Williams was dead for six or seven years at the time of the preparation of the book *Trinidad and Tobago: The Independence Experience 1962-1987,* Ryan was still bold to call the most powerful resident intellectual in Trinidad and Tobago between 1948 and 1981 – Dr Eric Williams himself – "a philistine".[7]

This brings us the question of an assessment of the man himself, Dr Williams. While he was alive, his tremendous power over the PNM party machine and over the machinery of government made it unwise for residents, even scholars, to criticise him on grounds outside the limits of public policy. In Trinidad and Tobago even his historical writings in question elsewhere were protected by his political power. Anyone who lived in Trinidad and Tobago and talked politics on the verandah must have heard the view that the Doctor was strangely enigmatic. A great deal of such comments went in the direction of a belief that he had personality defects which adversely affected public affairs. The Doctor could go into long periods of silence on urgent public matters; he could disappear from public view for weeks; he could raise up favourites and then cast them down without explanations; he could be ambivalent, devious, inscrutable. He was only accountable to Parliament and the nation when he felt like giving an account. He struck fear into the hearts of some senior civil servants and even Cabinet colleagues and inhibited them from taking responsible initiatives. Here was a West Indian statesman, politician and scholar, a fit subject for a psychobiographical study, the only approach to which so far has been Ramesh Deosaran's attempt to uncover the secret source of his drive for power.[8] Williams was never a simple man. The mystery surrounding the imperial seclusion in which he died, or chose to die, has done nothing to improve his image as a complicated man.

The Achievements in Education

The achievements of the PNM government in the expansion of education between 1956 and 1981 were most impressive and the development of educational opportunity is probably the social gain of which that party is most proud.[9] The PNM would gladly acknowledge that of the three broad levels of education –

primary, secondary and post-secondary – it was at the secondary level that the biggest success was scored. Primary education for all, or virtually for all, was already established in the country by 1956; very high levels of university education was out of the question, and was never a social demand of the people or a goal of the politicians; it was therefore at the level of secondary education that the greatest aspirations of the majority peaked. Secondary education was the highest expectation of the greatest number. It was at this level that government's provision for, and planning of, education was most openly a response to social needs. The government gave the people what they wanted: large-scale access to secondary schools; after the revolution in oil prices and the decision to enter heavy industry, the expansion of secondary education took on, to a greater degree than before, the additional objective of providing the manpower requirements of the nation. But the flag of social demand waved over the spread of secondary education at all times; 'free' secondary education, declared in 1960, was a far more popular achievement than any reform of the secondary school curriculum in the direction of technical/vocational education.

Post-secondary education, taken here to mean university education, remained without protest education for a small minority. The PNM government enlarged that minority significantly by the development of UWI St Augustine and by its programme of scholarships for nationals at foreign universities; it was, however, unlikely that at any one time more than 3,000 nationals were studying at universities at home and abroad. The government's expansion of opportunities at this level ran ahead of popular political pressure for this type of education. University scholarships in certain fields went unused for lack of suitable candidates. At all times, on the other hand, the social demand for secondary education outstripped the provision of places, creating a bottleneck in the passage from primary to secondary schools. By removing children between the ages of 11 and 15 years from the primary school to the secondary school sector, the government at first made worse the problem of inadequate secondary school places which it then failed to solve, especially before 1976, up to the high level of aroused public expectation. On the other hand from the 1970s the government increasingly was able to meet the total demand for primary school places, redefined to cover only children between 6 and 11 years of age.

How impressive were the gains? In 1956 there were 15 recognised denominational and government secondary schools with 7,430 students; in 1969/1970 there were 27,627 students in such schools; and in 1981 the figures had risen to 86,831 students in secondary schools. The PNM politicians never ceased quoting such figures. Of course, a considerable number of students were in the dreaded double shift schools. The number of students passing annually from primary to secondary schools via the Common Entrance Examination grew by leaps and bounds: from 225 in 1956 (College Exhibitions) to 5,370 in 1969/1970, to 18,474 in 1976 and with a slight fall to 18,384 in 1981. By 1983 about 85 percent of the

11+ age group in primary schools were entering the junior secondary schools, and about 63 percent of the junior secondary population moved on to the senior secondary (comprehensive) schools. It was secondary education for the masses, a considerable achievement, but still short of the promised five years of free secondary education for all. The demand for secondary school places, especially in the prestige schools, was always greater than the supply, causing the Common Entrance Examination to remain a traumatic experience for many children. The construction of junior secondary schools and senior comprehensive schools enabled the government to provide more new secondary school places in the 1970s than in all the previous years of the twentieth century. These schools were enormous structures each capable of disgorging well over a thousand students into the streets at lunch time. The solidity of these buildings, with well planned work areas and improved teaching environment, expressed powerfully the importance of secondary education. In many districts the new junior secondary or senior secondary school was the most massive building in the neighbourhood.

In 1935 when expenditure on education was running at about 9 percent of revenues, Director of Education Captain Cutteridge decided that this level of expenditure was enough. In the 1920s expenditure had been in the order of 6 percent of revenues. Under the PNM regime expenditure on education, using another sort of measuring rod, increased steadily from being 2.6 percent of GDP and 14 percent of the budget in 1960 to 3.2 percent of GDP and 17.9 percent of the budget in 1970. The PNM government eventually got into the position where education was the single largest sector of recurrent expenditure, indeed nearly 6 percent of GDP by the early 1980s. After the oil bonanza of the 1970s the government put aside more money for selected areas of education than it could spend in the immediate future. Money was then no problem.[10]

To the extent that one can judge actual expenditure from the three Five-year Plans of 1958-1962, 1964-1968, and 1969-1973, one can observe that the rhythm of government expenditure on different types of education down to the edge of the oil revolution was quite different. In the late 1950s and early 1960s (First Five-year Plan 1958-1962), the emphasis was on building new government secondary schools, on teacher training and on technical education in the form of the John Donaldson Technical Institute. More money was also allocated to primary education than in each of the subsequent two Five-year Plans. It was a remarkable fact that the government expenditure on primary education declined substantially in the second half of the 1960s up to the start of the oil boom. Even expenditure on secondary education declined in the second half of the 1960s, not for lack of interest, but while the government decided on the model of secondary schools it was going to adopt. The decline in expenditure on primary and secondary education in the second half of the 1960s (Second Five-year Plan 1964-1968) was to the benefit of expenditure on university education, and on the scholarship programme to prepare professionals. This was the period of the early development of the St Augustine campus requiring increased capital and recurrent funding.

In the early 1970s (Third Five-year Plan 1969-1973), expenditure on secondary education outran mightily the funding of all other sectors of the education system as the very expensive junior secondary schools were established. After the oil boom started there was more money for everything, though the policy of external borrowing for capital expenditure was not completely abandoned. Expenditure on primary education came back heavily into the picture as the government began to rebuild many dilapidated school buildings. With such a programme in the context of the reduction of the primary school population, the government seemed to have brought under control the problems of the supply of primary school places, at least on the global level.

The government built three large teacher training colleges: Mausica Teachers' College, Corinth Teachers' College and Valsayn Teachers' College; and was able to raise the level of trained teachers from 49.2 percent (1965/1966) to 64.3 percent in 1975/1976, to nearly 92 percent in 1983. This commendable achievement however related only to the provision of primary school teachers; the most dynamic sector of the system, secondary schools, had an inadequate supply of teachers, although it drew recruits from all sectors of the education system. The supply of teachers qualified in practical, vocational or technical subjects remained woefully deficient and the government was very slow, remarkably so, in developing a training wing at the John Donaldson Technical Institute. It was quite an uphill struggle to achieve reasonable standards of work because the recruits had serious educational deficiences, and the programme was only part-time. So that the problem faced by the Ministry of Education was both quantitative and qualitative. In the early 1970s the government had to resort more than ever before to the recruitment of technical/vocational teachers, nationals and foreigners, from abroad; and a fair response was met from persons attracted by reasonably good salaries; but the problem of a ready supply of trained – or even untrained – technical/vocational teachers for certain crafts remained unsolved.

The Question of Equality of Opportunity

The expansion of education of all types was essential to the PNM goal of – or rather obsession with – equal opportunity for all in education. On one level considerable progress was made towards this goal by the massive increase of secondary school places. The distribution of boys and girls within secondary schools improved to the benefit of girls. Before 1956 the pattern was that boys had more school places in the public secondary schools and girls were better represented in private secondary schools. For example, in 1957 the split in the public secondary schools was 5,203 boys and 3,878 girls; by 1968/1969 the

27,435 students in public secondary schools were split evenly between boys and girls. The main reason for this change was the construction of coeducational secondary schools by the government in contrast to the churches' predilection for single sex secondary schools. The expansion of the public secondary school sector caused a decline in the number of children in the private school sector in the 1970s, possibly reducing what appeared to have been a preponderance of girls in that sector.

A most successful aspect of the government policy of equalizing educational opportunity was the spread of secondary schools to rural areas. The Christian churches had already started such a trend before the advent of the PNM; still in 1956, it was a fact that secondary school places were heavily concentrated in urban areas, meaning Port of Spain and San Fernando. In that year as many as 7,536 of the total of 10,639 secondary school places (70.8%) were in Port of Spain and San Fernando; in 1966/1967 this had been lowered to 14,773 out of 26,164 (56.4%); and it fell lower in the 1970s with the location of larger junior secondary and senior secondary comprehensive schools outside the two main towns. The churches also reversed the major direction of their pre 1956 policy: 50 percent of their new secondary schools between 1958 and 1970 were in the countryside. Even private secondary schools gravitated more than previously to the countryside.

High Failure Rates in Schools

Since the method of teaching, examination and certification remained the same as in the era when secondary education was for the few, the expansion of secondary education was accompanied by a new phenomenon – large failure rates in public secondary schools. For many failure and frustration, not success and self-esteem, began to be the predictable outcome of secondary schooling. By 1964 a remarkable drop in the achievement of students in public secondary schools judged by the convenient but inadequate measuring rod of the GCE O level and Cambridge School Certificate examination had occurred: in that year only 30.7 percent passed, whereas in 1956/1960 the average annual rate of success was 73.8 percent.[11] In 1966 the rate of success was only 26.5 percent. The crisis dragged down academic achievement at the once mighty QRC, and this college never fully recovered down to 1981.[12] Although there were particular subjects in which students from the new government secondary schools sometimes outscored students from the prestige denominational secondary schools and from QRC, the latter group of schools usually did better than the new government secondary schools. The new government secondary schools were staffed by a disproportionately high percentage of non-university teachers; and most important they had admitted a large number of children with a wider range of abilities and talents many of whom had serious deficiencies in literacy and numeracy. In the latter 1960s the pass rate for GCE O level examination in government and denominational secondary schools, especially the former, was decidedly worse than in 1966. The trend towards poor results in these colleges persisted in the 1970s, although the prestige schools recruited the best students from the primary schools.[13]

Another set of poor results faced the educators when the early batches of the junior secondary school graduates, having reached the senior comprehensive schools, took the GCE O level of Cambridge or London University, or later the CXC Ordinary level examination. From the late 1970s the majority of craft courses were examined by local examinations devised by the National Examinations Council. Nevertheless results in these local examinations were extremely poor, the failure rate for senior comprehensive students in 1980 being 91 percent.[14] This prompted some persons to suggest that students doing craft courses in senior comprehensive schools should not be judged at all by examination success, but by the general dissemination of skills useful in employment. Students who failed examinations might very well have benefited from participation in the programmes. Suggestions for the reform of examinations have usually gone in the direction of making them easier to pass.

Some of the public scrutiny which focused on poor examination results in the secondary schools was occasionally transferred to the primary schools; and there the verdict on quality was also unfavourable. It was observed that many pupils were leaving primary schools without being literate. No systematic evaluative studies were done on the causes for poor examination performance at the secondary level, or for illiteracy at the primary level. Illiteracy, however, was not a genuinely new trend for those who did not finish the primary school course. Where it applied to pupils who had reached the upper grades of the primary schools, it was something relatively new. The weaknesses in the enlarged secondary school population between the 1960s and 1981 represented the transference of some of the faults of the primary schools into the secondary school sector. The price for a rapid rate of secondary school expansion was poor examination results.

Education and Social Revolution

It is evident that the expansion of secondary education brought new opportunities for attendance at a public secondary school to children of working class parents. In a study in 1972 of the students of Form V and Form VI in all 45 public secondary schools (before the advent of junior secondary schools), Ambrose Dotting found that 59.8 percent of their fathers and 69.9 percent of their mothers had only primary school education or less than this attainment.[15] It was common knowledge in the island that a high proportion of secondary school students in the 1960s and the 1970s were first generation secondary school children. Other studies have shown clearly that the new government secondary schools of the early 1960s, and of course the junior secondary schools and the senior comprehensive schools of the 1970s, have drawn heavily on children of the Indian and black working class. It is inconceivable that any such result would have been found by a study of the public secondary schools in 1956. At that time secondary schools charged fees which, though unchanged for more than half a century, were still high enough to keep out working class children, except those on scholarships. Evidence of the rising access of working class people to secondary schools came from a study of Ishmael Baksh. He showed that in the early 1980s nearly half of the students in the grammar schools (or prestige schools) were of lower class origins.[16] Some of these students probably moved up later into prestigious and well paid professions, hence securing upward social mobility. By 1981 a wide cross-section of middle class occupations and jobs would have been fertilized by black and Indian secondary school graduates of working class origins.

Like so many governments in other countries Dr Williams and the PNM had great faith in the ability of expansion of education facilities to promote the highly desired equality of opportunity and social justice. As indicated earlier one goal was careers open to talent. But it has been shown by studies both in developed and Third World countries that such expansion might in fact contribute far less than expected to the elimination of inequality. Equalizing educational opportunity was a complex problem. First of all there were various kinds of equality of educational opportunity, classified by one researcher, Ishmael Baksh, as equality of access, equality of participation, equality of education results and equality of effects of education on life chances.[17] The vital question behind these categories were: did students of different socioeconomic groups (not to mention sexes) have equal access to schools, equal access to specific kinds of schools, equal rates of success in schools and equal chance of getting employment? The PNM government was consistently interested in only the first kind of equality, namely equality of access to secondary level education. The chosen instrument of equality of access was the Common Entrance Examination to determine academic merit which in turn determined access to secondary schools. Studies have indicated that children from higher socioeconomic groups performed better in this examination than children of lower socioeconomic groups, because of superior home environment and parental support, better teachers and schools, even perhaps the cultural bias of the examination. (Strange to say the question of superior performance in this examination by girls or boys hardly elicited any interest.) Superior performance in turn helped the higher socioeconomic groups (including many whites, Chinese and students of Syrian or Lebanese descent) to get into the prestige schools; also working in this direction was the fact of residential proximity – urban and suburban homes – to the prestige schools. The goal of equal access to secondary school, as in Jamaica, was flawed fundamentally by the absence of a single type of secondary school and by the wide gap in prestige between junior secondary schools and the grammar type schools, especially the prestige grammar schools founded before the advent of the PNM government.[18] That the PNM government succeeded in increasing the access of working class children to secondary schools was clear enough; equality of participation in different types of schools was more elusive. A disproportionately large number of children of lower class origins were distributed in the junior secondary schools, and a disproportionately large number of children from the higher socioeconomic groups could be found in the grammar schools.

After emancipation education became a factor in social stratification and by 1939 a significant educated middle class of non-whites existed. This process continued during and after World War II, and during the long regime of Dr Eric Williams and the PNM it accelerated to the point where some scholars now feel justified in speaking of a social revolution in the country which involved downward mobility for some whites and upward educational and social mobility for thousands of Indians, blacks and coloureds. The lingering influence of caste among the Indians and of race, colour and family tradition among the rest of the population seemed to have been swamped by a meritocracy. According to Selwyn Ryan,

> the old male white dominated social order has largely passed away . . . and in the new protean order which has replaced it, academic achievement and new wealth are the most important resources which generate and promote social mobility, and not the values ascribed to the aristocracy of the skin . . .

Another researcher, Rhoda Reddock, has recently shown that although substantial sectors of the population experienced no social mobility between 1960 and 1980 and Indian and black women experienced lower rates of social mobility than their male counterparts, the most significant overall pattern for Indians, blacks and coloureds (and Chinese) is that of pronounced educational mobility. Women, including Indian women whose education had been so neglected in the early twentieth century, have been substantial beneficiaries of social and educational mobility. This must surely rank among the great contributions of Dr Williams and his party to the building of contemporary Trinidad and Tobago.[19]

It must be said at once that scholarly assessment of the inadequacies of the education system to secure equality of participation in various types of schools did not dampen public confidence in, and support for, the education system. The fact that the system often shunted students to secondary schools which matched their social class origins was not an area of great public concern. As long as the distribution to secondary schools was made through a competitive examination and not by ascriptive factors of race or colour, it looked like a fair system. There was no important body of opinion critical of the impact of education policies on social structure. Indeed the very opposite was the case: what was perceived was the favourable effect of education policies upon the life chances of thousands of working class children.[20] It followed (leaving aside the prickly question of transfers after the initial placements) that for the most part the public and the government thought that students were sent to the secondary schools they deserved; and although many Indians felt that adult Indians were victims of the PNM myth of careers open to talent, the analysis of Indian disadvantage in employment was not apparently extended backwards to the younger generation of Indians in the secondary schools of the 1970s.

Race, Social Integration and Technical/Vocational Education

What can be said about racial integration? No reliable evaluative studies have been done. To the extent that under the PNM regime government secondary schools became the biggest sector of the secondary school provision, accepting students of all races and religions, these schools could reasonably be presumed to have made a contribution to social harmony among students, particularly between blacks and Indians. Racial mixing also had ample opportunity in denominational secondary schools attended by all the racial varieties in the country. On the other hand, Hindu and Muslim schools still taught almost no one but Indians. There might have been some government schools which from their location were dominated numerically by Indian students; others by black students. The system of schools buses was designed simply to get children to school, not to promote racial integration. The schools had to operate in an environment which exerted considerable countervailing non-integrative influences at least as powerful as the integrative tendencies of many schools. There seems today no easy answer to the question of the effects of schools on social integration. If race relations between blacks and Indians were better in 1981 than in the early 1960s – and some scholars think they were [21] – perhaps the role of the schools should not be overlooked among the factors contributing to this happy outcome. But it was still possible for an Indian scholar, completely forgetting the schools, to assert in 1992 that the "PNM for the first 24 years after independence, did little to build bridges of cooperation between Indians and Creoles".[22]

It is a matter of regret that there was a paucity of evaluative studies of the technical/vocational input into education since 1972. An exception were two studies by Theodore Lewis of some graduates of the senior comprehensive schools. Lewis concluded that the technical/vocational graduates were doing better on the job market than their non-vocational schoolmates.[23] This was not surprising, since the needs of the construction industry still ran ahead of the supply of trained craftsmen and technicians. In the absence of sufficient studies government officials and the public tended to confuse intention with results. It would be interesting to ascertain from systematic evaluative studies to what extent technical/vocational education was by 1986 more popular with students and parents than in 1972; if employers were more satisfied with recruits into industry than in 1972. And of course there was the enormously complex question whether technical/vocational education contributed in any significant way to increased productivity or economic development from 1972 to 1986. To date these questions have to be answered tentatively by guesswork, and by unsystematic feedback from persons close to technical/vocational education. It is obvious that the technical/vocational thrust was the cause of serious misgivings; yet faith in its capability to contribute to the lowering of unemployment and the development of the economy always remained high. Neither the government nor educators in general were worried by the cautious, indeed sceptical assessment in the international literature of the transforming potential of technical/vocational education. Fortunately for the country the technical/vocational input was first seriously made during the oil boom when unemployment was substantially reduced. At any other time before the 1970s – or indeed since the end of the oil boom – the industrial environment would have been less auspicious to such a large dose of technical/vocational education. The fact that technical or vocational education does not create jobs – which the society is learning in the post-oil boom era – might have been missed in the 1970s because the technical/vocational input and the new jobs came at the same time. Although the education system impacted positively on social structure, it is not so clear that it had a similar effect on industry or on national development in general.[24]

There is also the question of wider changes in the political and social values of the country needed to maximise the effectiveness of technical/vocational education. For technical/vocational education to contribute significantly it needs to be supplemented meaningfully by structural changes in the political economy of a country; for example, minimum structural changes should include income redistribution to attract graduates into agricultural or craft employment; changes in methods of hiring to ensure that graduates of technical/vocational schools are employed in preference to other persons; changes in attitudes to work in order to banish the stigma attached to some forms of manual labour, as well as improvement in working conditions in industries.[25] A whole culture involving changed attitudes towards hard work has to be created and new discipline inculcated. In Third World countries with restricted resources and a legacy of neocolonialism, the ideal structural changes to maximise the effectiveness of technical/vocational education move in a direction away from the democratic pluralist state towards an authoritarian state. Dr Williams and the PNM chose not to limit greatly personal freedoms in order to foster national economic goals.

The success of technical/vocational education also demanded a rethinking of the nature of education, the methods of teaching and the methods of assessment. The ideas of the public on these matters were set by long experience with academic education in secondary grammar schools. Technical/vocational education was an innovation which had to fight against the entrenched values and methods of traditional education, supported by powerful elites who were not – even those who functioned in the modern sectors of the economy – the prime advocates of the vocationalisation of the curriculum of secondary schools. Business firms preferred in-firm training of their own craftsmen and technicians, or training in technical institutes. More than ten years were needed for technical/vocational education in secondary schools to legitimate itself as valid education; but the process could have gone further if there were parallel facilitative innovations in the political economy and value system of the country.

Education and Decolonisation

Dr Eric Williams insisted that he inherited a colonial system of education; in the course of the long PNM regime almost everything that was undesirable or wrong about education was said to be of a colonial nature. It becomes then a point of interest to attempt to discover how far the PNM government could be said to have decolonised the education system. One way to proceed is to identify the features of the system that were repeatedly decried as colonial. These included excessive clerical control entrenched in the dual system; inequality of access to secondary schools to the benefit of privileged groups presumed to be mostly whites or near whites; the hiatus between primary and secondary education and consequently discrimination against primary school teachers; the lack of integration in the teaching service; the academic/classical content of education; the absence of a technical/vocational bias; the dependence on external examination and under-expenditure by government on education. There were other allegations about the colonial nature of education; but these were less serious. For example, it was sometimes said that the excessive urban location of secondary schools before 1956 was a legacy of colonialism.

The PNM government reversed significantly every one of these colonial features, but without eliminating any completely except underexpenditure on education. The government and teachers also went very far in many subject areas in West Indianising what was taught. Not much progress was made in the elimination of external examinations for traditional or academic subjects; the historic and unrelenting rejection of City and Guilds of London examinations in respect of technical/vocational subjects was not followed immediately by similar nationalistic action in respect to other subjects. Also a vital test of decolonisation was the fact that the churches were still a powerful influence in the education system. On the criteria of the overambitious PNM government itself, one would have to credit it with only a partial or incomplete decolonisation of education. This accords with the general incomplete state of decolonisation in other components of the political economy of the nation. The economy was incompletely decolonised; so too the political structures despite the advance to a republican constitution. It has been suggested that in small West Indian nations with inadequate resources and no will to stage revolutionary breaks with the past, partial or incomplete decolonisation is likely to be permanent.[26]

An Assessment 1956-1986

By adopting other, though vaguer criteria about the nature of colonialism in education, it is possible to make a more severe indictment of the decolonisation process in Trinidad and Tobago. But first, let us acknowledge that Dr Williams, as historian, scholar and political leader who never forgot the baneful effects of the plantation system and slavery, did possess in his intellectual armoury a more comprehensive understanding of colonialism than was reflected officially by the party or the government. Although Dr Williams in the later 1960s abated his early rhetoric against the agents of colonialism, his response on the level of thought (for instance, in the Chaguaramas Declaration and Perspectives for the New Society) to the Black Power movement indicated that he still understood the pervasiveness of colonialism as a system of ideas against which the youths were in rebellion.[27] It seemed true, however, that Williams at all times saw more clearly as the object for action the adverse institutional outcomes of colonialism rather than its adverse psychological outcomes. Hence his or the government's agenda for the decolonisation of education did not really face the actual challenge of building a decolonised mentality in the youths, except in so far as the West Indianisation of the curriculum was invoked, more than promoted. In particular, the mandatory teaching of West Indian history was at best an overrated anti-colonial purgative. To aim publicly and openly at reshaping of the consciousness of youths beyond the respectable ideal of racial tolerance, and showing loyalty to the flag and nation was to transgress the limits of democratic freedom to which Williams was absolutely pledged.

To argue then for education policies that would consciously promote revolutionary decolonisation was to ask for more than Dr Williams and the PNM could deliver within the confines of the political economy they chose to promote. Radical critics of the decolonisation process in education (or generally) who would prefer to see not just attempted reversals of colonial institutions, but drastically different systems or forms of alternative education – however vaguely conceived – must necessarily be highly disappointed with the PNM regime.[28] In Caribbean countries such as Trinidad and Tobago effective revolutionary decolonisation along these lines could hardly stop short of the birth of the socialist state which the PNM always rejected.

[13]

Epilogue
1981-1986

> In Trinidad and Tobago there now exists the basic infrastructure for the provision of a relatively comprehensive formal system of education which encompasses the primary to the tertiary level.
>
> *The Imperatives of Adjustment. Draft Development Plan 1983-1986, p. 116*

The Imperatives of Adjustment

Here we will consider briefly a few significant developments in education between the death of Dr Eric Williams in March 1981 and the spectacular defeat of the PNM regime in 1986. Although the country was still prosperous in 1981, the economists knew that trouble was immediately ahead in view of falling oil prices coupled with a decline in crude oil production. In the last term of the PNM in office (1981-1986), it could be said that in respect to education, the emphasis was to resist expansion. The operation of state-owned heavy petrochemical industrial plants consumed millions of dollars of government revenues and there was increasingly less money to finance other schemes. Money had in fact become a problem again.

The government felt rightly that a comprehensive system of education already existed with free provision for about 80 percent of those who qualified for secondary education. Since 1956 greater opportunities for education, apparently endless education, had been the good fortune of the country. There was clearly no very urgent case for continued expansion of the education system at the primary or secondary levels though some primary school buildings were in very poor condition. It was sometimes said by officials that the goal of free education for 100 percent of those who qualified for secondary school should be reached by 1985 and that several new primary schools were needed in new housing districts.[1] But these needs did not constitute a very urgent case for expansion if government

Epilogue 1981-1986

revenues were under great pressure. A task force, chaired by William Demas, the most respected economist in the country, was asked to prepare a medium term economic programme for the country. This was published under the title *The Imperatives of Adjustment. Draft Development Plan 1983-1986*. The country was trying to find its way back to integrated economic planning after its abandonment in the oil boom years. This Demas report said clearly that there was no alternative to reduced government expenditure and to a lowering of the standard of living. This report envisaged new capital expenditure on a few secondary schools and 20 new primary schools; but these buildings could only be financed by loans, and since they were not seen as investment which could expand the productive base of the country, they were assigned such a low priority that the clear intention was that they were not to be attempted. However the report stopped short of recommending reduction of expenditure on education, although the advice that wages in the public sector should be frozen was a warning to teachers.[2] The level of expenditure on education in the first half of the 1980s was apparently left static.

The year 1983 marked the official end of the period covered by the previous Education Plan (1968-1983). There was no great sense of urgency to make another education plan, understandably since planning presupposes new expenditure. What followed as planning was on a totally less meticulous scale than in the Education Plan of 1968-1983. When the new Education Plan (called the Successor Education Plan 1985-1990) was unveiled and discussed, it also (like the Imperatives of Adjustment) envisaged new capital expenditure on secondary and primary schools and did not speak to the need for any sort of reduction. However figures relating to how much anything would cost were tucked away uninvitingly (as if not meant to be read) at the very end of the plan, and the main emphasis was declared to be not expansion, but the improvement of the quality of education. Hence a great deal of attention was paid to training and evaluation.[3]

The Concern for Quality

The education authorities and the government seemed convinced that the curriculum revolution had solved the problem of relevance in education, and that with expansion at a level justifying self-congratulation the only deficits were in relating to quality. (Ten years later nobody was so sure that relevance was not a problem.) Thinking in the country among educators was turning in the direction of the deficit in quality in the late 1970s. A concern for quality was already apparent in the three reports of the Teacher Education Committee (1979-1980) chaired by Dr C. V. Gocking. The main burden of these reports was the need for the training of all teachers, even those in peripheral sectors of the education system, and for the periodic retraining of those in mainstream educational institutions.[4] This concern for quality was carried forward after 1981 and could be seen for example in the acceptance of the recommendation of the Examination Review Committee that general science and social studies should be incorporated into the Common Entrance Examination.

Another example of concern for quality might be observed in relation to the teaching of specialised crafts in the senior comprehensive schools. There was a low-keyed debate between the 'generalists' and the 'specialists', between those who favoured only a general pre-technical orientation in the senior comprehensive schools to be followed by on-the-job training and those who preferred specialised vocational training inside these schools plus on-the-job training. The debate was not about the effectiveness of specialised vocational training inside schools to foster economic development, but over the alleged unpreparedness of youths for specialised craft training at age 14+. In 1984 Professor Max Richards of the Faculty of Engineering, UWI, chaired a Working Party investigating this matter. It recommended that general technical/vocational education be given to the age group 14+ in senior comprehensive schools, and that specialised craft training be postponed until after age 16+ (Form V).[5] This was the direction of the St Clair King Committee of May 1982: it recommended the continuation of specialised craft courses, but wanted them revised to reflect general technical training.

There were two other matters which might usefully be mentioned in this epilogue. The question of the 'national norm' for secondary schools, in other words the two-tier secondary school system, received some attention, but the direction of thinking showed some falling away from the former determination to have a single system so evident in the conclusions of previous Working Parties. For example, in 1982 the St Clair King Committee was set up and asked to consider converting junior secondary schools and senior secondary schools into full-time five-year schools. This amounted to an inquiry whether government secondary schools should use the same organisational model as the denominational secondary schools. The committee saw positive advantages in having, not any one norm, but a diversity of school types as actually existed. This was said to make for a dynamic school system. If a norm was needed at all, it should be the division of the secondary school life into two basic cycles (not schools), in other words into cycle one (Forms I-III) and cycle two (Forms IV-V), with the two-tier curriculum then existing in the junior secondary and senior comprehensive schools. Such a recommendation in favour of diversity of schools, or the use of the five-year secondary school model of the churches, was basically contradictory to long established PNM policy.

Another example of thinking on the problems of organizing the education system which might have displeased Dr Williams, if he was alive, came from a committee appointed by government to look further into "national ownership and joint management of schools". This committee under the chairmanship of the Tobagonian Victor Bruce reported in May 1981. It had no clerics on it, yet some of its recommendations and its tone generally bore testimony to the influence of the churches' views on education. The committee favoured the argument that increased government subsidies to church schools under joint management arrangements did not necessitate government ownership of the school buildings so aided, or so managed. It saw no need to express "national ownership" in this way. It saw no need to change the name of a school under joint management to reflect the increased government financial input.[6] Together with the recommendation after "arduous discussion" of the St Clair King Committee for a multi-type secondary school system which would allow churches to continue their five-year (and seven-year) schools, the recommendations of the Victor Bruce Committee constituted significant rethinking in a direction contrary to standard PNM policy in education. In fact on several matters relating to the structure and spirit of the education system as set up in the era of Eric Williams, there were reversals and modifications in the 1980s and early 1990s.[7]

And there was Tobago. Relations between the Tobago House of Assembly and the Trinidad government did not improve in the last term of the PNM The chief bone of contention related to interpretation and implementation of the Tobago House of Assembly Act, particularly the size and timing of the transfer of funds from the central (Trinidad) government to the Tobago House of Assembly. Mr A. N. R. Robinson, then chairman of the Tobago House of Assembly, described that Assembly as a form of Crown Colony government and in 1982 used his majority in it to threaten the central government with secession unless it offered "terms and conditions acceptable to the authorised representatives of the people of Tobago".[8] Robinson and his controlling party in the Tobago House of Assembly drew up a Tobago Development Plan 1981-1990 in which important changes in education were sketched. These would require nothing less than the complete control of education in Tobago by the Tobago House of Assembly. Although the plan frowned on "massive structures" and "ultra-modern equipment", the most expensive part of it would be the establishment of the superior layer of post-secondary schools which Tobago had always lacked: a teachers' college, a technical college, and finally what looked like a degree-granting institution, namely a College of Arts, Science and Technology, possibly in association with UWI. The plan also called for changes in the curriculum of the secondary and primary schools mostly in the direction of technical/vocational education of a type thought most relevant to Tobago: fishing, boat building and tourism. A very extensive programme for the insertion of Tobago's folklore into the schools was envisaged.[9] Hardly any part of the education programme seemed capable of realisation without a drastic improvement in the relations between the Tobago House of Assembly and the central government. This could have been done first of all by new legislation, but essentially the problem was a political one between an opposition party entrenched in Tobago and in the Tobago House of Assembly and on the other hand the PNM government in Trinidad under great economic pressure.[10]

Appendix

THE CONCORDAT

The Minister of Education and Culture wishes to clarify, for general information, some of the proposals on Education with reference to the reorganisation of Education so far as these proposals affect the Denominational Boards of Management, the Governing Bodies and Principals of Assisted Secondary Schools.

1. In relation to property, the ownership and right of direct control and management of all denominational primary and secondary schools will be assured to the Denominations in whatever modifications of the existing system that may subsequently be introduced in the new Education Ordinance, and all existing rights, so far as property is concerned, will be respected.

2. In denominational schools no books or apparatus, to which the denominational authority formally objects, will be introduced or imposed.

3. In denominational schools (unless the Denomination concerned otherwise gives its consent) the religion of the particular Denomination which owns the school will be taught exclusively and by teachers professing to belong to that Denomination. In Government schools all recognised religious Denominations will have access through their accredited representatives during the times specified in the time-table for the teaching of Religion to the pupils belonging to their faith.

   Pupils attending the schools of a Denomination not of their own faith will not be compelled to take part in the religious exercises or lessons of that Denomination.

4. The right of appointment, retention, promotion, transfer and dismissal of teachers in primary schools will rest with the Public Service Commission.
   A teacher shall not be appointed to a school if the denominational Board objects to such an appointment on moral or religious grounds. Similarly, if a teacher be found unsatisfactory on these very grounds, moral or religious, the denominational authority shall have the right to request his removal to another school after due investigation. For these reasons it is proposed (provided the legal and constitutional arrangements allow) that vacancies as they occur in all schools should be advertised and applications submitted in the first instance to the respective Board of Management which will examine them and forward them all, with their recommendations, to the Public Service Commission for final action.

Appendix

Secondary Schools

5. The existing relationship between Government and the Governing Bodies and teachers in Assisted Secondary Schools will remain, subject however to negotiated change inevitable with the introduction of free secondary education and to a system of inspection of these schools by persons authorised to do so by the Ministry of Education and Culture. The Governing Bodies of these schools will continue to be responsible for the administration of these schools and for their maintenance, repair and furnishing. These schools will continue to qualify for Government aid.

    The Principals of Assisted Schools will make available a minimum of 80 per centum of the first form entry places to those who, by passing the test, qualify on the results of the Common Entrance Examination for free secondary education. The Principals will be represented on the panel of examiners to be set up to administer the test.

    The Principals will be free to allocate up to 20 per centum of the remaining places, as they see fit, provided that the pass list of the Common Entrance Examination serve to provide the pupils.

    Entry above the first form will be under the control of the Ministry of Education and Culture and will require the approval of the Minister.

6. Where the need arises for disciplinary reasons or unsatisfactory progress to remove a pupil from the school, the right to request such removal will remain with the Principal who may for the same reason suspend a pupil pending investigation. Authority to expel a student is vested solely in the Cabinet. For disciplinary reasons the same principle will apply to Primary Schools.

7. All new Central schools may be established only by government for the simple reason that these schools are to be fed from the primary schools of all Denominations as well as Government schools which may be in the area served by the Central school. When however the need arises for converting an existing denominational school into a secondary school, the denominational character of that school will be allowed to remain.

8. The selection of teachers for training at the Teachers' College is to remain solely with the Ministry of Education and Culture. Selection of teachers for training in the existing denominational training colleges may be made by the Denominational Boards, but such selection must be approved by the Ministry of Education and Culture.

9. It is the desire of the Government that all teachers be trained at the Teachers' College under Government supervision and administration. Government will however respect the rights of the existing training colleges conducted by the Denominations; but no expansion of these facilities will be allowed without the expressed permission of Government.

Signed by Hon. J. S. Donaldson
Minister of Education and Culture
on behalf of Cabinet on 22 December 1960 and published on 25 December 1960

Notes

Chapter 1

1. *Centenary Record of the Sisters of St Joseph of Cluny 1836-1936* (Trinidad, 1936), pp. 31-37.
2. C. Campbell, "The transition from Spanish law to English law in Trinidad before and after emancipation", *Some Papers on Social, Political and Economic Adjustments to the Ending of Slavery in the Caribbean* (Barbados, 1976), pp. 25-52.
3. The Shouter Baptists had no schools; and the mission stations sponsored by the Baptist Missionary Society from 1843 to about 1892 hardly had any schools. See Eudora Thomas, *A History of the Shouter Baptists in Trinidad and Tobago* (Ithaca, 1987); J. Hackshaw, *The Baptist Denomination* (1992), pp. 54-58.
4. C. Campbell, "Education and black consciousness: the amazing career of Captain J. Cutteridge in Trinidad 1921-1942", *Journal of Caribbean History* 18 (1984): 35-66.
5. C. Campbell, "The establishment of Queen's Collegiate School in Trinidad 1857-1867", *Caribbean Journal of Education* 2, no. 2 (Dec. 1975): 71-86.
6. C. Campbell, "The dual mandate of the Imperial College of Tropical Agriculture 1922-1960", *Jamaican Historical Review* 16 (1988): 1-16.
7. C. Campbell, "New perspectives on secondary education in Trinidad and Tobago 1926-1935", in *Education in the Caribbean: Historical Perspectives*, edited by Ruby King (UWI, 1988), pp. 145-62.
8. C. Campbell, "The College Exhibition in Trinidad and Tobago 1870-1938", *History Teachers Journal*, no. 2 (March 1983): 42-53.
9. C. Campbell, "Charles Warner and the development of education in Trinidad 1838-1870", *Journal of Caribbean History* 10 and 11 (1978): 54-81.
10. See J. Houk, "The Orisha religion in Trinidad: a study of culture process and transformation" (PhD diss., Tulane University, 1992).
11. This paragraph has benefited from the seminal analysis in M. Archer, *The Sociology of Educational Expansion: Take-off, Growth and Inflation in Educational Systems* (London, 1982).
12. H. Johnson, "Crown Colony government in Trinidad" (DPhil diss., University of Oxford, 1969), pp. 365; 403-5.
13. C. L. R. James, *Life of Captain Cipriani: an Account of British Government in the West Indies* (Lancashire, 1932), p. 45; also A. Hamel-Smith, "Education and the East Indians in Trinidad 1900-1938" (Postgraduate seminar paper, UWI, 1979), pp. 17-23.
14. See D. Ramsaran, *Breaking the Bonds of Indentureship: Indo-Trinidadians in Business* (St Augustine, 1993).
15. Catholic News (hereafter quoted as CN), 7 Aug. 1920, Editorial.
16. L. Braithwaite, "Social stratification in Trinidad", *Social and Economic Studies* 3, nos. 2 and 3 (Oct. 1953): 97-98.
17. For recent attempts to explain the relative success of blacks and Indians in business, see S. Ryan and L. A. Barclay, *Sharks and Sardines: Blacks in Business in Trinidad and Tobago* (St Augustine, 1992), and D. Ramsaran, *Breaking the Bonds*, op. cit.
18. See T. Millett, *The Chinese in Trinidad* (Port of Spain, 1993), pp. 37-59.
19. C. Campbell, *Cedulants and Capitulants: the Politics of the Coloured Opposition in the Slave Society of Trinidad*

Notes to Chapter 2

1783-1838 (Port of Spain, 1992), chap. 1.

20. For the career of one such scholar, see S. Ryan, *The Pursuit of Honour: the Life and Times of H. O. B. Wooding* (St Augustine, 1990).
21. A leading scholar who supports changes in the post-emancipation period is B. Brereton. See "Social organisation, and class, racial and cultural conflicts in 19th century Trinidad", in *Trinidad Ethnicity*, edited by K. Yelvington (London, 1993), pp. 33-55. The social scientists are less likely to perceive any important change: see Ralph Henry, "Notes on the evolution of inequality in Trinidad and Tobago", in Yelvington, *Trinidad Ethnicity*, op. cit., p. 64.
22. Lloyd Braithwaite, "Social stratification", op. cit., pp. 46-48; 57; 122-26.
23. Y. Malik, *East Indians in Trinidad: a Study of Minority Politics* (Oxford, 1971), pp. 17-18; *Trinidad and Tobago: the Independence Experience 1962-1987*, edited by S. Ryan (St Augustine, 1988), p. 217.
24. C. Campbell, "Education and black consciousness", op. cit.
25. V. Judges, "Recent trends in English education", *International Review of Education* 1 (1955): 264-65.
26. R. H. E. Braithwaite, *Moral and Social Education* (Port of Spain, 1991), pp. 10-21.
27. C. E. Beeby, *The Quality of Education in Developing Countries* (Cambridge, Mass., 1966).
28. G. Guthrie, "Stages of educational development? Beeby revisited", *International Review of Education* 26, no. 4 (1980): 411-35; also C. Beeby, "The thesis of the stages fourteen years later", *International Review of Education* 26, no. 4 (1980): 451-72.
29. For the words of this memorable calypso, see *Voiceprint: an Anthology of Oral and Related Poetry from the Caribbean*, edited by S. Brown, M. Morris and G. Rohlehr (London, 1989), pp. 129-30.

Chapter 2

1. Report of the West Indies Royal Commission 1945 (Moyne Report).
2. T. S. Simey, *Welfare and Planning in the West Indies* (Oxford, 1946), p. 165.
3. S. A. Hammond, *Education in St Vincent* (Kingstown, 1943)
4. Apart from contributing to the education section of the Reports of the Comptroller of Welfare and Development, Hammond wrote the following pamphlets: *The Cost of Education* (Bridgetown, 1943); *Education in St Vincent* (Kingstown, 1943); *Education in Grenada* (St George's, 1943); *St Lucia: Memorandum on Education* (Castries, 1943); *Education in Dominica* (Bridgetown, 1944); *Education in Jamaica* (Kingston, 1944); *The Development of Secondary Education in Grenada* (St George's, 1946).
5. For some of the struggles, see S. Craig, *Community Development in Trinidad and Tobago 1943-1973: from Welfare to Patronage*, ISER Working Paper, no. 4 (St Augustine, 1974).
6. For these activities, see Annual Reports of the Colony of Trinidad and Tobago 1946-1954.
7. Much of this dispute can be seen in CO 318/467, for instance, Roman Catholic Archbishop to Acting Governor Wright, 22 June 1944; Roman Catholic Archbishop to Robert Patrick, 5 Nov. 1943, and comments by Colonial Office officials.
8. CO 295/630, Governor Bede Clifford to Oliver Stanley, 9 Dec. 1943; also 295/630, Telegram from Bede Clifford to British government, 7 April 1945.
9. For example, see CP 27 of 1946, Educational Policy and Development Programme.
10. For figures, see Appendices of Reports of Directors of Education for 1946-1949.
11. H. Ramsing, "The historical development of Muslim schools in Trinidad and Tobago" (Caribbean Study thesis, UWI St Augustine, 1969); also R. Mohammed, "The socioeconomic fac-

Notes to Chapter 2

tors responsible for the emergence of Islamic schools in Trinidad" (Caribbean Study thesis, UWI St Augustine, n.d.).

12. S. Ryan, *Race and Nationalism in Trinidad and Tobago: a Study of Decolonisation in a Multiracial Society* (St Augustine, 1974), p. 147; also *Trinidad Guardian* (hereafter quoted as TG), 1 and 18 April 1954, articles by Bhadase Maraj praising Joseph.
13. R. Bissoon, "The growth of the Sanatan Dharma Maha Sabha of Trinidad and Tobago Incorporated" (Caribbean Study thesis, UWI St Augustine, 1980), p. 19.
14. *Port of Spain Gazette* (hereafter quoted as POSG), 1 Feb. 1955, Lecture by Eric Williams.
15. POSG, 6 Sept. 1952.
16. *Observer*, April 1943; *Trinidad Presbyterian*, June and August 1946.
17. POSG, 19 July 1952.
18. Unclassified documents, RVI, List of persons to sit examinations, 1949; also Unclassified documents, RVI, Return of registered apprentices, June 1959.
19. By 1948 motor mechanics formed the largest single category of apprentices (109 of total of 442): see Unclassified documents, RVI, Minutes of BIT, 1948. See also C. Dyer, *History of Industrial Education and Training in Trinidad and Tobago* (Trinidad, 1994), pp. 214-26.
20. C. Dyer, *History of Industrial Education*, op. cit., pp. 214-26, and passim.
21. Unclassified documents, RVI, Minutes of BIT, 25 April 1951.
22. The Petroleum Association of Trinidad estimated that it could use 30 to 40 university-level recruits each year; see Report of the West Indies Committee of the Commission on Higher Education in the Colonies (1945) (Irvine Committee), Evidence of Petroleum Association 1944, UWI files.
23. Education in Trinidad and Tobago: Report of the Working Party, 1954 (The Missen Report), p. 28.
24. The Missen Report, p. 43.
25. The Missen Report, pp. 92-95.
26. The Missen Report, p. 93.
27. C. Stephens, "St George's College 1953-1987: a historical perspective" (DipEd thesis, UWI St Augustine, 1987).
28. Administrative Report of the Director of Education for 1945 (Trinidad, 1947), p. 3.
29. For an aborted Chinese private school in Port of Spain in 1943, see Carlton Chinapoo, "Chinese immigration into Trinidad 1900-1950" (MA thesis, UWI, 1988), pp. 92-93.
30. H. R. D'Aeth, *Secondary Schools in the British Caribbean* (London, 1956), p. 114; also Report of Committee on Grants-in-Aid to Assisted Secondary Schools, 1956 (Trinidad, 1957).
31. N. Thut, "Economic, social and administrative difficulties in expanding education", in *World Year Book of Education 1965*, edited by G. Bereday (London, 1965), pp. 98-111. Also see Nicholas Hans, "Meeting the demand in advanced and developing countries", in the same *Yearbook*, pp. 126-37.
32. J. M. Lee and Martin Petter, *The Colonial Office, War and Development Policy: Organisation and the Planning of a Metropolitan Initiative 1939-1945* (London, 1982), chap. 1; also John Flint, "The failure of planned decolonisation in British Africa", *Africa Affairs* 82, no. 328 (July 1983): 389-411.
33. H. Grimal, *Decolonisation: the British, French, Dutch and Belgian Empires 1919-1963* (London, 1965), pp. 133-57; 214-27; 287-321.
34. H. Johnson, "The West Indies and the conversion of the British official classes to the development idea", *Journal of Commonwealth and Comparative Politics* 15, no. 1 (March 1977): 55-83.
35. Trinidad and Tobago Five-year Economic Programme, vol. II (1950-1955), Appendix II.
36. Hansard Legislative Council Debates, 25 May 1956, speech of the Financial Secretary. In another source the number of school places was said to be 42,000. Perhaps this figure includes

new Hindu and Muslim schools for which the government was not primarily responsible. See Digest of Statistics on Education 1950-1956, Table 11, p. 3 (Central Statistical Office, Government of Trinidad and Tobago).
37. Annual Report of the Director of Education 1947 (Trinidad, 1948), pp. 21-23.
38. O. Mathurin, Review of Gomes' autobiography (Through a Maze of Colour) in Caribbean Studies 14, no. 4 (Jan. 1975): 73-81. For a social history of the Portuguese in Trinidad, see Jo-Anne Ferreira, The Portuguese of Trinidad and Tobago: Portrait of an Ethnic Minority (St Augustine, 1994).
39. Hansard Legislative Council Debates, 14 Jan. 1949; 21 Jan. 1949, speeches of Albert Gomes and others; also 8. C. Campbell, "The College Exhibition in Trinidad and Tobago 1870-1938", History Teachers Journal, no. 2 (March 1983): 42-53
40. The Missen Report, p. 74.
41. CO 318/467, Memorandum from Roman Catholic Archbishop of Port of Spain to Acting Governor Wright, 7 June 1944; also Roman Catholic Archbishop of Port of Spain to Director Patrick, 5 Nov. 1943.
42. M. Archer, "History of Bishop's High School, Tobago 1925-1981" (mimeograph, n.d.), p. 15.
43. See C. Campbell, The Young Colonials: a Social History of Education in Trinidad and Tobago 1834-1939 (Kingston, 1996).
44. D. Niddrie, Land Use and Population in Tobago: an Environmental Study (London, 1961), p. 47.
45. See R. Pemberton, "Towards a reevaluation of the contribution of the West Indian peasantry: a case study of Tobago 1900-1949 (MA thesis, UWI, 1984).
46. M. Archer, "History of Bishop's High School", op. cit., p. 5.
47. Hansard Legislative Council Debates, 17 Jan. 1947; 30 April 1948; 31 July 1950, speeches of James.
48. Hansard Legislative Council Debates, 2 Feb., 1951; 2 March 1951; 9 Dec. 1952; 6 Dec. 1954, speeches of James. If James had any role in the reopening and government take-over of the Black Rock Moravian school it was not apparent from his speeches in Parliament. See Norrel London, "Policy and practice in education in the British West Indies during the late colonial period" History of Education 24, no. 1 (1995): 91-104.
49. There were several letters to the press over these incidents, but it appears that there were delicate aspects not made public. See TG, 8 Jan. 1960, article by 'Interested'; also TG, 1 Aug. 1960, letter from H. A. McNish.
50. Unclassified documents, RVI, Minutes of BIT. S. Granger to BIT (Port of Spain, 9 Oct. 1947), on behalf of the Tobago Peasants and Industrial Workers Union (Roxborough).
51. POSG, 28 July 1955, letter from 'Peter and Paul'(Scarborough) to editor.

Chapter 3

1. Hansard Legislative Council Debates, 4 Nov. 1949, see Table.
2. Report of the West Indies Committee of the Commission on Higher Education in the Colonies (1945) (The Irvine Committee), Evidence of R. S. Jordan, 1944. UWI files.
3. Commission on Higher Education, op. cit., Note on colonial students in the United Kingdom by J. L. Keith, 11 Dec. 1943.
4. Commission on Higher Education, op. cit., Evidence of Fr Boniface, 1944.
5. Commission on Higher Education, op. cit., Evidence of J. Wight, 29 March 1944 [document indicates 1943, but this might be an error].
6. Commission on Higher Education, op. cit., Memorandum and notes of evidence, 1944. See evidence of J. Wright of QRC, 29 March 1944.
7. C. Chinapoo, "Chinese immigration into Trinidad 1900-1950" (MA thesis, UWI, 1988), p. 100.
8. Trinidad Presbyterian, Aug. 1948. Other references to Indians going to and returning from universities can

be found in the *Trinidad Presbyterian* 1944-1945.
9. For calculations of rate of registration of Indian doctors and lawyers between 1941 and 1952/54, see Ivar Oxaal, *Black Intellectuals and the Dilemmas of Race and Class in Trinidad* (Cambridge, Mass., 1982), pp. 88-89.
10. Annual Report of the Director of Education for 1948 (Trinidad, 1949), Appendix VI.
11. For list of teachers with extraordinary qualifications, see Commission on Higher Education, op. cit., Memorandum and notes of evidence 1944, Trinidad and British Guiana, Evidence of Trinidad and Tobago Teachers' Union.
12. TG, 18 Feb. 1963, article on Harry Joseph.
13. C. Campbell, "The dual mandate of the Imperial College of Tropical Agriculture 1922-1960", *Jamaican Historical Review* 16 (1988): 1-16.
14. Ibid.
15. Commission on Higher Education, op. cit., Memorandum and notes of evidence, Trinidad and British Guiana. Notes from Ayra Pratinidhi Sabha, 24 Feb. 1944. The *Indian Journal* (Observer) also carried articles insisting on the urgency of the problem of illiteracy among Indians, see *Observer* Feb. 1942; March 1942.
16. Commission on Higher Education, op. cit., Evidence of Noel Bowen, Registrar General, 8 March 1944. A university giving Arts degrees was declared to be foolishness, but not a university turning out persons trained in useful occupations.
17. *Teachers Herald*, January 1945, edited by Alex Brown; also *Priestly Diaries* 11, 1 May 1944.
18. Commission on Higher Education, op. cit., Memorandum and notes of evidence 1944, Memorandum of the Why Not Discussion Group.
19. Trinidad students comprised 18.2 percent, 19.8 percent, and 20.7 percent of the total students at UCWI in 1953, 1954 and 1955 respectively. See Report of the Committee appointed to review the policy of the UCWI (Dec. 1957-Jan.1958) (The Cato Committee), Appendix III.

Chapter 4

1. For academic career of Williams, see E. Williams, *Inward Hunger: the Education of a Prime Minister* (London, 1969); and I. Oxaal, *Black Intellectuals and the Dilemmas of Race and Class in Trinidad* (Cambridge, Mass., 1982), chaps. 4-6
2. There appears to have been some expectation that Williams was to do a Diploma in Education after his first degree, but it is doubtful that he was under a bond to return to Trinidad. See E. Williams, *Inward Hunger*, pp. 43-44; and C. Palmer, Introduction to the 1994 edition of Williams' *Capitalism and Slavery* (North Carolina, 1994).
3. E. Williams, *Inward Hunger*, op. cit., pp. 71-80. In a recent article on Caribbean intellectuals in the USA in the 1930s and 1940s, no notice was taken of Eric Williams, signifying perhaps his focus on academic life and on developments in the West Indies, see V. Franklin, "Caribbean influences on Afro-Americans in the USA" in *Intellectuals in the Twentieth Century Caribbean*, edited by A. Hennessy (London, 1992), pp. 179-90.
4. For Williams' understanding of the political significance of the work of Beryl McBurnie in the late 1940s and early 1950s, see M. Ahye, *Cradle of Caribbean Dance: Beryl McBurnie and the Little Caribe Theatre* (Trinidad, 1983), pp. 31-39; 138-39.
5. P. Sutton, "The historian as politician: Eric Williams and Walter Rodney", in *Intellectuals in the Twentieth Century Caribbean*, edited by A. Hennessy, op. cit., pp. 98-114.
6. E. Williams, *Inward Hunger*, op. cit., chap. 9; also K. Post, *Strike the Iron: a Colony at War, Jamaica 1939-1945* (New Jersey, 1981), vol. 1.
7. C. Palmer, Introduction, op. cit.

8. S. Cudjoe, *Movement of the People: Essays on Independence* (Ithaca, 1993), pp. 14-16.
9. E. Williams, "The proposed British West Indian university", *School and Society* 63 (Jan.-June 1946).
10. Ibid., 245.
11. Ibid.
12. Eric Williams, "Education in dependent territories in America", *Journal of Negro Education* 15 (1946).
13. S. A. Hammond, "Education in the British West Indies", *Journal of Negro Education* 15 (1946).
14. E. Williams, "Education in dependent territories", op. cit., 548.
15. Ibid., 549.
16. S. A. Hammond, "Education in the British West Indies", op. cit., 440.
17. E. Williams, "Education in dependent territories", op. cit., 549.
18. S. A. Hammond, "Education in the British West Indies", op. cit., 444-45.
19. E. Williams, "Education in dependent territories", op. cit., 547.
20. Ibid., 550.
21. E. Williams, *Education in the British West Indies* (Port of Spain, 1950), p. 31.
22. Ibid., p. 32.
23. See C. Campbell, *The Young Colonials: a Social History of Education in Trinidad and Tobago 1834-1939* (Kingston, 1996), chap. 2.
24. For instance, Williams would probably have agreed with most of the main ideas in the undebated Council Paper of 1946 which emanated from colonial officials; see CP 27 of 1946.
25. See C. Campbell, *The Young Colonials*, 97-104.
26. *Clarion*, 8 May 1948, Editorial. The French creole editor of the *Clarion* (party organ of the Labour Party) wrote several articles in 1948 and 1949 hostile to Cutteridge, Hayden, Hogben, and Hammond – all English education experts. Divine justice was said to have reached Cutteridge who allegedly was in England (in retirement) in a "wheeled chair and wearing a bib", (*Clarion*, 8 May 1948, Editorial).
27. E. Williams, "The need for instructional materials related to the Caribbean environment", in *Education in the Caribbean* (Port of Spain, 1956).
28. E. Williams, *Inward Hunger*, op. cit.; for reports of his speeches, see POSG, 2 Sept. 1954; 5 Sept. 1954; 30 Sept. 1954; 20 April 1955; 29 April 1955; 1 May 1955; 19 May 1955; 29 May 1955.
29. For the debate between Williams and Dom Basil Matthews on Aristotle, see POSG, 1 Dec. 1954; also see Ivar Oxaal, *Black Intellectuals*, op. cit., pp. 104-5.
30. See DeWilton Rogers, *The Rise of the People's National Movement. In the Beginning: an Excursus and a Biography* (Port of Spain, n.d.); also Rhoda Reddock, *Women, Labour and Politics in Trinidad and Tobago: a History* (London, 1994), chap. 11.
31. *Trinidad Chronicle*, 21 Oct. 1956.

Chapter 5

1. For a recent study that emphasises the alleged positive role of a younger generation of Indians, including Rienzi, see Solomon Agyemang, "A study of radical political thought in colonial Trinidad 1919-1950" (MSc thesis, UWI, 1989), chap. 3; also see Teresa Cardinez, "Politics in Trinidad and Tobago 1946-1956: from personal politics to ethnic based parties" (MPhil thesis, UWI, 1990), chap. 3.
2. For careers of Cipriani, Rienzi and Butler, see Kelvin Singh, *Race and Class Struggles in a Colonial State: Trinidad 1917-1945* (The Press UWI, 1994).
3. The literature on British decolonisation is dominated by the process in Africa and India, with only slight mention of the West Indies. See Rudolph Von Albertini, *Decolonisation: the Administration and Future of the Colonies 1919-1960* (reprint, Hadleigh, 1982), pp. 175-83; and J. Flint, "The failure of planned decolonisation in British

Africa", *Africa Affairs* 82, no. 328 (July 1983): 389-411.
4. For government's use of wartime conditions to frustrate the trade unions, see A. Gomes, *Through a Maze of Colour* (Port of Spain, 1974), pp. 57-68.
5. T. Cardinez, "Politics in Trinidad", op. cit., pp. 117-39.
6. In writing this chapter the author drew generously on materials from several contributors to a recent publication on the political economy of Trinidad between 1962 and 1987. See *Trinidad and Tobago: the Independence Experience*, S. Ryan (St Augustine, 1988).
7. S. Ryan, *The Independence Experience*, op. cit., pp. 141-59; also R. Henry, "The state and income distribution in an independent Trinidad and Tobago", in *The Independence Experience*, edited by S. Ryan (St Augustine, 1988), pp. 477-79.
8. I. Oxaal, *Black Intellectuals and the Dilemmas of Race and Class in Trinidad* (Cambridge, Mass., 1982), pp. 129-33.
9. For the biography of Dr Capildeo, see I. Oxaal, *Black Intellectuals*, op. cit., chap. 9.
10. *The Independence Experience*, edited by S. Ryan, op. cit., pp. 221-22; also John La Guerre, "Race relations in Trinidad and Tobago", in *The Independence Experience*, edited by S. Ryan (St Augustine, 1988), pp. 193-205.
11. *The Independence Experience*, edited by Selwyn Ryan, op. cit., pp. 144-59; also Selwyn Ryan, "The limits of executive power", in *Eric Williams: the Man and the Leader*, edited by Ken Boodhoo (New York, 1986), pp. 65-82.
12. I. Oxaal, *Black Intellectuals*, op. cit., p. 177.
13. R. Henry, "The state and income distribution", op. cit., pp. 477-79.
14. A. Payne, *Governments, Intellectuals and International Relations: the Politics of the University of the West Indies 1968-1984*, Occasional Papers in Caribbean Studies, no. 7, Centre for Caribbean Studies, University of Warwick (Warwickshire, c. 1993).
15. For a comprehensive record of the Black Power movement, see *Power: the Black Power Revolution 1970, a Retrospective*, edited by S. Ryan and T. Stewart (St Augustine, 1995).
16. S. Cudjoe, *Movement of the People: Essays on Independence* (Ithaca, 1993), pp. 31-49.
17. Rosina Wiltshire-Brodber, "Trinidad and Tobago's foreign policy 1962-1987: an evaluation", in *The Independence Experience*, edited by Selwyn Ryan (St Augustine, 1988), p. 288.
18. R. Ramlogan, "Trinidad and Tobago's iron and steel industry in perspective: analysis and prospects" (MSc thesis, UWI, 1985), chap. 6.
19. *The Imperatives of Adjustment: Draft Development Plan 1983-1986. Report of the Task Force appointed by Cabinet to formulate a multi-sectoral development plan for the Republic of Trinidad and Tobago* (Trinidad, 1984), pp. 1-2.
20. S. Ryan, *Revolution and Reaction: Parties and Politics in Trinidad and Tobago 1970-1981* (St Augustine, 1989), pp. 74-94.
21. Rosina Wiltshire-Brodber, "Trinidad and Tobago's foreign policy", op. cit., p. 290.
22. *Imperatives of Adjustment*, op. cit., pp. 1-4.

Chapter 6

1. E. Williams, *Inward Hunger: the Education of a Prime Minister* (London, 1969), p. 283.
2. TG, 1 Aug. 1956, Speech of Williams at Woodford Square.
3. For nationalism and the churches' role, see S. Stewart, "Nationalist educational reforms and religious schools in Trinidad", *Comparative Education Review* 25, no. 2 (June 1981): 183-201.
4. For Roman Catholic fears of growing government power in education, see Memoranda received from national organisations on Draft Second Five-year Plan 1964/68, Memorandum of Finbar Ryan, Archbishop of Port of

Notes to Chapter 6

Spain, 2 Sept. 1963; also Memorandum of St Mary's College Union, 13 Sept. 1963.
5. For a recent copy of this rare document, see *Sunday Guardian*, 15 Sept. 1991 (Appendix 1).
6. TG, 4 May 1967, article on Lutchmi Hindu College; TG, 17 Oct. 1965, Speech of Williams at Woodford Square. In 1974 some principals said they selected students from the 'merit list', but not in order of merit; see *Sunday Guardian*, 13 Oct. 1974, full page advertisement by heads of denominations.
7. Memoranda received from national organisations on Draft Second Five-year Plan 1964/68, Memorandum of St Mary's College Union, 13 Sept. 1963; also [Archbishop Ryan], the Catholic Church and the Draft Education Act (c. 1965), pp. 3-9.
8. TG, 9 Dec. 1965, Speech by Williams in Parliament.
9. *Sunday Guardian*, 13 Oct. 1974.
10. TG, 17 Oct. 1965, Speech by Williams at Woodford Square; also Hansard Parliamentary Debates (HOR), 8 Dec. 1965, speech by Williams on Education Act.
11. The Committee on General Education 1959 (The Maurice Report), p. 23.
12. See testimony of an ex-teacher, S. Doodnath, *A Short History of the Early Presbyterian Church and the Indian Immigrants in Trinidad 1845-1945* (Port of Spain, 1983), pp. 69-73.
13. For a description of the interlocking duties and powers of the Teaching Service Commission and Boards of Management, see Report of the Teaching Service Commission (Dec. 1980), pp. 5-10.
14. C. Campbell, *Colony and Nation: a Short History of Education in Trinidad and Tobago* (Kingston, 1992), pp. 12-13.
15. Cabinet Proposal on Education (Trinidad, 1960).
16. Selwyn Ryan, "The limits of executive power", in *Eric Williams: the Man and the Leader*, edited by Ken Boodhoo (New York, 1986), pp. 65-82.
17. See for example, Address of Dr Cuthbert Joseph, Minister of Education at the Annual Convention of the Trinidad and Tobago Anglican Teachers' Association at Holiday Inn, 10 June 1977.
18. Report of the Joint Committee between government and the Roman Catholic authorities on the hand-over of seven primary schools by the Roman Catholic Board of Management and the Cabinet decisions thereon (Trinidad, 1978).
19. Ibid.
20. In 1986 the PNM said 42 denominational schools were under joint management, see *PNM General Election Manifesto 1986*, pp. 12-13.
21. Report on the offer by the Roman Catholic Education Authority to hand over to government seven primary schools subject to certain conditions relating to their management (1978), Appendix III, Archbishop Pantin to Minister of Education, 22 March 1978.
22. Final report of the Working Group appointed by the late Prime Minister on national ownership and joint management of schools (Trinidad, May 1981).
23. TG, 27 Oct. 1974.
24. Ibid.
25. I. Baksh, "Education and equality of opportunity in Trinidad and Tobago", *Caribbean Journal of Education* 13, nos. 1 and 2 (1986): 6-24.
26. In its 1986 election manifesto, perhaps in an effort to seek the broadest based support, the PNM declared that it had "maintained the dual education system". See *PNM Election Manifesto 1986*.
27. Statistics on Public Education 1983/1984 (Ministry of Education, Planning Division, Port of Spain, Nov. 1985).
28. M. Holmes, "The place of religion in public education", *Interchange: a Quarterly Review of Education* 24, no. 3 (1993): 205-23.

Chapter 7

1. *PNM Major Policy Documents*, vol. 1, The People's Charter (Port of Spain, n.d.), p. 30.
2. Ibid., pp. 30-31.
3. Ibid., p. 50.
4. H. M. Phillips, "Trends in educational expansion in developing countries", in *World Year Book of Education 1967*, edited by G. Bereday (London, 1967), p. 386.
5. See Memoranda received from national organisations on Draft Second Five-year Plan 1964/1968.
6. See Concordat, Appendix 1.
7. Ignoring the role and overall responsibility of the Ministry of Education for education policy, The Maurice Report pilloried the directors of education for the predilection for denominational schools; see The Committee on General Education 1959 (The Maurice Report), pp. 6-7.
8. For a critique of faulty school building by the churches, see Education in Trinidad and Tobago: Report of the Working Party, 1954 (The Missen Report), pp. 30-32.
9. TG, 18 Jan. 1961, Case of Bejucal Hindu School.
10. Hansard Parliamentary Debates (HOR), 14 Dec. 1962, speech of Ramdeen.
11. Draft Second Five-year Plan 1964/1968, p. 127; also C. Hauch, *Educational Trends in the Caribbean: European-affiliated Areas* (Washington, DC, 1960), pp. 70-71.
12. C. Dyer, "A study to determine curriculum content for industrial arts in the junior secondary schools of Trinidad and Tobago" (PhD diss., Arizona State University, 1974), p. 136.
13. *PNM Major Party Documents*, no. 1. General Election Manifesto 1961. These figures are accurate though taken from a highly political document.
14. Hansard Legislative Council Debates, 26 April 1957, speech of Dr Solomon.
15. C. Campbell, "The dual mandate of the Imperial College of Tropical Agriculture 1922-1960", *Jamaican Historical Review* 16 (1988): 14-16.
16. Hansard Legislative Council Debates, 12 April 1961, Budget speech of Dr Williams.
17. Draft Second Five-year Plan 1964/1968, p. 34.
18. The Maurice Report, op. cit., pp. 9-13.
19. For a critique of the Maurice Report, especially from Dr Forrester, see TG, 21 Aug. 1960; 30 Aug. 1960; 31 Aug. 1960; 16 Sept. 1960; 23 Sept. 1960; 30 Sept. 1960.
20. Hansard Legislative Council Debates, 25 July 1960, speech of Lionel Seukeran.
21. R. Henry, "The interface between education and employment in Trinidad and Tobago", in *Report on Conference on Educational Research in Trinidad and Tobago 20-22 July 1981*, edited by E. Gift, C. Harvey, P. Mark and G. Williams (St Augustine, 1984), pp. 64-67.
22. Hansard Legislative Council Debates, 24 April 1959 and 12 April 1960, speech of Lionel Seukeran.
23. Hansard Parliamentary Debates (HOR), 28 May 1965, speech of B. Ramdeen. The chief opposition spokesmen on education were Ramdeen and Seukeran.
24. Hansard Parliamentary Debates (Senate), 14 Jan. 1972, speech of Carlton Gomes, Minister of Education.
25. Interview with Albert Alleyne, July 1984.
26. For an insider account of changes in the Ministry of Education in respect to educational planning and the UNESCO report, see W. Emanuel, "Educational planning for development: a critical analysis of recent work and its relevance to Trinidad and Tobago" (MA thesis, University of Newcastle-upon-Tyne, 1970).
27. Draft Plan for Educational Development in Trinidad and Tobago 1968-1983 (Trinidad, 1968), pp. 95-98.
28. The Missen Report, pp. 94-95.
29. Ibid., pp. 35-39.
30. Hansard Parliamentary Debates, 14 Jan. 1972, speech of Carlton Gomes, Minister of Education.

Notes to Chapter 7

31. See speech of Dr Williams at the inauguration of The National Cultural Council, 1971, quoted in Narsaloo Ramaya, "Towards the evolution of a national culture: Indian music in Trinidad and Tobago", paper presented at the Third Conference on East Indians in the Caribbean 1984, St Augustine, UWI.
32. M. Alleyne and S. Syrimis, "Manpower studies: stock and demand for technicians and craftsmen" (Ministry of Education, 23 June 1969).
33. Draft Education Plan, op. cit, pp. 54-55.
34. "The still small voice: comments of secondary school students on teachers, schools, education etc. 1971-1981", edited by H. R. Braithwaite (School of Education, UWI St Augustine, mimeo, 1981), p. 1; also TG, 3 May 1971, article on school rebellion at Woodbrook Secondary School. Also "Document from the United Freedom Fighters of Trinidad", *Pan-African Journal* 8, no. 2 (1975): 203-26.
35. Report of the Curriculum Committee appointed by Dr the Rt Hon Eric Williams, Prime Minister, at the Chaguaramas Consultation on Education, held in October 1974 (The Valdez Report 1975), pp. 36, 54-55.
36. Ibid., pp. 43-53.
37. Hansard Parliamentary Debates (HOR), 26 July 1968, speech of Bhadase Maraj; 24 May 1968, speech of R. Bholai.
38. Hansard Parliamentary Debates (HOR), 1 Dec. 1970, speech of A. Lequay.
39. Hansard Parliamentary Debates (HOR), 13 June 1969, speech of L. A. Wright.
40. Hansard Parliamentary Debates (HOR), 24 Jan. 1969, speech of R. Bholai; 13 June 1969, R. Rambachan; see also Debates on Five-year Development Plan and Draft Education Plan on 13 June 1969; also 7 Dec. 1969, speech of Dr J. Bharath; 4 Dec. 1969, speech of S. H. Shah; 15 Dec. 1970, speech of H. Hanoomansingh.
41. In September 1966, in a party speech, Dr Williams claimed that the opposition proposed that "the education system should be based on small village schools of 25 and of 40 or 50 large comprehensive schools with an intake of 1,000 or 5,000 and teaching up to the General Degree of London University". He proceeded to show how ridiculous and expensive it would be. See "A review of the political scene: an address by the political leader to the special PNM convention, 11 September 1966".
42. Memorandum on the role and status of the private secondary schools of Trinidad and Tobago (Association of Principals of Private Secondary Schools, Port of Spain, 1968), Appendix 2B, Table 2.
43. Prime Minister's proposals to Cabinet on education, 18 Sept. 1975, enclosures, Letter from heads of religious bodies to Prime Minister, 30 July 1975; also TG, 7 July 1975, article by education reporter.
44. National Consultation on Education held at Convention Centre, Chaguaramas, 17 Oct. 1974.
45. E. Williams, "Education and decolonisation: address to Caribbean Union conference", August 1974.
46. *Sunday Guardian*, 13 Oct. 1974, full page advertisement by heads of denominations; also National Consultation on Education, 17 Oct. 1974, op. cit., speeches of Fr Valdez and Sr Xavier. Perhaps the prestige school that entered most willingly into a technical/vocational programme was Fatima College; see Address of Dr Cuthbert Joseph (Minister of Education) at Fatima College, 22 Jan. 1978.
47. See various 1975 plans (attached to Prime Minister's proposals to Cabinet on education, 18 Sept. 1975).
48. TG, 1 Aug. 1975, article by staff reporter.
49. Prime Minister's proposals to Cabinet on education, 18 Sept. 1975.
50. TG, 31 May 1975, article by staff reporter; TG, 7 July 1975, article by education reporter; TG, 1 Aug. 1975, article by staff reporter.
51. *Express*, 18 June 1975, Speech by Minister of Education, Carlton Gomes.

52. Prime Minister's proposals to Cabinet on education, 18 Sept. 1975.
53. Ibid.
54. Prime Minister's proposals to Cabinet on the implementation of Cabinet's decisions on education (Ministry of Education and Culture, Government of Trinidad and Tobago, 1979).
55. The lower birth rate was probably a reflection of substantial emigration in the 1960s; see Jack Harewood, "Human resources", in *The Natural Resources of Trinidad and Tobago*, edited by St G. E. Cooper and P. R. Bacon (London, 1981), pp. 168-69.
56. Hansard Parliamentary Debates (Senate), 15 Dec. 1977, speech of Dr Joseph, Minister of Education.
57. Accounting for the Petrodollars, p. 10, Appendix 4A.
58. Draft Education Plan, op. cit., p. 37.
59. TG, 15 March 1976. Other useful articles can be found in TG, 23 April 1975; *Express*, 18 June 1975; *Express*, 14 Nov. 1975; TG, 10 Dec. 1975; *Express*, 11 Dec. 1975; TG, 12 Dec. 1975; TG, 30 Jan. 1978; TG, 27 Jan. 1978; TG, 8 April 1978; *Express*, 19 Oct. 1978
60. For a summary of NIHERST in relation to UWI, see Selwyn Ryan "Republic of Trinidad and Tobago White Paper on National Institute of Higher Education (Research, Science and Technology)", *Caribbean Studies* 17, nos. 3-4 (Oct. 1977 [1978]): 183-93.
61. Hansard Parliamentary Debates (Senate), 13 Dec. 1977, speech of Mervyn Desouza.
62. For more on the NIHERST fiasco see G. Williams and C. Harvey, *Higher Education in Trinidad and Tobago: a Focus on Organisational Development and Change* (Caracas, 1985), pp. 83-101.
63. Hansard Parliamentary Debate (Senate), 13 Dec. 1977, speech of Horne.
64. Hansard Parliamentary Debate (Senate), 13 Dec. 1977, speech of Dr Sammy.
65. See Report on teacher education and training for the primary level (Trinidad, January 1980); also Report on teacher education and training for secondary education and for tertiary and further education (Trinidad, August 1980).

Chapter 8

1. C. Campbell, "Tobago and Trinidad: problems of alignment of their educational systems at union 1889-1931", *Antilla* 1, no. 3 (April 1987): 21-27.
2. In 1960 the question of Tobago's independence was much discussed in relation to the West Indies federation; see TG, 14 and 26 Aug. 1960, letter from 'A firm supporter'; also 30 Aug. 1960, Tobago secession.
3. An exception was a disastrous hurricane in September 1963 which destroyed two schools and damaged several others, and generally crippled the island; see Report of the Tobago Planning Team (1963).
4. *Trinidad Chronicle*, 12 Jan. 1957, Speech of Williams in Tobago; also *Trinidad Chronicle*, 16 Jan. 1957.
5. Hansard Legislative Council Debates, 7 June 1957, speech of James.
6. National Consultation on Education held at Convention Centre, Chaguaramas, 17 Oct. 1974, speech of Victor Wheeler, principal of Scarborough School (Tobago).
7. M. Archer, "History of Bishop's High School, Tobago 1925-1981" (mimeo, n.d.), p. 5.
8. *Express*, 24 April 1975; for a defence of Bishop's High School, see TG, 16 June 1975, letter from Lionel Mitchell; see also I. Caesar, *Vignettes of Tobago* (Trinidad, 1984), p. 118, comments by Eric Roach.
9. Hansard Parliamentary Debates (HOR), 17 Nov. 1978, speech of Dr Winston Murray.
10. Hansard Parliamentary Debates (Senate), 18 Sept. 1980, speech of J. Donaldson.
11. It appears that the situation was favourable as late as 1974, see National Consultation on Education, op. cit., speech of Wheeler, and rejoinder by

Dr Williams. As late as 1977, Wheeler continued to suggest that Tobago, from an availability of sufficient secondary school places, could lead the way in democratising secondary education. See Victor Wheeler, "Democratising secondary education in Tobago" (2d part of five government broadcasts from 13 Aug.-Sept. 1977).

12. A survey in 1994 showed that 37.2 percent of the 11-16 age group in Tobago were in secondary school, a proportion among the lowest in the nation. See A study of the secondary school population in Trinidad and Tobago: Placement patterns and practices, Summary Report (Centre for Ethnic Studies, UWI St Augustine, 1994), p. 10.

13. Hansard Parliamentary Debates (HOR), 14 Jan. 1977, speech of Robinson.

14. See TG, 5 April 1984 for ruling of a High Court judge that the Tobago House of Assembly did not have exclusive responsibility to implement government policy.

15. For a recent hard-hitting survey of alleged PNM discrimination against Indians, see R. Premdas, "Ethnic conflict in Trinidad and Tobago: domination and reorientation", in *Trinidad Ethnicity*, edited by Kelvin Yelvington (London, 1993), pp. 136-60.

16. For the view that Indians had a majority, if illegal black immigrants were discounted. See National Consultation on Education, op. cit., speech of Capildeo, pp. 56-57.

17. Ramesh Deosaran, "Some issues in multiculturalism: the case of Trinidad and Tobago in the post-colonial era", *Ethnic Group* 3 (1981): 199-213.

18. Ibid., pp. 218-25. For expression of dissatisfaction by Hindus over the place of Indian culture in secondary schools, see Sandra Gajrag, "Indian cultural presence in the secondary school system of Trinidad and Tobago: images and perceptions" (DipEd thesis, UWI St Augustine, 1984); also Kamala Tewarie, "Integration and multiculturalism: a dilemma in the school system in Trinidad and Tobago" (paper presented at the Third Conference on East Indians in the Caribbean, UWI St Augustine, 1984).

19. *Trinidad Presbyterian*, June 1956; March 1957; Sept. 1959, Editorial; July 1959; March and Nov. 1960.

20. For many of the problems of the church in the mid twentieth century, see G. Legge, Report of a preliminary survey of the Presbyterian Church of Trinidad and Grenada, Oct.-Nov. 1965, pp. 81-85.

21. Y. Malik, *East Indians in Trinidad: a Study of Minority Politics* (Oxford, 1971), p. 34.

22. E. Williams, "Address at Tagore Centenary Celebrations delivered at Queen's Hall, Port of Spain, 6 May 1961" (Office of Premier, pamphlet, 1961), pp. 29-30.

23. TG, 18 Jan. 1961; see case of the Bejucal Hindu School.

24. Hansard Parliamentary Debates (HOR), 24 Jan. 1969, speeches of R. Bholai and A. Baksh.

25. Hansard Parliamentary Debates (HOR), 26 July 1968, speech of Bhadase Maraj; 24 May 1968 and 24 Jan. 1969, speech of Bholai.

26. Hansard Parliamentary Debates (HOR), 15 Dec. 1970, speech of H. Hanoomansingh.

27. TG, 24 April 1987, report of conference paper of Kamala Tewarie. See also Brader Brathwaite, *Teaching Inside-out: Reflections and Research from a Trinidadian Educator* (Tunapuna, Trinidad, 1992), pp. 45-47.

28. For some of these Hindu youth organisations, see S. Vertovec, "Religion and ethnic ideology: the Hindu Youth Movement in Trinidad", *Ethnic and Racial Studies* 13, no. 2 (April 1990): 225-49.

Chapter 9

1. National Consultation on Education held at Convention Centre, Chaguaramas, 17 Oct. 1974,

Notes to Chapter 10

speeches of Frank Byam, Frederick Powder.
2. In the 1970s, for example, nutrition centres, home economics centres (formerly domestic science) and woodwork centres attached to primary schools were closed, see Report on teacher education and training for the primary level (Jan. 1980), Appendix 1, p. 21.
3. Education in Trinidad and Tobago: Report of the Working Party, 1954 (The Missen Report), p. 44.
4. The Carnegie Project in Primary School Organisation Trinidad and Grenada 1968-1970: an evaluation by J. Raymond Gerberich, (Institute of Education, 1974).
5. See for example, *The Language Arts Syllabus 1975: Comments and Countercomments*, edited by L. D. Carrington and C. B. Borely (rev. ed, St Augustine, Nov. 1978).
6. The Missen Report, op. cit., pp. 44-45. For criticism of excessive testing and examination, see Committee on General Education 1959 (The Maurice Report), p. 18; also Historic Education Documents, vol. 16, R. T. Green, Memorandum on the Common Entrance Examination as a selection procedure, 15 March 1966, pp. 10-11; also TG, 31 Jan. 1964, speech of Senator Donald Pierre.
7. For an explanation of the Common Entrance tests as originally introduced, see Historic Education Documents, vol. 16, P. E. Vernon, Summary of discussion and recommendations on selection for secondary education in Trinidad and Tobago, 7 Sept. 1960.
8. By 1982 it was estimated that about 600 graduate teachers in secondary schools were without professional training, see The Imperatives of Adjustment: Draft Development Plan 1983-1986. Report of the Task Force appointed by Cabinet to formulate a multi-sectoral development plan for the Republic of Trinidad and Tobago (Trinidad, 1984), p. 119.
9. Caribbean Union Teachers' College, a private multi-purpose college run by the Seventh-Day Adventists, began training teachers in 1960. See Report on teacher education, op. cit., Appendix 1, p. 17.
10. National Consultation on Education, op. cit., speech of Fr Valdez, pp. 49-50.
11. Report on teacher education, op. cit., p. iv.
12. Perhaps the most elaborate published formula for revamping teacher training was put forward in 1974, see Report of the Curriculum Committee (The Valdez Report), Sept. 1975, pp. 13-23. Previously the Maurice Report had also indicated the need for comprehensive changes, see The Maurice Report, pp. 58-70.
13. Report on teacher education, op. cit., pp. 43-50.
14. E. Gift (compiler), "Report to the Board of Education of Teacher Training on the final practical teaching exam" (mimeo, n.d.)
15. P. Mark, "A critique of practices in teacher education in Trinidad and Tobago" (St Augustine, School of Education, Jan. 1979).
16. For a useful survey of the problems, see N. Moore, "The teachers' colleges of Trinidad and Tobago: their purpose, performance and possibilities" (DipEd thesis, UWI St Augustine, 1978).

Chapter 10

1. The only writer in Trinidad and Tobago who displayed any knowledge of this literature is Theodore Lewis, and he came on the scene too late. See Theodore Lewis, "Labour market outcomes of comprehensive education in Trinidad", *Caribbean Journal of Education* 3, nos. 1-2 (1976): 44-48.
2. For some brief reservations by a visiting UNESCO expert, see S. Syrimis, Proposal for the establishment of a national vocational training scheme (Ministry of Education, 3 July 1969), p. 11; also more elaborately, see M. Alleyne and S. Syrimis, The supply of

craftsmen (Ministry of Education, 2 July 1969).
3. Draft Plan for Educational Development in Trinidad and Tobago 1968-1983 (Trinidad, 1968), pp. 18-21.
4. Fr Pedro Valdez, "Our secondary schools in relation to the needs of our times", *Educational Journal of Trinidad and Tobago* (July 1965): 21-24. See also J. Boatswain, "A study of the teaching of practical subjects in secondary schools 1956/1966" (Caribbean Study thesis, UWI St Augustine, 1969).
5. C. Dyer, "A study to determine curriculum content for industrial arts in the junior secondary schools of Trinidad and Tobago" (PhD diss., Arizona State University, 1974), pp. 135-40.
6. UNESCO Education Planning Mission Trinidad and Tobago, March-June 1964 (Paris, 1964); also UNESCO Trinidad and Tobago Educational Planning (May-Aug. 1965), by C. E. Gurr (Paris, 1966).
7. Education Planning Mission, op. cit., pp. 20-28; 58-59.
8. Vocational Training in Trinidad and Tobago (National Training Board, Aug. 1972), p. 12.
9. For a criticism of the underemphasis on technical/vocational education in the Education Plan by Ministry of Planning and Development officials while requesting a loan from the Inter-American Development Bank, see Proposal for a technical education project, part 1; vocational centre, part 2 (c. 1971).
10. At the National Consultation on Education in 1974, Victor Wheeler, principal of Scarborough School (Tobago) suggested the abandonment of the plan for separate vocational schools and the combination of technical/vocational education with senior secondary schools on ground of reduced cost and additional prestige for technical/vocational education. See National Consultation on Education held at Convention Centre, Chaguaramas, 17 Oct. 1974.
11. Draft Education Plan, op. cit., p. 18-21; 33-37.
12. Prime Minister's proposal to Cabinet, 18 Sept. 1975 (Port of Spain, 1975), pp. 5-8.
13. Vocational Training in Trinidad and Tobago (National Training Board, Aug. 1972), p. 83.
14. A good statement of the problem of choice between specialised vocational education and general education can be found in E. Stanley, *Planning Occupational Education and Training for Development* (New York, 1971).
15. C. Harvey, "Practitioner's perception of an innovative school system in a developing country: a qualitative analysis" (PhD diss., University of Toronto, 1981), pp. 167-274.
16. Report of the Working Party on Craft Training and National Apprenticeship Scheme (Government of Trinidad and Tobago, 1975).
17. A government appointed committee had insisted that specialised training start at age 16. But this committee was not important; see Report of the Working Party on Craft Training, op. cit.
18. For recent examinations of problems of technical/vocational training in these schools, see S. Samaroo, "A critique of vocational education in the senior comprehensive schools in Trinidad and Tobago" (DipEd thesis, UWI St Augustine, 1988), and M. Sambury, "An assessment of technical vocational education in the senior comprehensive schools of Trinidad and Tobago" (DipEd thesis, UWI St Augustine, 1991).
19. C. Harvey, "Practitioner's perceptions of an innovative school system", op. cit., pp. 165-264.
20. For discussions towards this scheme, see Tripartite meeting on training for the construction industry (Ministry of Education, July 1977), verbatim notes of proceedings.
21. Report of the Committee appointed to report on the scheme for short-term apprenticeship, utilising the resources of unemployed O level graduates in the proposed process industries (June 1976).
22. For an exaggerated view of the responsibility of private industry to train, see

A. Alleyne, "The role of technical/vocational education and training, science and technology as components of the education scheme for the future development of Trinidad and Tobago, 3 Feb. 1984" (paper prepared but apparently not read at Ministry of Education in-house seminar, St Francois School, Feb. 1984).

23. For problems of youth camps, see National Task Force on Youth. First interim report (Dec. 1971).

24. Alexander Riley, "Placement and functioning of youth camp graduates in the economy of Trinidad and Tobago. Report on field study for diploma course in youth studies 1975/76" (mimeo, May 1976), pp. 11-25; also National Task Force on Youth, op. cit.

25. For recommendations for programmes at these centres, see Report on trade centres under the control of Community Development (Ministry of Education, 8 July 1972).

26. Privately run trades centres. Paper submitted to Youth Subcommittee of National Training Board (Ministry of Planning and Development, c. 1972). The St Bede Vocational School, and the extraordinary SERVOL were outstanding examples run by the Roman Catholic Church. Founded (SERVOL) in 1971 by a Roman Catholic priest, by 1980 it had 4 'Life Centres' and 12 pre-schools. For a comprehensive appreciation of SERVOL, see Ron Weber, "Scaling up Jacob's ladder: community development in Trinidad and Tobago", *Grassroots Development: Journal of the Interamerican Foundation* 14, no. 1 (1990): 23-34.

27. For parental and student resistance to technical/vocational education at Arima government school in early 1970s, see National Consultation on Education, op. cit., speech of Jean Warner.

28. Claudia Harvey, "Practitioner's perceptions of an innovative school system", op. cit., pp. 167-274.

29. E. Williams, *Education in the British West Indies* (Port of Spain, 1950), pp. 45-46.

30. National Task Force on Youth, op. cit.; also National Consultation on Education, op. cit., speech of Bascombe. By 1975 agriculture apparently had been made compulsory at all youth camps, see Report of the Working Party on Craft Training, op. cit., p. 23.

31. UNESCO Educational Planning Mission, Trinidad and Tobago (Paris, 1964), p. 76. This school was one of the surviving federal institutions.

Chapter 11

1. Memoranda received from national organisations on Draft Second Five-year Plan 1964/65, op. cit., Memorandum of Finbar Ryan, Archbishop of Port of Spain, 2 Sept. 1963; also CN, 23 March 1967, speech of Rev Fr Connolly at Fatima College prize-giving.

2. V. Gopaul-Maharagh, "The social effects of the American presence in Trinidad during World War II (1939-1945)" (MA thesis, UWI, 1984), chap. 10; TG, 24 Feb. 1943.

3. Trinidad and Tobago Council Papers, nos. 1-47, 1951, Address of His Excellency the Governor, Sir Hubert Rance, 19 Oct. 1951.

4. Hansard Legislative Council Debates, 13 May 1949, Ordinance to Amend Education Ordinance.

5. For evidence of a decline of a sense of rivalry in the Presbyterian Church, see G. Legge, Report of a preliminary survey of the Presbyterian Church of Trinidad and Grenada, Oct.-Nov. 1965.

6. For an analysis of the New Primary School Syllabus of 1975, see C. Harvey, "Educational change and its impact on national development in Trinidad and Tobago 1962-1987", in *Trinidad and Tobago: the Independence Experience 1962-1987*, edited by S. Ryan (St Augustine, 1988), pp. 354-55.

7. In 1966 the Anglican primary school at Sixth Company had only 10 Anglican children out of a total of 120 on roll. The Baptists were very strong in

Notes to Chapter 11

this district. See *Anglican Review*, Sept. 1966. For a recent article on this subject see C. MacKenzie, "Denominational primary schooling: the case of Trinidad and Tobago", *International Review of Education* 37, no. 2 (1991): 211-26.

8. For a variety of outcomes in government secondary schools in respect to religious instruction, see F. Rampersad, "The role of religious education in secondary schools in Trinidad and Tobago" (DipEd thesis, UWI St Augustine, 1988).

9. Sandra Stewart's estimate of PNM hostility to religious instruction appears exaggerated. See S. Stewart, "Nationalist educational reforms and religious schools in Trinidad", *Comparative Education Review* 25, no. 2 (June 1981): 198-99.

10. For a mine of information about religious instruction in schools, see Conference on the Church [Roman Catholic] and Education, Port of Spain, 11-13 Oct. 1973; also John Thornley, "Christianity and education", in *New Horizons, Naparima Teachers' College Diamond Jubilee Issue, 1894-1969* (Port of Spain, 1969), pp. 59-60.

11. Annual Report of the Director of Education, 1946 (Trinidad and Tobago, 1948), p. 8.

12. See, for instance, the proposal for the education of girls in the undebated Council Paper of 1946 (CP 27 of 1946).

13. *Trinidad Chronicle*, 4 Oct. 1956, Role of J. S. Donaldson and DeWilton Rogers.

14. Annual Report of the Director of Education for 1948 (Trinidad and Tobago, 1949), Appendix 6. For the names of such Indian females, see Shameen Ali, "A social history of East Indian women in Trinidad since 1870" (MPhil thesis, UWI, 1993), p. 132.

15. See R. Taitt, "Women in the PNM" (MA thesis, UWI, 1990). Also R. Reddock, *Women, Labour and Politics in Trinidad and Tobago History* (London, 1994), pp. 297-307.

16. P. Mohammed, "Studies in education and society: a review of educational research in Trinidad and Tobago". Paper prepared for seminar in Education and Society in the Caribbean, sponsored by Research Institute for the Study of Man, Faculty of Education, Mona, Jamaica (St Augustine, 1989), pp. 19-20, 51-52; also see Address of Minister of Education, Dr Cuthbert Joseph on the occasion of the Speech Day Exercises of the St Francois Girls' High School, Thursday, 16 Feb. 1978, at Queen's Hall (Parliamentary Library, Port of Spain).

17. Final report of the National Commission on the Status of Women (Jan. 1976), Table 3. Statistics on the relative position of male and female teachers can be found in the Report of Teaching Service Commission (Dec. 1980).

18. For elaboration of the subject of gender differentiation in secondary schools, see J. Foreman, "Schooling, gender and development in Trinidad and Tobago" [work in progress], *EDC Occasional Papers*, no. 7 (June 1984): 15-33.

19. Report of the National Commission on the Status of Women for 1981, p. 4.

20. For a useful chapter on the cultural environment of Trinidad at the time of McBurnie's emergence, see Felix Harrington " 'On with the Dance Friends': Beryl McBurnie, pioneer, educator and catalyst in Caribbean dance" (Diploma in Dance paper, Jamaica School of Dance, May 1982), chap. 3; also M. Ahye, *Cradle of Caribbean Dance: Beryl McBurnie and the Little Carib Theatre* (Trinidad and Tobago, 1983), chap. 1.

21. M. Anthony, *Heroes of Trinidad and Tobago* (Port of Spain, 1986), p. 110.

22. I. Boodhoo, "A curriculum model in art education for the primary schools of Trinidad and Tobago" (PhD diss., University of Indiana, 1974), pp. 71-74.

23. For sketchy attempts at a history of Music Festivals, see *Express*, 21 March 1984, article by Jeremy Taylor; also *TG*, 27 Jan. 1980, article by David Johnsone.

Notes to Chapter 11

24. *Trinidad and Tobago Music Festival Silver Jubilee Brochure 1947-1972*, pp. 45-64. List of champions through the years.
25. For a critique of government indifference to art education, see Memoranda received from national organisations, op. cit., submission of Trinidad and Tobago Art Society, 27 Sept. 1963.
26. Interview with Isaiah Boodhoo, 7 Aug. 1985.
27. For music, see A. Pierre, "A survey into the facilities existing in Trinidad and Tobago for the training of music teachers" (UWI School of Education thesis, 1974); also E. Palmer, "Evaluating a creative arts programme in a developing nation (Trinidad and Tobago)" (DEd, Columbia University, 1980), pp. 31; 138-39. For more recent criticisms of the teaching of the Arts, see D. Bernard, "The place of drama in education and the drama teacher in secondary schools" (DipEd thesis, UWI St Augustine, 1991); also A. Salazar, "The importance of the Arts in Education" (DipEd thesis, UWI St Augustine 1991).
28. The failure to establish a single library service is legendary. For one proposal for integration, see Report of a Committee to consider the integration of the Library Services of Trinidad and Tobago into a National Library and to make recommendations thereon (The Best Committee) (mimeo, 26 July 1968). For a timid presentation of the case for more libraries, see Memoranda received from national organisations, op. cit.; Memorandum of Library Association of Trinidad and Tobago, 16 Sept. 1963. For a brief recent account of this fiasco, see L. Ackbarali, "National planning for the library and information service of Trinidad and Tobago" (PhD diss., Columbia University, 1992).
29. C. Campbell, *Colony and Nation: a Short History of Education in Trinidad and Tobago* (Kingston, 1992), p. 31.
30. Education Department Annual Report 1949, p. 33.
31. Annual Report of the Director of Education for 1948, op. cit., p. 28.
32. TG, 14 April 1949 and 9 June 1949, explanations of Director Hogben.
33. Hansard Parliamentary Debates, 13 Aug. 1982, statement of Overand Padmore, Minister of Education. It is not clear whether these schools wanted aid while remaining purely private or whether they wished to become assisted schools. One college (St Anthony's College) became an assisted school.
34. *Indian Centenary Review: 100 Years of Progress 1845-1945*, edited by M. Kirpalani, et al. (Port of Spain, 1945), p. 54.
35. In a recent article Norrel London used the protest of parents over the closure of the Black Rock Moravian School in Tobago (1949-1950) as evidence that they had not been socialised into docility by the schools. Possibly quite true; but since, presumably, several years had elapsed since leaving primary schools, their behaviour should be accounted for by other factors. See N. London, "Policy and practice in education in the British West Indies during the late colonial period", *History of Education* 24, no. 1 (1995): 91-104
36. Selwyn Ryan, "The limits of executive power", in *Eric Williams: the Man and the Leader*, edited by Ken Boodhoo (New York, 1986), pp. 65-82. Also TG, 15 Oct. 1974; Express, 14 Oct. 1974.
37. Historic Education Documents, vol. 16, Memorandum on the Common Entrance Examinations as a selection procedure, by R. T. Green (March 1966).
38. Historic Education Documents, vol. 9, First report of Examination Review Committee (June 1980).
39. Teacher Education Committee, Report on nursery education 3-5 years (Jan. 1980).
40. The Gocking Reports referred to in the last five paragraphs are the three reports (1979-1980) stated in the bibliography under Reports on Education.
41. TG, 12 Nov. 1961, speech of electioneering Dr Capildeo.

42. C. Campbell, "The dual mandate of the Imperial College of Tropical Agriculture 1922-1960", *Jamaican Historical Review* 16 (1988): 1-16; also TG, 20 Nov. 1961, statement by Arthur Lewis on the development of UWI.
43. TG, 1 Oct. 1984.
44. C. Campbell, "The St Augustine campus of UWI: success and excess", *Jamaican Historical Review* 16 (1988): 58-59.
45. UWI Vice Chancellor's Report 1963-1964, Appendix 3, Table 6.
46. Ibid., p. 60.
47. Ibid., p. 48.
48. Accounting for the Petrodollars 1973-1983 (Trinidad and Tobago, 1984), p. 10, Table 4a.
49. For a recent analysis of these issues, see A. Payne, *Governments, Intellectuals and International Relations: the Politics of the University of the West Indies 1968-1984*, Occasional Papers in Caribbean Studies, no. 7, Centre for Caribbean Studies, University of Warwick (Warwickshire, c. 1993).
50. Report of a Committee appointed to consider problems of secondary and primary education in Trinidad, Barbados, Leeward Islands and Windward Islands 1931-1932 (The Marriott/Mayhew Report).
51. E. Williams, *The Negro in the Caribbean* (Washington, DC, 1942), p. 76.
52. UNESCO Trinidad and Tobago Educational Planning (1965), by C. E. Gurr (Paris, 1966); also *Daily Gleaner*, 12 July 1987, p. 3a for World Development Report 1987.
53. For several comparisons between the British West Indies and Africa in the 1930s, see W. W. Macmillan, *Warning from the West Indies* (London, 1936).
54. For the plans of some African countries in respect to universal primary education, see R. C. Smith, *Progress towards Universal Primary Education: a Commonwealth Survey* (London, 1979); see also *International Review of Education* 29, no. 2 (1983), special issue on the universalisation of primary education.

Chapter 12

1. See bibliography, section on Reports on Education, for a short list of Reports/Working Parties.
2. For a review of research on education since 1950, see P. Mohammed, "Studies in education and society: a review of educational research in Trinidad and Tobago". Paper prepared for seminar in Education and Society in the Caribbean, sponsored by Research Institute for the Study of Man, Faculty of Education, UWI Mona, Jamaica (St Augustine, 1989).
3. For two recent severe assessments of Dr Williams by a black, and Indian, scholar, see S. Cudjoe, *Movement of the People: Essays on Independence* (Ithaca, 1993), pp. 6-60; and Ralph Premdas, "Ethnic conflict in Trinidad and Tobago: domination and reconciliation", in *Trinidad Ethnicity*, edited by K. Yelvington (London, 1993), pp. 136-39.
4. *The Independence Experience*, edited by S. Ryan, op. cit., pp. 155-59.
5. Ibid., p. 145.
6. Ibid., p. 156.
7. Ibid., p. 157.
8. R. Deosaran, "A psychological portrait of political power", in *Eric Williams: the Man and the Leader*, edited by K. Boodhoo (New York, 1986), pp. 13-28.
9. The PNM government in 1984 produced its own assessment of the Education Plan, but it was so political as to be of limited use. See Assessment of the Plan for Educational Development in Trinidad and Tobago 1968-1983 (Ministry of Education, Oct. 1984). The World Bank and IDB also made assessments in relation to their loans, but these are classified documents.
10. For a number of special education funds, see Accounting for the Petrodollars 1973-1983 (Trinidad and Tobago 1984), pp. 6-11.
11. However nearly 50 percent were third-grade certificates, see The Committee on General Education 1959 (The

Notes to Chapter 13

12. TG, 3 Feb. 1963, QRC Old Boys' Dinner; Express, 25 Oct. 1982, article by Anthony Milne.
13. A. Atwell, "Barriers to achievement in secondary education in Trinidad and Tobago", in Reports on Conference on Educational Research in Trinidad and Tobago, 20-23 July 1981 (School of Education, UWI St Augustine), pp. 24-30.
14. See for example, A Compendium of Statistics on Examinations in Secondary Schools and Technical Institutes (compiled by Ministry of Education and Culture, 1981).
15. A. Dotting, "Secondary education and employment in Trinidad and Tobago: implications for educational planning" (EdD diss., Columbia University, 1973), pp. 147-51.
16. I. Baksh, "Education and equality of opportunity in Trinidad and Tobago", Canadian and International Education Review 11, no. 2 (1982): 23.
17. I. Baksh, "Educational expansion and opportunity in Trinidad and Tobago", Canadian and International Education Review 11, no. 2 (1982): 27-42.
18. For a recent explanation of the complexities of Common Entrance placement, see A study of the secondary school population in Trinidad and Tobago: Placement patterns and problems. A research project (Centre for Ethnic Studies, UWI St Augustine, 1994), pp. 227-61.
19. Social and Occupational Stratification in Contemporary Trinidad and Tobago, edited by S. Ryan (St Augustine, 1991), pp. 58-79; Rhoda Reddock, "Social mobility in Trinidad and Tobago 1960-1980", in Social and Occupational Stratification, op. cit., pp. 210-33. For more on gains of Indian girls in secondary schools, see A study of the secondary school population ... Summary Report, op cit., p. 5.
20. West Indian Digest Monthly, May 1981, article by Selwyn Ryan.
21. S. Ryan, "Popular attitudes towards independence, race relations and the People's National Movement", in Trinidad and Tobago: the Independence Experience 1962-1987 (St Augustine, 1988), p. 227.
22. R. Premdas, "Ethnic conflict in Trinidad and Tobago", op. cit., p. 110.
23. T. Lewis, "Labour market outcomes of comprehensive education in Trinidad", Caribbean Journal of Education 3, nos. 1-2 (1976): 60-62.
24. C. Harvey, "Educational change and its impact on national development in Trinidad and Tobago 1962-1987", in Trinidad and Tobago: the Independence Experience, edited by S. Ryan (St Augustine, 1988), pp. 345-81.
25. K. Lillis, "Problems associated with vocational education in less developed countries", in Education and Development edited by R. Garrett (London, 1984), pp. 172-99.
26. For discussion of decolonization, see The Newer Caribbean: Decolonisation, Democracy and Development, edited by P. Henry and C. Stone (Philadelphia, 1983), pp. 1-122.
27. P. Sutton (comp), Forged from the Love of Liberty. Selected Speeches of Dr Eric Williams (London, 1981), pp. 162-70; also see Eric Williams Speaks: Essays on Colonialism and Independence, edited by S. Cudjoe (Wellesley, 1993), pp. 92-99.
28. See for instance, S. Cudjoe, Movement of the People, op. cit., pp. 6-60.

Chapter 13

1. TG, 6 July 1979, speech of Dr Cuthbert Joseph, Minister of Education.
2. The Imperatives of Adjustment: Draft Development Plan 1983-1986. Report of the Task Force appointed by Cabinet to formulate a multi-sectoral development plan for the Republic of Trinidad and Tobago (Trinidad and Tobago, 1984), pp. 121-23.
3. Education Plan 1985-1990 (Trinidad and Tobago, Ministry of Education 1985).
4. Teacher Education Committee. Report on nursery education 3-5 years

Notes to Chapter 13

(Trinidad and Tobago, 1979); Teacher Education Committee, Report on teacher education and training for the primary level (Trinidad and Tobago, 1980); Teacher Education Committee, Report on teacher education and training for secondary education and for tertiary and further education (Trinidad and Tobago, Aug. 1980).

5. Report of the Cabinet-appointed Committee to examine the content, organisation and administration of technical/vocational education in secondary schools (Port of Spain, 1984) (The Richards Report), pp. 2-4.

6. Report of the Working Group appointed by the late Prime Minister on national ownership and joint management of schools (May 1981).

7. See for instance the recommendations of the Education Policy Paper (1993-2003) by the National Task Force on Education (Ministry of Education, Trinidad and Tobago, 1993).

8. Report of the Tobago House of Assembly for year ending Dec. 1982 (Trinidad and Tobago, 1983).

9. The Tobago Development Plan 1981-1990.

10. If a recent psychological survey of Tobago youths is correct, the gap between Tobago and Trinidad will not be closed by their generation, see G. Gray, "The aspirations of youths and the education system in a developing society: the Tobago case" (MSc thesis, UWI, 1990), pp. 167-70.

Bibliography

A.   PRIMARY SOURCE

Official/Semi-official Documents

CP 78 of 1887, Report on public instruction in Trinidad 1885-1887.
Hansard Legislative Council Debates 1939-1962.
Report of the Agricultural Policy Committee of Trinidad and Tobago, Part 1 (1943).
(Sir Frank Stockdale), Development and Welfare in the West Indies 1940-1942 (HMSO, London, 1943).
CO 295/630, Correspondence between Governor Bede Clifford and certain government officials.
CO 318/467, Correspondence between Roman Catholic Archbishop of Port of Spain and certain government officials.
Commission on Higher Education in the Colonies (The Irvine Committee). Memorandum and notes of evidence 1944.
Report of the West Indies Royal Commission 1945 (The Moyne Report).
Unclassified documents, Royal Victoria Institute, List of persons to sit examinations 1949; Return of registered apprentices June 1959; (Letter) A. Hodgson to Hopkins, 14 June 1940; Minutes of Board of Industrial Training 1945-1948.
CP 27 of 1946, Educational Policy and Development Programme Trinidad and Tobago Five-year Economic Programme, vol. 2 (1950-1955).
Annual Reports of the Colony of Trinidad and Tobago 1946-1955.
Annual Reports of Director of Education 1946-1957.
Digest of Statistics on Education 1950-1956 (Central Statistical Office, Government of Trinidad and Tobago).
Minutes of Board of Industrial Training 1956-1978.
Correspondence of Board of Industrial Training 1956-1965.
Report of the Team which visited Tobago March/April 1957 (Development and Welfare in the West Indies, Bulletin no. 34) (The Frampton Report).
The Concordat 1960.
Cabinet proposals on Education (July 1960).
Williams, Eric. 1961. "Address at Tagore Centrnary Celebrations delivered at Queen's Hall, Port of Spain, 6 May" (Office of the Premier, pamphlet).
Hansard Parliamentary Debates (Senate) 1963-1986.
Hansard Parliamentary Debates (House of Representatives) 1963-1986.
Report of the Tobago Planning Team (1963).
Draft Second Five-year Plan 1964-1968.

Bibliography

Act no. 1 of 1966, An Act to make better provision for the promotion of education in Trinidad and Tobago.
Draft Plan for Educational Development in Trinidad and Tobago 1968-1983 (1968).
Draft Third Five-year Plan 1969-1973.
Prime Minister's further report to Cabinet on education (2 Oct. 1975).
Prime Minister's proposals to Cabinet on education (18 Sept. 1975).
White Paper on National Institute of Higher Education (Research, Science, and Technology) 1977.
Prime Minister's proposals to Cabinet on the implementation of Cabinet's decision on education (Ministry of Education, Government of Trinidad and Tobago, 1979).
The Tobago Development Plan 1981-1990.
Report of the Tobago House of Assembly for year ending Dec. 1982 (Government Printing Office, Port of Spain, 1983).
Assessment of the Plan for Educational Development in Trinidad and Tobago 1968-1983 (Government of Trinidad and Tobago, Ministry of Education, Oct. 1984).
Accounting for the Petrodollars 1973-1983 (Government Printing Office, Port of Spain, 1984).
The Imperatives of Adjustment: Draft Development Plan 1983-1986. Report of the Task Force appointed by Cabinet to formulate a multi-sectoral development plan for the Republic of Trinidad and Tobago (Government Printing Office, Port of Spain, 1984).
The Successor Education Plan 1985-1990 (Ministry of Education, 1985).

Reports on Education

CP 168 of 1916, Report of the Education Commission appointed by Sir G. R. LeHunte on 16 June 1914 (Government Printing Office, Port of Spain, 1916).
Report of a Committee appointed to consider problems of secondary and primary education in Trinidad, Barbados, Leeward Islands and Windward Islands 1931-1932 (HMSO, 1933) (The Marriott/Mayhew Report).
CP 16 of 1940 Report of the Special Committee on Vocational Education 20 Feb. 1939.
Report of the West Indies Committee of the Commission on Higher Education in the Colonies (HMSO, 1945) (The Irvine Report).
CP 27 of 1946, White Paper on government education policy. Education in Trinidad and Tobago: Report of the Working Party 1954 (The Missen Report).
Report of Committee on Grants-in-Aid to Assisted Secondary Schools, 1956 (Government Printing Office, Port of Spain, 1957).
Report of the Committee appointed to review the policy of the UCWI (Dec. 1957-Jan. 1958) (The Cato Committee).
The Committee on General Education 1959 (The Maurice Report).
Historic Education Documents, Trinidad and Tobago, vol. 16. P. E. Vernon, Summary of discussions and recommendations on selection for secondary education in Trinidad and Tobago, 7 Sept. 1960.
Cabinet Proposal on Education (Government Printing Office, Port of Spain, 1960, pamphlet).
Memoranda received from national organisations on Draft Second Five-year Plan 1964/1968.

Bibliography

UNESCO Education Planning Mission to Trinidad and Tobago, March-June 1964 (UNESCO, Paris, 1964).

(Archbishop Finbar Ryan), The Catholic Church and the Draft Education Act 1965 (n.d., pamphlet).

Legge, G. Report of a preliminary survey of the Presbyterian Church of Trinidad and Grenada, Oct.-Nov. 1965.

UNESCO Trinidad and Tobago Educational Planning, May-Aug. 1965, by C. E. Gurr (UNESCO, Paris 1966).

Historic Education Documents, Trinidad and Tobago, vol. 16. R. T. Green, Memorandum on the Common Entrance Examination as a selection procedure, 15 March 1966.

The Catholic Church and the Draft Education Act 1966 (by the Roman Catholic Church).

Memorandum on the role and status of the private secondary schools of Trinidad and Tobago (Association of Principals of Private Secondary Schools, Port of Spain, 1968).

Report of a Committee to consider the integration of the Library Services of Trinidad and Tobago into a National Library and to make recommendations thereon, 26 July 1968 (The Best Committee).

Tripartite Committee on Technical/Vocational Education (1969).

M. Alleyne and S. Syrimis, Manpower studies: Stock and demand for technicians and craftsmen (Ministry of Education, 23 June 1969).

M. Alleyne and S. Syrimis, The supply of craftsmen (Ministry of Education, 2 July 1969).

S. Syrimis, Proposal for the establishment of a national vocational training scheme (Ministry of Education, 3 July 1969).

National Task Force on Youth. First interim report (Dec. 1971).

Proposal for a technical education project, part 1; vocational centre, part 2 (c. 1971).

Report of the Education Working Party (Chaguaramas Secondary School Conference) April 1972.

Report on trade centres under the control of Community Development (Ministry of Education, 8 July 1972).

Vocational training in Trinidad and Tobago (National Training Board, Aug. 1972).

Paper submitted to Youth Subcommittee of National Training Board (Ministry of Planning and Development, c. 1972).

Conference on the Church [Roman Catholic] and Education, Port of Spain, 11-13 Oct. 1973.

Eric Williams, Education and decolonisation: Address to Caribbean Union Conference, August 1974.

National Consultation on Education held at Convention Centre, Chaguaramas, 17 Oct. 1974.

The Carnegie Project in Primary School Organisation, Trinidad and Grenada 1968-1970: an evaluation by J. Raymond Gerberich (Institute of Education, 1974).

Report of the Curriculum Committee appointed by Dr the Rt Hon Eric Williams at the Chaguaramas Consultation on Education, held in October 1974 (The Valdez Report), Sept. 1975.

Report of the Working Party on Craft Training and National Apprenticeship Scheme (Port of Spain, 1975).

Report of Working Party on Education, Jan. 1976 (The St Clair King Report).

Bibliography

Final report of the National Commission on the Status of Women (Jan. 1976).

Report of the Committee appointed to report on the scheme for short-term apprenticeship, utilising the resources of unemployed O level graduates in the proposed process industries (June 1976).

Tripartite meeting on training for the construction industry (Ministry of Education, July 1977), verbatim notes of proceedings.

Report of the Joint Committee between government and Roman Catholic Church authorities on the hand-over of seven primary schools by the Roman Catholic Board of Management and Cabinet decisions thereon (Government Printing Office, 1978).

Report of the offer by the Roman Catholic Education authority to hand over to government seven primary schools subject to certain conditions relating to their management (1978).

Statement by the Minister of Education to House of Representatives on the implementation of the agreement on the handing over of denominational primary schools to government under the new management agreement based on a joint venture between church and state (27 April 1979).

Teacher Education Committee. Report on nursery education 3-5 years (Oct. 1979).

Report of the Teaching Service Commission (Dec. 1980). Teacher Education Committee, Report on teacher education and training for the primary level (Trinidad and Tobago, Jan. 1980).

Teacher Education Committee, Report on teacher education and training for secondary education and for tertiary and further education (Trinidad and Tobago, Aug. 1980).

Report of Working Group appointed by the late PM on national ownership and joint management of schools (May 1981) (The Bruce Report).

Final report of the Working Group appointed by the late PM on national ownership and joint management of schools (Government Printing Office, Trinidad, May 1981).

Report of the National Commission on the Status of Women for 1981.

Historic Education Documents, vol. 9 (Feb. 1983). First report of Examination Review Committee (June 1980).

The GCE O level 'failure' rate (by C. V. Gocking and L. J. Edgehill), 1981.

Final report of Working Group appointed to consider the feasibility of converting senior secondary and senior comprehensive schools into full-time five-year schools (May 1982).

Historic Education Documents, vol. 9. Second report of Examination Review Committee (Nov. 1982).

Historic Education Documents, vol. 9. Third report of Examination Review Committee (Dec. 1982).

Historic Education Documents, vol. 15. Further report of Examination Review Committee (1983).

Historic Education Documents vol. 15. Fifth report of Education Review Committee (July 1983).

Summary report of Project Concern: a follow-up study of graduates of the senior comprehensive schools and the on-the-job training programme (by T. Lewis, K. Martin and R. Boddie, Aug. 1983).

Report of the Cabinet-appointed Committee to examine the content, organisation and administration of technical/vocational education in secondary schools (Port of Spain, 1984) (The Richards Report).

Bibliography

A. Alleyne, The role of technical/vocational education and training, science and technology as components of the education scheme for the future development of Trinidad and Tobago, 3 Feb. 1984 (paper prepared but apparently not read at Ministry of Education in-house seminar, St Francois School, Feb. 1984).

Education Policy Paper (1993-2003) by the National Task Force on Education (White Paper) (Ministry of Education, Trinidad and Tobago, 1993).

A study of the secondary school population in Trinidad and Tobago: Placement patterns and practice. A research project (Centre for Ethnic Studies, UWI St Augustine, 1994). See also the Summary Report, 1994.

Newspapers/Journals

Anglican Review, Sept. 1966.

Catholic News, 7 Aug. 1920.

Clarion, 8 May 1948.

Daily Gleaner, 12 July 1987.

Express, 14 Oct. 1974; 24 April 1975; 18 June 1975; 14 Nov. 1975; 11 Dec. 1975; 19 Oct. 1978; 27 Jan. 1980; 25 Oct. 1982; 24 Feb. 1984; 28 Feb. 1984; 29 Feb. 1984; 1 March 1984; 4 March 1984; 21 March 1984.

The Observer, Aug. 1943; Nov. 1943; Aug. 1946.

Port of Spain Gazette (Weekly), 19 Oct. 1931; 19 July 1952: 6 Sept. 1952; 2 Sept. 1954; 5 Sept. 1954; 30 Sept. 1954; 1 Dec. 1954; 1 Feb. 1955; 20 April 1955; 29 April 1955; 1 May 1955; 19 May 1955; 29 May 1955; 28 July 1955.

Priestly Diaries, 1 May 1944.

The Spectator, July 1949; April 1950.

Teachers Herald, Jan. 1945.

Tobago Educational Review 1972.

Trinidad Chronicle, 4 Oct. 1956; 21 Oct. 1956; 12 Jan. 1957.

Trinidad Guardian 14 April 1949; 9 June 1949; 18 May 1955; 1 Aug. 1956; 8 Jan. 1960; 1 Aug. 1960; 14 Aug. 1960 ; 21 Aug. 1960; 26 Aug. 1960; 30 Aug. 1960; 31 Aug. 1960; 16 Sept. 1960; 23 Sept. 1960; 30 Sept. 1960; 18 Jan. 1961; 12 Nov. 1961; 20 Nov. 1961; 3 Feb. 1963; 8 Feb. 1963; 31 Jan. 1964; 17 Oct. 1965; 9 Dec. 1965; 17 Oct. 1965; 22 Nov. 1967; 3 May 1971; 31 May 1971; 29 July 1971; 13 Oct. 1974; 15 Oct. 1974; 27 Oct. 1974; 23 Dec. 1974; 23 April 1975; 31 May 1975; 8 June 1975; 12 June 1975; 16 June 1975; 7 July 1975; 8 July 1975; 10 Dec. 1975; 12 Dec. 1975; 15 March 1976; 27 Jan. 1978; 8 May 1978; 30 June 1978; 6 July 1979; 27 Jan. 1980; 5 April 1984; 1 Oct. 1984; 24 May 1987.

Trinidad Presbyterian, 1943-1964.

Weekly Guardian, 28 April 1923; ll Oct. 1924; 23 Oct. 1926; 20 Nov. 1926.

West Indian Digest Monthly, May 1981.

Books

Ahye, M. 1983. *Cradle of Caribbean Dance: Beryl McBurnie and the Little Carib Theatre*. Trinidad and Tobago: Heritage Cultures.

Anthony, M. 1986. *Heroes of Trinidad and Tobago*. Port of Spain: Circle Press.

Bibliography

Archer, M. 1982. *The Sociology of Educational Expansion: Take-off, Growth and Inflation in Educational Systems*. London: Sage Publications.

Baptiste, F. 1988. *War, Cooperation and Conflict: the European Possessions in the Caribbean, 1939-1945*. Westport: Greenwood Press.

Beeby, C. E. 1966. *The Quality of Education in Developing Countries*. Cambridge, Mass.: Harvard University Press.

Bereday, G., ed. 1965. *The World Year Book of Education, 1965*. London: Evans Brothers.

Bereday, G., ed. 1967. *The World Year Book of Education, 1967*. London: Evans Brothers.

Boodhoo, K., ed. 1986. *Eric Williams: the Man and the Leader*. New York: University Press of America.

Brathwaite, B. 1992. *Teaching Inside-out: Reflections and Research from a Trinidadian Educator*. Tunapuna, Trinidad: Gloria V. Ferguson Ltd.

Braithwaite, R. H. E. 1991. *Moral and Social Education*. Port of Spain: Paria Publishing Co.

Brereton, B. 1981. *A History of Modern Trinidad 1783-1962*. Port of Spain: Heinemann.

Brown, S., M. Morris, and G. Rohlehr, eds. 1989. *Voiceprint: an Anthology of Oral and Related Poetry from the Caribbean*. London: Longman.

Caesar, I. 1984. *Vignettes of Tobago*. Trinidad.

Campbell, C. 1992. *Colony and Nation: a Short History of Education in Trinidad and Tobago*. Kingston: Ian Randle Publishers.

Campbell, C. 1992. *Cedulants and Capitulants. The Politics of the Coloured Opposition in the Slave Society of Trinidad 1783-1838* Port of Spain: Paria Publishing.

Campbell, C. 1996. *The Young Colonials: a Social History of Education in Trinidad and Tobago*. Kingston: The Press UWI.

Carrington, L. D. 1978. *UNESCO Report 1978: Education and Development in the English-speaking Caribbean*. Paris: UNESCO.

Carrington, L. D., and C. B. Borely, eds. 1978. *The Language Arts Syllabus 1975: Comments and Counter-comments*. Rev. ed, St Augustine: UWI School of Education.

Cooper, G. E., and P. R. Bacon, eds. 1981. *The Natural Resources of Trinidad and Tobago*. London: Edward Arnold.

Craig, S. 1974. *Community Development in Trinidad and Tobago, 1943-1973: from Welfare to Patronage*. ISER Working Paper, no. 4. St Augustine: ISER.

Cudjoe, S., ed. 1993. *Eric Williams Speaks: Essays on Colonialism and Independence*. Wellesley: Calaloux Publications.

Cudjoe, S. 1993. *Movement of the People: Essays on Independence*. Ithaca: Calaloux Publications.

D'Aeth, H. R. 1956. *Secondary Schools in the British Caribbean*. London: Longman.

Doodnath, S. 1983. *A Short History of the Early Presbyterian Church and the Indian Immigrants in Trinidad 1845-1945*. Port of Spain: The author.

Dyer, C. 1994. *History of Industrial Education and Training in Trinidad and Tobago*. Trinidad: HEM Enterprises.

Ferreira, J. 1994. *The Portuguese of Trinidad and Tobago: Portrait of an Ethnic Minority*. St Augustine: ISER.

Garrett, R., ed. 1984. *Education and Development*. London: Croom Helm.

Gomes, A. 1974. *Through a Maze of Colour*. Port of Spain: Key Caribbean Publications.

Bibliography

Grimal, H. 1965. *Decolonisation: the British, French, Dutch and Belgian Empire, 1919-1963*. London: Routledge and Kegan Paul.

Hackshaw, J. 1992. *The Baptist Denomination*.

Hammond, S. A. 1941. *Education in Jamaica*. Kingston: Government Printing Office.

Hammond, S. A. 1943. *The Cost of Education*. Bridgetown: Advocate.

Hammond, S. A. 1943. *Education in Grenada*. St George's: Government Printing Office.

Hammond, S. A. 1943. *Education in St Vincent*. Kingstown: Government Printing Office.

Hammond, S. A. 1943. *Memorandum on Education in St Vincent*. Kingstown: Government Printing Office.

Hammond, S. A. 1943. *St Lucia: Memorandum on Education*. Castrties: Government Printing Office.

Hammond, S. A. 1944. *Education in Dominica*. Bridgetown: Advocate.

Hammond, S. A. 1946. *The Development of Secondary Education in Grenada*. St George's: Government Printing Office.

Hauch, C. 1960. *Educational Trends in the Caribbean: European-affiliated Areas*. Washington, DC: US Government Printing Office.

Henry, P., and C. Stone, eds. 1983. *The Newer Caribbean: Decolonisation, Democracy and Development*. Philadelphia: Institute for Study of Human Issues.

Hennessy, A., ed. 1992. *Intellectuals in the Twentieth Century Caribbean*. London: Macmillan.

James, C. L. R. 1932. *Life of Captain Cipriani: an Account of British Government in the West Indies*. Nelson, Lancashire: Coulton and Co.

Kirpalani, M. 1945. *Indian Centenary Review: 100 Years of Progress 1845-1945*. Port of Spain: n.p.

Lee, J. M., and M. Petter. 1982. *The Colonial Office, War and Development Policy: Organisation and the Planning of a Metropolitan Initiative, 1939-1945*. London: Institute of Commonwealth Studies.

Lewis, G. 1968. *The Growth of the Modern West Indies*. New York: Monthly Review Press.

Macmillan, W. W. 1936. *Warning from the West Indies*. London: Faber and Faber.

Malik, Y. 1971. *East Indians in Trinidad: a Study of Minority Politics*. Oxford: Oxford University Press.

Millett, T. 1993. *The Chinese in Trinidad*. Port of Spain: Inprint Publications.

Niddrie, D. 1961. *Land Use and Population in Tobago: an Environmental Study*. London: Geographical Publications.

Oxaal, I. 1982. *Black Intellectuals and the Dilemmas of Race and Class in Trinidad*. Cambridge, Mass.: Schenkmann Publishing.

PNM. 1986. *General Election Manifesto*. Port of Spain: PNM Publishing.

PNM. N.d. *PNM Major Policy Documents*, vol. 1. Port of Spain: PNM Publishing.

Payne, A. c. 1993. *Governments, Intellectuals and International Relations: the Politics of the University of the West Indies 1968-1984*. Occasional Papers in Caribbean Studies, no. 7, Centre for Caribbean Studies, University of Warwick, Warwickshire.

Post, K. 1981. *Strike the Iron: a Colony at War, Jamaica 1939-1945*, vol. 1. New Jersey: Humanities Press.

Ramsaran, D. 1993. *Breaking the Bonds of Indentureship: Indo-Trinidadians in Business*. St Augustine: ISER.

Reddock, R. 1994. *Women, Labour and Politics in Trinidad and Tobago: a History*. London: Zed Books.

[Roman Catholic Church]. 1936. *Centenary Record of the Sisters of St Joseph of Cluny, 1836-1936*. Port of Spain: Yuille's Printers.

[Roman Catholic Church]. 1973. *Conference on the Churches and Education*. Port of Spain.

Rogers, D. N.d. *The Rise of the People's National Movement. In the Beginning: an Excursus and a Biography*. Port of Spain: The author.

Ryan, S. 1974 [1972]. *Race and Nationalism in Trinidad and Tobago: a Study of Decolonisation in a Multiracial Society*. Reprint, St Augustine: ISER.

Ryan, S. 1975. *The Disillusioned Electorate: the Politics of Succession in Trinidad and Tobago*. Port of Spain: Inprint Caribbean.

Ryan, S. 1989. *Revolution and Reaction: Parties and Politics in Trinidad and Tobago 1970-1981*. St Augustine: ISER.

Ryan, S. 1990. *The Pursuit of Honour: the Life and Times of H. O. B. Wooding*. St Augustine: ISER.

Ryan, S., ed. 1988. *Trinidad and Tobago: the Independence Experience 1962-1987*. St Augustine: ISER.

Ryan, S., ed. 1991. *Social and Occupational Stratification in Contemporary Trinidad and Tobago*. St Augustine: ISER.

Ryan, S., and Lou Anne Barclay. 1992. *Sharks and Sardines: Blacks in Business in Trinidad and Tobago*. St Augustine: ISER.

Ryan, S., and T. Stewart, eds. 1995. *Power: the Black Power Revolution 1970*. St Augustine: ISER.

Sherlock, P., and R. Nettleford. 1990. *The University of the West Indies: a Caribbean Response to the Challenge of Change*. London: Macmillan.

Singh, K. 1994. *Race and Class Struggles in a Colonial State: Trinidad, 1917-1945*. Kingston: The Press UWI.

Simey, T. S. 1946. *Welfare and Planning in the West Indies*. Oxford: Oxford University Press.

Smith, R. C. 1979. *Progress towards Universal Primary Education: a Commonwealth Survey*. London: Commonwealth Secretariat.

Stanley, E. 1971. *Planning Occupational Education and Training for Development*. New York: Praeger Publishers.

Sutton, P., comp. 1981. *Forged from the Love of Liberty: Selected Speeches of Dr Eric Williams*. London: Longman Caribbean.

Thomas, E. 1987. *A History of the Shouter Baptists in Trinidad and Tobago*. Ithaca: Calaloux Publications.

Trinidad and Tobago Music Festival Silver Jubilee Brochure 1947-1972.

Von Albertini, R. 1982. *Decolonisation: the Administration and Future of the Colonies 1919 1960*. Reprint, Hadleigh, Essex: Africana Publishing.

Yelvington, K., ed. 1993. *Trinidad Ethnicity*. London: Macmillan.

Williams, E. 1942. *The Negro in the Caribbean*. Washington, DC: Associates in Negro Folk Education.

Williams, E. 1950. *Education in the British West Indies*. Port of Spain: Guardian Commercial Printery.

Williams, E. 1964. *History of the People of Trinidad and Tobago*. London: André Deutsch.

Williams, E. 1969. *Inward Hunger: the Education of a Prime Minister*. London: André Deutsch.

Williams, E. 1994 [1964]. *Capitalism and Slavery*. Reprint, Chapel Hill: University of North Carolina Press.

Williams, G. and C. Harvey. 1985. *Higher Education in Trinidad and Tobago. A Focus on Organisational Development and Change*. Caracas: CRESALC-UNESCO.

Articles

Anthony, M. 1970. "Archdeacon Streetly - pioneer in technical education". *Anglican Review* (November).

Alleyne, M. 1972. "Educational planning in Trinidad and Tobago". *Caribbean Studies* 11, no. 4.

Atwell, A. 1981. "Barriers to achievement in secondary education in Trinidad and Tobago". In *Reports on Conference on Educational Research in Trinidad and Tobago, 20-23 July 1981*, 24-30. School of Education, UWI St Augustine.

Baksh, I. 1982. "Educational expansion and opportunity in Trinidad and Tobago". *Canadian and International Education Review* 11, no. 2.

Baksh, I. 1986. "Education and equality of opportunity in Trinidad and Tobago". *Caribbean Journal of Education* 13, nos. 1 & 2 (January-April).

Beeby, C. E. 1980. "The thesis of the stages fourteen years later". *International Review of Education* 26, no. 4.

Braithwaite, L. 1953. "Social stratification in Trinidad". *Social and Economic Studies* 2, nos. 2 & 3 (October).

Brathwaite, R. H. E. 1981. "Plus ça change". *Trinidad and Tobago Education Forum* 2, no. 1 (June).

Brereton, B. 1993. "Social organisation and class, racial and cultural conflict in nineteenth century Trinidad". In *Trinidad Ethnicity*, edited by K. Yelvington, 33-54. London: Macmillan.

Campbell, C. 1975. "The establishment of Queens' Collegiate School in Trinidad 1857-1867". *Caribbean Journal of Education* 2, no. 2 (December).

Campbell, C. 1976. "The transition from Spanish law to English law in Trinidad before and after emancipation". In *Some Papers on Social, Political and Economic Adjustments to the Ending of Slavery in the Caribbean*, 25-52. Barbados: ACH.

Campbell, C. 1978. "Charles Warner and the development of education in Trinidad 1838-1870". *Journal of Caribbean History* 10 and 11.

Campbell, C. 1983. "The College Exhibition in Trinidad and Tobago 1870-1938". *History Teachers Journal*, no. 2 (March).

Campbell, C. 1984. "Education and black consciousness: the amazing career of Captain J. Cutteridge in Trinidad, 1921-1942". *Journal of Caribbean History* 18.

Campbell, C. 1987. "Tobago and Trinidad: problems of alignment of their educational systems at union 1889-1931". *Antilla* 1, no. 3 (April).

Campbell, C. 1988. "The dual mandate of the Imperial College of Tropical Agriculture 1922-1960". *Jamaican Historical Review* 16.

Campbell, C. 1988. "New perspectives on secondary education in Trinidad and Tobago 1926-1935". In *Education in the Caribbean: Historical Perspectives*, edited by R. King, 145-62. Kingston: UWI.

Bibliography

Campbell, C. 1988. "The St Augustine campus of UWI: success and excess". *Jamaican Historical Review* 16.

Campbell, C. 1988. "The university of our dreams: centralisation versus decentralisation in the planning of the University of the West Indies, 1943-1944". *Jamaican Historical Review* 16.

Deosaran, R. 1981. "Some issues in multiculturalism: the case of Trinidad and Tobago in the post-colonial era". *Ethnic Group* 3.

Deosaran, R. 1986. "A psychological portrait of political power". In *Eric Williams: the Man and the Leader*, edited by K. Boodhoo, 13-28. New York: University Presses of America.

Document from the United Freedom Fighters of Trinidad *Pan-African Journal* 8, no. 2 (1975).

Flint, J. 1983. "The failure of planned decolonisation in British Africa". *Africa Affairs* 82, no. 328 (July).

Foreman, J. 1984. "Schooling, gender and development in Trinidad and Tobago" [work in progress]. *EDC Occasional Papers*, no. 7 (Department of Education in Developing Countries, University of London, Institute of Education, June).

Franklin, V. 1992. "Caribbean influences on Afro-Americans in the USA". In *Intellectuals in the Twentieth Century Caribbean*, edited by A. Hennessy, 179-90. London: Macmillan.

Guthrie, G. 1980. "Stages of educational development? Beeby revisited". *International Review of Education* 26, no. 4.

Hammond, S. A. 1946. "Education in the British West Indies". *Journal of Negro Education* 15.

Hans, Nicholas. 1965. "Meeting the demand in advanced and developing countries". In *World Year Book of Education 1965*, edited by G. Bereday, 126-37. London: Evans Brothers.

Harewood, J. 1981. "Human resources". In *The Natural Resources of Trinidad and Tobago*, edited by St G. E. Cooper and P. R. Bacon, 168-69. London: Edward Arnold.

Harvey, C. 1988. "Educational change and its impact on national development in Trinidad and Tobago, 1962-1987". In *Trinidad and Tobago: the Independence Experience, 1962-1987*, edited by S. Ryan, 345-80. St Augustine: ISER.

Henry, R. 1984. "The interface between education and employment in Trinidad and Tobago". In *Report on Conference on Educational Research in Trinidad and Tobago 20-22 July 1981*, edited by E. Gift, C. Harvey, P. Mark, and G. Williams, 64-67. St Augustine: UWI.

Henry, R. 1988. "The state and income distribution in an independent Trinidad and Tobago". In *Trinidad and Tobago: the Independence Experience, 1962-1987*, edited by S. Ryan, 471-94. St Augustine: ISER.

Henry, R. 1993. "Notes on the evolution of inequality in Trinidad and Tobago". In *Trinidad Ethnicity*, edited by K. Yelvington, 56-80. London: Macmillan.

Holmes, M. 1993. "The place of religion in public education". *Interchange: a Quarterly Review of Education* 24, no. 3.

Johnson, H. 1977. "The West Indies and the conversion of the British official classes to the development idea". *Journal of Commonwealth and Comparative Politics* 15, no. 1 (March).

Judges, V. 1955. "Recent trends in English education". *International Review of Education* 1.

La Guerre, J. 1988. "Race relations in Trinidad". In *Trinidad and Tobago: the Independence Experience, 1962-1987*, edited by S. Ryan, 193-206. St Augustine: ISER.

Lewis, T. 1976. "Labour market outcomes of comprehensive education in Trinidad". *Caribbean Journal of Education* 3, nos. 1-2.

Lewis, T., and M. Lewis. 1985. "Vocational education in the Commonwealth Caribbean and the United States". *Comparative Education* 21, no. 2.

Bibliography

Lillis, K. 1984. "Problems associated with vocational education in less developed countries". In *Education and Development*, edited by R. Garrett, 172-99. London: Croom Helm.

London, N. 1991. "An experiment in education provision during economic hardship: a Third World example". *Educational Management and Administration* 19, no. 3.

London, N. 1993. "The impact of economic adjustment on educational facilities planning in Trinidad and Tobago". *Educational Management and Administration* 21, no. 2.

London, N. 1995. "Policy and practice in education in the British West Indies during the late colonial period". *History of Education* 24, no. 1.

MacKenzie, C. 1991. "Denominational primary schooling: the case of Trinidad and Tobago". *International Review of Education* 37, no. 2.

Mathurin, O. 1975. Review of A. Gomes' autobiography *Through a Maze of Colour*. *Caribbean Studies* 14, no. 4 (January).

Mohammed, P. 1989. "Studies in education and society: a review of educational research in Trinidad and Tobago". Paper prepared for seminar in Education and Society in the Caribbean, sponsored by Research Institute for the Study of Man, Faculty of Education, Mona, Jamaica (ISER, St Augustine).

Palmer, C. 1994. Introduction to 1994 reprint of Eric Williams' *Capitalism and Slavery*. In *Capitalism and Slavery*, by E. Williams, xi-xxi. Chapel Hill: University of North Carolina Press.

Parris, C. 1983. "Personalisation of power in an elected government: Eric Williams and Trinidad and Tobago, 1973-1981". *Journal of Inter-American Studies and World Affairs* 25, no. 2 (May).

Phillips, H. M. 1967. "Trends in educational expansion in developing countries". In *World Year Book of Education 1967*, edited by G. Bereday, 382-98. London: Evans Brothers.

Premdas, R. 1993. "Ethnic conflict in Trinidad and Tobago: domination and reconciliation". In *Trinidad Ethnicity*, edited by K. Yelvington, 136-60. London: Macmillan.

Reddock, R. 1991. "Social mobility in Trinidad and Tobago 1960-1980". In *Social and Occupational Stratification in Contemporary Trinidad and Tobago*, edited by S. Ryan, 210-33. St Augustine: ISER.

Ryan, S. 1978. "Republic of Trinidad and Tobago White Paper on National Institute of Higher Education (Research, Science and Technology)". *Caribbean Studies* 17, nos. 3-4 (October 1977).

Ryan, S. 1986. "The limits of executive power". In *Eric Williams: the Man and the Leader*, edited by Ken Boodhoo, 65-82. New York: University Press of America.

Ryan, S. 1988. "Popular attitudes towards independence, race relations and the People's National Movement". In *Trinidad and Tobago: the Independence Experience 1962-1987*, edited by S. Ryan, 217-28. St Augustine: ISER.

Stewart, S. 1981. "Nationalist educational reforms and religious schools in Trinidad". *Comparative Education Review* 25, no. 2 (June).

Sutton, P. 1982. "Dr Eric Williams and politics in Trinidad". *Caribbean Societies* 1 (Collected Seminar Papers, no. 29, Institute of Commonwealth Studies, University of London).

Sutton, P. 1984. "Trinidad and Tobago: oil capitalism and the 'presidential power' of Eric Williams". In *Dependency under Challenge: the Political Economy of the Commonwealth Caribbean*, edited by A. Payne and P. Sutton, 43-76. Manchester: Manchester University Press.

Sutton, P. 1992. "The historian as politician: Eric Williams and Walter Rodney". In *Intellectuals in the Twentieth Century Caribbean*, edited by A. Hennessy, 98-114. London: Macmillan.

Thornley, J. 1969. "Christianity and education". In *New Horizons, Naparima Teachers College Diamond Jubilee Issue, 1894-1969*. Port of Spain: Rahaman Printing.

Thut, N. 1965. "Economic, social and administrative difficulties in expanding education". In *World Year Book of Education 1965*, edited by G. Bereday, 98-111. London: Evans Brothers.

Valdez, P. 1965. "Our secondary schools in relation to the needs of our times". *Educational Journal of Trinidad and Tobago* (July).

Vertovec, S. 1990. "Religion and ethnic ideology: the Hindu Youth Movement in Trinidad". *Ethnic and Racial Studies* 13, no. 2 (April).

Webber, R. 1990. "Scaling up Jacob's ladder: community development in Trinidad and Tobago". *Grassroots Development: Journal of the Interamerican Foundation* 14, no. 1.

Whitehead, C. 1989. "The 'two-way pull' and the establishment of university education in British West Africa". *History of Education* 16, no. 2.

Whitehead, C. 1989. "The impact of the Second World War on British colonial education policy". *History of Education* 18, no. 3.

Williams, E. 1945. "The idea of a British West Indian university". *Harvard Educational Review* 15.

Williams, E. 1946. "Education in dependent territories in America". *Journal of Negro Education* 15.

Williams, E. 1946. "The proposed West Indian university". *School and Society* 63 (January-June).

Williams, E. 1956. "The need for instructional materials related to the Caribbean environment". In *Education in the Caribbean*. Port of Spain: Caribbean Commission Central Secretariat, Kent House.

Wiltshire-Brodber, R. 1988. "Trinidad and Tobago foreign policy 1962-1987". In *Trinidad and Tobago: the Independence Experience 1962-1987*, edited by S. Ryan, 281-302. St Augustine: ISER

Unpublished Theses and Papers

Ackbarali, L. 1992. "National planning for the library and information service of Trinidad and Tobago: a case study". PhD diss., Columbia University.

Agyemang, Solomon. 1989. "A study of radical political thought in colonial Trinidad, 1919-1950". MSc thesis, UWI.

Ali, S. 1993. "A social history of East Indian women in Trinidad since 1870". MPhil thesis, UWI.

Archer, M. N.d. "History of Bishop's High School, Tobago 1925-1981". Mimeo.

Beekhee, C. 1974. "The first Maha Sabha secondary educational institute of Trinidad: a study of the Sangre Grande Hindi College 1954-1974". Caribbean Studies thesis, UWI St Augustine.

Bernard, D. 1991. "The place of drama in education and the drama teacher in secondary schools". DipEd thesis, UWI St Augustine.

Bisnauth, D. 1977. "The East Indian immigrant society in British Guyana 1891-1930". PhD diss., UWI.

Bissoon, R. 1980. "The growth of the Sanatan Dharma Maha Sabha of Trinidad and Tobago Incorporated". Caribbean Studies thesis, UWI St Augustine.

Boatswain, J. 1969. "A study of the teaching of practical subjects in secondary schools 1956-1966". Caribbean Studies thesis, UWI St Augustine.

Bibliography

Boodhoo, I. 1974. "A curriculum model in art education for the primary schools of Trinidad and Tobago". PhD diss., University of Indiana.

Braithwaite, H. R., ed. 1981. "The still small voice: comments of secondary school students on teachers, schools, education etc. 1971-1981". Mimeo, School of Education, UWI St Augustine.

Campbell, C. 1973. "The development of education in Trinidad 1834-1970". PhD diss., UWI.

Cardinez, T. 1990. "Politics in Trinidad and Tobago 1946-1956: from personal politics to ethnic based parties". MPhil thesis, UWI.

Chinapoo, C. 1988. "Chinese immigration into Trinidad 1900-1950". MA thesis, UWI.

Chapman, L. 1991. "Basic needs fulfilment as government policy: a case study of Trinidad and Tobago 1956-1981". PhD thesis, Vanderbilt University.

Dotting, A. 1973. "Secondary education and employment in Trinidad: implications for educational planning". EdD diss., Columbia University.

Dyer, C. 1974. "A study to determine curriculum content for industrial arts in the junior secondary schools of Trinidad and Tobago". PhD diss., Arizona State University.

Emmanuel, W. 1970. "Educational planning for development: a critical analysis of recent work and its relevance to Trinidad and Tobago". MA thesis, University of Newcastle-upon-Tyne.

Gajraj, S. 1984. "The Indian cultural presence in the secondary school system of Trinidad and Tobago: images and perceptions". DipEd thesis, UWI St Augustine.

Gift, E., comp. N.d. "Report to the Board of Education of Teacher Training on the final practical teaching exam". Mimeo.

Gopaul-Maharagh, N. 1984. "The social effects of the American presence in Trinidad during World War II, 1939-1945". MA thesis, UWI.

Gray, G. 1990. "The aspirations of youths and the education system in a developing society: the Tobago case". MSc thesis, UWI.

Hamel-Smith, A. 1979. "Education and the East Indians in Trinidad 1900-1938". Postgraduate seminar paper, UWI.

Harrington, Felix. 1982. " 'On with the Dance Friends': Beryl McBurnie, pioneer, educator and catalyst in Caribbean dance". Diploma in Dance paper, Jamaica School of Dance.

Harvey, C. 1981. "Practitioners' perceptions of an innovative school system in a developing country: a qualitative analysis". PhD diss, University of Toronto.

Houk, J. 1992. "The Orisha religion in Trinidad: a study of culture process and transformation". PhD diss., Tulane University.

Isaac, A. 1979. "Unequal development of Trinidad and Tobago: a preliminary study". MA thesis, Carlton University.

Johnson, H. 1969. "Crown Colony government in Trinidad". DPhil diss., University of Oxford.

Lewis, T. 1983. "An analysis of the effects of senior comprehensive schooling on the labour market performance of a sample of vocational and non-vocational graduates in Trinidad and Tobago". PhD diss., Ohio State University.

Mark, P. 1979. "A critique of practices in teacher education in Trinidad and Tobago". UWI St Augustine, School of Education.

Mohammed, F. 1982. "The impact of the oil boom of 1973/1974 on the local construction industry of Trinidad and Tobago". MSc thesis, UWI.

Bibliography

Mohammed, P. 1987. "Women and education in Trinidad and Tobago 1938-1980". MSc thesis, UWI.

Mohammed, R. N.d. "The socioeconomic factors responsible for the emergence of Islamic schools in Trinidad". Caribbean Studies thesis, UWI St Augustine.

Mohammed, T. 1987. "Acquisition of construction technology in Trinidad and Tobago". MSc thesis, UWI.

Moore, N. 1978. "The teachers' colleges of Trinidad and Tobago, their purpose, performance and possibilities". DipEd thesis, UWI St Augustine.

Palmer, E. 1980. "Evaluating a creative arts programme in a developing nation, Trinidad and Tobago". DEd diss., Columbia University.

Pemberton, R. 1984. "Towards a re-evaluation of the West Indian peasantry: a case study of Tobago 1900-1949". MA thesis, UWI.

Pierre, A. 1974. "A survey into facilities existing in Trinidad and Tobago for the training of music teachers". Mimeo, UWI School of Education.

Ramaya, Narsaloo. 1984. "Towards the evolution of a national culture: Indian music in Trinidad and Tobago". Paper presented at the Third Conference on East Indians in the Caribbean, UWI St Augustine.

Ramlogan, R. 1985. "Trinidad and Tobago's iron and steel industry in perspective: analysis and prospects". MSc thesis, UWI.

Rampersad, F. 1988. "The role of religious education in secondary schools in Trinidad and Tobago". DipEd thesis, UWI St Augustine.

Ramsing, H. 1969. "The historical development of Muslim schools in Trinidad and Tobago". Caribbean Studies thesis, UWI St Augustine.

Ramrekersingh, A. 1975. "The conflict between the Roman Catholic Church and the State in secondary education 1955-1975". Department of Education paper, Institute of Education, UWI St Augustine.

Salazar, A. 1991. "The importance of the arts in education" DipEd thesis, UWI St Augustine.

Samaroo, S. 1988. "A critique of vocational education in senior comprehensive schools in Trinidad and Tobago". DipEd thesis, UWI St Augustine.

Sambury, M. 1991. "An assessment of technical vocational education in the senior comprehensive schools of Trinidad and Tobago". DipEd thesis, UWI St Augustine.

Stephens, C. 1987. "St George's College 1953-1987: a historical perspective". DipEd thesis, UWI St Augustine.

Taitt, R. 1990. "Women in the PNM". MA thesis, UWI.

Tewarie, K. 1984. "Integration and multi-culturalism: a dilemma in the school system of Trinidad and Tobago". Paper presented at the Third Conference on East Indians in the Caribbean, UWI St Augustine.

Wheeler, V. 1977. "Democratising secondary education in Tobago". Second part of five government broadcasts from 13 August-September.

Wheeler, V. 1992. "Work, the comprehensive school and specialised craft in Trinidad and Tobago: an analysis". MA thesis, UWI.

Williams, Eric. 1966. "A review of the political scene: an address by the political leader to the special PNM convention, 11 September 1966".

Index

Abdullah, Rev Clive: in conflict between government and churches, 87
Adult education, 20
Adult suffrage, 23
Agricultural education, 107; calls for, 16; and ICTA, 52; in junior secondary schools, 166; lack of emphasis on, 101; and link to technical/vocational education, 165; in primary schools, 113-114; private enterprise and, 165; promotion of, 14
Ali, Moulvi Ameer, 26
Alleyne, Albert, 108
Anglicisation: role of education in, of Trinidad, 2
Anglo-American Caribbean Commission: Eric Williams and the, 58-59; establishment of, 58
Anthony, Michael, 173
Apprentice Trade School: government takeover of, 101
Apprentices: Indians as, 29; masters and, in Tobago, 45; oil companies and employment of, 28; registration of, 28; Trinidad and Tobago Electricity Company and, 29; World War II and employment opportunities for, 28
Apprenticeship: inception of, 4; schemes for, in industries, 126
Art: and craft, after the 1960s, 175; in schools, 174
Arya Pratinidhi Sabha: and opposition to university for Trinidad, 53
Asquith Commission, 52
Association of Principals of Private Secondary Schools, 117

Bar examinations: for West Indian students, 49
Barbados: and education, 194-195
Beacham, Dennis: and administration of Bishop's High School, 44
Beeby, C.E.: on stages of development of primary education, 17-18

Best, Lloyd, 75; on education and blacks, 11
Bishop Anstey High School, 3, 10, 94
Bishop's High School, Tobago, 3, 10, 42; enrolment at, 1946, 43; establishment of, 131; functioning of, 134; as grammar school, 43
Black Power movement, 106; causes and results of, 74-75; effects of, 107
Blacks: and disagreement with Indians over politics, 69-70; education and social mobility of, 11; political alliance of Indians and, 79; relations between Indians and, 72-73; and support for university for Trinidad, 53; and university education overseas, 49
Board of Education, 97
Board of Industrial Training (BIT): and assistance from Trinidad Leasehold Limited, 28; control of, by Ministry of Education, 100-101; oil companies and assistance to, 28; on technical training in Tobago, 45; and trades training, 4, 16; work of, in south Trinidad, 27, 28
Boards of Management: of denominational schools, 104, 181
Book grants, 124-125
Boolai, Rampersad, 141
Bowles, Dr Sylvan, 42, 134
Boys: Indian, and Cambridge School Certificates, 27
Boys' Model School, 9-10
Braithwaite, Lloyd: on social stratification, 13; assessment of views of, on race and class, 13-14
British Council: work of, in Trinidad, 50
Bruce, Victor, 42; and committee on joint management, 92, 214
Budget: and education, 102
Bursar system: of training of primary school teachers, 115
Butler riots, 19; effect of, on trades training, 27
Butler, Uriah, 70

Index

Cabildo schools, 1
Cambridge School Certificates: increase in holders of, 33; and Indian boys, 27; private secondary schools and, 178
Canadian Presbyterian Mission: and ecumenism, 138; and education of Indian women, 171; and education of Indians, 2, 10-11; education policy of, 138; membership of, 138; and preparation of Indians for College Exhibitions, 26-27; social influence of, 6; and university training for Indians, 49
Capildeo, Dr Rudranath, 140
Capildeo, Simboonath, 26, 140
Capitalism and Slavery, Eric Williams, 57
Caribbean: recommendation of study of, in secondary schools, 114
Caribbean Examinations Council (CXC), 183
Caribbean Plan: for primary schools, 144
Caribbean Research Council, 58
Caribbean Union College: and teacher training, 149
Carmichael, Stokely, 75
Carnegie Foundation: and funding of Caribbean Plan, 144; and project in school organisation, 144
Chaguaramas Trade School, 100, 154
Chamberlain, Joseph: and promotion of agricultural education, 14; and imperial development of the British Caribbean, 14
Charlotteville Methodist School, 42
Child labour: defence of, 9
Chinese immigrants: and education in China, 49
Church: and calls for revision of Education Plan, 120; conflict between government and, 85-86, 87; conflict between government and, over dual system, 39, 40; PNM Charter on role of, in education, 86; and provision of education in Trinidad, 5; and relationship with PNM government, 82; role of, in elementary education, 2; social influence of, 6
Church rivalry: and expansion of education opportunities, 7-8, 39-40
Cipriani, Captain, 70; and modern nationalist movement, 69
City and Guild of London Institute: abolition of examinations of, 108
Civil service: Indians in, 76
Code of Regulations, 89

College Exhibitions, 5; increase in number of, 38, 99; Indians and, 26-27; in Tobago, 45, see also Common Entrance Examinations
College of the Immaculate Conception (CIC), 3; prestige attached to, 94; rivalry between QRC and, 10, 40
College of Liberal Arts: opening of, 102
Colonial Development and Welfare: establishment of, 19-20; and expenditure on school building, 35; influence of, on education system, 21
Coloureds: and support for university in Trinidad, 53
Common Entrance Examination: and girls, 172; increased secondary school places under, 71, 84-85; influence of, on teaching in primary schools, 145-146; rethinking of, 182-183; and students for secondary schools, 94; in Tobago, 135. *See also* College exhibitions
Community development, 20
Compulsory attendance. *See* School attendance
Concordat, 74, 82, 85, 89, 96, 104; conscience clause in, 169; text of, 216-217
Conference on Secondary Schools: Eric Williams and, 113
Constitution: rights of parents under, 86
Constitutional Commission: appointment of, by Eric Williams, 76
Corinth: teacher training college at, 123, 203
Council for Legal Education: and bar examinations for West Indians, 49
Crafts, 30; implementation of specialised training in, 160-162; introduction of, in schools, 16
Creolisation: of Indians, 14
Crime: increase in, in post-war period, 167-168
Culture: teaching of subjects related to, 175-176
Curriculum development: calls by Eric Williams for West Indianisation, 67; for primary schools, 125; preparation of West Indian oriented, 115; for primary schools, in post-war Trinidad, 30-31; recommendation of Caribbean studies in, 114
Curriculum reform: Captain Cutteridge and, 16; NJAC on, 113; objectives of, 15-16
Cutteridge, Captain J, 2; and curriculum reform, 16
Cutteridge Code (1935): review of, 24

Index

Dancing: Indian, in schools, 173; in Roman Catholic girls' schools, 174; in schools, 173-174
Daniel, Captain William, 31
Demas, William: on capital expenditure in schools, 213
Democratic Action Party, Tobago, 132
Democratic Labour Party, 72
Des Vignes Road Moravian School, Tobago, 42
Development: and education, 35
Development Plan for Tobago, 133
Development scholarships, 101
Devenish, Dr S., 56
Director of Education: decrease in powers of, 23
Domestic science: in primary schools, 30
Donaldson, John, 68
Draft Education Plan. *See* Fifteen-year Education Plan (1968-1983)
Drama: in secondary schools, 173
Dual system: conflict between government and churches over, 39, 40; Eric Williams on, 65; functioning of, 7; government control over schools under, 81; Hindu schools under, 26; increase in number of church secondary schools under, 98; Moyne Commission on, 30; Muslim schools in, 26; reorganisation of, under PNM, 83; role of government in, 39

Eastern Caribbean Farm Institute, 101, 165, 166
Economic strategies: search for new, by PNM government, 76
Ecumenism: and Presbyterian Church policy, 138
Education: in Barbados, 194-195; as beneficiary of increase in number of degrees, 50-51; and blacks, 11; and budget, 102; change in attitudes towards, 34-35, 40; churches role in provision of, 5; comparison of, with Africa, 195-196; constitutional changes affecting, after World War II, 23; criticism of changes in, 116-117; criticisms of denominational, 87-88; democratisation of system of, 103; and development, 35; effect of abolition of slavery on, 1; effect of oil price rise on spending on, 118; equal opportunity for, 203-204; Eric Williams on West Indian, 60; financing of, 24; and government control, 82; government subsidy of, 8; grievances relating to, in Tobago, 45; higher, and relation to manpower needs, 124; increased pace of higher, in post-war period, 50; influence of Colonial Development and Welfare on, 21; management of, 180-182; objective of church in, 2; PNM Charter on role of church in, 86; qualitative improvements in system of, 182; and race, 3, 208; reformers of, in early twentieth century, 66; reorientation of system of, 107-108; responses to expansion and reorientation in system of, 105; role of, in anglicisation of Trinidad, 2; role of, in decolonisation, 210-211; and social integration, 81, 88-90; and social transformation, 20, 205-208; support for expansion of, 34; in Tobago, 130; White Paper on, 1946, 25, 33

Education in the British West Indies, Eric Williams, 65

Education Act (1966), 82, 89-90; and consolidation of education system, 84
Education, agricultural. *See* Agricultural education
Education Fund: establishment of, 118
Education, industrial: Foster Commission on, 27
Education Plan: calls for revision of, 120, 121; execution of, 1948-55, 34; national consultation on, 119; review of, 121
Education planning: aim of, 125; promotion of, by UNESCO, 108, 109-110
Education policies: assessment of, of PNM government, 198-200; challenge to, from radicals, 15; change in direction of, 121; criticisms of, by Indians, 140; and Legislative Council, 23; and PNM, 70-71, 117; of Presbyterian Church, 138; in Tobago, 134
Education, primary: compulsory, 24-25; increased expenditure on, 34; Missen Report on, 144; reforms in, in the 1960s, 144; role of the church in, 2; subordination of, to secondary education, 143
Education, secondary: achievements of PNM in relation to, 83; demand for, 119; expansion of, 106-107; formulation of model for, 109; free, debates on introduction of, 37-38; free, institution of, 71; increased access to, 71; influence of English model on, 3; opportunities for, for girls, 3; role of examinations in, 4-5; and social mobility, 3, 11; in Tobago, 3; universalisation of, 152

Education, technical/vocational, 3; degree of specialisation in, 159-160; effect of, on school curriculum, 158-159; evaluation of, 208; girls and, 172-173; government involvement in, 100; and link to agricultural education, 165; and oil boom, 153; on-the-job training and, 162; in public secondary schools, 152-153; reasons for change in government thinking on, 156-157; in secondary modern schools in the 1950s, 154; social status of, 164; suggestions for, in Draft Education Plan, 112; syllabus of, in senior comprehensive school, 158; in Tobago, 44-45; UNESCO mission on, 155; variety of, 163; youth camps and, 154-155

El Socorro Islamic school, 25-26

Elementary education. *See* Education, primary

Emergency Teacher Training College, 101-102

Engineers: oil industry and training of, 30

Examinations: high failure rate of, 204-205; role of, in education system, 39, 115; in secondary school selection system, 4-5; and upward mobility, 5

Examinations Review Committee, 183; on the Common Entrance Examination, 213

External degrees: availability of, in the West Indies, 48

Family life education: in secondary schools, 129

Farm scholarships, 101

Farm schools: construction of, 118; in Tobago, 134

Fatima College, 32

Federation: Eric Williams on, 59

Fifteen-year Education Plan (1968-1983), draft, 90, 95; and definition of two-cycle secondary system, 110-111; management of, 181-182; and suggestions for technical/vocational training, 112, 155-156; on trained teachers for technical/vocational schools, 112

Five-year Development Plan: of 1958-1962, 100; income tax and financing of, 102; 1964-1968, on technical/vocational education, 155

Five-year Economic Programme (1950-1955): and education expansion programme, 35

Foster Commission: recommendations of, 27

Free coloureds: education of, in pre-emancipation Trinidad, 1

French creoles: and resistance to anglicisation of Trinidad, 7

Ghany, Abdul, 26

Ghany, Noor, 26

Girls: increased access to secondary education for, 172; Indian, and secondary education, 27; technical/vocational training for, 172-173; University scholarship for, 40

Girls' Model School, 9-10

Gocking, C.V., 91, 183; and enquiry into teacher training system, 129; on nursery education, 184; recommendations of Committee chaired by, 185-186

Gomes, Albert: and defence of teachers, 171; on free secondary education, 37, 38

Gomes, Carlton, 128, 157

Government: and aid for Muslim schools, 26; conflict between churches and 85-86, 87; conflict between churches and, over dual system, 39, 40; and control of teacher appointment in denominational schools, 19; role of, in dual system, 39; role of, in higher degree programmes, 47

Government expenditure: on schools, 7

Government Training College, 32; establishment of residential branch of, 148

Grammar schools: social demand for, 31

Grosvenor, E.B., 42

Grow More Food Campaign: and social transformation, 20; Tobago's contribution to, 43

Guidance counselling: in secondary schools, 129

Haig Girls' School, 177

Hammond, S.A.: criticism of views of, by Eric Williams, 61-64; effect of recommendations of, 21-22; influence of, on education system, 21; objectives of, 20; recommendations of, 20-21

Hanoomansingh, Hans, 141

Health care: for primary and secondary school students, 124

Hill, Errol, 176

Hindi, 25; demands for recognition of, as second language, 26; Eric Williams on teaching of, 26

Hindu schools: in the dual system, 26, 131; establishment of, 11; and government aid,

Index

100; increase in number of, 137-138; primary, 25
Hindus: and defence of role of religion in education, 139-140; and preservation of culture, 142
History, West Indian: contribution of Eric Williams to, 57, 59; Eric Williams on teaching of, in secondary schools, 105; mandatory course in, at St Augustine campus, 188
Hogben, Sidney, 33; on religious instruction in schools, 168
Hopkins, Moreland: on a West Indian university, 53
House Scholarships (Tobago), 42

Ibbertson, Dora: criticisms of, by creoles, 62
Ideal High School, 177
Imperial College of Tropical Agriculture (ICTA), 4; contribution of, to education in the West Indies, 52
Income tax: and financing of Five-year Development Plan, 102
Indians: accusations of prejudice against, by PNM government, 100; as apprentices, 29; attitude of Eric Williams to schools of, 139; birth rate of, 136; boys, and Cambridge School Certificates, 27; and College Exhibitions, 26; creolisation of, 14; and criticisms of PNM education policies, 140; and disagreement with blacks over politics, 69-70; in Education Department, 180; effect of separate schooling for, 41; females and employment as teachers, 51; and formation of opposition party, 72; girls, and secondary education, 27; and Island Scholarships, 26-27; political alliance of blacks and, 79; and political power, 136-137; primary education of children of, 2; race consciousness of, 11; recognition of culture of, 137; relations between blacks and, 72-73; and social mobility, 11; and theological training, 49; trades training and, 29; and university education, 49; university education for female, 49
Industrialisation: as a result of the oil boom, 78
Integration: effect of separate schooling of Indians on, 41; schools and social, 88-90, 112
Irvine Committee: on university education for the West Indies, 52-53
Island Scholars: and political leadership, 12

Island Scholarships, 5; increase in number of, 101, 124; Indians and, 26-27

James, A.P.T.: and nationalism in Tobago, 43-44, 133; as Tobago spokesman, 132
John Donaldson Technical School, 100, 163; construction of, 154; and leadership in technical/vocational education, 107-108; and training of technical teachers, 123
Joint Management system: and economic thrust of government, 93; functioning of, 91-93; between Roman Catholic church and government, 91; teachers and, 93
Jones, Rev. Ivor, 43; dismissal of, 44
Joseph, Cuthbert, 128
Joseph, Roy, 26, 38, 100, 105; criticism of by Eric Williams, 67; and defence of teachers, 171
Jordan, Rawle, 3; on external degrees, 47
Junior Technical School, San Fernando, 4
Juvenile delinquency: in secondary schools, 160-170

Keenan, Patrick, 22

Language: English as official, 139; Hindi and Urdu in schools, 139
Legislative Council: and education policy, 23; increase in powers of elected members of, 23
Little Carib Movement, 67, 173, 176

MacAlister, H.W., 42
Malik, Yogendra, 14
Manpower: needs of 1970s, 157; survey of, 112
Maraj, Bhadase, 25, 137, 141; criticism of, by Eric Williams, 72
Maraj, James: and the Caribbean Plan for primary schools, 144
Marriott, James, 21
Masson, Norbert, 107-108
Maurice Committee Report: on church schools, 89, 98; philosophical assumptions underlying, 103-104; recommendations of, 103-104, 109
Maurice, J. Hamilton, 98
Mausica Teachers' College, 102, 148, 203
Mayhew, Arthur, 21
McBurnie, Beryl, 173
Middle class: formation of, 12; widening of educated, 41

Index

Millette, James, 75
Ministry of Education: and Draft Fifteen-year Education Plan, 108; establishment of Planning Unit in, 108; powers of, 85; Publications Branch of, 115
Ministry of Tobago Affairs: abolition of, 131
Missen Report, 109; on the dual system, 30; on primary education, 144; on religious instruction, 30; on secondary modern schools, 31
Mount Hope Medical Complex, 192, 194; building of, 124
Moyne Commission, 109; recommendations of, 19
Music Festivals: impact of, 174; lack of Indian element in, 175
Muslim schools: in the dual system, 26, 131; establishment of, 11; government aid for, 26; increase in number of, 137, 138-139; primary, 25, 26

Naipaul, Vidia, 27
Naparima Girls' High School, 3, 27, 49
Naparima Training College, 32, 149; tertiary training for graduates of, 49
National Alliance for Reconstruction (NAR), 79
National Commission on the Status of Women, 173
National Examination Council for Technical and Vocational Education: establishment of, 108
National Institute of Higher Education (NIHE): establishment of, 126
National Institute of Higher Education (Research, Science and Technology) (NIHERST), 126, 127-129; criticisms of plans for, 128
National Joint Action Committee (NJAC), 75; on school curricula, 113
National Organisation of Revolutionary Students: on school curricula, 113
National Pre-school Education Project, 123
National Training Board, 159; and on-the job training scheme, 162-163
Nationalism: in the Commonwealth Caribbean, 132, 187; development of, in post-war period, 69-70; Eric Williams and, 68, 89; in Tobago, 43; in Trinidad, 62-63
Neehall, Rev Roy, 138
Negro in the Caribbean, Eric Williams, 57

New Primary School Syllabus: implementation of, 145
New World Group, 75
Nursery education: improvements in, 184-185

Oil industry: and assistance to BIT, 28; and employment of apprentices, 28; non-white supervisors in, 30; and trades training, 29; and training of engineers, 30
Oil prices: collapse of regime of high, 80; effect of reduction in, on government policies, 80; effect of rise in, 77, 78, 118; and technical/vocational education, 153
Orisha religion, 6
Osmond High School, 177

Pantin, Fr Anthony: and conflict between government and the churches, 87
Parents: rights of, under Independence Constitution, 86
Patrick, Robert: as director of education, 22; suggestions of, 22
People's Democratic Party (PDP), 72
People's Education Movement, 68, 171
People's National Movement (PNM): and accusations of prejudice against Indians, 100; achievements of, in education expansion, 200-203; assessment of education policies of, 198; Charter of, on role of church in education, 86, 98; economic strategies of 71, 76; education policies of, 70-71; and expenditure on education, 202-203; formation of, 68; goals of, in relation to education, 97; and government ownership in the 1970s, 77; government and relationship with the church, 82; and lack of focus on women, 172; and loss of popular black support, 76; women in campaign of, 172
Petroleum technology: training in, 123-124
Pluralism, cultural: of Trinidad society, 7
Point Fortin Trade School, 154
Polytechnic Institute, 100
Pre-school education. *See* Nursery education
Presbyterian church. *See* Canadian Presbyterian Mission
Public Service Commission. *See* Teaching Service Commission
Pupil teacher scheme, 147

Queen's Collegiate School, 3

Index

Queen's Royal College (QRC), 3; prestige attached to, 94; rivalry between CIC and, 10, 40

Race: accusations of prejudice against Indian schools, 100; discrimination against primary school teachers on basis of, 88; and education, 3, 208
Race consciousness: separate education of Indians and, 11
Ramcharan, Sylvia: academic achievement of, 27
Ramdeen, Balgobin, 140
Ramkessoon, Rawle, 42, 50
Rance, Governor Hubert, 168
Reddock, Rhoda: on social mobility and education, 207
Religious instruction: in curriculum of primary schools, 168; Eric Williams on, in schools, 168-169; Missen Report on, 30; role of, in schools, 167-170
Richards Committee: recommendations of, 160
Rienzi, Adrian Cola, 70
Robinson, A.N.R., 42, 215; political career of, 131-132; as Prime Minister, 80; status of, in Tobago, 131
Robinson, E.A.: and support for child labour, 9
Rogers, DeWilton, 68
Roman Catholic Church: and defence of denominational schools, 86; influence of, in Trinidad, 6; and objection to government control of education, 6-7; and resistance to anglicisation of Trinidad, 7; social doctrine of, 6, 86; and surrender of some primary schools, 91
Roman Catholic Women's College, 32, 149
Ryan, Count Finbar, 22, 87
Ryan, Selwyn, 14; on PNM, 198-199

St Clair King Report: on Common Entrance Examination, 183
St George's College, 31
St Joseph's Convent, 2; and education of girls, 3; prestige attached to, 94
San Fernando Technical College, 100
Sanatan Maha Sabha: criticism of, by Eric Williams, 72; schools of, 25, 137
Scholarship and National Training Fund: establishment of, 124

Scholarships: and financing of university education, 50; *see also* Island Scholarships
School attendance, 40
School building: Colonial Development and Welfare and expenditure on, 35; programme for, 35-36; programme for senior secondary schools, 121; and repair, 90-91, 122; in Tobago, 42; use of denominational, 104
School bus service, 125
School enrolment: during World War II, 32-33; in post-war period, 33, 34, 36; in Tobago, 42, 43
School feeding: programme of, 124
School gardens: establishment of, 16
School libraries: development of, 176-177; improvements in, 124
School places: expansion of, 32, 106; shortage of, in Tobago, 135
School uniforms: grants for, 124
Schools: durability of denominational, 96; government expenditure on, 7; quality of, in Tobago, 42-43; and social integration, 88-90, 142; and sports, 124
Schools, cabildo: before emancipation, 1
Schools, elementary. *See* Schools, primary
Schools, government: aim of, 5; Charles Warner and, 5-6; Dr Eric Williams and, 5-6
Schools, Hindu. *See* Hindu schools
Schools, junior secondary: accomplishments of early students in, 126; agricultural education in, 165-166; establishment of, 111, 118; opposition to, 120; recommended establishment of, 19; revision of plans for, 121; quality of, 118; shift system in, 120, 183; and technical/vocational education, 153, 154
Schools, Muslim: establishment of, 11
Schools, nursery: expansion in number of, 123
Schools, primary: agriculture in, 113; Beeby on stages of development of, 17-18; curriculum development in, in post-war period, 30-31; curriculum reform, for 12-15 year olds in, 99; enrolment in, 36-37, 99, 122; expansion of, 99; new curriculum for, 125; new syllabus for, 145, 169; outside influences in the founding of, 2; overcrowding in, 106; in post-emancipation Trinidad, 2; quality of, in 1920s and 1930s, 18; race discrimination against teachers in, 88; religious instruction in curriculum of, 168; in Tobago, 42

Schools, private secondary: and Cambridge Certificate holders, 178; expansion in number of, 117; role of, in education, 177-180; in Tobago, 117

Schools, secondary: denominational, government control of, 84, 85; development of, in nineteenth century, 3; drama in, 173; enrolment in, 1834-1902; expansion of facilities for, 9-10; expectations of government from two-cycle system of, 111; family life education in, 129; growth of private, 10; guidance counselling in, 129; increase in enrolment (1946-1952), 37; increase in number of, 98-99; increase in number of, under dual system, 98; prestige attached to, 94-95; Roman Catholics in establishment of, 2; and social integration, 81; and social prestige, 3-5; syllabus of, 31; technical/vocational education in public, 152-153; in Tobago, 134-135

Schools, secondary modern: lack of social demand for, 31; technical/vocational education in, in the 1950s, 154; in Tobago, 134

Schools, senior comprehensive, 111; building of, 121; difficulties faced by, 125-126; technical/vocation education in, 158; in Tobago, 134

Schools, teacher training: establishment of, 4

SERVOL, 164

Seukaran, L.F., 140

Shift system: in junior secondary schools, 120, 183

Shouter Baptists, 6

Simab, Maulana Nazir Ahmed, 26

Simey, T.S., 20

Sinnanan, A.S., 140

Skills training, 4

Slavery: effect of abolition of, on education, 1

Smith, Kathlyn: academic achievement of, 27

Social mobility: of Blacks, 11; after emancipation, 12-14; Indians and, 11, Rhoda Reddock on, 207

Social prestige: secondary schools and, 3-5

Social stratification: assessment of Braithwaite's views on, 13-14; Lloyd Braithwaite on, 13

Social welfare: attitudes to, 8-9

Social Welfare Department, 21

Solomon, Patrick, 101

Sports: and schools, 124

State of Emergency: declaration of, 75

Tapia, 75

Teacher education: improved standards of, 17-18

Teacher Education Committee: views of, on nursery education, 184

Teacher training: consolidation of, 147-150; developments in, 146-147; durability of model of, 1956-1981, 151; enquiry into system of, 129; expansion in, 123; government involvement in, 83-84; model of, 1956-1981, 150; programmes for, 107; for secondary schools level, 147; at university level, 186; during World War II, 32

Teachers: bursar system of training, 115; employment opportunities for non-white, 51; government control over, in denominational schools, 84; increase in number of, 36; Indian women as, 51; in-service training for, 116, 192-193; and Joint Management system, 93; and participation in politics, 24; of primary schools, with degrees, 51; of primary schools in Tobago, 45; ratio of trained secondary school, 102; recognition of needs of primary school, 23-24; shortage of, 129; training of primary school, 185; training of technical/vocational, 101, 159; untrained, in primary schools, 145; upgrading of salaries for secondary school, 102

Teachers' Economic and Cultural Association, 65, 171

Teaching Service Commission: responsibility of, 88; role of, 84

Textbooks: preparation of West Indian oriented, 115; Williams on West Indianisation of, 66-67

Theatre: need for West Indian, 176

Tobago: A.P.T. James and nationalism in, 43-44; BIT on technical classes in, 45; and College Exhibitions, 45; Common Entrance Examinations in, 135; culture of, in schools, 136; desire for control of schools in, 136; development plan for, 133; education in, 130; education needs of, 133; Eric Williams' analysis of problems of, 133; and grievances relating to education, 45; and Grow More Food campaign, 43; nationalism in, 43; performance of the PNM in, 131; primary school teachers in, 45; primary schools in, 42; quality of schools in, 42-43; school buildings in, 42; school enrolment in, 42; secondary education in, 3, 43, 134-135; separatist outlook in, 130, 131, 132; shortage of secondary

Index

places in, 135; status of A.N.R. Robinson in, 131
Tobago House of Assembly: and authority over schools, 136; establishment of, 131; and relations with Trinidad government, 215
Tobago Peasants and Industrial Workers Union: on technical classes in Tobago, 44-45
Trades training: BIT and, 4, 16; centres for, 107, 155, 164; and Indians, 29; oil industry and, 29; in South Trinidad, 27-28; women in centres, 172
Training: degree of specialisation for technical/vocational, 159-160; expansion of opportunities for, 101; on-the-job, and technical/vocational education, 162
Trinidad Leasehold Limited: and assistance to BIT, 28
Trinidad and Tobago Electricity Company: and apprentices, 29
Trinidad and Tobago Historical Society, 67
Trinidad and Tobago Teachers' Union, 171
Trinidad and Tobago Unified Teachers' Association: in school management, 181
Trinidad and Tobago Welfare Ltd, 21

UNESCO: and management of education system, 129; and promotion of education planning, 108, 109-110; recommendations of, regarding secondary schools, 109-110; and technical/vocational education, 155
United British Oilfields of Trinidad: and apprenticeship training, 30
United National Independence Party (UNIP), 75
University: arguments for and against a West Indian, 53-54; Eric Williams on a West Indian, 60-61; Irvine Committee on West Indian, 52-53
University College of the West Indies (UCWI): branch of, in Trinidad, 102; consequences of establishment of, 54-55
University degrees: non-whites with, 46-47
University education: blacks and, 49; Chinese immigrants and, 49; developments in, 102; increase in, 49-50; for female Indians, 49; Indians and, 49; for women, 171-172
University of London: degrees from, 47, 48
University scholarship: for girls, 4; *see also* Island Scholarship

University of the West Indies (UWI): emergence of St Augustine campus of, 187-194; and Eric Williams, 126-127; Faculty of Agriculture of, 187, 190-192; student enrolment at St Augustine campus, 189; West Indian history as mandatory at St Augustine campus, 188

Valdez Working Party: on agriculture in secondary schools, 113, 114; and secondary school curriculum, 113
Valsayn Teachers' College, 203-204
Van Leer Foundation: and pre-school education, 123

Warner, Charles: and education policy, 88-89; and government schools, 5-6
West Indian Histories, 31, 115
West Indian Readers, 2, 16, 115
West Indian Tobacco Company: and agricultural education, 165
Wheeler, Victor: on education needs of Tobago, 133
Whites: on university for Trinidad, 53
Why Not Discussion Group: and support for a West Indian university, 53-54
Williams, Dr Eric, 4; academic achievements of, 56-57; on adult education, 64; and analysis of problems of Tobago, 133; and the Anglo-American Caribbean Commission, 58-59; assessment of, 200; attitude of, to Indian schools, 139; and the Black Power movement, 74-75; *Capitalism and Slavery*, 57; and compromise with opponents, 74; and Conference on Secondary Schools, 113; contribution of, to West Indian History, 57, 59; and criticism of anti-nationalist forces, 71-72; and criticism of S.A. Hammond's views, 61-64; on curriculum reform, 63; on dual control of education, 65; *Education in the British West Indies*, 64, 65; on education in the West Indies, 60; esteem for, in Trinidad, 59; final years of, 79-80; and government schools, 5-6; and nationalist movement, 68; *The Negro in the Caribbean*, 57; opposition of, to churches' role in education, 86; pan-Caribbean perspective of, 57; and politicisation of cultural affairs, 67; on religious instruction in schools, 168-169; and revision of education plan, 121; strategies to counter policies of, 73-74; on teaching of Hindi in schools, 26; on

Index

teaching of West Indian history in secondary schools, 105; and UWI, 126-127, 193; on West Indian federation, 59; on West Indian university, 60-61; on West Indianisation of textbooks, 66-67

Women: and education, 170-173; and equal pay, 171; National Commission on the Status of, 173; in PNM campaign, 172; as primary school teachers, 170; thinking on role of, in society, 171; and university education, 171-172; university education for Indian, 49, 171

Woodbrook Secondary School: disturbances at, 113

Wooding, H.O.B., 56

Woodwork: in primary schools, 30

World War II: effect of, on employment of apprentices, 28

Youth camps: for boys, 107; establishment of, 163; and technical/vocational education, 154-155

www.ingramcontent.com/pod-product-compliance
Lightning Source LLC
Chambersburg PA
CBHW050842230426
43667CB00012B/2115